FOUNDATIONS AND
IN EARLY CHILDHOOD
EDUCATION

BICENTENNIAL
1807
WILEY
2007
BICENTENNIAL

THE WILEY BICENTENNIAL—KNOWLEDGE FOR GENERATIONS

*E*ach generation has its unique needs and aspirations. When Charles Wiley first opened his small printing shop in lower Manhattan in 1807, it was a generation of boundless potential searching for an identity. And we were there, helping to define a new American literary tradition. Over half a century later, in the midst of the Second Industrial Revolution, it was a generation focused on building the future. Once again, we were there, supplying the critical scientific, technical, and engineering knowledge that helped frame the world. Throughout the 20th Century, and into the new millennium, nations began to reach out beyond their own borders and a new international community was born. Wiley was there, expanding its operations around the world to enable a global exchange of ideas, opinions, and know-how.

For 200 years, Wiley has been an integral part of each generation's journey, enabling the flow of information and understanding necessary to meet their needs and fulfill their aspirations. Today, bold new technologies are changing the way we live and learn. Wiley will be there, providing you the must-have knowledge you need to imagine new worlds, new possibilities, and new opportunities.

Generations come and go, but you can always count on Wiley to provide you the knowledge you need, when and where you need it!

WILLIAM J. PESCE
PRESIDENT AND CHIEF EXECUTIVE OFFICER

PETER BOOTH WILEY
CHAIRMAN OF THE BOARD

FOUNDATIONS AND CHANGE IN EARLY CHILDHOOD EDUCATION

Martha T. Dever
Utah State University

Renée C. Falconer
George Mason University

BICENTENNIAL
1807
WILEY
2007
BICENTENNIAL

JOHN WILEY & SONS, INC.

This work is dedicated to our grandchildren
Isabelle, Molly, Sawyer, Rhya, Abigail, and Hannah.
May all their teachers envision a just and peaceful world.

Vice President and Publisher: *Jay O' Callaghan*
Executive Editor: *Christopher T. Johnson*
Acquisitions Editor: *Robert Johnston*
Senior Editorial Assistant: *Katie Melega*
Editorial Assistant: *Eileen McKeever*
Production Editor: *Nicole Repasky*
Senior Illustration Editor: *Sandra Rigby*
Senior Photo Editor: *Jennifer MacMillan*
Marketing Manager: *Emily Streutker*
Designer: *Hope Miller*
Production Management Services: *Ingrao Associates*
Media Editor: *Sasha Giacoppo*
Cover Photo: *Lisette LeBon/SUPERSTOCK*
Interior Design: *GGS Services, Inc.*
Photo Researcher: *Elyse Rieder*
Bicentennial Logo Design: *Richard J. Pacifico*

Chapter Opener 1 *PhotoDisc/Getty Images • Masterfile • PhotoDisc/Getty Images • Grace/Zefa/Corbis Images*
Chapter Opener 2 *PhotoDisc/Getty Images • Masterfile • PhotoDisc/Getty Images • Hulton Archive/Getty Images*
Chapter Opener 3 *PhotoDisc/Getty Images • Masterfile • PhotoDisc/Getty Images • Jeff Greenberg/The Image Works*
Chapter Opener 4 *PhotoDisc/Getty Images • Masterfile • PhotoDisc/Getty Images • Bill Losh/Taxi/Getty Images*
Chapter Opener 5 *PhotoDisc/Getty Images • Masterfile • PhotoDisc/Getty Images • Syracuse Newspaper/Dick Blume/The Image Works*
Chapter Opener 6 *PhotoDisc/Getty Images • Masterfile • PhotoDisc/Getty Images • Spencer Grant/PhotoEdit*
Chapter Opener 7 *PhotoDisc/Getty Images • Masterfile • PhotoDisc/Getty Images • Lawrence Migdale/Pix Photography*
Chapter Opener 8 *PhotoDisc/Getty Images • Masterfile • PhotoDisc/Getty Images • Myrleen Ferguson Cate/PhotoEdit*
Chapter Opener 9 *PhotoDisc/Getty Images • Masterfile • PhotoDisc/Getty Images • Laura Dwight Photography*
Chapter Opener 10 *PhotoDisc/Getty Images • Masterfile • PhotoDisc/Getty Images • Michael Newman/PhotoEdit*
Chapter Opener 11 *PhotoDisc/Getty Images • Masterfile • PhotoDisc/Getty Images • Bob Daemmrich/PhotoEdit*
Chapter Opener 12 *PhotoDisc/Getty Images • Masterfile • PhotoDisc/Getty Images • Michael Krasowitz/Taxi/Getty Images*
Chapter Opener 13 *PhotoDisc/Getty Images • Masterfile • PhotoDisc/Getty Images • Michael Newman/PhotoEdit*
Chapter Opener 14 *PhotoDisc/Getty Images • Masterfile • PhotoDisc/Getty Images • Lawrence Migdale/Pix Photography*

This book was set in 10.5/12 Minion by Preparé, Inc. and printed and bound by Courier Kendallville, Inc. The cover was printed by Courier Kendallville, Inc.

This book is printed on acid free paper. ∞

To order books or for customer service, please call 1-800-CALL WILEY (225-5945).

Library of Congress Cataloging-in-Publication Data
Dever, Martha T.
    Foundations and change in early childhood education / Martha T. Dever, Renée C. Falconer.
        p.   cm.
    ISBN-13: 978-0-471-47247-6 (pbk.)
        1. Early childhood education.   I. Falconer, Renée C.   II. Title.

LB1239.23.D48 2008
372.21--dc22   2006030326

Printed in the United States of America
10 9 8 7 6 5 4 3 2 1

About the Authors

Martha Taylor Dever. I have worked in early childhood education for over 35 years. I began my career in a part-time position as a first grade reading teacher and eventually became a kindergarten teacher. As a novice teacher, I thought the most important thing for me to do was plan and implement structured learning experiences for children in my class. I provided open-ended activities (e.g., play, art) when they had completed their "lessons." By my second year of teaching, I realized that children were far more engaged in the open-ended learning experiences; so, I took their lead and incorporated "lessons" into those open-ended activities. In that particular social–political context, my ideas were so unique that the local paper featured my class under the heading "*Kindergarten Isn't What It Used to Be.*" I was hooked; I loved teaching.

As one who loves change, I began teaching adults when my local community college asked me to teach some classes so candidates could be certified as child care directors. The more I taught, the more I studied. As demographics in early care and education became more and more diverse, my interest in foundational issues increased.

Today, I am very passionate about the well-being of teachers and children of the twenty-first century who are in early care and education. As a grandmother, I have great personal interest too. Writing this book is my way of sharing all that I have learned with you who are the future of teaching.

Renée C. Falconer. I completed my teacher education over 40 years ago, in 1966, in Britain. It is sobering to reflect that the children in my first class will now be almost fifty years old. During my teacher preparation courses my outlook and beliefs about educational environments were imbued with Piaget's theories, the child-oriented British Infant School approach to early and the concept of project based learning. During my many years as a classroom teacher I had the privilege and joy of teaching in Britain, Canada, Australia, the United States, and the International School in Kenya. For many of those years I taught first grade or multiage primary classes with highly diverse groups of children, and the learning environment I created reflected the beliefs about early childhood education that I developed in my teacher education program.

I have always been intrigued by ideas about how children learn and grow, and my time working with children from various cultures helped me realize that childhood is a universal construct and children from all cultures play, laugh, and cry. It is not *what* children learn that is the core of their being, but *how* they learn; this will mold their future contribution to the society in which they grow and hopefully flourish.

The heart of the matter for all of us who are educators is to thoroughly analyze and understand what we mean by education. Is it merely to develop skills necessary to join the workforce and earn a living, or is it a larger issue that has ramifications for the global society and quality of life in another 40 years? For the sake of my grandchildren, I hope that the latter is the answer.

Preface

The inspiration for this text came out of our many conversations as mothers, grand-mothers, friends, former teachers of young children, authors, professors, and, most of all, advocates for the well-being of young children and their families. As professors who teach foundations of early childhood education courses, we wanted to write a book that would help us give you a broad introduction to the field, its joys and challenges. We have great pride in our profession and want to have a positive impact on your careers as early childhood professionals.

The primary goal of this text is to help you understand early childhood issues and best practices, and ways to advocate on behalf of young children. It takes you through the historical evolution of early childhood education with a primary focus on issues and practices today. Five themes are central to our text and woven throughout the chapters. The first and most prominent theme is *children*. The other themes include *advocacy, diversity, social–political environments,* and *professional development.*

Children. The needs and well-being of children and their families are central to everything we do as early childhood professionals. Hence, we begin the text with a focus on children in our chapter on the social view of children, past and present. This chapter provides a view into the lives of children over time and the influence of the social–political contexts in which they lived.

Woven throughout subsequent chapters is content related to the developmental and cultural needs of young children. This is important information for early child-hood educators who must create physically and psychologically safe learning environments for young children. Scholars have identified developmental patterns and benchmarks yet acknowledge that there is individual variation in patterns and timing of growth. As early childhood professionals, we must understand the developmental continuum on which young children are continually evolving, and the individual uniqueness of each child, in order to teach effectively, develop appropriate curriculum, make good management decisions, and be strong advocates for young children and their families.

Advocacy. As early childhood professionals, we have an understanding of the needs of young children and their families that others may not have. From our own experiences advocating to state legislators, we know that when we express ourselves in reasoned and socially appropriate ways, we can create changes that have a positive impact on the lives of children. As early childhood professionals, each of us is in a prime position to educate parents, community members, and policy makers about the needs of young children and to be advocates. Whatever form your advocacy takes, everything you learn from this text will support you as an advocate for young children.

Diversity. The great cultural diversity of our nation, past and present, provides the foundation for our free society. With many different voices to be heard, it has been our challenge and our privilege to embrace the many ways of knowing and living in our great nation.

The cultural aspects of the human existence shape who we are, what we value, and how we live. We live in an increasingly culturally diverse society and this is reflected in the culturally diverse populations of children in early childhood care and education. It is imperative that early childhood educators have adequate knowledge and understanding to teach for social justice and equal human rights, and so they can adequately meet the needs of all children in their early childhood settings. This text develops the diversity theme in a unique way because it highlights the breadth of difference present in our human existence. We address difference related to age, gender, class, ability, religion, sexual orientation, and ethnicity. For example, we have woven discussion of religious difference throughout the text because we believe that, whether you are atheist, Protestant, Catholic, Jewish, Muslim, Hindu, a member of a subgroup, or any other religion, your identification with that group is core to who you are. (We certainly acknowledge diversity within groups too.) Ignoring this aspect of culture can be likened to ignoring your ethnicity or gender.

Socio-political Environments. Having been early childhood professionals for many years, we have been fascinated to note how the social–political environment impacts our jobs and thus, the lives of children and their families. For example, we both remember vividly the years of the Cold War and the anti-communist sentiment in the United States. This sentiment led to an increased emphasis on math and science teaching in our nation's schools when the Russians, not us, launched the first space satellite. History is thick with such examples, which has led to our view that children and their families live in particular social–political contexts and these contexts the shape children's lives. We wrote this text to highlight the social–political contexts in which families live and to illuminate the influence of particular contexts. Events, ideas, our professional beliefs, and the work of early childhood professionals grow out of particular contexts, which is why we situated the content of this text in context.

Professional Development. As we look back 40 years or more to our teacher education programs, we realize how much our attitudes, beliefs, and practice have changed from then until now. As research emerges and stories are told, we constantly have new information to think about that has an impact on our professional lives. In your role as a student, you have entered the professional world of early and, in this role, you are developing your attitudes, beliefs, and practices related to early childhood education. Having been a student for many years, you bring some attitudes, beliefs, and practices to your teacher education experience from the onset. As you continue through your program, those attitudes, beliefs, and practices are likely to alter. This text includes a feature titled *My Developing Professional View* which gives you periodic opportunities to articulate your attitudes, beliefs, and practices. This view will evolve throughout your career.

Organization

Part 1 of the text sets the historical context for early childhood education today. Chapter 1 traces society's view of childhood over time. Chapter 2 continues by describing social and philosophical trends over time and the scholars whose work contributed to those trends. It is organized by eras (colonial era, industrial era, progressive era, etc.) so that readers can consider trends and contributions of scholars in particular contexts. Chapter 3 examines the influence of cultural diversity, the social view of childhood, and sociopolitical factors. The evolution of school governance relative to policy development and court rulings, past and present, is also addressed.

Part 2 focuses on the role of early childhood educators working in infant, toddler, preschool, kindergarten, and primary grade settings. Chapter 4 lays the foundation for examining early childhood contexts by discussing the role of early childhood educators, including professional qualifications for working in various early childhood settings, and giving an overview of best practices. Subsequent chapters discuss and describe contemporary issues, trends, and practices specific to the age and developmental stage of children they serve. Highlighted in the discussion of programs are contemporary characteristics of programs, scholars who influenced each, and the research base.

Part 3 addresses issues and practices related to guiding and assessing young children. It further illuminates the role of early childhood educators in relation to management, child guidance, assessment, and working with linguistically diverse children and their families.

Part 4 discusses key issues related to working with families and communities including families who have children with special needs. Other family and community issues examined include variation in family configurations and values and child abuse. High-quality early childhood environments and the role of technology are addressed in this section. Chapter 14 culminates the text by focusing on important issues for early childhood educators, in the twenty-first century.

Pedagogical Features

Boxed Features. The boxed features are designed to extend your understanding of the themes of the text. The *Focus on Children* box exemplifies characteristics of young children based on our actual observations. Again, based on actual observations, *Focus on Diversity* exemplifies differences among children. The *Advocating for the Child* feature describes aspects of public attitude and policy that impact the lives of children and their families, whereas *Focus on History* makes connections between the present and the past. *Window into the Classroom* chronicles happenings in real classrooms, and *Theory into Practice* makes suggestions for practice based on theory and research.

Many states are requiring a professional portfolio as part of teacher licensure where you articulate your beliefs about teaching and learning and provide evidence of those beliefs. Whether you are required to develop a portfolio or not, you will be asked on many occasions to share your philosophy of education. The *My Developing Professional View* feature invites you to articulate what you believe about the central topic of the chapter.

End of Chapter Features. Suggestions for additional learning experiences are provided at the end of each chapter. *Enrichment Activities* can be used either as in-class or as out-of-class projects. *For Further Reading* and *Professional Development Resources* provide resources for learning more about a particular topic. The *Self-Assessment* feature is designed to help you assess your learning from the chapter.

Acknowledgments

We have been fortunate to work with a wonderful team at John Wiley & Sons, including Brad Hanson (formerly of Wiley), Jay O'Callaghan, Vice President and Publisher, Robert Johnston, Acquisitions Editor, Katie Melega, Senior Editorial Assistant, Eileen McKeever, Editorial Assistant, Emily Streutker, Marketing Manager, and Nicole Ferrato, Marketing Assistant. In addition, we want to express our gratitude to the production and design team, especially Nicole Repasky, Harry Nolan, Hope Miller, Sandra Rigby, Jennifer McMillan, and Suzanne Ingrao of Ingrao Associates.

We are also very grateful for the feedback and suggestions provided by the many reviewers and wish to express our thanks to each of them. Their constructive suggestions and innovative ideas strengthened our work immeasurably.

Reviewers

Beena Achhpal, *Southern Connecticut State University*
Rachel Adeodu, *Northeastern Illinois University*
Sally Adler, *Washtenaw Community College*
Ola Aina, *College of Charleston*
Junie Albers, *University of Central Florida*
Jennifer Aldrich, *Central Missouri State University*
Jerry Aldridge, *University of Alabama, Birmingham*
Sharon Allen, *Portland Community College*
Keri Altig, *University of Nevada Las Vegas*
Sarah Jane Anderson, *Mount Ida College*
Barbara Barton, *Three Rivers Community College*
Alice Beaudreau, *Capital Community College*
Michael J. Bell, *West Chester University*
Teresa Bennett, *Eastern Illinois University*
Jacques Benninga, *California State University, Fresno*
JaneAnn Benson, *Grand Rapids Community College*
Barbara Biles, *Joliet Junior College*
Beverly Boals, *Arkansas State University*
Barbara Boyle, *Bucks County Community College*
Anne Broughton, *Northern Kentucky University*
Dana Bush, *Eastern Kentucky University*
Stacy Burr, *Clemson University*
Takiema Bunche-Smith, *Borough of Manhattan Community College*
Melissa Burnham, University of Nevada, Reno
Tim Campbell, University of Central Oklahoma
Dong Hwa Choi, *Indiana State University*
Susan Christian, *Patrick Henry Community College*
Chris Coberly, *Alabama A and M University*
Layna Cole, *Minnesota State University, Moorhead*
Judy Collmer, *Dallas County Community College District*
Kathleen Cummings, *Suffolk County Community College, Riverhead*
Alison Drake, *College of DuPage*
Vanese Delahoussaye, *Houston Community College*
Alika Hope Despotopoulos, *Manhattan Community College*
Beth Engelhardt, *Sinclair Community College*
Judie Erickson, *Snow College*
Gretchen Espinetti, *Kent State University*
MaryBeth Evans, *University of Southern Mississippi*
Karen Falcone
Colleen Finegan, *Wright State University*
Sufian Forawi, *University of Akron*
Teresa Frazier, *Thomas Nelson Community College*
Connie Gassner, *Ivy Tech State College*
Eugene Geist, *Ohio University, Athens*
Bonnie Good, *Delta College*
Rhonda Harrington, *Arkansas State University*
Jill Harrison, *Delta College*
Craig Hart, *Brigham Young University, Provo*

Jeanne Helm, *Richland Community College*
Eileen Hughes, *University of Alaska*
Janet Imel, *Ivy Tech State College, Central*
Sai Jambunathan, *New Jersey City University*
Susan Johnson, *Northern Virginia Community College, Loudoun*
Tricia Giovacco Johnson, *Montclair State University*
Rose Jones, *University of Southern Mississippi*
Donna Jones, *Arkansas State University*
Judy Judd, *California State University, Sacramento*
Lori Keith, *University of North Texas*
Elisa Klein, *University of Maryland, College Park*
Denise Knight, *San Bernadino Community College District*
Janice Kroeger, *Kent State University*
Sheri Leafgren, *Kent State University*
Mary Leidy, *Metropolitan Community College*
Leslie L. Loughmiller, *Texas State University*
Jeri Lupton, *Ventura College*
Jamie Mabry, *Aiken Technical College*
Mary Ann Maggitti, *West Chester University*
Arlene Martin, *Kean University*
Carol Mollard, *University of Nebraska, Kearney*
Selina Mushi, *Northeastern Illinois University*
Farol Nelson, *Utah State University*
Melanie Nollsch, *Kirkwood Community College*
Leigh M O'Brien, *Montclair State University*
Patricia Oliff, *Temple University*
Penelope Orr, *Florida State University*
Debra Pierce, *Ivy Tech State College*
Helen Mele Robinson, *Borough of Manhattan Community College*
Margaret Rodriguez, *El Paso Community College*
Kim Ruebel, *Georgia Southern University*
Angela Salmon, *Florida International University*
Meera Shin, *Kean University*
Debbie Simpson, *Middle Tennessee State University*
Diane Sparks, *Grand Rapids Community College*
Gloria Spinella, *Rowan University*
Dolores Stegelin, *Clemson University*
Ruth Supler, *Minnesota State University, Moorhead*
Kevin Swick, *University of South Carolina*
Barbara Thompson, *University of Kansas*
Louis Warren, *East Carolina University*
Kathleen Watkins, *Community College of Philadelphia*
Susan Weaver, *Oklahoma State University*
Alan Weber, *Suffolk County Community College, Selden*
Brenda Wolodko, *University of Toledo*
Melinda Young, *University of Nebraska, Kearney*
Glenna Zeak, *Pennsylvania State University, University Park*
Nillofur Zobairi, *Southern Illinois University*

Brief Contents

Part 1: Evolution of Early Childhood Education

1. View of Childhood: Past and Present   1
2. History of Social, Political, and Philosophical Trends   21
3. Governance of Early Education and Care: Past and Present   53

Part 2: Early Childhood

4. Role of Early Childhood Educators in Children's Lives   69
5. Infants and Toddlers   91
6. Preschool and Kindergarten   113
7. Early Childhood: The Primary Grades   139

Part 3: Guiding and Assessing Young Children

8. Guiding Children's Behavior in Early Childhood Settings   161
9. Assessing the Child in Early Childhood Settings   187
10. Children Who Are Linguistically Diverse   207

Part 4: Supporting and Advocating for Young Children in the Twenty-first Century

11. Children with Special Needs   227
12. The Impact of Environments and Technology on Young Children   249
13. Children and Their Families   275
14. Issues and Advocacy in Early Childhood Education in the Twenty-first Century   297

Contents

Part 1: Evolution of Early Childhood Education

1 View of Childhood: Past and Present 1

Ancient View of Childhood 2
    Ancient Native American View of Childhood 3
    Ancient Greek View of Childhood 4
    Ancient Roman View of Childhood 4

Children as Miniature Adults 5
    Child Guidance 6
    Reformation Era (1400–1600) 6

Children as Sinful 6
    African-American and Native American Children 6
    Child Guidance 7
    Native Americans 7
    European Americans 8

Children as Blank Slates 8

Children as Children 8
    Jean-Jacques Rousseau 8
    Johann Heinrich Pestalozzi 9
    Children as Children Continues 10
    Native American Children 11
    Child Guidance 11
    African-American Children 11

Standardization of Childhood 11
    Native American Children 12
    Children with Disabilities 12
    Child Guidance 12

Modern Views of Childhood 13
    The Sensual Child 13
    The Malleable Child 13
    The Hurried Child 13
    Child Guidance 14
    Behavior Modification 15
    Democratic Behavior Guidance 15

Children Today 16
    Miniature Adults 16
    Readiness 16
    Child-Centered Learning Environments 16

Children as Our Future 16
Summary 17
Enrichment Activities 17
Self-Assessment 18
For Further Reading 18
References 19

2 History of Social, Political, and Philosophical Trends 21

Precolonial Times 22
    Native Americans 22
    European Influence 22

Colonial Era 24
    Social-Political Environment 24
    Early Childhood Education 25
        Dame Schools 25
        Latin Grammar Schools 25

Industrial Era 25
    Social, Political Environment 25
        Common Schools 26
        Origin of the Testing Movement 27
        Educating African-Americans 28
        Educating Native Americans 28
    Early Childhood Education 28
        Origin of Kindergarten 28

Progressive Movement 30
    Social, Political Environment 30
        The Testing Movement 31
    Educational Theories 31
        Progressive Educators 31
    Early Childhood Programs 32
        Schooling for Children of Color 32
        Schooling for Children with Disabilities 33
        Nursery Schools 33
        Bank Street 33
        Kindergarten 33

Montessori Education   34

The Child Study Movement   **34**
  Social, Political Environment   **34**
    The Testing Movement   35
  Early Childhood Theories   **35**
    Constructivism   35
    Behaviorism   37
    Self-Actualization Theory   38
    Maturationism   38
  Early Childhood Programs   **39**
    Children with Disabilities   39
    Waldorf Schools   39

Post World War II and the Great Society   **39**
  Social, Political Environment   **39**
    The Great Society   40
  Early Childhood Theories   **41**
    Behaviorism   42
    Psychosocial Theory   42
  Early Childhood Programs   **42**
    Reggio Emilia   42
    High/Scope   44
    Head Start   44
    Children with Disabilities   44

Accountability Movement   **45**
  Social, Political Environment   **45**
    The Testing Movement   45
  Early Childhood Programs   **46**
    Open Education   46

Electronic Age   **47**
  Social, Political Environment   **47**
    The Testing Movement   47
  Early Childhood Theories   **48**
  Early Childhood Programs   **49**
Summary   49
Enrichment Activities   50
For Further Reading   51
Professional Development Resources   51
Self-Assessment   51
References   51

**3   Governance of Early Care and
Education: Past and Present**   **53**

Oversight for Early Care and Education   **54**
  Administrative Reform   **54**
    Scientific Management   55
    Nursery Schools   55
    Governance of Early Care and Education
      Today   55
    Critique of Centralized Governance   56

**Federal Policies Affecting Early Childhood
Education**   **57**
    Postwar Years   57
    Children with Disabilities   58

The Era of the Great Society   59
The Era of Accountability   59
Entering the Twenty-First Century   59

The History of Bilingual Education   **61**

The Relationship of Church and State   **62**
    Colonial Era   62
    Industrial Era   63
    History of Roman Catholic Schools   64
    The Progressive Era   64
    The Twentieth Century   65
    Separation of Church and State Today   66
Summary   67
Enrichment Activities   67
For Further Reading   67
Professional Development Resources   68
Self-Assessment   68
References   68

Part 2: Early Childhood

**4   The Role of Early Childhood
Educators in Children's Lives**   **69**

Preparing to Be an Early Childhood Educator   **70**
    Child Care and Pre-K Programs   70
    Grades K–3   70
    Professional Development   71
  Philosophies of Learning   **72**
  Brain-Based Development   **73**
    Multiple Intelligences   74
  Constructivism   **76**
  Behaviorism   **76**
  Maturation   **77**

Appropriate Practices   **78**
  Developmentally Appropriate Practice   **78**
  Culturally Relevant Practice   **79**
  The Value of Play   **79**
    Play and Social–Emotional Development   81
    Play and Cognitive Development   82
  Your Role in Supporting Children's Play   **82**
    Support from Outside the Play   82
    Support from Inside the Play   83
  Curriculum Development   **83**
    Infants and Toddlers   84
    Children Ages 3–8   84
    Integrated Curriculum   84

Advocacy   **87**
Summary   88
Enrichment Activities   88
For Further Reading   89
Professional Development Resources   89
Self-Assessment   90
References   90

5 Infants and Toddlers **91**

**Developmental Characteristics of Infants
and Toddlers** **92**
  Language Development **92**
    Theories of Language Acquisition 92
    Stages of Language Development 96
    Reading to Infants and Toddlers 97
    Language Is Cultural 98
    Delayed Language Development 98
  Cognitive Development **99**
    Egocentrism 100
    Reasoning 100
  Physical Development **100**
  Social–Emotional Development **101**
    Impulse Control 101
    Attachment 101
    Temperament 102
  Play **103**
    Supporting Infant and Toddler Play 103

Programs for Infants and Toddlers **104**
  Child Care **104**
  Reggio Emilia **105**
  Early Head Start **106**
  Montessori **106**

Creating an Antibias Environment **107**
Summary 109
Enrichment Activities 109
For Further Reading 110
Professional Development Resources 110
Self-Assessment 110
References 111

6 Preschool and Kindergarten **113**

**Developmentally and Culturally Appropriate
Programs for Three- to Five-Year-Olds** **114**
  Language Development 114
  Cognitive Development 116
  Social–Emotional Development 117
  Physical Development 118
  Programs for Three- to Five-Year-Olds **118**
  Head Start 119
  High/Scope 121
  Bank Street 123
  Reggio Emilia 123
  Waldorf 124
  Montessori 125
  Teaching Antibias Attitudes **127**

Child Care **128**
  Types of Child Care **128**
    Center Based Child Care 128
    Employer Sponsored Care 129
    Home Child Care 129
    Church or Temple Care Centers 129
    Nannies 129

  Quality in Child Care **129**
    Funding Quality Care 130
Kindergarten **130**
  Readiness **131**
  Retention and Academic Redshirting **132**
    Benefits Cannot Be Consistently
      Substantiated 132
    Sociocultural Issues 132
    Developmental Kindergartens
      and Transitional First Grade 133
    Entrance Age 133
    An Alternative 133
  Half-Day/Full-Day Kindergarten **134**
  Kindergarten Curriculum **134**

Summary 135
Enrichment Activities 136
For Further Reading 137
Professional Development Resources 137
Self-Assessment 137
References 138

7 Early Childhood: The Primary Grades **139**

**Developmental Considerations for Primary
Grade Children** **140**
  Language and Literacy Development 140
  Cognitive Development 140
  Physical Development 143
  Social–Emotional Development 144

**Antibias Classrooms in the Primary
Grades** **144**
  Literacy Learning 144
  Antibias Instructional Strategies **146**
    Integrating Content about Diversity into
      the Curriculum 147

**Curriculum and Effective Teaching
in the Primary Grades** **150**
  Child-Centered Environment **151**
  Explicit Instruction **151**
    Direct Instruction 151
  Balanced Literacy **151**
    National Reading Panel Report 153
  **Extension of Programs for 3- to 5-Year-Olds
    into Primary Grades** **153**
    Play in the Primary Grades 153
    Before and After School Programs 154

**Classroom and Calendar Configurations
in Primary Grades** **154**
  Multiage Grouping 154
  Looping 155
  Homeschooling 155
  Year-round and Traditional Schools **156**
  Educating Homeless Children **157**

Summary 158
Enrichment Activities 158

For Further Reading   159
Professional Development Resources   159
Self-Assessment   159
References   160

Part 3: Guiding and Assessing Young Children

8 Guiding Children's Behavior in Early Childhood Settings   161

Encouraging Environments   162
    Infants   162
    Toddlers   162
    Preschoolers and Kindergarteners   163
    Primary Grade Children   166

Managing Environments and
Guiding Behavior   168
    General Considerations for
    Guiding Behavior   169
        Choices   169
        Praise   169
        Punishment   170
    Developmentally Appropriate Guidance
    Strategies   170
        Infants   170
        Toddlers   171
        Preschoolers and Kindergarteners   173
        Primary Grade Children   175
        Children with Special Needs   177
    Cultural Considerations   178
        Individualism vs. Collectivism   179
        Understanding Roles   180
    Supporting Nonviolent Behavior   181
        Bullying   183

Summary   184
Enrichment Activities   184
For Further Reading   185
Self-Assessment   185
References   186

9 Assessing the Child in Early Childhood Settings   187

Types of Assessment in Early Childhood
Settings   188
    Observation   188
        Anecdotal Records and Field Notes   189
        Audio/Video and Photographic Recordings   190
        Checklists   191
    Portfolios   191
        Reflection   192
        Purposes   193
        Age Appropriate Portfolios   193
    Home Visits   194

    The Work Sampling System   194
    Standardized Tests   195
    Linking Assessment and Curriculum   195

Assessment Issues   196
    Align Assessment with the Nature of the Child   196
        Infants and Toddlers   197
        Preschool, Kindergarten, and Primary
            Grade Children   197
    Standardized Testing in Early
    Childhood Settings   197
        Developmental Considerations   197
        Inappropriate Labels   198
        High-Stakes Testing   198
    Cultural Issues in Assessment   199
        Culturally and Linguistically Diverse Children 200
        Barriers to Accurate Assessment   200
        Culturally Appropriate Assessment   201
    Assessing Children and Programs   202

Summary   203
Enrichment Activities   204
For Further Reading   205
Self-Assessment   205
References   205

10 Children Who Are Linguistically Diverse   207

The Challenge   208
    The Controversy   208

Linguistic Differences   210
    Dialects   210
        Dialect Errors: Points to Consider   210
        Black English   211
        Role of the Early Childhood Educator   211
    Accents   212
    Sign Language   212
    Speakers of Languages Other than English   213
        Bilingual Education   213
        English as a Second Language   214
        Nonverbal Communication   215

Acquiring a Second Language   215
    Theories of Second Language Acquisition   215
    Language Acquisition Stages   216
    Factors Affecting Second Language
        Acquisition: Social, Emotional,
        and Cognitive   220
    Loss of the First Language   222

Summary   223
Enrichment Activities   224
For Further Reading   224
Professional Development Resource   224
Self-Assessment   225
References   225

Part 4: Supporting and Advocating for Young Children in the Twenty-first Century

11 Children with Special Needs   227

Causes of Exceptionalities	228
Genetic	229
Prenatal Conditions	229
Birth and Postbirth Complications	229
Exceptionalities and the Role of Early Childhood Educators	229
Assessment of Exceptionalities	230
Labeling	231
Attention Deficit Hyperactivity Disorder	231
The Role of Early Childhood Educators	232
Autism	232
The Role of Early Childhood Educators	233
Behavior Disorders	233
The Role of Early Childhood Educators	233
Developmental Delays	233
The Role of Early Childhood Educators	234
Down Syndrome	234
The Role of Early Childhood Educators	234
Gifted	235
Role of Early Childhood Educators	235
Language and Hearing Disabilities	236
The Role of Early Childhood Educators	236
Learning Disabilities	237
The Role of Early Childhood Educators	238
Physical Disabilities	238
The Role of Early Childhood Educators	238
Visual Disabilities	239
The Role of Early Childhood Educators	239
Early Childhood Environments for Children with Disabilities	239
Inclusion	239
Infants and Toddlers	240
Preschool and Kindergarten	240
Primary Grades	241
Early Intervention and Early Childhood Special Education	242
Abuse and Neglect	242
The Role of Early Childhood Educators	243
Provide Quality Care and Education	243
Develop Reciprocal Relationships with Families	243
Recognize When Children Are at Risk	243
Understand and Assist Families	244
Build on Strengths	244
Be Informed	244
Antibias Environments for Children with Special Needs	244
Teaching about Differences	245
Summary	246
Enrichment Activities	246
For Further Reading	247
Professional Development Resources	247
Self-Assessment	248
References	248

12 The Impact of Environments and Technology on Young Children   249

Indoor Environments	250
Child-Centeredness	250
Scheduling Considerations	252
Room Arrangements	254
Infants and Toddlers	254
Preschool and Kindergarten	255
Primary Grades	257
Inclusive Environments	259
Outdoor Environments	259
Gross Motor Activity	260
Creative Play	260
Appreciation of Nature	260
The Social Environment	260
Teaching for Social Justice	261
Teach Questioning	262
Perspective Taking	262
Rethinking Curriculum	263
Take Action	264
Inequity in School Funding	264
Quality Schools for All	267
The Role of Technology in Early Childhood Environments	268
NAEYC Position on Technology and Young Children	268
Media Violence	269
Technology and Parenting	270
Antibias Technology Environments	271
Equitable Access	271
Assistive Technology	271
Summary	271
Enrichment Activities	272
For Further Reading	273
Professional Development Resources	273
Self-Assessment	273
References	274

13 Children and Their Families   275

Diverse Family Beliefs, Attitudes, and Practices	276
Stages of Cultural Identity	276
Cultural Progression in Our Diverse Nation	277
European American Families	277
African-American Families	278
Asian-American Families	279
Biracial Multiethnic Families	280
Gay and Lesbian Families	280

Hispanic American Families   280
Jewish American Families   281
Native American Families   282
Parents with Disabilities   283
Children of Divorce and Blended Families   283
Families Living in Poverty   **284**
Poverty and Resources   284
Poverty and Language   285
The Role of Early Childhood Educators   285

Involving Parents from Diverse Populations   286
Types of Parental Involvement   287
Barriers to Parent Involvement   288

Antibias Environment   289
Family Literacy   **290**

Using Community Resources   290
Family Friendliness   291
Resources   292
Invited Guests   293

Summary   293
Enrichment Activities   293
For Further Reading   294
Professional Development Resources   295
Self-Assessment   295
References   296

14 Issues and Advocacy in Early Childhood in the Twenty–first Century   297

View of the Child   298
Sociopolitical Influences   **299**
Poverty   **299**
Health and Well-being   **300**
Commerce, Industry, and Business   **303**
Metaphor of the Market for Schooling   **303**
High-Stakes Testing   **305**
Diversity   306
Teaching in a Diverse Society   **306**
Advocacy   308
Professional Development   **309**
Curriculum   **310**
Summary   311
Enrichment Activities   311
Self-Assessment   312
For Further Reading   312
Professional Development Resources   313
References   313

Index   **314**

View of Childhood: Past and Present

Children are our greatest natural resource; cultivate them. Children today are the laborers, professionals, parents, decision makers, and voters of tomorrow. They will be in charge of our democracy and productivity and they are our only hope for realizing a peaceful and just world. While all citizens are entitled to *life, liberty, and the pursuit of happiness,* not all are born with equal opportunity to achieve that goal. Some citizens come from nonmainstream groups that have historically been denied opportunities in schools and the workplace. For example, non-native English speakers often encounter challenges in schools and work environments. High-quality early education and care provide perhaps the best opportunity to create equal opportunity for all.

This is an exciting time to become an early childhood educator. Decades of research have illuminated the importance of the early years (birth to age 8) to human development, because during those years, the trajectory of an individual's life is set. Studies (Reynolds, Temple, Robertson, & Mann, 2001; Schweinhart, 2004; Schweinhart, Barnes, & Weikart, 1993) suggest that high-quality early education and care result in fewer juvenile arrests, lower school drop-out rates, lower rates of grade retention, and fewer special education placements later in life. These positive effects translate into significant savings to taxpayers.

We begin this text by examining how the social, economic, political, and scientific environment of any society drives its view of childhood and, hence, the lives of children. Social factors such as the needs of the family or religious values coupled with scientific knowledge, political attitudes, and availability of resources influence how children are viewed, how their developmental and learning needs are met, and how expectations for their behavior are determined. Over time, society's view of childhood has affected services and programs for children, including their care and education.

As you read about groups of people in this and subsequent chapters (e.g., ancient Greeks, Native Americans, Puritans), we will refer to some cultural norms within groups of people because it helps us understand the general beliefs and values that bind that group of people. For example, we note that Puritans grounded their strict disciplinary child raising practices in their religious belief that humans were inherently sinful. However, it is equally important to avoid stereotyping and to acknowledge that there are many differences among members of any particular group. Not all women are the same. Not all Hispanics are the same. Not all Jews are the same, and so on.

You can test this notion by trying the following exercise. In a group, decide on a culture all of you have in common (e.g., Christian, female). Then, generate a list of stereotypical characteristics for that group. Now, go through those characteristics and decide how many of them apply to you and to others in the group. We are certain that your list does not describe all of you perfectly.

This chapter sets the stage for the study of foundations of early childhood education by describing the history of views of childhood and child guidance. Beginning with the *ancient view of childhood*, subsequent views are discussed including *children as miniature adults, children as sinful, children as blank slates, children as children, standardization of childhood, modern views of childhood, and children as our future.*

After reading this chapter, you will understand:

► How society's view of children evolved over time.

► Social, economic, political, and scientific factors that influenced society's view of children over time.

► Scholars who have influenced our society's view of children.

► The evolution of child guidance practices.

► Contributors to practice in child guidance.

Ancient View of Childhood

The presence of Native Americans in North America dates back to ancient times. Furthermore, over time European cultures have contributed to beliefs and lifestyles in the United States. Following is a brief overview of the view of childhood in Native American and European cultures that have influenced our view of children in the United States today (Figures 1.1 and 1.2).

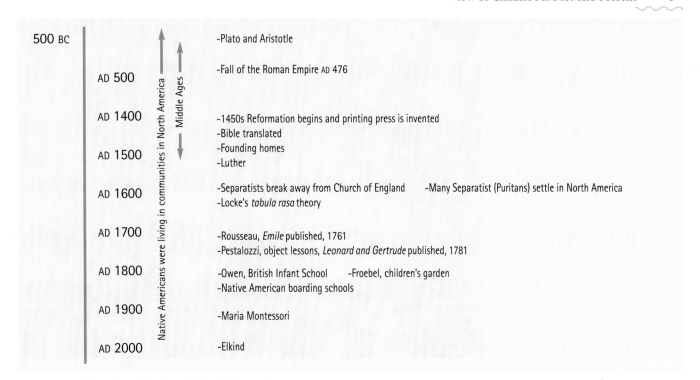

Figure 1.1. Time line of influential scholars and events.

```
500 BC ─┬─                    -Plato and Aristotle

   AD 500 ─┤                    -Fall of the Roman Empire AD 476


   AD 1400 ─┤                   -1450s Reformation begins and printing press is invented
                                -Bible translated
   AD 1500 ─┤                   -Founding homes
                                -Luther

   AD 1600 ─┤                   -Separatists break away from Church of England    -Many Separatist (Puritans) settle in North America
                                -Locke's tabula rasa theory

   AD 1700 ─┤                   -Rousseau, Emile published, 1761
                                -Pestalozzi, object lessons, Leonard and Gertrude published, 1781

   AD 1800 ─┤                   -Owen, British Infant School    -Froebel, children's garden
                                -Native American boarding schools

   AD 1900 ─┤                   -Maria Montessori


   AD 2000 ─┤                   -Elkind
```

Native Americans were living in communities in North America

Middle Ages

Figure 1.2. Time line of images of childhood.

```
500 BC ─┬─                    -Native Americans—Children as part of community
                              -Greeks—Children will shape the future
                              -Romans—Education leads to strong moral character
   AD 500 ─┤

                              -Children as as miniature adults
   AD 1400 ─┤

   AD 1500 ─┤                 -Universal schooling

   AD 1600 ─┤                 -Children as sinful
                              -Children as blank slates

   AD 1700 ─┤                 -Children as children
                              -Child-centered education

   AD 1800 ─┤                 -Standardization of childhood
                              -Native American boarding schools

   AD 1900 ─┤                 -Children as sensual, malleable, and hurried

   AD 2000 ─┤                 -Children as our future
```

Ancient Native American View of Childhood

Millions of Native Americans inhabited North America long before the arrival of Europeans. The indigenous peoples lived in many different ways across what we now call North, Central, and South America. The early Native Americans spoke over 200 different languages, some of which exist today. In general, Native Americans viewed humans (and thus children) holistically. That is, all beings were made up of spirit, mind, and body and the ultimate goal of education was connection of the individual to the Supreme Creator (Locust, 1988).

Hulton-Deutsch Collection/CORBIS.

Native American children were generally viewed as part of the community within the family, tribe, and nation. Through observation, imitation, and instruction, children learned gender specific skills in the context of daily living and at the feet of their elders. Play was a primary activity where boys played the role of hunters, warriors, and athletes while girls played the role of mother, farmer, and homemaker. Toys such as dolls and bows with arrows resembled the tools of adults (Reagan, 2005).

Ancient Greek View of Childhood

The ancient Greek scholars Plato (427–347 BC) and Aristotle (384–322 BC) were strong proponents of education for young children. They believed that education was important to a society's strong moral fiber. As the children learned the skills of the society, the future took shape. Plato believed that young children should learn in their natural environment through observation and playing at the feet of their mothers. During this era, formal education began at age 6 and was reserved primarily for male children destined to become political leaders or clergy.

Aristotle felt that large families often led to a life of poverty so he advocated for small families. As a result, some babies, particularly females, were abandoned and eventually died from exposure (Osborn, 1975). Aristotle advocated for abortion as preferable to the practice of infanticide.

Ancient Roman View of Childhood

Ancient Romans modeled schooling after the teachings of Plato and Aristotle, and shared their view that education was the means to a strong moral society. As with the Greeks, young children learned at home. The Romans had some community schools where formal education began around age 7. Unlike the Greeks, however, they provided schooling for both male and female children. With the fall of the Roman Empire in AD 476, Germanic rule came about (Castle, 1961). Under the new rule, schools were sponsored by churches and reserved for males who were on a career path to become clergy. They were responsible for reading scripture and writing religious manuscripts.

The rise of Christianity caused a change in the attitudes about infanticide. Because early Christian leaders considered all children to have a soul (Osborn, 1975), infanticide was eventually deemed a pagan practice. Thus, some families who wished to be rid of a child would place their infant in a basket adorned with ornaments, and leave the infant in a public place hoping someone would find and keep him/her.

Children as Miniature Adults

The epoch of the Middle Ages (500–1500) was one of great unrest in Europe and many families were struggling to survive. During this time, childhood was almost nonexistent because as soon as children could function without constant care from their mothers, they became apprentices in the world of work. Children were property, valued primarily for what they would bring to the family and community when they were old enough to contribute, usually around age 7 or 8. Children's developmental needs were not understood or considered during this period.

Boys were valued more highly than girls because they grew into stronger laborers and they could inherit property. (The *Focus on Diversity* illuminates a common social attitude about girls.) Although discouraged, infanticide was still practiced, particularly for girls and for children with disabilities. To rid themselves of a child, parents might suffocate the child while lying in bed, because by doing this intent to kill was difficult to prove.

Foundling homes, the precursor to orphanages, were established as an alternative to infanticide. Thus, any child who was not able to contribute to the survival of the family might be subject to either abandonment in a Foundling Home or infanticide (Colon & Colon, 2001). Infant and child mortality rates were high during this period.

Focus on Diversity

Gender Attitudes of the Past

Throughout the period of the Middle Ages in Europe, boys continued to be valued more highly than girls. The birth of a girl was often rationalized by the fact that she may someday give birth to a boy. From the pulpit, females were reminded of their status as second-class citizens and women were reminded that they were subordinate to their husbands.

Following is a 15th-century French proverb that characterizes the value of women to society:

A good horse and a bad horse need the spur.
A good woman and a bad woman need the stick.
A woman who talks like a man and a hen that crows like a cock are not worth keeping. (p. 320)

Schooling for young girls consisted primarily of learning to spin, cook, and sew. Because the nearest physician might be many miles away, most girls also learned the skills of a midwife and how to mix commonly needed medicines.

Owing to the Protestant view that all citizens needed to be literate in order to read Scripture and talk with God, schools for girls eventually began to appear. However, attendance was usually limited to girls from the most prominent families.

Have you had any similar observations or experience that reflect this view?

Source: Colon, A. R., with Colon, P. A. (2001). *A history of children: A socio-cultural survey across millennia.* Westport, CT: Greenwood Press.

Child Guidance

Child guidance practices are influenced by a society's view of children. Consistent with the view of children as miniature adults, they were expected to act like adults. Those children who did not meet expectations were harshly punished with practices like withholding food or dunking a child in cold water. It was not unusual for a child to die as a result of punishment.

Reformation Era (1400–1600)

By the 1500s Europe was enjoying economic growth due to increases in commercial trade. The *Renaissance* period which emerged toward the end of the Middle Ages revived interest in literature, art, and culture. Economic and political turbulence began to diminish, although there was still unrest due to the Protestant opposition to the Roman Catholic Church. Henry VIII, who opposed the pope because he would not allow him to divorce his wife, started his own church, declaring himself its head. Many European countries were establishing national autonomy which further weakened the power of the Catholic church.

With economic and political strife lessened, societies were free to take another look at childhood. A move in Europe to provide education for all children, male and female, was led by clergyman Martin Luther (1483–1546), who believed that all children needed to learn to read the Bible to acquire intellectual, spiritual, and physical good health. Translation of the Bible from Latin into other languages and the invention of the printing press in the 1450s gave birth to universal schooling in Europe. There were now materials and venues for teaching children how to read.

Educational leaders, who were also the religious leaders, influenced the emergence of childhood. Many taught that life was not about the human existence, as we know it; rather, it was about eternal life. The earthly duty of humans was to become worthy of the fruits of heaven rather than the den of hell. This ideal coupled with the emergence of universal schooling gave birth to childhood, or a time between dependency and apprenticeships that was designated for learning to read the Bible.

Children as Sinful

By the early 17th century, a revolution of sorts was taking place in England. While there had been long-standing differences between the Catholics and the Church of England, a group known as the *Puritans* or *Separatists* was breaking away from the Church of England, creating a third, contentious group. The Puritans wanted to simplify worship by getting rid of the traditional incense, robes, and crosses. They were persecuted in England, which led many to leave and settle in New England.

The Puritans believed that humans were inherently sinful. Any misbehavior on the part of a child was evidence of the devil's influence, and that influence had to be eradicated. There were two ways to eradicate the influence of the devil from the child; one was to beat the devil out of the child and the other was for the child to read and study the Scriptures. Most teachers and parents adhered to this belief, so children endured harsh beatings and long periods of recitation of the Scripture and catechism if they misbehaved.

African-American and Native American Children

African-Americans and Native Americans were living in America during this period. Africans first came to America as indentured servants alongside white indentured servants. In exchange for their passage to America, indentured servants agreed to work for their sponsors for a particular period of time. However, colonists found it more economically advantageous to have slaves rather than indentured servants because, unlike slaves, indentured servants had to have some

Pierre Delliette, 1702. Courtesy of the Peabody Museum of Archaeology and Ethnology.

goods and services provided, and they would eventually be freed (Banks, 2003). Eventually, African-Americans became slaves with no rights. Children of slaves were not educated, lived in substandard conditions, and were often malnourished. Their lives as laborers began as soon as they were able to handle duties on the plantation or as house servants.

As more Europeans arrived in America, cultural conflict arose between Europeans and Native Americans. There were great differences in their religious practices and lifestyles. Most Europeans practiced Christianity, while Native Americans held deep spiritual beliefs about the world of living things and sought to live in accord with all living things. European immigrants viewed Native Americans as heathen and wanted to convert them to their Christian, European ways.

Native Americans were dying from diseases brought to America by the Europeans. To escape conflict and disease, Native American children were rapidly moving west with their families, because the West was not yet populated by European immigrants.

Child Guidance

Given what we know about family values during this era, what would you predict about child guidance practices among Native Americans and European Americans? Each culture's view of children is reflected in their guidance practices.

Native Americans

In general, Native Americans viewed their young children holistically and parents sought to nurture the spirit, mind, and body in concert. A common Native American practice was to place infants in cradle boards strapped on the mother's back. This was believed to instill discipline and to help infants learn about their natural world as they lay still and peacefully in the cradle board surrounded by nature (Morey & Gilliam, 1974).

In general, behavior guidance of young Native American children was accomplished by modeling and the wisdom of the elders. That is, desirable behavior was explained but primarily modeled by parents and other adults. When children misbehaved, they were asked to think about their behavior and what they learned. Logical consequences (Chapter 8) were often applied.

European Americans

European American child guidance practices varied across social class and religious orientation. There were generally three family types among the European settlers in the 17th and 18th centuries: the *genteel*, the *moderate*, and the *evangelical* (Wortham, 1992). The genteel parents were affluent and their children enjoyed the finest toys and clothing, had access to libraries, and were often raised primarily by nurses or servants. Parents and children often had distant relationships.

The moderate parents set limits for their children and expected obedience. Authority over their children was often extended to grandparents and other extended family. The evangelical parents taught their children to love and to fear both God and their parents. These parents held total power over their children and demanded obedience and submission, often by inflicting severe punishment; such practices extended to schools.

Children as Blank Slates

John Locke (1632–1704) was a 17th-century scholar who is best known for his book *Some Thoughts Concerning Education*, published in 1693. It was written as a manual on good breeding and education of children. In his treatise, Locke asserted the *tabula rasa* theory; that is, at birth, the infant's mind was a blank slate. Rather than having innate characteristics, Locke believed the infant's mind was blank at birth, ready to learn through experience.

Locke was a British physician who earned his living as a teacher of the sons of British aristocrats. He believed that children were best educated at home by their parents or tutors because schools were places of social ills. He felt that isolating children would prevent them from developing bad social habits (Beatty, 1995). He emphasized the importance of "natural education," whereby children learn through play and by doing.

Locke implored parents to instill good character in their children. He was opposed to physical punishment; rather, parents should teach their children through their model and expectations. He believed parents should assert their will on their children and appeal to their desire to please authority.

Locke also noted that children vary in their temperaments and that parents should study their children to understand their individual natures. He asserted that young children learn through practice, not memorization of rules. Learning experiences should reflect the needs of individual children such that programs are tailored to children, not children to programs.

Locke's ideas about nurturing children through sensory experiences and adult modeling have had much influence in early childhood education over the years. Sensory experiences were a large part of Maria Montessori's program (Chapter 2) and are present in early childhood programs today.

Children as Children

The 18th century saw a shift in the social view of childhood in Europe. Scholars were beginning to assert that human nature was essentially good, that children were not inherently sinful, and that education must allow their goodness to unfold. While many people in North America at this time still held to the Puritan beliefs that children were inherently sinful, this new view would eventually make its way to the colonies.

Jean-Jacques Rousseau

Rousseau (1712–1778) was a French philosopher who lived during a period of Western history known as the Age of Enlightenment, which was a time that un-

earthed a modern view of the world (Anchor, 1967). He did not adhere to the supernatural order of the world; rather, he introduced ideas about living according to natural law (Anchor, 1967). Rousseau's ideas about education for young children would turn schooling in Europe and subsequently North America in a new direction. He believed in the natural goodness of children and that childhood should be prolonged and protected rather than exploited. He asserted that mothers should breast-feed their infants, and fathers should mentor their children.

A naturalist, Rousseau wrote and published the book *Emile* in 1761; it was one of the most radical writings of the time on child rearing and education. The book chronicles the life of a fictitious boy, Emile, who was raised on an island, untainted by social ills. His education came from the natural environment as he learned through his senses. Rousseau believed that children learn as they experience rain, care for living things, and so on.

Rousseau was one of the first scholars to suggest that children's development evolves in stages and that young children have a unique way of viewing the world. Similar to Locke, he believed that very young children should not be engaged in formal learning, but rather should learn through play and active experiences with nature and objects. He believed that young children need to be allowed to develop in their own way with the support the natural environment provides.

Like Locke, Rousseau did not believe in schools for children, because he considered them to be an unnatural environment. Unlike Locke, however, he felt the home was also an unnatural environment. He believed children should be given to male tutors to be educated in the natural environment away from society and its ills.

According to Rousseau, girls should be educated differently than boys. He viewed men as strong and active, and women as weak and passive. This characterization of women was embodied in Sophie, Emile's wife, who was dependent and docile. She was trained to stay in her place and educated for the sole purpose of meeting Emile's needs and caring for their children.

Jean-Jacques Rousseau.

If Rousseau lived today, he would probably oppose teaching children through memorization and assessing them with paper/pencil tests. More likely, he would make the school yard and the community his classroom.

Johann Heinrich Pestalozzi

Many credit Pestalozzi (1746–1827) with formalizing early education. Unlike Locke or Rousseau, he was a teacher of young children, and was particularly concerned about the lives of children living in poverty. He cared deeply, not about changing

Johann Heinrich Pestalozzi.
The Granger Collection.

their social class, but about teaching them to be independent. In fact, he taught many poor children in the natural environment on his farm until it became insolvent.

Pestalozzi was quite impressed with Rousseau's *Emile*. He embraced the notion of children learning in their natural environment. He also highlighted the importance of the first year of life and acknowledged that young children learn through their senses. Unlike Rousseau, Pestalozzi saw the home as the ideal natural environment. In his 1781 book, *Leonard and Gertrude*, he introduced the peasant teacher, Gertrude, who taught children to count steps as they went from one room to another and to count the threads while spinning (Beatty, 1995).

Pestalozzi is also known for his *object lessons*, curriculum where children learn by doing rather than memorizing. His objects were to be manipulated as children learned to count or stack, and as they learned what objects can do (e.g., slide, roll). Adults created a climate that supported healthy interactions and learning to read. He believed that, while gaining knowledge was important, children's development was more important. Thus, the aim of object lessons was primarily to support development, and acquisition of knowledge was secondary (Hughes, 2001).

Similar to his predecessors, Pestalozzi felt schools were unhappy places. They were not child-centered nor did they provide children with the affection they needed. By the early 19th century, his ideas began to appear in English advice manuals, which were widely read by parents in North America. Thus, the seeds of child-centered education were planted in the United States.

Children as Children Continues

Subsequent scholars promoted the child-centered curriculum for young children. Robert Owen (1771–1858) wanted young children to be educated in groups outside the home. Concerned about the effects of industrialization on poor children, he believed in the importance of socializing them in the ways of the culture, even at the expense of their individualism. Thus, he initiated the British Infant School (Chapter 2).

Friedrich Froebel (1782–1852), the father of kindergarten, also promoted the child-centered curriculum. It was Froebel's ideas about the child-centered curriculum that would finally make their way to the United States (Chapter 2).

Native American Children

Since the end of the American Revolution, Indian nations had been establishing various relationships with the U.S. government and negotiating possession of land. For example, the Cherokee negotiated sovereignty and equal status with Americans. While many other tribes maintained their traditional ways, the Cherokee wrote a constitution, printed newspapers in their native language, and became landowners and slave holders, and some converted to Christianity (White, 1993). While Native American children were influenced by these changes, they did not attend school with European American children; they continued to be educated within their tribes.

Child Guidance

The dawn of the 19th century and the industrial revolution heralded reform in disciplinary practices in public schools. Friedrich Froebel and others asserted their belief that the nature of children was essentially good. Froebel had a strong faith in children's inherent ability to learn and advocated for educational activities to be experiential rather than rote, meaningful rather than mundane. He did not agree that brutal punishment to enforce memorization of facts and appropriate behavior was supportive of children's learning and development.

Although many forms of punishment remained, corporal punishment diminished. New child guidance approaches sought to instill an internalized authority rather than external control based on fear. For example, rather than harsh punishment, the child might be asked to sit out of a game as a consequence for misbehaving during the game. Activities were more engaging as object lessons replaced recitation, and classroom management was now built into the learning activities (e.g., picture guides for giving directions). Teachers of this era used rewards, promotion, and demotion as incentives.

African-American Children

In the post-Civil War period, many African-American children had access to schooling. Disciplinary approaches for them were not based on affectionate authority or internal control as they were for European American children. Many felt it was inappropriate to provide affectionate authority or internal control because African-Americans were considered an inferior race. Known as racial paternalism, the authority of a paternalistic and purportedly superior race was instilled (Butchart, 1998).

Standardization of Childhood

By the late 19th century, children did not necessarily need to work for the families to survive, and society shifted its view of childhood to see it as a time of innocence. In Europe and the United States, a uniform social view of children emerged, one that aligned with the ways of the cultural mainstream, and many children did not fit the mold. Juvenile delinquency was on the rise by

Bettmann/Corbis Images.

the turn of the 20th century, and welfare agencies and juvenile correctional institutions had been created to address issues of child poverty and crime.

Unlike Europe, the United States treated boys and girls similarly with regard to education. They walked to school together and sat side by side in classes. Because African-American children were considered to be inferior to European American children, their schools were separate. Fewer resources were put into schools for African-American children than for white children.

Native American Children

By the mid-19th century, the Indian reservation was viewed as a laboratory for creating social change, and Native Americans were indoctrinated in white ways (Nabokov, 1993). Children, traditionally educated within the tribe, were taken from their homes and sent to boarding schools where they learned the English language, dressed in the school uniforms of white children, cut their hair, and ate the food of white people. This attempt to assimilate Native Americans into the ways of the white mainstream and to force them to disregard their native cultures created a long-term negative impact on the cultural identities of many Native Americans.

Children with Disabilities

Until this point in time, children with disabilities were usually considered a burden to their families. This view changed when, in the early 20th century, theories emerged suggesting that intelligence was not fixed and scholars were asserting that the environment could have an effect on mental growth. J. McVicker Hunt argued that nature sets the bounds of individual intelligence but nurture determines whether or not individual intellectual potential is realized. Scholars began taking an interest in the needs of children with disabilities.

The well-known studies of Skeels and Dye (Skeels, 1966) found that 3-year-old orphans moved to a nurturing environment developed more advanced intelligence than 3-year-olds who stayed in the orphanage with minimal nurturing. These events led to increased interest and study of the needs of children with disabilities. Eventually, federal legislation on behalf of children with disabilities emerged (Chapter 3).

Child Guidance

As the 20th century dawned, corporal punishment was still an accepted means of disciplining children, although it was uncommon in early childhood settings. The belief in children's inherent goodness was promoted through the writings and teachings of Maria Montessori and John Dewey, who did not accept that children were inherently sinful. They believed that children are best guided by engaging them in meaningful and interesting experiences. Object lessons, which had replaced recitation, now gave way to the project method. Along with more developmentally appropriate and meaningful learning experiences, educators like Dewey and Montessori promoted preventative discipline (discussed later in this chapter) that was designed to teach rather than control.

The first organized new approach to discipline was promoted by Fritz Redl and William Wattenberg in the 1950s. They advised teachers to assess the cause of misbehavior and then react appropriately. Reaction options included sending nonverbal cues and moving closer to children in an effort to support self-control, helping the children deal with whatever provoked the misbehavior, and encouraging appropriate behavior.

The early 20th century saw the hiring of more administrators to provide surveillance over schools. These administrators also attended to the physical environment, believing that ventilation, lighting, and other physical characteristics of the environment impacted learning. Psychologists who introduced a therapeutic view of behavior and discipline were added to school personnel, and interventions were developed to address behavior problems (Butchart, 1998).

Modern Views of Childhood

David Elkind (1931–) was one of the most prolific writers of the late 20th century on the view of childhood that continues today. He noted that, historically, the view of childhood resulted from the social, political, and economic conditions of the time. Modern images of children were purported to be scientific in origin but may not have been any more valid than those images grounded in social, political, and economic conditions. He further asserted that modern images of childhood lead to the miseducation of young children (Elkind, 1993), and included *the sensual child, the malleable child* (Elkind, 1993), and *the hurried child* (Elkind, 1981).

The Sensual Child

Grounded in Freudian theory, the view of the sensual child implies that children whose sexual instincts were unduly repressed were destined to become neurotic (Elkind, 1993). For parents and educators, this meant that children needed to be allowed to express themselves through play, art, and other mediums. Children with healthy opportunities for self-expression would develop healthy personalities and, hence, have healthy intellectual development. Elkind believed that, whereas excessive repression may produce neuroses, some repression is necessary for healthy coexistence. Self-expression at all costs is inappropriate. For example, children must be taught not to express anger by striking another but can appropriately express it in a painting.

The Malleable Child

Elkind (1993) posited a view that children are more amenable to social change than adults. This circumstance creates tension between generations of rigid adults and their more flexible children. Adults are products of their upbringing and thus are rigid and inadaptable, whereas children are free of habits of the mind and thus are more able to adapt to social changes. That is, children can adapt to changes brought about by technology, changing styles in clothing, and so on. Conversely, familial issues such as divorce or relocation of the family are difficult for young children to understand; it is likely that adaptation in these circumstances will be more challenging for children than adults.

The prominence of computers in classrooms is one way to exemplify the concept of the malleable child (Elkind, 1993). Young children will interact with computers and learn about what they can do. The miseducative step would be to begin teaching programming before young children are interested, knowledgeable about what computers can do, and able to learn the skills of programming. In sum, there are things that young children are not yet able to learn. Elkind believed that early childhood is not the time to learn about everything.

The Hurried Child

By the late 20th century, adults in the United States were living amid often competing demands of home, work, and recreation. Single working parent and dual working parent families were common. If child raising added to adult stress, then hurrying children to grow up eased that stress and enabled parents to enlist children's support in carrying the load (Elkind, 1981). Does that idea—hurrying children to

| Table 1.1 | Mothers with Children under Age 6 Participating in the Workforce |

Year	Number	Percent of Total
1980	6,538,000	46.8
1985	8,215,000	53.5
1990	9,397,000	58.2
1999	10,322,000	64.4
2000	10,316,000	65.3

Source: Children's Defense Fund. (2001). The state of America's children, 2001 (p. 48). Washington, DC: author.

grow up and help carry the load—sound familiar? It seems the image of children as miniature adults resurfaced from the Middle Ages.

Grounded in social, political, and economic circumstances as well as science, intellectual development was one sphere where children seemed hurried to grow up.

Several factors influenced the hurried child concept. During the 20th century new research-based information highlighted the importance of early stimulation. Furthermore, the strong focus on children during the *Great Society* of the 1960s and the emphasis on achievement during the *Cold War* (Chapter 2) influenced adult attitudes about hurrying children's intellectual development. Finally, mothers were entering the workforce in increasing numbers during the later part of the 20th century, and more young children were enrolled in child care and preschool programs, a perfect forum for instruction. Table 1.1 shows the late 20th-century trend of mothers of young children entering the workforce in increasing numbers.

All of these circumstances changed the social view of precocity in children (Elkind, 1981). Where highly precocious children once caused suspicion, new emphasis and attitudes elevated intellectual achievement and precocity to a level of importance. Child prodigies, once deemed odd and socially inept, were now many parents' dream.

Children were hurried in other ways as well. Children's clothing gradually took on an adult look. Children were enrolled at very young ages in activities like swimming, dance, and sports, and they were entered in competition at very young ages.

Evans/Three Lions/Getty Images, Inc.

In other words, children's lives were very adult-like.

During the later half of the 20th century, most children had access to TV and other media, and this made them the target for marketing, a sort of commercializing of childhood. Appealing ads for food and toys of all kinds were directed at even the youngest children.

Child Guidance

By the mid- to late 20th century, society's view was that children needed to be nurtured. Harsh punishment was considered inappropriate and, if excessive, was considered abusive from both social and legal perspectives. Many theories of behavior guidance surfaced, each generally aligned with one of two different approaches, *behavior modification* and *democratic behavior guidance*. The trend to use these child guidance strategies continues today.

Behavior Modification

Grounded in the work of B. F. Skinner (1971), behavior modification is based on the assumption that the environment shapes the child's behavior. Behavior modification may take many forms but there is one underlying principle: To change the behavior one determines under what conditions the behavior happens and then restructures the environment to reshape the behavior. For example, if a child regularly forgets to bring toys in from outdoor play, she is stopped at the door and asked to retrieve the toys. She receives praise when she remembers to bring the toys in on her own.

Behavior modification came into prominent use in the 1960s and involved procedures designed to modify the environment to reinforce desirable behavior and, concurrently, to avoid reinforcing undesirable behavior. Behavior modification was commonly used with young children.

Democratic Behavior Guidance

By the 1970s, scholars like Dreikurs, Glasser, and others were promoting democratic means of behavior guidance as most appropriate for teaching children to thrive in a democratic society. They promoted strategies that help children to be self-governing in appropriate ways. Like earlier scholars such as Herbart, Pestalozzi, Froebel, Montessori, and Dewey, these later scholars advocated for structuring a physical and social environment that would encourage appropriate behavior.

Three themes were woven throughout the writings of these scholars. First, the goal of behavior guidance was to teach children self-control. Second, to develop self-control, children needed to have their needs met. Finally, children needed to live in a positive environment with opportunities to interact in meaningful ways.

Rudolf Dreikurs (1897–1972). Rudolf Dreikurs was a medical doctor who wrote extensively about democratic methods of behavior guidance. He contended that what children need is to have their emotional needs met for a positive sense of contact, power, protection, and withdrawal (Dreikurs, Grunwald, & Pepper, 1982). When these needs are not met, children use inappropriate behaviors in an attempt to have them met. For example, if a child does not experience positive contact, s/he will engage in annoying attention-getting behavior in an attempt to feel connected, because negative contact is better than no contact at all. The role of the teacher or caregiver is to give the child attention when s/he is behaving appropriately and avoid giving attention to inappropriate behavior if possible. Dreikurs promoted the use of logical and natural consequences (Chapter 8) rather than punishment (Dreikurs et al., 1982).

William Glasser (1925–). Glasser was a medical doctor whose ideas about behavior guidance had a great impact in schools in the latter part of the 20th century. In his book *Schools Without Failure* (Glasser, 1969), Glasser suggested that unless we provide schools where children can be successful we will continue to encounter problems. He further noted that students make a choice to behave the way they do; schools may aggravate their tendency to misbehave or to fail.

Glasser promoted the notion that children need school experiences that help them meet their needs for belonging, power, fun, and freedom. He asserted that traditional discipline practices did not meet this objective (Glasser, 1969). He implored teachers to look at the teaching environment and the curriculum, assess how children's needs are being met, and then adjust as necessary. He also promoted the use of class meetings as a vehicle for teachers and students to collaboratively solve problems (Chapter 8).

David Young-Wolff/PhotoEdit.

Children Today

The past image of children as miniature adults has resurfaced in many images also of children today. Other ideas such as *readiness* and *child-centered curriculum* had their origin in eras past. Can you think of other ideas present today that had their origin in the past?

Miniature Adults

Pockets of current society reflect the view of children as miniature adults. Although many countries including the United States strive to protect children from exploitation in the workplace by enforcing child labor laws, this is not the case in some less industrialized countries. In some countries, children are needed contributors to the well-being of the family and thus put in long hours working in factories and fields. Some U.S. businesses outsource labor to those countries as a means of widening their profit margins.

Across the United States and other Westernized countries, the image of children as miniature adults is evident as children's lives mirror those of adults. For example, movies and electronic toys with adult themes, sensual adult dolls, and motorized toys are all marketed to children.

Readiness

Locke's idea about molding programs to the needs of children rather than expecting children to mold to program expectations is found in some contemporary debates. One side of the debate is this: In the midst of calls for accountability on the part of teachers and schools (Chapter 2), curriculum has been rapidly taking on expectations for the next grade level. Those on the other side of the debate suggest we should learn what the child needs and then mold learning experiences to meet those needs. This concept of readiness is discussed further in Chapter 6.

Child-Centered Learning Environments

Scholars as far back as Plato and including Rousseau and Pestalozzi declared the importance of a child-centered learning environment. They asserted the importance of the natural learning environment and the dangers of translating learning into mere memorization of facts. Pestalozzi's concept of the peasant teacher is a precursor to the integrated curriculum, a developmentally appropriate approach for young children. This image of children as children will be revisited in Part 2 of this text. Other scholars whose work informs early education and care are discussed in Chapter 2.

Children as Our Future

The unique developmental needs of young children are often set aside by other images of children. The early childhood community implores us to create an image of childhood that is based on what we know about them developmentally, culturally, and individually. The *Focus on Diversity* depicts some proverbs from several cultures about childhood. Think about what each one means. Again, we pose the proverb with which this chapter began: *Children are our greatest natural resource; cultivate them.*

As we make our way through the 21st century, the rights of children must be must be central in all that we do. Historically, children, and many adults, have been excluded from social, economic, and political processes due to differences in gender, social class, ability, religion, or ethnicity. If children are to thrive as our greatest

Paul Conklin/PhotoEdit.

Focus on Diversity

Proverbs provide insight into cultural attitudes. What attitude does each of these express?

It takes a village to raise a child. (Africa)
Children should be seen and not heard. (United Kingdom)
What children prepare will not be enough for dinner. (Ethiopia)
A tree should be bent while it is still young. (South Africa)
When a child knows how to wash his hands, he eats with his elders. (Ghana)
The egg should not be smarter than the duck. (Vietnam)
Children are innocent like angels; they can't do any harm. (Pakistan)
Spare the rod and spoil the child. (Puritans)
You don't have to be old to be wise. (Nigeria)

natural resource, adults must develop a view of childhood that extends human rights to each child, regardless of differences.

Adults must think and act differently on behalf of children than we have in the past. Respect for their developmental stages, levels of maturity, individual natures, cultural identities, and human rights must be paramount. We must protect them from harm and exploitation, provide them with experiences that support their growth and development, and teach them to respect the human rights of all people. Early childhood educators are well positioned to meet the challenge of educating parents and policy makers about the needs and rights of young children.

 My Developing Professional View

What is your current view of children and their place in society?

SUMMARY

The social, political, and economic environments in which children lived have shaped images of children in the past. Whether children were viewed as miniature adults, sinful, or hurried, images of children at various times and in various places were influenced by the environments in which they existed. More recently, scientific inquiry has provided knowledge and altered our view of childhood.

This chapter sets the stage for this text. We will take a broad look at events, issues, and trends that shape the lives of children, past and present. Ideally, this will lead each of you to thoughtful consideration and advocacy for young children of the 21st century.

ENRICHMENT ACTIVITIES

Individual Activities

1. Building on the brief discussions related to gender and education in this chapter, research the issue further to determine how educational opportunities for young girls have been different than for boys over time. Write an overview of your findings.

2. Review the proverbs listed in the *Focus on Diversity* in this chapter. Write one to three sentences for each that captures its meaning.

3. Interview one or two parents in your community. What is their view of childhood? Does it fit with any of the paradigms discussed in this chapter? What do they expect early education and care to provide for their children?

4. Interview one or two early childhood educators in your community. What is their view of childhood? Does it fit with any of the paradigms discussed in this chapter?

Cooperative Activity

5. In your cooperative groups, have each group member select a topic of interest to learn more about historical views of childhood (e.g., evolution of children's literature, evolution of children' clothing, a particular era). Individually research your topic and teach what you learn to the members of your group.

Advocacy Activity

6. Examine copies of your local newspapers for a recent period of a few weeks (libraries have back copies). Identify an issue related to the social view of childhood (e.g., less outdoor play in primary grades to increase instructional time, coloring contests for young children, beauty contests for little girls). Write a letter to the editor taking a position on behalf of young children.

⟩ SELF-ASSESSMENT

1. The social, economic, and political climate has historically influenced our view of childhood. List three examples to exemplify this. For example, Christians believed infanticide to be a pagan practice; thus infanticide diminished with the rise of Christianity in ancient Rome.

2. A society's view of childhood impacts how parents and educators guide children's behavior. For example, the Puritans believed children were sinful and thus practiced beating the devil out of them. Give another example of the connection between a society's view of childhood and child guidance practices.

3. Write a one-page overview of the early concept of the child-centered curriculum.

4. Write a one- or two-sentence proverb that reflects your attitude about children.

Scenario

A 6-year-old child is struggling with learning tasks. The child does not know how to read and does not always recognize letters and letter sounds correctly. Select a person from this chapter (e.g., Pestalozzi, Native American elder, Elkind), take his/her perspective, and discuss, in general, how you would address this child's needs from the character's perspective.

⟩ FOR FURTHER READING

Burton, H. W., & Provenzo, E. F. (1999). *History of education and culture in America.* Englewood Cliffs, NJ: Prentice-Hall.

Colon, A. R., with Colon, P. A. (2001). *A history of children: A socio-cultural survey across millennia.* Westport, CT: Greenwood Press.

Dreikurs, R., Grunwald, B. B., & Pepper, F. C. (1982). *Maintaining sanity in the classroom: Classroom management techniques,* (2nd ed.). New York: Harper & Row.

Elkind, D. (1981). *The hurried child.* New York: Addison-Wesley.

Elkind, D. (1987). *Miseducation.* New York: Alfred A. Knopf.

Elkind, D. (1993). *Images of the young child.* Washington, DC: National Association for the Education of Young Children.

Skinner, B. F. (1974). *About behaviorism.* New York: Random House.

Wortham, S. C. (1992). *Childhood 1892–1992.* Wheaton, MD: Association for Childhood Education International.

REFERENCES

Anchor, R. (1967). *The enlightenment tradition.* New York: Harper & Row.

Banks, J. A. (2003). *Teaching strategies for ethnic studies.* New York: Allyn and Bacon.

Beatty, B. (1995). *Preschool education in America: The culture of young children from the colonial era to the present.* New Haven, CT: Yale University Press.

Butchart, R. E. (1998). Punishments, penalties, prizes, and procedures: A history of discipline in U.S. schools. In: R. E. Butchart & B. McEwan (Eds.), *Classroom discipline in American schools: Problems and possibilities for democratic education* (pp. 19–36). Albany, NY: State University of New York.

Castle, E. B. (1961). *Ancient education and today.* Baltimore, MD: Penguin Books.

Children's Defense Fund. (2001). *The state of America's children, 2001.* Washington, DC: author.

Colon, A. R., with Colon, P. A. (2001). *A history of children: A sociocultural survey across millennia.* Westport, CT: Greenwood Press.

Dreikurs, R., Grunwald, B. B., & Pepper, F. C. (1982). *Maintaining sanity in the classroom: Classroom management techniques* (2nd ed.). New York: Harper & Row.

Elkind, D. (1981). *The hurried child.* New York: Addison-Wesley.

Elkind, D. (1993). *Images of the young child.* Washington, DC: National Association for the Education of Young Children.

Glasser, W. (1969). *Schools without failure.* New York: Harper & Row.

Hughes, J. L. (2001). *Froebel's educational law for all teachers.* Grand Rapids, MI: Froebel Foundation, USA.

Locust, C. (1988). Wounding the spirit: Discrimination and traditional American Indian belief systems. *Harvard Educational Review, 58*(3), 317.

Morey, S. M., & Gilliam, O. L. (Eds.). (1974). *Respect for life.* Garden City, Waldorf Press.

Nabokov, P. (1993). Part four: Long threads. In B. Ballantine & I. Ballantine (Eds.), *The Native Americans: An illustrated history* (pp. 301–383). Atlanta: Turner Publishing.

Osborn, D. K. (1975). *Early childhood education in the historical perspective* (3rd ed.). Athens, GA: Daye Press.

Reagan, T. (2005). *Non-Western educational traditions: Indigenous approaches to educational thought and practice* (3rd ed.). Mahwah, NJ: Lawrence Erlbaum Associates.

Reynolds, A. J., Temple, J. A., Robertson, D. L., & Mann, E. A. (2001). Long-term effects of an early childhood intervention on educational achievement and juvenile arrest. *Journal of American Medical Association, 285*(18), 2339–2346.

Schweinhart, L. J. (2004) *The High/Scope Perry Preschool study through age 40.* http://www.highscope.org/Research/homepage.html. Retrieved September 2006.

Schweinhart, L. J., Barnes, H. V., & Weikart, D. P. (1993). *Significant benefits: The High/Scope Perry Preschool study through age 27.* Ypsilanti, MI: High/Scope Press.

Skeels, H. (1966). Adult status of children with contrasting early life experiences. *Monographs of the society for research in child development, 32*(2).

Skinner, B. F. (1971). *Beyond freedom and dignity.* Indianapolis, IN: Hackett Publishing.

White, R. (1993). Part three: Expansion and exodus. In B. Ballantine & I. Ballantine (Eds.), *The Native Americans: An illustrated history* (pp. 211–299). Atlanta: Turner Publishing.

Wortham, S. C. (1992). *Childhood 1892–1992.* Wheaton, MD: Association for Childhood Education International.

History of Social, Political, and Philosophical Trends

There are several reasons to examine the history of social, political, and philosophical trends in early childhood education. Think back in your own life. What have you learned from the past that influences you today? By understanding the roots and historical evolution of early childhood education, we can better understand our role as early childhood educators today. Trends resurface or develop over time. A careful examination of the past gives us insight into how early childhood education theories and ideas have developed and influenced current practices.

Organized chronologically by eras, this chapter examines the history of social, political, and philosophical trends and scholars who have influenced those trends. Using eras as a framework for examining history provides chronology and context for understanding the past. The chapter begins by looking at *precolonial times*. Then, periods are examined in chronological order: *colonial era, industrial era, progressive movement, child study movement, post World War II and the Great Society, accountability movement*, and the *electronic age*. Woven throughout the discussion is historical information related to several topics that are developed in subsequent chapters.

After reading this chapter you will understand:

▶ Native American lives and early childhood practices in precolonial times.

▶ Early influences on early childhood education.

▶ The evolution of educational theories and their influence on early childhood education.

▶ Past social and political contexts in which young children lived.

▶ The evolution of testing.

▶ Contributors to thought in early childhood education.

▶ The origin of many early childhood programs.

Precolonial Times

In the United States of America, we often think of our history as beginning with Columbus' "discovery" of America and the pilgrims' arrival more than 100 years later. However, the land we now know as the United States of America was inhabited long before the arrival of Columbus and the Pilgrims. Native Americans lived on this continent for centuries prior to the immigration of Europeans. Thus, any exploration of our history is incomplete without examining the lives of Native Americans. We also examine Europe in precolonial times because early childhood education in America has been highly influenced by early European scholars. Figure 2.1 outlines the major historical eras and events.

Native Americans

In Chapter 1, we introduced some Native American child raising practices. Generally, mothers of young Native American children kept them close by their sides for the first years of life. As children got older, their education took place in the tribe as they interacted with adults and observed their model as apprentices. Eventually children learned gender appropriate skills.

The Granger Collection.

The education of young children in Native American families varied based on the family lifestyle. For example, some families were farmers while others were hunters, and the children had to learn the appropriate skills. The early Native American lifestyle had limited influence on the lifestyles of European immigrants. Native Americans living in the Northeast taught early immigrants how to farm and survive off the land; yet the pilgrims did not adopt the Native American spiritual ways or family practices.

European Influence

In Chapter 1, we discussed how the invention of the printing press created a need for universal education for children. In fact, the impact of the printing press might be likened to the development of technology literacy today. Technological advances continue to change the world as we know it! By the 16th century, universal education was promoted by clergymen such as Martin Luther and John Comenius, as a means of promoting Christianity.

Martin Luther (1483–1546). In the 16th century, the Protestant Reformation was prompted by Martin Luther, who taught that people, not the Roman Catholic Church, were authors of their own salvation. He asserted that in order for the Bible to be available for everyone to read, it had be translated from Latin (the Catholic tradition) into the many languages of Christians throughout Europe. After Luther translated the Bible into German himself, many other translations followed. With the Bible available in multiple languages, learning to read became a requisite skill for children.

John Amos Comenius (1592–1670). Comenius was born at the end of the Reformation era (Chapter 1) as nations were becoming autonomous and religious strife abounded. Ordained as a Moravian minister (Czech Republic), Comenius believed that education was the key to bringing about peace among nations. Comenius advocated for international, universal education and believed that it should begin in the early years. He felt that all humans were born in the image of God and that education provided the best way to grow in that image.

Comenius thought that mothers should organize nursery schools for their young children. The nursery schools would not provide formal education; rather, young children would prepare for school as they learned through play, songs, and games. He believed that every school should be a mirror of society,

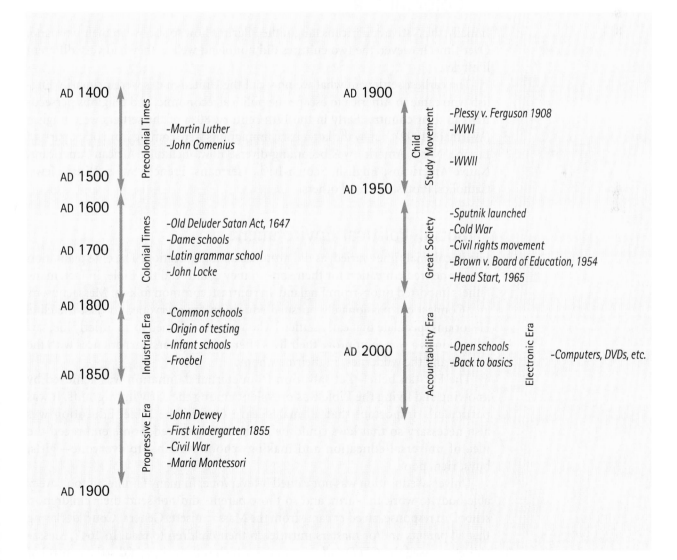

Figure 2.1. The major historical eras and events.

and objects used in learning experiences should come from real life. Other principles for early childhood education set forth by Comenius included the following (Sadler, 1966):

▶ Combining instruction with play.

▶ Encouraging intellectual and physical activity as well as spontaneous effort.

▶ Encouraging cooperative effort and honest rivalry.

▶ Limiting abstractness in learning activities.

▶ Stressing direct observation and learning through the senses.

▶ Offering variety to avoid boredom.

Among Comenius' noted works is his book *Orbis Pictus*, the first picture book for children. He believed that young children should not read or even learn the names of objects unless they could look at the objects. In other words, he believed that the presence of objects or pictures of them was critical to good teaching. Comenius' notion that we should teach children in ways they are best able to learn is paramount in a child-centered learning environment today (Chapter 4). Such ideas would continue to surface in the work of later scholars.

Colonial Era

Initially, the Native Americans taught the Pilgrims how to survive in their new land. Over time, however, the two cultures did not blend well as they had very different lifestyles.

The earliest settlers in what we now call the United States were primarily English who came to America to escape the political, economic, and religious persecutions in their country. Early in the 17th century, 80% of the settlers were English (Wortham, 1992), but by the latter part, immigrants were coming from other parts of Europe. North America was becoming diverse now, including African-Americans, Native Americans, English, Scotch-Irish, Germans, French, Swiss, Welsh, Jews, Catholics, Protestants, and others.

Social-Political Environment

Life in colonial times varied, as did attitudes about education. The elite plantation owners desired education for their sons so they could read the Bible. In fact, many fathers imported tutors from England. In contrast, common folks of Massachusetts and Connecticut passionately pursued education for everyone, not just the elite. Historians speculate that early settlers, who were accustomed to an orderly life, saw education as a way to improve their lives after suffering harsh experiences with the climate and the wilderness in their new home.

The Puritan belief that salvation from eternal damnation was achieved by knowing and living the Bible was prevalent among the early immigrants. It was particularly important that all males learn to read the Bible. Education was also necessary so that laws could be studied and obeyed. Some embraced the idea of universal education and making school available to everyone—girls, boys, rich, poor.

Universal education was not valued by everyone. In many families, it took every able body to work the farm, and so those parents did not send their children to school. In response, an edict came from the Massachusetts General Court declaring that all parents and/or masters must teach their children to read. In 1647, Massachusetts passed the *Old Deluder Satan Act*, which is the origin of district control of school systems today. This law decreed that any community with 50 or more households had to provide a teacher for the children, and the teacher was to be paid by the community members.

Early Childhood Education

In colonial times, education for young Native American children continued to take place in the tribes while schools for children of the immigrants were communal. The education of young girls was limited to the dame schools. Young boys attended dame schools and then either became apprentices (e.g., blacksmith, carpenter) or went on to Latin grammar schools.

Dame Schools

Most children of immigrants began their schooling in a dame school, which was typically in the home of an older woman. The curriculum consisted of learning letters and interpreting the Lord's Prayer and the catechism (questions and answers about the Christian doctrine). The woman would go about her household chores while listening to boys and girls read their *hornbooks* and *New England primers.*

17th-Century English Hornbook. The Granger Collection.

Latin Grammar Schools

Boys who were on track to become magistrates and ministers went on to the Latin grammar school, but attendance was not free. Only children of affluent parents were able to attend. From the Latin grammar school, many went on to Harvard, eventually to become political leaders.

Industrial Era

In the early 19th century, Eli Whitney's invention of the cotton gin heralded the industrial era. Urban populations grew as people moved from farms to mill towns and found work in factories. The United States had an open-door policy regarding immigration, and immigrants were rapidly entering the United States primarily to escape hardships in Europe. In the mid-1800's the influx was primarily Irish and German, followed by British and Scandinavians. The 9 million people in the country in 1820 grew to 31 million by 1860 (Braun & Edwards, 1972).

Social, Political Environment

During this era, children attending schools and working as apprentices were primarily from affluent families. Those from less affluent families were working in the factories because job opportunities were plentiful and this was a way to help support their families. Because so many children were not in school or apprenticeships, the effect of schools and apprenticeships as transmitters of cultural values was diluted. Moreover, poverty and crime abounded in the rapidly growing country. Much of the citizenry believed that education for all was the only way to stabilize the workforce, strengthen the economy, and combat crime.

Focus on Diversity

How the Lives of Children Differed in Colonial Times

The lives and education for young children were anything but equal in colonial times. If children were African-American, Native American, or poor, they encountered many problems.

African-American Children. During colonial times, children of African-American descent lived in slavery on the plantations of the Southeast. Usually, they lived in substandard homes and were undernourished; they frequently suffered cruelty at the hands of their owners. Usually, by the age of 6, they were working in the cotton fields, not attending schools.

It was not unusual for African-American families to be torn apart by sales. Owners sold slaves one by one to the highest bidder, often separating parents from their children and siblings from each other. Young African-American children were often left feeling isolated and abandoned.

Native American Children. When the first Pilgrims arrived in America, the Native Americans assisted them and the two groups got along. However, subsequent generations of immigrants viewed the Native Americans as heathens and conflicts began. Thus, Native Americans began moving west, further away from the immigrants.

Furthermore, Native Americans were not resistant to the diseases the immigrants brought from Europe and many died. Native American children continued to be educated in the tribe, as was the tradition.

Poor Children. Children living in poverty were often orphaned, sold by their parents, or taken in by more affluent families to work as servants or to learn a craft or trade. Others lived in a workhouse with their families, where labor was traded for a place to live. The workhouse had abysmal living conditions.

A social norm of the era was that idleness was the devil's workplace. Thus, it was important for children to learn to work to save them from being idle. By the dawn of the industrial era, abusive child labor became an issue.

Source: Adapted from Wortham, S. C. (1992). *Childhood 1892–1992.* Wheaton, MD: Association for Childhood Education International.

Common Schools

The 1830s through the 1840s was the period of the common school movement in the United States. Common schools were distinct from schools already in existence, because they were standardized within each state and designed for specific social and political purposes (Spring, 1986). Based on the principle that human nature could be shaped and given direction through common experiences, schools were institutionalized through the common school movement. Ideals of the common school movement included the following (Spring, 1986):

▶ The belief that if socially diverse groups of children were taught a common social–political ideology in common schools, hostility among diverse groups would decrease.

▶ Provision of common knowledge among citizens to link governmental policy with social, economic, and political problem solving.

▶ Creation of state control of schools to carry out government policies.

The citizens of New York created the position of State Superintendent of Schools in 1812, the first state to do so. In the decades to follow, other states did the same. Horace Mann, the first Secretary of the Massachusetts Board of Education and the "father of the common school," edited the *Massachusetts Common School Journal*, which served to articulate and promote leading educational ideas of the time (Spring, 1986). Mann and others promoted the idea of common schools, believing that public schools were important for all children, not just the elite. They called for public support and control for schools. Although the notion of the common school quickly became popular, few common schools actually existed.

As common schools eventually caught on, men began voting to levy taxes to support them (and in turn a strong economy). Eventually, voters determined that property taxes would be used to support schools, and states began to offer aid to districts only if they taxed themselves. This placed the states in control of schools; they could set standards and regulate teacher education.

Initially, common schools existed only at the elementary level. Secondary schools were attended only by the tuition-paying, college-bound elite. However, the *Kalamazoo Case of 1874* resulted in public support for secondary schools, and by 1900, graded schools were the norm. Normal schools for teacher education also emerged.

Origin of the Testing Movement

In the mid to late 19th century, the testing movement began in Europe, and by the beginning of the 20th century, it had made its way to schools in the United States. This movement saw the development of statistical techniques, a focus on the individual, and concepts such as mental age (MA) and intelligence quotient (IQ).

At this time, scientists and scholars generally believed that intelligence was fixed and static, but Charles Darwin promoted the importance of studying early behaviors as a means of understanding human development. This led to studies of infants and a new awareness of the importance of infancy and the early years to later development. The foundation was now laid in the United States to focus on early education and care.

The Granger Collection.

Educating African-Americans

A few schools existed for African-American children in the early years of the colonies, because they, too, needed to read the Bible to lead useful lives. The schools were funded by free African-Americans, African-American churches, and fraternal organizations (Wortham, 1992). However, following the Revolutionary War in the late 18th century, teaching of African-American children was forbidden. In fact, severe penalties were inflicted on those who tried to educate them. During the reconstruction effort following the Civil War in the mid-19th century, schools for African-American children came about again and *the Freedman's Bureau* was established to aid in building the schools.

Although inferior to white schools, about 4,000 schools for black children were built. But the Freedman's Bureau was dismantled in 1875 and African-Americans were left to create schools on their own. Southern whites had very negative attitudes about educating African-American children; so much so that teachers of African-American children were often denied room and board and sometimes their school buildings were destroyed. This, of course, discouraged many from becoming teachers for African-American children.

Educating Native Americans

Young Native American children were educated in their tribes. By age 6 or so, most were sent to boarding schools (Chapter 1), which were controlled primarily by the Bureau of Indian Affairs (BIA). The cultural mainstream, predominantly white and Christian, did not understand Native American spirituality and their respect for nature. This motivated many white missionaries to establish one-room schools to teach Christian ways to Native American children.

Early Childhood Education

During the industrial era, the traditional agrarian family gave way to more distinct roles for family members. Many fathers were wage earners outside of the home, mothers were homemakers, and children were dependents rather than producers. These new and distinct family roles became the national ideal, and many felt schooling for young children was an intrusion on time with mother in the home. For many, the expectation was that young children would learn at home with their mothers.

Other Americans wanted to educate their young children outside of the home, and the British infant school (highlighted in the *Focus on Children*) was the primary model. Infant school methods, based on the teachings of Rousseau and Pestalozzi (Chapter 1), were used to teach young children, infancy through age 5.

Indigent mothers were encouraged to send their children to charity infant schools so they could be socialized and saved from the influences of the home. Mothers were encouraged to read about good child rearing and educational practices. By the mid-19th century the focus on preschool children increased, particularly for those children living in tenements and ghettos. Practices now reflected a belief in original sin but in the natural goodness of children.

Origin of Kindergarten

Friedrich Froebel (1782–1852), known as the *father of kindergarten*, was born in Germany, the son of a Lutheran minister. He promoted early childhood education and training for early childhood teachers. Following an unhappy childhood, he was apprenticed to a forester at age 15, and during his 2-year apprenticeship studying plants, he became very interested in organic growth. From this experience, he developed his own sense of order and harmony with nature (Beatty, 1995). This and the religious influence of his father would permeate his teaching philosophy in the future.

Froebel started *kindergarten*, German for *children's garden*, in Germany for children ages 2–6. Influenced by scholars like Comenius and Pestalozzi, he believed in the natural unfolding of young children. After careful observation he would prepare an environment designed to meet the children's learning needs.

Froebel is known for his gifts and occupations. Gifts are objects that children manipulate and examine to learn what they can do and how they are used in everyday life. Initially, Froebel's gifts were objects such as a cylinder or cube. Today, gifts include realistic play props, clay, and other manipulatives. His idea of occupations includes creative craft activities with paper, paint, pencils, and so on. Songs were also a part of his curriculum.

Froebel believed that children learn through play, yet adults must not merely leave them to play alone. He believed adults were responsible for facilitating learning through play by the way they structured the environment. For example, appropriate props must be provided to encourage content for play.

Focus on Children

What the British Infant School Was Like

The British infant school, which preceded the kindergarten movement in Europe by several decades, resulted from the work of a social reformer named Robert Owen (1771–1858) from Newton Walls. Owen believed that the environment shaped who the child would become, and that the trajectory for children's lives was set at a young age. Furthermore, he was committed to creating an institutionalized social environment for young children, particularly those of poor factory workers. Owen saw schools as a way to combat the influence of the family and to strip children of individualism, for promoting homogeneous social behaviors (Beatty, 1995). That is, schools were an arm of society that could engineer social improvement for the society.

Owen aligned his philosophy with that of Rousseau and Pestalozzi; his first school served children ages 18 months to 5 years. He believed that traditional academic education made young children unhappy and that they learn best with objects, not books. The teacher's job was to amuse children. Yet, owing to his commitment to institutionalize social behavior, his school had a factory-like atmosphere (Beatty, 1995).

Contemporary British infant schools in Great Britain continue to reflect Owen's initial beliefs. Many are still located in poor, working-class neighborhoods. Weber (1971) characterizes 20th century British infant schools as informal. She suggested that *informal education* "refers to the setting, the arrangements, and the teacher–child and child–child relationships" (p. 11). She noted further that relationships within the learning atmosphere "maintain, re-stimulate if necessary, and extend what is considered to be the most intense form of learning, the already existing child's way of learning through play and through the experiences he seeks out for himself" (p. 11).

To combat the negative influence of an urban environment, effort was put into creating the schools with aesthetic appeal. Each has aesthetically pleasing outdoor play areas, and children alternate time indoors with time outdoors (Weber, 1971).

The British infant school, where children are grouped *family style* (mixed age), still emphasizes hands-on learning and amusement through play. For example, children work in small groups with sand, clay, and musical instruments. Cleanliness is very important.

The distinctive characteristics of Froebel's teaching for young children included these (Hughes, 2001):

▶ Child as the chief agent in his own development.

▶ Fostering of unity between the child and his creator.

▶ Self-activity which reveals children's inner conceptions.

▶ Early training of sensations and emotions.

▶ Importance of children's individuality.

▶ Nature study.

▶ Educational value of cooperation, experiential learning, symbolism, and play.

▶ Balance between spontaneity and control.

▶ Women as teachers.

Think back on your own early education experiences. Do you recall any evidence of Froebel's philosophy in your experiences?

In the 1850s, Mrs. Carl Schurz learned about Froebelian methods in Germany and returned to open the first U.S. kindergarten in Watertown, Wisconsin (Hill, 1942). She later met a wealthy Bostonian and teacher, Elizabeth Peabody, who championed appropriate education for young children in America. Together, they promoted the view that kindergarten was a supplement to mothers' nurturing.

Elizabeth Peabody corresponded with William Harris, the Superintendent of Schools in St. Louis, and eventually convinced him to sponsor the first public kindergarten. Susan Blow was the founder of the first public kindergarten opened as an experiment in St. Louis. This increasing number of proponents of the Froebelian philosophy and the public school endorsement ignited the spread of kindergarten in the United States.

⟩ Progressive Movement

The U.S. population grew rapidly during the last half of the 19th century. Many European American families moved west and settled, eventually creating large cities. Inventions like the telephone, electricity, and farm implements were changing lifestyles. As more European Americans moved west, the lives of Native Americans were changed as well. Industry expanded and disrupted their way of life (e.g., hunting, living off of the land) and they eventually moved onto reservations.

⟩ Social, Political Environment

Families in the urban–industrial climate became mobile as more and more fathers worked in industry or on the railroads. The common school was a way of life and more children were attending school because they no longer worked on farms. Laws regulating and limiting child labor were gaining momentum. With the prominence of industry, higher levels of literacy were needed if children were to grow up and make a living.

Progressive education was a humanitarian effort intended to improve the lives of children from all backgrounds. It was intended to meet the needs of the evolving urban–industrial society. Influenced by scholars of the era, a more child-centered curriculum was designed to replace existing rigid curricula.

The Testing Movement

The testing movement was greatly hastened in the early 20th century in the United States in response to increased immigration and World War I. Compulsory school attendance and increasing numbers of immigrants created new challenges for educators striving to meet the needs of a diverse population of children. The outbreak of World War I heralded a call for procedures and instruments to ensure selection of capable inductees. Standardized tests provided a means to accomplish this because they were easy and inexpensive to administer and score and, in the minds of many, made for easy comparisons among individuals and groups. The governments of France and the United States funded scientists to develop tests to measure mental ability for use in schools and other contexts.

Early in the 20th century, Frenchman *Alfred Binet* was asked by the French government to develop a test to measure mental ability in order to identify children who were in need of special education. Based on the belief that mental ability was genetically fixed and manifested through the sensory functions of the body, most testing instruments of the time were sensory tests. Binet, however, suggested that reasoning, comprehension, and judgment were better measures of mental ability and, with his colleague *Theodore Simon*, constructed a test on that premise. The test was translated into English by *Henry Goddard* in 1908, and the IQ test soon came into use in the United States.

Tests to measure aptitude and achievement emerged over the next decades, as publication of reviews of tests and lists of tests became big business in the United States. Still, assessment in public school classrooms was achieved primarily through context specific, teacher-developed measures. Standardized tests were not widely used in public schools and were nearly unheard of in the primary grades.

Corbis-Bettmann.

John Jackson/The Image Works.

﹛ Educational Theories

The progressive approach to education was initially asserted by Francis Parker and subsequently, John Dewey. Although their ideas met with some criticism, they were implemented broadly, particularly in kindergarten.

Progressive Educators

Francis A. Parker introduced progressive education in 1875 when he was superintendent of schools in Quincy, Massachusetts. Impressed with his observations of child-centered pedagogical innovations in Europe, Parker was committed to implementing new ideas in the United States. His efforts were controversial. Parker later became principal of the Cook County Normal School in Chicago where the children of Professor John Dewey (University of Chicago) were enrolled.

John Dewey (1859–1952). The progressive education movement was fueled by John Dewey, perhaps the best known progressive educator. Born and raised in the United States, Dewey viewed his own childhood education as boring and uninteresting. In his position as professor of philosophy at the University of Chicago and Columbia University, he spoke and wrote broadly about teaching and learning. He recognized the need for education to respond to the changing patterns of economic and family life (Dewey, 1899). Children no longer needed to learn skills to work on the family farm; rather, they needed a much broader array of skills. For example, children needed to learn to read if they were to secure employment in the now industrialized society.

Dewey rejected traditional education and called for a child-centered curriculum with social interaction, experiential learning, and opportunities to solve real-life problems. He was critical of Froebel's ideas for educating young children because he felt that children were merely imitating teachers. He asserted that school is life and that school experiences should reflect children's daily lives rather than merely preparing them for something later (Dewey, 1910). He urged teachers to capitalize on children's interests and weave the traditional aspects of schooling into projects, field trips, and problem solving.

The concept of *continuity* was at the core of Dewey's notion of experiential learning. Dewey's concept of continuity means that some experiences are *miseducative* and set a negative trajectory for future experiences. Some experiences are *neutral*; they neither support nor impede growth. On the other hand, *educative* experiences are positive and set a trajectory for positive growth (Dewey, 1938).

Let's say, for example, that you ask a child to pass a napkin to each of her peers for snack time. That experience would be educative if the child is learning the math concept of one-to-one correspondence and you help her count each time she sets a napkin in front of a child. On the other hand, if the activity is routine and the child has done it many, many times before, it would be neutral. The same activity would be miseducative if you ask her to pass the napkins as a punishment, and she is focused on being angry with you and not on the task at hand. Similarly, learning to read is educative if it is enjoyable and provides opportunities for children, but miseducative if it is meaningless and not enjoyable. Whether a task is educative or not is relative to the individual child engaging in the task.

Early Childhood Programs

Now that the common school prevailed, it became necessary to address educational needs of all children. Native American children attended boarding schools, African-American children attended segregated schools, and there were limited educational opportunities for children with disabilities. Owing to the success of kindergarten, nursery schools for very young children were emerging.

Schooling for Children of Color

Following the Civil War and subsequent Indian Wars, Native American children were attending federally funded boarding schools, and some segregated schools existed for African-American children. These schools were meagerly funded in comparison to schools for white children. Many whites believed that African-Americans were destined to work as laborers rather than professionals; thus, schools did not need to prepare them for professional careers. African-Americans who had become skilled tradesmen were creating an African-American middle class; nevertheless, low occupational status, high mobility, and high death rates due to poor living conditions continued to plague the African-American culture.

Many African-Americans, including Booker T. Washington, founder of the Tuskegee Institute, fought against prejudice and advocated for African-Americans' right to education. The 1908 case of *Plessy v. Ferguson* resulted in the establishment of separate but equal educational facilities. Separate education for blacks and whites was established, but equality was not achieved. Courts did not feel that cases of inequality were successfully established (Wortham, 1992); thus, segregated schools and separate and unequal conditions would endure for quite some time.

Schooling for Children with Disabilities

With the progressive era came educational opportunities for children with disabilities. While a few services and private programs for children with disabilities existed, there were not yet any programs in public schools. Among advocates for education for children with disabilities were *Alexander Graham Bell* (a speech therapist as well as an inventor) and *Elizabeth Farrell*, a public school teacher in New York. Farrell organized classes for children who did not fit well in public schools and started the National Council for Exceptional Children. The council addressed needs of children who had giftedness as well as those who had physical, mental, and emotional disabilities.

Nursery Schools

By the 1920s, new educational theories brought about increased focus on childrens' learning needs during the early years. Early childhood educators had noticed that children were flourishing in kindergarten and they were interested in providing out of home experiences for children ages 2–4.

Kindergarten, now part of public schools, was beginning to look more like formal schooling, while nursery school teachers took pride in implementing the latest, research-based best practices with young children. Many nursery schools were supported by philanthropic foundations and met the needs of many different populations of children.

Bank Street

The Bank Street approach to early childhood education was born out of the progressive era. Under the direction of *Lucy Sprague Mitchell*, the Bank Street model originated in the Bureau of Educational Experiments. The curriculum, influenced by John Dewey and other progressive educators, was child-centered and focused on engaging children in meaningful learning experiences. This model is discussed in detail in Chapter 6 where we take a closer look at models of early childhood education.

Kindergarten

As the 19th century came to a close, kindergarten flourished. The number of public school kindergartens and settlement kindergartens to

Corbis-Bettmann.

support children of poverty increased. Kindergarten educators were slowly breaking from Froebelian methods to embrace the ideas of progressivism. For example, Eudora Hailmann rejected the rigidity of Froebelian methods and added things like sand tables and doll houses to her curriculum. Others added science, art, and free play. Adoption by some of the new progressive philosophy created controversy in kindergarten education between progressives and nonprogressives.

Montessori Education

The work of Maria Montessori (1870–1952) has been highly influential in early childhood education. The first woman in Italy to become a physician, Montessori was initially concerned with childhood diseases, but her interest was soon captured by problems of mental retardation in young children. After successfully teaching some children with mental disabilities to read, she decided that children would benefit from special education interventions at a young age. Later in her career, her methods were used with typically developing children (Montessori, 1967).

Maria Montessori grounded her teaching in five basic principles:

▶ Respect for the Child. Children need freedom to choose activities in which they will engage. Children's individual needs must be respected and addressed.

▶ Absorbent Mind. Children learn by living and doing.

▶ Sensitive Periods. Children have periods which are optimal for learning certain things. Teachers must observe and identify those periods.

▶ Prepared Environment. Children learn best in a prepared environment where they are not heavily reliant on adult assistance.

▶ Autoeducation. In a carefully prepared environment, children educate themselves.

Reflect on your own early educational experiences; do you recall any that reflect Maria Montessori's theory?

The Child Study Movement

On the heels of the progressive movement, the child study movement further changed early childhood education by generating new theories and knowledge about how young children learn and develop. This movement was influenced by Darwin's theory that humans are not a fixed species but one that changes, develops, and evolves.

Social, Political Environment

Early in the 20th century, high infant and maternal mortality among the poor, and inadequately prepared World War I recruits illuminated the need to better understand child development and the influence of the early years on later development. Under the leadership of *G. Stanley Hall* and *Arnold Gesell*, centers for child study were established where parents and teachers could learn about effective ways to work with young children. Scholars focused on identifying characteristics of normally functioning young children, the influence of heredity and environment on intelligence, and development of better instruments for assessing young children (Kelley & Surbeck, 2000). Early childhood education and development was now a respected discipline for study and research.

In 1916, Lucy Sprague Mitchell and others carried out a series of studies on child development to identify techniques for analyzing and interpreting children's complex behaviors. At the same time, behaviorists like *Edward Thorndike* and *John Watson* were doing experiments to learn about structuring environments to support children's learning. Thorndike and Watson brought further legitimacy to the study of children by demonstrating that appropriate stimuli improved children's learning.

With new knowledge about how young children learn and develop, nursery schools and kindergartens for young children flourished until the time of the stock market collapse in 1929. This economic crisis called for some budget cuts and kindergarten was often one of the programs eliminated. However, the economic crisis had the opposite effect on nursery schools. The federal government provided monetary support for nursery schools so that women could enter the workforce and help support their families (Wortham, 1992).

The Testing Movement

The testing movement escalated during the child study movement. Many educators and policy makers believed testing was a way to more efficiently manage schools as well as identify skills needed in various work environments. In this social–economic–political climate, standardized tests became very useful.

Early Childhood Theories

Early childhood curriculum and instruction should be based on what we know about how children learn, and the era of the child study movement heralded many new theories. The most prominent theories in early childhood education were constructivism, behaviorism, maturationism, psychosocial theory, and self-actualization theory.

Constructivism

Two contemporaries of this period posited constructivist theories: Jean Piaget and Lev Vygotsky. Although their theories differed in some ways, both viewed children as active constructors of knowledge. Vygotsky, a social constructivist, emphasized social interaction as key to the learning process.

Jean Piaget (1896–1980). Piaget is the theorist most aligned with constructivism. Born in Switzerland, Piaget was a biologist who also studied psychology and became well known and respected for his contributions to understanding intellectual development. His work led him to ponder the nature of knowledge, how it is acquired, and whether one can gain an objective understanding of the world (Ginsburg & Opper, 1969).

While studying with Theodore Simon in Paris, Piaget was asked to develop a standardized intelligence test and it was this assignment that sent his future in a new direction. As he questioned children, he became fascinated with the patterns he noted in their incorrect responses. This set him on the path to his theory about how children learn.

Through his extensive work with young children, Piaget posited that they construct knowledge as they actively engage with people and objects in their environment. For example, as an infant examines and drops a ball, she learns what the ball can do.

Piaget believed that mental development begins at birth. He also believed that cognitive structures are formed as a result of encounters with the environment, and that changes in mental development are cumulative. Like Montessori, he believed that teachers could structure a stimulating environment that would support young children's development. Concepts included in his theory are as follows:

Adaptation. Piaget believed that the functional and psychological aspects of humans interact to assist them to adapt to their environment. Humans *assimilate* new experiences into existing mental *schemes*, or *accommodate* the schemes to encompass the new situation (Piaget, 1962). Children change their understanding by first assimilating new information into an existing mental schema, and then accommodating that information to refine their understanding. The schema now includes the new experience of the phenomenon. For example, a child encountering a sheep for the first time may observe the four legs and a tail, and immediately equate it with his pet dog. After hearing the goat bleat, seeing the hooves, watching it being milked, and being told by an adult that it is a goat, the child accommodates the new information. The child's understanding is now expanded to include a new animal phenomenon, "goat."

Equilibration. This is the state of mental balance that humans try to achieve as they engage in assimilation and accommodation. For example, when the child added the concept of goat to his mental schema, he was making sense of his experience with the goat. Equilibration or self-regulation allowed him to do this.

Stage Theory. Piaget noted that children of the same ages tended to give similar incorrect responses. His theory suggests that although intellectual development is individual, children of the same general age think in similar ways. The *Focus on Children* is an overview of Piaget's stages of intellectual development.

Play. Piaget found that play supported cognitive development and symbolic thinking (Piaget, 1962).

Lev Vygotsky (1896–1934). Born in Russia, Vygotsky was a teacher of psychology, literature, and theater. Although he died of tuberculosis at the young age of 38, he made great contributions to the understanding of how young children learn.

Vygotsky's theory is labeled sociocultural because he believed the social environment highly influenced development. Children learn through social interaction. Vygotsky conceptualized the *zone of proximal development* which is "the distance between the actual developmental level as determined by independent problem solving and the level of potential development as determined through problem solving under adult guidance or in collaboration with more capable peers" (Vygotsky, 1978, p. 86). Think about something you learned recently. Did someone assist you as you worked in your zone of proximal development?

Vygotsky did not ascribe to stage theory as Piaget did. However, he did note a remarkable cognitive shift that happens around age 2 (toward the end of what Piaget called the sensorimotor stage). As this developmental shift takes place, children's use of language transforms their activity to a level not attained by other forms of animal life (Vygotsky, 1978). Young children develop as symbolic thinkers and their ability to think symbolically transforms their play. During the preverbal time, the meaning of the object drives the play. For example, a child might pretend to drink from a cup. While the cup is being used in a pretend and playful way, it is being used as cups are intended to be used. When young children develop the ability to think symbolically, they are able to assign meaning to objects and that assigned meaning then drives the action of the play (Vygotsky, 1966). Now the cup can be a hat, a boat, a doll bed, anything a child can imagine it to be. Think about a time when you observed children assigning meaning to objects during play.

Focus on Children

Piaget's Stages of Development

Sensorimotor Stage, Birth to Age 2

Infants and toddlers explore the social and physical world through their senses. They develop object permanence, or the understanding that objects continue to exist when they cannot be seen. For example, an infant with object permanence will look for an object if it disappears.

Laura Dwight Photography

Preoperational Stage, Ages 2–6

Young children are beginning to use symbols to stand for objects, events, and people. This is manifest in symbolic play and oral language. For example, a child is thinking symbolically when she pretends a hanger is a purse during play.

Laura Dwight Photography

Concrete Operational Stage, Ages 6–12

Primary age children can reason and use logic, but still need a concrete base for their thinking. Symbolic thinking is manifest in their ability to read, write, and use number symbols. For example, primary grade children can learn to add and subtract but need actual objects to set before them to visualize the operations.

Elizabeth Crews

Formal Operational Stage, Acquired Around Ages 12–14

When children reach this stage, they no longer need a concrete referent for thinking about their world. They apply logic to real and hypothetical problems.

Digital Vision/Getty Images, Inc.

Behaviorism

Around the turn of the 20th century, behaviorism emerged out of the need on the part of some scientists for a precise research methodology for understanding human behavior. Early behaviorists studied animals' responses to stimuli to understand the stimulus–response relationship. *Ivan Pavlov (1849–1936)* was a Russian physiologist who, through the study of animal behavior, developed the theory of *classical conditioning* (Pavlov, 1928). Observing a dog, he discovered that food, a stimulus, resulted in salivation, a response. He further observed that other stimuli associated with food generated the same response (associating a bell with food, for example).

Edward Thorndike (1874–1949). Building on the work of his contemporary Pavlov, Thorndike further developed the behaviorist theory by explaining the role of experience in the relationship between a stimulus and a response. He observed that when stimulus–response experiences are repeated, they are strengthened (Thorndike, 1935). For example, if a child is given a candy bar for sitting quietly, and that candy bar is desirable to the child, repeated awarding of a candy bar will increase the behavior of sitting quietly. However, he also observed that punishment does not necessarily weaken the behavior; rather, punishment may merely lead to other behaviors. Thus, if the same child is scolded (punished) for running wildly around the room, she may begin to cry (another behavior) but still does not demonstrate the behavior of sitting quietly (Thorndike).

John Watson (1878–1958). Also a contemporary of Pavlov and Thorndike, Watson was known as the *father of behaviorism* because he gave the philosophy its name. Watson asserted that we cannot understand thinking or mental activity; rather, we can only observe behavior (Watson, 1925). Behaviorist principles would gather steam later with the work of B. F. Skinner.

Self-Actualization Theory

Abraham Maslow believed that all humans, regardless of gender, race, age, or culture, are motivated by certain needs (Maslow, 1954). His self-actualization theory provides a hierarchy of needs for the human condition, and has implications for how to best meet the needs of children. For example, if children are hungry or feel physically unsafe because of abuse, they are not going to be able to focus on learning tasks until their basic physical needs have been met. The *Focus on Children* is an overview of Maslow's hierarchy of needs.

Maturationism

The maturationist theory, influenced by Rousseau's idea that children need to develop naturally, was further developed at the Gesell Institute during the child study movement. Arnold Gesell (1880–1961) was a psychologist and physician who asserted that children have an internal clock that governs their development, and the individual's internal clock influences development more than environmental factors. The unfolding of children's development is genetically determined and uneven; that is, children often grow in spurts (Gesell & Ilg, 1943).

Gesell's most notable contribution to early childhood education is the identification of developmental benchmarks that are useful in assessing children's development over time. For example, Gesell's work is reflected in the concept of school readiness, where early childhood educators evaluate children's development against benchmarks to determine readiness to enter school (Chapter 6). While Gesell's work was very influential, he also had critics who felt focusing on norma-

Focus on Children

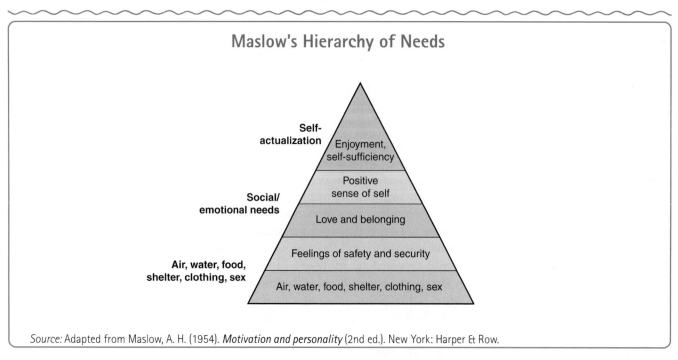

Maslow's Hierarchy of Needs

Source: Adapted from Maslow, A. H. (1954). *Motivation and personality* (2nd ed.). New York: Harper & Row.

tive data would prevent teachers and caregivers from addressing individual differences. Some scholars felt that his data were not normed on diverse populations of children (Wortham, 1992).

Early Childhood Programs

The study of child development focused some attention on the needs of children with disabilities, although there were no federal mandates for special education yet. Waldorf schools were a new program that started in Germany.

Children with Disabilities

Recall from the discussion of the progressive era that tests to measure development and intelligence were emerging. Having been translated into English, they were now more commonly used in the United States. Henry Goddard of the Vineland Training School established testing seminars for teachers and advocated for early diagnosis of disabilities (Kelley & Surbeck, 2000). As a result of his advocacy and work, children with disabilities were placed in special classes with teachers trained to meet their needs. This was a precursor to the special education classes of today.

Juila Cumes/The Image Works.

Waldorf Schools

At the beginning of the 20th century, *Rudolf Steiner (1861–1925)* was asked to organize a school for the children of workers at the Waldorf Astoria cigarette factory in Germany. Named Waldorf schools (Chapter 6), they serve children from preschool through high school in the United States today.

Steiner believed that the domains of body, soul, and spirit developed in concert and that humans go through identifiable developmental stages from childhood to adulthood. He felt that early childhood programs needed to address the needs of the whole child, and that young children should be protected from all evil. Included in what Steiner considered evil was highly formal, structured education for young children.

Initially, Waldorf schools served preschool and kindergarten children. The curriculum encompassed play and other motor activities as well as art and creativity. Children also engaged in everyday tasks such as cooking, washing dishes, and sweeping floors.

Post World War II and the Great Society

The 1930s and 1940s were years of the economic crisis created by the Great Depression and the U.S. involvement in World War II (WWII). This period had a significant effect on early childhood education. The growth of kindergarten came to a halt due to budget cuts during the Depression, while nursery schools experienced rapid growth to accommodate mothers entering the workforce as part of the war effort. With the growing body of knowledge about development, debates erupted about what constituted best practices in early education and care.

Social, Political Environment

The 1950s saw a great shift in the social, political, and economic climate of the United States. The postwar years were economically flush, and the U.S. involvement in postwar reconstruction in Europe led to increased international involvement. Simultaneously, tension rose between the East and the West. This tension, known as *the Cold War*, was primarily between the United States and England with their democratic governments and Russia with its communist government.

During the period of the Cold War, the communists were taking over Eastern Europe and the United States felt it was imperative to stop communist power and rule. This tension bred competition. For example, the United States and Russia engaged in a race for space, each trying to develop a space program superior to the other's. In 1957, Russia successfully launched an earth satellite, Sputnik, something the United States had not yet accomplished. To be competitive, the United States needed a well-educated population, and this prompted a new emphasis on math and science in public schools. Federal money was appropriated to support college scholarships for students who achieved well in math and science.

The decade of the 1950s set the stage for the Great Society of the 1960s. Issues of poverty were more easily addressed in the flush economic times of the postwar years. Investigation into the lives of families living in poverty unearthed information that would have a profound effect on early childhood education by drawing attention to inequities in living conditions, health care, and educational opportunities. Early interventions were viewed as the only way to eradicate the negative effects of poverty and oppression. Civil disobedience by African-Americans in the South (e.g., bus boycott, lunch counter sit-ins) set the stage for the forthcoming civil rights movement. New knowledge from the child study movement supported a focus on the needs of children with disabilities. Women who had filled needed gaps in the workplace during the war wanted to maintain the identity and independence that working outside the home offered them.

The Great Society

President Lyndon Johnson took office in November of 1963 following the assassination of President John F. Kennedy. His administration is best known as the period of *the Great Society*, a time when significant and lasting social change would take place. The Great Society on the home front was balanced by anticommunism sentiment and entrance into the war in Vietnam, a move that fueled much antiwar sentiment.

The War on Poverty. Still fully immersed in the Cold War in the mid-1960s, the Johnson administration initiated a *war on poverty* that brought about new federal funds to support families living in poverty. Funded through the Economic Opportunity Act (Chapter 3), the components of the War on Poverty included (1) training and education leading to employment, (2) VISTA, a domestic peace corps, and (3) community action programs.

Civil Rights. The purpose of the civil rights movement was to guarantee the constitutional rights of all citizens to be free, to vote, and to enjoy equal protection under the law (Bok, 1992). The landmark case of *Brown v. Board of Education* in 1954 (Kansas) ended school segregation. However, after decades of marginalization, a disproportionate number of African-Americans were living in poverty in urban areas while a disproportionate number of European Americans settled in the suburbs. Of course, this demographic perpetuated school segregation.

The Civil Rights Act of 1964 was intended to end the apartheid in the South and to provide equal rights to all. However, prejudice and discrimination abounded during this period. For example, some districts still implemented poll taxes (Bok, 1992) which prevented the poor (of which a disproportionate number were African-Americans) from voting. Cases of African-American lynchings sometimes went unsolved.

Children with Disabilities. During this time of much social change, the needs of children with disabilities gained attention. The move was influenced by the work of Piaget and McVicker Hunt, who posited that intelligence is not fixed and highlighted the importance of environmental influence on children's development. Because of the testing movement there were instruments to diagnose various disabilities. Significant social legislation (Chapter 3) was passed that provided funds and opportunities for children with disabilities.

Corbis-Bettmann.

Changing Role of Women. The women's movement gained momentum during the period following WWII and the decade of the Great Society. The movement was influenced by the War on Poverty because many people living in poverty were women heads of household. Traditional gender-based employment was reconsidered to enhance women's opportunities to find jobs (Bok, 1992). Training programs to assist women entering the workforce flourished.

The Testing Movement. To this point, testing in the primary grades continued to be limited to teacher-developed instruments, particularly relating to reading and math skills. Even if standardized measures were used, the scores were confidential and did not appear on the front page of newspapers. Scientists were discovering that tests for young children had poor predictive validity because test scores did not correlate between children's early and later years. In fact, this finding was further proof that intelligence was not genetically endowed, fixed, or easily quantifiable (Kelley & Surbeck, 2000). Scholars including J. McVicker Hunt and David Elkind continued to assert that intelligence is not fixed, and that mental ability is only one part of intelligence. This lies at the heart of debates today about the usefulness of standardized tests for young children.

The War on Poverty led to increased involvement of the federal government in schools and to an increase in standardized testing to measure children's progress and identify their needs. Continuous funding of Head Start (a federally funded preschool program) was contingent on students making academic gains, and those gains were primarily measured by standardized instruments.

With more testing in early childhood, new tests for use in preschools and kindergarten were developed. For example, kindergarten teachers were noticing an obvious gap in children's developmental levels when they entered school, which led to the development of instruments to assess readiness for kindergarten.

Early Childhood Theories

Early childhood scholars continued to posit theories of early childhood education. The behaviorist theory became widely used in early care and education at this time, and Erik Erickson's psychosocial theory came about.

Behaviorism

Building on the work of his predecessors, B. F. Skinner was speaking and writing extensively during this period about the principles of behaviorism. Programs such as the well-known DISTAR (Chapter 7) reflecting the behaviorist principles came into use.

B. F. Skinner (1904–1990). Skinner was a successor of Thorndike and Watson and is probably the most well-known behaviorist scholar. Writing for over four decades in the mid to late 20th century, Skinner had a great impact on learning theory in educational and therapeutic settings.

Skinner's predecessors believed that there was no way to understand mental events or the thoughts and ideas of a being because there was no objective way for scientists to agree on what the being was learning. In other words, we can understand behavior because it is observable but mental events are not, so they cannot be understood. Skinner took a bit different position on this issue by acknowledging that thoughts, feelings, and ideas exist and can be understood. However, our ability to understand them lies in what we can observe because observation is the only way to obtain a good description of mental events. In other words, we can describe behavior but cannot readily attribute the cause of it (Skinner, 1974).

Skinner is most well known for his theory of *operant conditioning*. He noted that a behavior is strengthened by its consequences, which he refers to as *reinforcers* (Skinner, 1974). He preferred the objective term *reinforcement* rather than the subjective term *reward*.

Although not used exclusively, Skinner's theory of operant conditioning was applied in early childhood settings to support learning. Early childhood educators shaped appropriate behavior and reinforced learning accomplishments with the use of reinforcements like praise or tangible rewards.

Psychosocial Theory

Psychosocial theory was posited by Erik Erikson (1902–1994), who believed that development happens in a social context and that cognitive and social development are entwined (Erikson, 1963). As Piaget did for intellectual development, Erikson proposed a stage theory of social development. His stages are fluid and ages attributed to each are approximate. The *Theory into Practice* highlights the first four stages of his theory.

Early Childhood Programs

During the mid-20th century, the work of Piaget and Vygotsky was translated into English, and the constructivist theory gradually made its way into teacher education programs in the United States. Programs for young children that emerged at this time were increasingly grounded in constructivism, particularly at the preschool level. Programs introduced here are discussed more fully in later chapters.

Reggio Emilia

The Reggio Emilia early childhood program got its name from the town in which it was conceived, Reggio Emilia, Italy. The Italians have a history of providing services and support for families with

Joack Moebes/Corbis Images.

young children that dates back to the early 19th century (Cadwell, 1997). Influenced by progressive educators like John Dewey, debates ensued in Italy about needed changes in early childhood programs.

Loris Malaguzzi (1920–1994). The Reggio Emilia school was started by Malaguzzi to support young children and families during reconstruction in post-WWII Italy. His school quickly became of interest to American educators, and Reggio Emilia schools began appearing in the United States. Influenced by Piaget, Vygotsky, and Montessori, Malaguzzi believed that children's energy and abilities should be liberated through education (Cadwell, 1997), and he implored teachers to listen to children and follow their lead. His principles of early childhood education include the following:

▶ Children are strong, rich, and capable.

▶ Education should focus on young children's relationships with family, teachers, and peers.

▶ Education must foster symbolic thinking via drawing, words, movement, dramatic play, music, and so on.

▶ The environment is a teacher.

▶ Teachers are partners, nurturers, and guides.

David Young-Wolff/PhotoEdit.

Theory into Practice

Implications of Erikson's Stages of Psychological Development

Stage	Task of the Stage	Adult Role
Trust vs. Mistrust, Birth to Age 1	Infants need to learn that the world is a psychologically and physically safe place.	Adults meet the needs of infants and respond to their distress. Without appropriate caregiver responses, infants learn to mistrust their world.
Autonomy vs. Shame, Ages 1–3	Toddlers are declaring independence in their world. They are learning that they are unique and autonomous beings.	Adults offer opportunities for toddlers to do things for themselves and assert their independence. They offer reasonable choice of activities, clothing, and food. Without these opportunities, toddlers learn to feel ashamed of their abilities.
Initiative vs. Guilt, Ages 3–5	Preschoolers are learning to take initiative as they expand their repertoire of accomplishments.	Adults provide an environment that invites safe exploration. They encourage initiative. Without this encouragement, children feel guilty when they take initiative.
Industry vs. Inferiority, Ages 5–12	Elementary age children are learning many new skills including reading, writing, soccer, swimming, dance, etc. They need to feel competent about new things they are learning to do.	Adults encourage and support children as they try new things. They acknowledge even small amounts of growth rather than belittling children for what they cannot do. Consistent criticism results in feelings of inferiority.

Source: Adapted from Erikson, E. (1963). *Childhood and society* (2nd ed.). New York: Norton.

▶ Teachers must be researchers. They must engage in discussion about their work and that of the children.

▶ Teachers must carefully consider how they will present children's thinking.

▶ Parents play an active role in their children's education.

High/Scope

The High/Scope Educational Research Foundation was founded by *David Weikart* in 1970 in response to the War on Poverty. The foundation developed and supported the High/Scope approach to early childhood education that is grounded in the constructivist philosophy. Its mission was to examine and provide quality early childhood education for children living in poverty.

As part of the War on Poverty, the government funded a large research project called the Perry Preschool Project. Headed by Weikart, the project was an investigation of the impact of preschool experiences on later school achievement. Later academic gains of young children identified as at-risk for school failure (High/Scope Educational Research Foundation, 2004) were examined for two groups of at-risk preschoolers, one that attended preschool and one that did not. Attendance in preschool was found to make a difference in achievement. Later, comparisons were made among the High/Scope approach, traditional nursery school, and a highly structured preschool. Findings from this study suggested the High/Scope approach provided the best support for achievement gains (High/Scope Educational Research Foundation, 2004).

The primary principles of the High/Scope approach include these:

▶ Children are active learners.

▶ Children's interests must be at the core of the curriculum.

▶ Teachers are facilitators of learning who pose open-ended questions and provide hands-on learning experiences.

Courtesy of PRO LOCO di SOLOGNO, www. sologno.it.

Head Start

Policy makers believed that early childhood education was a way to diminish the cycle of poverty in families. A component of the community action programs implemented as part of the War on Poverty, Head Start preschools came about in 1965. Head Start did not adopt a universal curriculum but required programs to address children's development in the areas of

▶ Language.

▶ Curiosity.

▶ Discipline.

▶ A positive sense of self.

Children with Disabilities

Now that the federal government was playing a significant role in the education of young children, efforts were made to address the needs of those with disabilities. Funds were available for preschool programs for young children with disabilities, and many were developed in communities across the nation. By 1972, the Economic Opportunity Act (Chapter 3) was amended to require that not less than 10% of available slots in Head Start be reserved for children with disabilities.

Accountability Movement

By the 1970s, increasing availability of federal and state resources for schools heralded a strong accountability movement nationwide. The federal government became more involved in educational funding and this resulted in legislation that affected preschool and school-age children, particularly those with disabilities. The testing movement characterized the accountability era as test scores became a way to hold school districts accountable for students' achievement.

Social, Political Environment

In the early 1970s, morale in the United States was low. Citizens were experiencing an economic recession; there was concern that we continued to send troops to fight in the civil war in Vietnam; and President Nixon's *Watergate* scandal (the first widespread exposure of dishonesty in the federal government) shook the faith of many citizens in the federal government. Although both President Nixon and his successor, President Carter, made great strides in developing good relationships with communist governments in Asia (The People's Republic of China, Korea), foreign and domestic problems seemed vast to many citizens.

By the 1970s, television was accessible to most children. Programming expanded and children became the target for marketing of toys and food. Television depicted violence more often and more graphically than before, and expanded programming and marketing aimed at children became a social concern for many who lobbied the federal government to regulate programming for children.

Courtesy of High/Scope Foundation.

The 1970s saw a change in families, with nearly half of all marriages ending in divorce. The higher frequency of divorce led to a rise in single-parent households and the number of mothers working outside the home. Many married women chose to work outside the home now that it was more socially acceptable.

The changing family demographics led to a great need for child care. However, high-quality care still eluded many families. Consumers could not absorb the cost of high-quality care, which required well-trained teachers and the best facilities. Many highly qualified early childhood professionals chose to work in public or private schools where salaries and benefits were higher.

The Testing Movement

The 1964 Maternal Child Health and Mental Retardation Act and the Economic Opportunity Act (Chapter 3) required the provision of educational and social opportunities for all children. In 1975, the federal government initiated PL 94–142 that mandated a free and appropriate education for all children age 3 and older. Continuation of funding for compensatory preschool programs, special education programs, and other related programs depended on evaluation that indicated children were showing achievement gains. Because policy makers perceived tests as an easy and inexpensive way to measure progress, test scores became the yardstick for measuring whether schools were meeting standards and whether educational innovations would be funded. The testing industry expanded as new measures were developed to reflect goals of various programs.

By the mid-1970s, testing was a regular practice in the primary grades and was frequently used as a basis for decisions to retain children or to track them by ability. Simultaneously, context-specific, teacher-developed assessments were becoming less important as teachers began to teach to mandated, standardized tests and rely on them as indicators of students' achievement. However, scholars (Shepard & Smith, 1988; Kelley & Surbeck, 2000) were finding that achievement tests for young children lacked reliability and validity; many had high error rates and poor predictive validity.

Testing and accountability led to the *pushed down curriculum* or next grade expectations. More formal and academic instruction aimed at teaching reading, writing, and math skills appeared in kindergarten and the primary grades. The trend even extended to preschool settings where educators were asked to prepare the children for an academic curriculum in kindergarten.

Lawrence Migdale/Pix Photography.

Early Childhood Programs

The accountability era was characterized not just by testing, but by the *back to basics* movement as well. This movement emphasized the teaching of basic skills as paramount to other kinds of learning experiences (e.g., inquiry, content learning). This created a trend toward more academic learning in preschool and kindergarten. This was a source of concern for many early childhood educators who believed young children learn best through active experiences and limited skills instruction.

Existing programs (e.g., Montessori, High/Scope) continued to flourish during the accountability movement, and more children were being placed in child care. In public schools, *open education* emerged as a new educational approach.

Open Education

Modeled after British schools, the open education concept came into practice in the United States in the 1970s. Although there was great variation in the British open schools, they generally reflected freedom of choice with regard to learning experiences, and curriculum was integrated across disciplines. For example, 7-year-olds might have lessons where science content is integrated with language arts (e.g., note taking, recording observations) and math (e.g., creating charts or graphs). The schools generally had open spaces and materials arranged for children to use with their learning activities.

In the United States, open education was often translated into open spaces. New schools were built with minimal walls so children had large spaces in which to work and move around. Some children were tracked across grade levels by ability, and groups of children moved from teacher to teacher for different subjects. Influenced by the accountability movement and back to basics foci, however, the curriculum remained fairly rigid.

Electronic Age

The period of the 1980s into the 1990s was a time of rapid change in industry and in families. Advances in technology improved the economic horizon and had a positive impact in the workplace and on personal lives. Large quantities of information could now be easily stored and quickly retrieved. Divorce rates rose and women increasingly worked out of the home.

Social, Political Environment

During the late 20th century, the effects of technology improved the economy for a period during the 1980s and 1990s, but the number of children in the United States living in poverty was increasing. The rate of families living in poverty rose 13% from 1980 to 1982 (Wortham, 1992). Tax reforms were favoring the wealthy while budget cuts took a toll on social programs for the poor.

Elizabeth Crews.

Immigration. Immigration into the United States continued as people moved in from eastern Europe, Cuba, Mexico, Vietnam, Laos, China, and Taiwan to name several. Some were refugees and others sought the American dream. Schools and child care centers were enrolling more children who were non-native English speakers. Urban schools might have 30 or more languages spoken, and educators struggled to meet the needs of all children. Certifications for working with English language learners (ELL) emerged in teacher education [English as a second language (ESL), bilingual education] (Chapter 10).

Technology. Few homes in the United States were without technology. In addition to TVs, computer games, videos, and DVDs became a new pastime. Children as young as 2 enjoyed technology, some to excess. Perhaps a reflection of the sedentary recreational activities that technology offered, childhood obesity was on the rise (Rimm, 2004). This constituted a new health threat for children who had been enjoying better health thanks to childhood immunizations.

Terrorism. Terrorist threats escalated in the late 20th and early 21st century. Radical groups committed terrorist acts around the world and, on September 11, 2001, struck on U.S. soil. That day, planes flown into the World Trade Center in New York City and the Pentagon in Washington, D.C., altered the lives of families in the United States indefinitely. With a need for increased security on planes and in public places, even the youngest of children would stand with their parents in long security lines and perhaps be frisked for weapons. Terrorist alerts and intelligence are the norm today in most corners of the world.

The Testing Movement

The demand for accountability remained strong and the testing movement continued into this era. Legislation that endorsed special education and related services for preschoolers continued to promote testing because standardized tests were deemed the best way to determine what services, if any, individual children needed.

In August 1981, then Secretary of Education, T. H. Bell, created a *National Commission on Excellence in Education* and charged the members to determine what was wrong with American education. Published in the now well-known *A Nation at Risk* (National Commission on Excellence in Education, 1984), the following quote summarizes the findings:

> *We have squandered the gains in student achievement made in the wake of the Sputnik challenge. Moreover, we have dismantled essential support systems which helped make those gains possible. We have, in effect, been committing an act of unthinking, unilateral educational disarmament. (p. 5)*

Standardized test scores served as the primary indicator of student achievement as the commission analyzed the state of U.S. schools.

A Nation at Risk (National Commission on Excellence in Education, 1984) became the subject of much debate and even criticism (Masini & Edirisooriya, 2000). For example, no one was able to clearly establish how the selected tests aligned with various curricula. So, perhaps the tests were not measuring what they were supposed to be measuring. Nonetheless, the report raised concern in the minds of policy makers, and the use of tests to measure student achievement escalated again. It now had a prominent place in the primary grades and, in some states, in kindergarten. Testing was used in federally funded prekindergarten (pre-K) programs but was still not prevalent in other pre-K settings.

Myrleen Cate/©Index Stock Imagery.

Testing now carried high stakes (life-altering consequences) and created tension among educators who were concerned that their students would not measure up. Some school districts published test scores in newspapers, which created even more tension for educators. For many early childhood educators, other means of assessment, such as observation and analysis of artifacts, gave way to an emphasis on test scores. More instructional time was spent teaching test taking skills. Prekindergarten educators now felt an increased responsibility to adequately prepare children for kindergarten; summer kindergarten preparation programs appeared in many communities.

In January of 2001, President George W. Bush signed the *No Child Left Behind* (NCLB) act into law, an action that would greatly change the lives of public school teachers and early childhood professionals. The law emphasized accountability, student achievement (based on test scores), and rigorous requirements for states to determine *adequate yearly progress* (AYP) of each public school. Early childhood educators were concerned about the well-being of children for whom tests were culturally biased (e.g., English language learners, children from cultures where tests are not valued).

Early Childhood Theories

Early childhood learned societies [e.g., the National Association for the Education of Young Children (NAEYC)] would have a great impact on early childhood education during this period. Some of these groups produced position statements to guide development of and practice in early childhood programs.

In 1987, the NAEYC published a research-based position statement on developmentally appropriate practice. The document was subsequently revised in 1997 to better address developmentally appropriate practices in diverse early childhood settings. Developmentally appropriate practice (DAP) and developmentally inappropriate practice (DIP) become household words for early childhood educators.

Also evolving at this time were research and theory about working with English language learners. Teacher education programs began offering majors and endorsements in English as a second language and bilingual education. Public schools sought teachers who were certified in ESL or bilingual education to better meet the needs of all children (Chapter 10). It was not unusual for school districts to be reported to the Office of Civil Rights (OCR) for not structuring an appropriate learning environment for ELL children. The OCR was called upon to enforce and oversee appropriate educational experiences for non-native English speakers.

Laura Dwight Photography.

Early Childhood Programs

Single and dual working parent families and high achievement expectations meant that early childhood programs were flourishing. Nearly all children attended kindergarten and well over half attended preschool or child care. Federal and state demands for high levels of accountability often

My Developing Professional View

Think about current social and political factors. What do you think is influencing early childhood care and education today?

led to developmentally inappropriate practice in early childhood settings, a concern to many early childhood educators. In many communities, pre-K and kindergarten educators were implementing an academic curriculum for large portions of the day. For example, in some pre-K settings, children were expected to learn letters and sounds so they could learn to read in kindergarten.

SUMMARY

This chapter has outlined the history of social, philosophical, and political trends in early childhood education within specific social–political contexts. The notion of the child-centered curriculum can be traced back for centuries, resurfacing during various periods. Our understanding of it today builds on the work of many past scholars in the field of early childhood education.

Children from minority groups, including those with disabilities, have traditionally received inferior educational opportunities. Initiated primarily in the decade of the Great Society, federal legislation and funds have increasingly supported programs for minority children and for children with disabilities. Having examined here the origin of many programs, we discuss their characteristics more fully in subsequent chapters.

The testing movement has greatly influenced education and practice with young children. This is particularly true in the past several decades when the amount of testing has increased and the stakes are high.

⟨ ENRICHMENT ACTIVITIES

Individual Activities

1. Access the website of the Froebel Foundation (http://www.froebelfoundation.org/) to learn more about the philosophy and practices for young children espoused by Friedrich Froebel and how they have evolved today.

2. Reflect on your own experiences with early education and care. Write a short reflective essay addressing the following questions. What do you think your early childhood educators believed about how children learn? What evidence do you have of that belief? Did you have a teacher that stood out in some way? Why?

3. Access the website of the Lyndon Johnson library (http://www.lbjlib.utexas.edu/). The site contains excepts from Johnson's diary and recorded phone conversations. Explore the site to learn more about the impact the era of the Great Society had on early childhood education and care. Write a brief overview of your findings.

4. Select one of the scholars discussed in Chapter 1 or Chapter 2 and learn more about his/her life and work. Write an overview of your findings.

Cooperative Activity

5. Select a topic (e.g., kindergarten, constructivism, Perry Preschool Project, girls and schooling) that you and your group members would like to learn more about. Divide the topic into subtopics so that there is one for each group member. For example, if you select the Perry Preschool Project as your topic, subtopics might include (1) the origin, (2) the High/Scope foundation, (3) research findings, and (4) educational philosophy and curricular materials. Research your individual subtopic and come back together as a group to prepare a formal presentation.

Advocacy Activity

6. An issue that has surfaced a few times in the history of education is the commitment to educating children as a means of stabilizing the workforce and the economy. For example, that commitment initiated the common school and lay at the foundation of the Great Society. Develop your personal position on this issue and write a letter to a legislator (or several) advocating strong legislative support for education in your state.

FOR FURTHER READING

Hill, P. S. (1942). *Kindergarten. A reprint from the American Educator Encyclopedia.* Chicago: United Educators.

National Commission on Excellence in Education. (1984). *A nation at risk.* Cambridge, MA: USA Research.

Singer, D. G. (1997). *A Piaget primer: How a child thinks.* Madison, CT: International University Press.

Tanner, L. N. (1997). *Dewey's laboratory school: Lessons for today.* New York: Teachers College Press.

Wortham, S. C. (1992). *Childhood 1892–1992.* Wheaton, MD: Association for Childhood Education International.

Zarefsky, D. (1986). *President Johnson's War on Poverty: Rhetoric and history.* Tuscaloosa, AL: University of Alabama Press.

Professional Development Resources

U.S. DEPARTMENT OF HEALTH AND HUMAN SERVICES
200 Independence Avenue SW
Washington, DC 20201
http://www.dhhs.gov/

CHILDREN'S DEFENSE FUND
25 E Street NW
Washington, DC 20001
http://www.childrensdefense.org/

SELF-ASSESSMENT

1. Thinking back over Chapters 1 and 2, write a brief overview of the early concept of the child-centered curriculum and the scholars who influenced it.

2. Briefly discuss the origin of kindergarten.

3. Identify some social, economic, and political influences on the testing movement over time.

4. Dewey noted that school *is* life for children. Considering his concept of continuity, explain what he meant.

5. Compare and contrast *constructivism* and *behaviorism*.

Scenario

As you observe in a kindergarten classroom, you notice one child who is continuously off-task. Although she is quiet and not disruptive, she does not seem to be interested in most classroom activities and does not engage in them. Taking the perspective of a scholar (e.g., Maslow, Skinner, Piaget) you have studied in this chapter, explain how you would approach this situation.

REFERENCES

Beatty, B. (1995). *Preschool education in America: The culture of young children from the colonial era to the present.* New Haven, CT: Yale University Press.

Bok, M. (1992). *Civil rights and the social programs of the 1960s: The social justice functions of social policy.* Westport, CT: Praeger Publishers.

Braun, S. J., & Edwards, E. P. (1972). *History and theory of early childhood education.* Belmont, CA: Wadsworth.

Cadwell, L. B. (1997). *Bringing Reggio Emilia home: An innovative approach to early childhood education.* New York: Teachers College Press.

Dewey, J. (1899). *The school and society.* Chicago: University of Chicago Press.

Dewey, J. (1910). *How we think.* Boston: Heath.

Dewey, J. (1938). *Experience and education.* New York: Touchstone.

Erikson, E. (1963). *Childhood and society* (2nd ed.). New York: Norton.

Gesell, A., & Ilg, F. L. (1943). *Infant and child in the culture of today: The guidance of development in home and nursery school.* New York: Harper & Brothers.

Ginsburg, H., & Opper, S. (1969). *Piaget's theory of intellectual development: An introduction.* Englewood Cliffs, NJ: Prentice-Hall.

High/Scope Educational Research Foundation. (2004). *Significant benefits: The High/Scope Perry Preschool Project.* Retrieved May 2004 from http://www.highscope.org/Research/PerryProject/

Hill, P. S. (1942). *Kindergarten. A reprint from the American Educator Encyclopedia.* Chicago: United Educators.

Hughes, J. L. (2001). *Froebel's educational law for all teachers.* Grand Rapids, MI: Froebel Foundation, USA.

Kelly, M. F., & Surbeck, E. (2000). History of preschool assessment. In B.A. Bracken (Ed.), *The psychoeducational assessment of preschool children* (3rd ed.), pp. 1–18. Boston: Allyn and Bacon.

Masini, D. E., & Edirisooriya, G. (2000, November). *Never a nation at risk: Exorcising the ghost of education past.* Paper presented at the meeting of the Mid-South Educational Research Association, Bowling Green, KY.

Maslow, A. H. (1954). *Motivation and personality* (2nd ed.). New York: Harper & Row.

Montessori, M. (1967). *The discovery of the child* (M. J. Costelloe, Trans.). Notre Dame, IN: Fides Publishers.

National Commission on Excellence in Education. (1984). *A nation at risk.* Cambridge, MA: USA Research.

Pavlov, I. P. (1928). *Lectures on conditioned reflexes* (W. Horsley Gantt, Trans.). New York: Liveright Publishing.

Piaget, J. (1962). *Play, dreams, and imitation in childhood* (C. Gattegno & F. M. Hodgson, Trans.). New York: W. W. Norton & Company.

Rimm, S. (2004). *Rescuing the lives of overweight children.* Emmaus, PA: Rodale Press.

Sadler, J. E. (1966). *J. A. Comenius and the concept of universal education.* New York: Barnes & Noble.

Shepard, L. A., & Smith, M. L. (1988). Escalating academic demand in kindergarten: Counterproductive policies. *The Elementary School Journal, 89*(2), 135–145.

Skinner, B. F. (1974). *About behaviorism.* New York: Vintage Books.

Spring, J. (1986). *The American school 1642–1985.* White Plains, NY: Longman.

Thorndike, E. L. (1935). *The psychology of wants, interests, and attitudes.* New York: D. Appleton-Century.

Vygotsky, L. (1978). *Mind in society.* Cambridge, MA: Harvard University Press.

Vygotsky, L. S. (1966). Play and its role in the mental development of the child. *Soviet Psychology, 12,* 62–76.

Watson, J. B. (1925). *Behaviorism.* New York: Norton.

Weber, L. (1971). *The English infant school and informal education.* Englewood Cliffs, NJ: Prentice-Hall.

Wortham, S. C. (1992). *Childhood 1892–1992.* Wheaton, MD: Association for Childhood Education International.

Governance of Early Care and Education: Past and Present

3

The nature of early care and education is greatly affected by how it is governed. Who makes policy decisions? What influences decisions about curriculum? As we examine early childhood governance from a historical perspective we see how our current structure and policies came to be.

Policies regulating early education and care grow out of the particular social, political, and economic contexts in which children live. Chapters 1 and 2 laid the foundation for understanding those contexts over time. This chapter builds on Chapters 1 and 2 as we look at governance of early education and care and specific factors affecting governance over time. It begins with a brief reflection on colonial times followed by a discussion of the significant administrative reform of public schools in the late 19th and early 20th centuries. Specific federal policies relevant to early childhood education and to children with disabilities are included. We also look at the role of public education and care regarding the issue of separation of church and state.

As a result of reading this chapter, you will understand:

▶ The history of governance of early care and education.

▶ Governance of early care and education today.

▶ The chronology of federal policy for early childhood education.

▶ Factors that influenced federal policy for early childhood education.

▶ The chronology of federal policy for early childhood special education.

▶ The evolution of policy regarding the relationship of church and state.

▶ The evolution of policy regarding bilingual education.

{ Oversight for Early Care and Education

The social communities of the early Europeans were religious monocultures where schools served as an arm of the particular community's religious tradition. School governance was handled at the community level. Even as states began mandating common schools under the *Old Deluder Satan Act* (Chapter 2), primary responsibility for governance remained at the community level.

Around the turn of the 20th century, the progressive era gave birth to the centralized governance of public schools that we have today. There was a shift from complete local control to one where policies were made and carried out in a bureaucracy.

{ Administrative Reform

During the period 1890–1920, major administrative reform took place in public school systems in the industrial North. The reform created centralized authority of public schools, placing it in the hands of policy makers, school boards, and superintendents, most of whom were isolated from the daily lives of families and young children. This centralization of school administration was shaped by philosophical underpinnings of capitalism; it was designed to be efficient and to produce social order (Snauwaert, 1993).

Social, Political, Economic Context. The decades of the 1870s and 1880s were a time of rapid industrialization in the North. The increased output of products led to intense competition, which in turn led to deflation and lower profits. Economic crisis loomed for many firms (Hobsbawm, 1987). On the heels of the Great Depression of 1893–97, industrialists consolidated their firms into large corporations to decrease competition and ensure higher profit margins (Snauwaert, 1993).

Consolidation was viewed as a way to control competition and ensure a high rate of profit without giving control to any one faction or firm. The move to consolidate was further perpetuated by the number of lawyers and bankers who profited financially by putting the mergers together. It was only a matter of time until

The Granger Collection.

Corbis-Bettmann.

this centralization of economic authority led to centralization in other social realms, including public schools. Bureaucracy in the administration of public schools was born from the social, political, and economic environment of the nation in general.

Scientific Management

Frederick Taylor's scientific management was used in the administration of new corporations in America, and his methods found their way into educational administration. Scientific management has four basic principles (Sergiovanni, Burlingame, Coombs, & Thurston, 1980):

J. P. Morgan Financier and Banker. Lebrecht Music & Arts/ The image Works.

▶ Replace intuitive methods of doing business by a scientific method of observation and analysis to obtain the best cost–benefit ratio.

▶ Select a person who can perform the job in the one best way.

▶ Cooperate and ensure that the work is being done according to established standards and procedures.

▶ Divide the work among managers and workers so that managers plan and supervise the work. (p. 44)

In the interest of efficiency, those management principles were applied to public schools. In business, total control of production lay in the hands of management, not workers; similarly, control of financial decisions, curriculum development, and standards for teachers were in control of centralized management—school boards and superintendents. The net effect was diminished autonomy for teachers as decision makers about curriculum and instruction in their classrooms.

Nursery Schools

The Great Depression of the 1930s and World War II in the 1940s (WWII) gave birth to federal involvement in nursery education and care (Chapter 2). Prior to that time, there was little federal involvement in nursery education. Nursery schools gained further momentum during the Great Society era (Chapter 2) of the 1960s.

Nursery schools were originally established in the 19th century to meet the developmental needs of young children, particularly those living in poverty. Nursery schools of the late 19th and early 20th centuries were operated by those who viewed the early years as critical developmental years. The schools provided opportunities for children to enjoy interesting activities, to learn through experiences, and to interact with other children and adults. Philanthropic organizations and private employers were the primary administrators of these nursery schools.

In the 1930s the Works Progress Administration (WPA), an arm of the federal government, created emergency nursery schools intended to stimulate the economy by creating jobs as well as to serve the needs of young children. With federal funding, nursery schools were now available to all children, not just those of the middle and upper classes. With oversight provided by public school administrators, nursery schools continued through the war years of the 1940s to address the needs of mothers working in the war industry. After the war ended, however, federal support for nursery schools declined.

Governance of Early Care and Education Today

Today, states regulate staff qualifications and health standards for early childhood settings, and provide curriculum and assessment guidelines for early childhood education in public schools. Decisions about specific aspects of the curriculum, schedules, and daily events are made within the school or center.

However, centralized school governance has remained the status quo in public schools since it was implemented over 100 years ago. Figure 3.1 depicts the governance structure for preschool and child care as well as early childhood settings in public schools. Although the federal government funds many initiatives for early care and education, the states have primary oversight, with the exception of Head Start programs. They also have the option to refuse participation in federal initiatives.

Critique of Centralized Governance

Centralized governance was designed to be efficient by placing decision making in the hands of a few. But centralized governance is not without critics. Some believe that teachers' knowledge of how young children learn often gets overlooked by policy makers. Expectations may be unrealistic because policy makers do not understand the context of schools. Can you think of some specific aspects of school that policy makers might not understand?

Critics feel that meeting the needs of all children is a more ideal goal than efficiency. Some suggest that public school governance might be better defined by the principles of participation, communication, association, nonviolence, and community (Snauwaert, 1993). In other words, parents, teachers, and community members have input into decisions affecting public schools, and their voices are heard at all levels—local, state, and national.

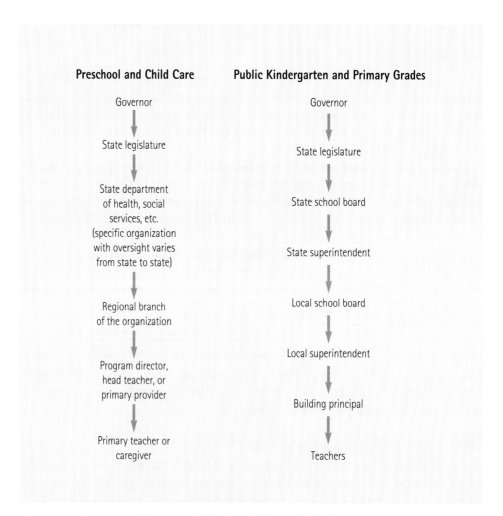

Figure 3.1. Governance structure for early care and education today.

Ellen B. Senisi.

Federal Policies Affecting Early Childhood Education

Recall from Chapter 2 that the progressive era brought about an interest in early childhood education. Nursery schools, including Patty Smith Hill's laboratory school at Columbia University, began opening in the first decades of the 20th century. Scholars studying young children were unveiling and applying new knowledge about how they grow and develop.

The social–political environment during the first half of the 20th century also turned attention to early childhood education. The federal government got involved in early care and education following two world wars and the Great Depression to address the needs of working mothers and children living in poverty. In turn, this led to federal legislation to benefit young children.

By 1940, nearly one-third of U.S. women worked in the war industry. To help these working mothers, the *Lanham Act* (legislation related to the WPA program) was initiated to establish war nurseries. Perhaps the best known of these nurseries was operated by the Kaiser Shipbuilding Company in Portland, Oregon. It was open for long hours each day and served children age 18 months to 6 years.

Early childhood educators hoped that the nursery schools would become permanent programs; however, that was not to be. The WPA and the Lanham Act programs halted in 1942 and 1946, respectively (Osborn, 1975). Nonetheless the stage was set, and state and federal initiatives for early childhood education were forthcoming.

Postwar Years

During the period following WWII, many mothers remained in the workforce, but without the federal nursery schools there were not enough facilities to care for their children. Private centers had long waiting lists and were too expensive for many. The demand for nursery schools increased when, during the period of the Cold War, many parents looked to early childhood educators for guidance in talking with their children about the atom bomb and other frightening things in the news. However, increased federally funded preschool programs remained illusive until the 1960s.

Children with Disabilities

Historically, practices of abandonment and infanticide were common for infants and young children with disabilities; yet, the field of special education has a long history. For example, a school for the deaf was established in Kentucky in 1823 and other states followed the lead. In 1852, Pennsylvania appropriated funds for the education of mentally handicapped children. In 1911, New Jersey adopted the first special education laws, and Minnesota established special education teacher certification requirements in 1915 (Weintraub & Ballard, 1982). Even with these initial efforts, the federal government did not enact policy and provide support for education for children with disabilities until the postwar years.

Advocating for the Child

Social Legislation Enacted during the Era of the Great Society

The period of the Great Society was one when significant and lasting social legislation was passed. Addressing issues related to poverty, civil rights, and children with disabilities, some of the policies enacted are highlighted below.

Training of Professional Personnel, 1958

This act provided funding for colleges and universities to train special education teachers.

Civil Rights Act, 1964

This act guaranteed the Fourteenth Amendment, which provides equal protection under the law. It enforced desegregation and set the stage for affirmative action.

Economic Opportunity Act, 1964

In the midst of tension related to civil rights, this act provided training, work, and the opportunity to live in dignity. This act administered Project Head Start, which required communities to implement programs for low-income preschool children. It was amended in 1972 to mandate that 10% of the openings be reserved for children with disabilities.

Elementary and Secondary Education Act, 1965

This act, which is in effect today, provided funds to schools serving low-income families, particularly elementary schools, to better meet the needs of at-risk students. Funding was determined by the number of low-income families in the school and could be spent on materials, food programs, and personnel. The act was expanded in 1966 to provide programs for Native American children, in 1967 to provide programs for non-native English speaking children, and in 1969 to define learning disabilities and model education for children with learning disabilities. It also addressed education for gifted and talented children.

Medicare and Medicaid, 1965

With working people enjoying health care benefits as part of employment compensation, a health care gap was created between the young and the elderly and the poor and more affluent (Bok, 1992). This act was designed to make health care more accessible for the poor and elderly.

Education for Handicapped Children, 1966

This provided funds to expand programs for preschool, elementary, and secondary children with disabilities.

Handicapped Children's Early Education Assistance Act, 1968

This act heralded a new focus on early childhood special education by funding early childhood programs with exemplary practices for children with disabilities.

Housing and Urban Development Act, 1968

To address issues of homelessness and substandard housing, this act subsidized low-income housing.

The Era of the Great Society

The period of the Great Society was one of significant social change, perhaps the most significant in our history for young children and their families. Federal initiatives abounded primarily to eradicate the effects of poverty. On the heels of decades of new scientific knowledge about how young children grow and develop (Chapter 2), federal policy makers focused on early education and its effects on intellectual development. Federally funded health and preschool programs were initiated, have been expanded, and continue to exist today. The *Advocating for the Child* highlights some of the federal legislation for young children and their families that was enacted during the 1960s or the era of the Great Society.

The Era of Accountability

Social factors spurred the federal government to organize the National Commission on Excellence in Education (Chapter 2) and charge them to examine the state of our nation's schools. These factors included continuing to address the needs of children and their families living in poverty. Higher divorce rates and social acceptance of working mothers meant more were entering the workforce and placing their young children in out-of-home care. There was also an increasing focus on achievement that came out of the competitive years of the Cold War (Chapter 2).

The commission published their findings in 1984 in *A Nation at Risk* (National Commission on Excellence in Education, 1984), and federal support and involvement in education increased. More legislation emerged that was designed to better serve the early care and educational needs of children living in poverty and of children with disabilities. The *Advocating for the Child* feature highlights some of the legislation during 1970–1990.

Even with these initiatives, families living in poverty often had to settle for substandard child care. The federal dollars used to subsidize child care were not enough for families to afford the highest quality (and consequently most expensive) child care. When we consulted with child care centers during this period, we found that many families struggled to make up a difference of 25 to 50 cents per hour which was the cost of child care in excess of the federal subsidy.

Entering the Twenty-First Century

The national focus on accountability continued into the 21st century. The period of the 1990s into the 21st century saw two significant pieces of legislation that affected young children: the *Goals 2000, Educate America Act* in 1993 and the *No Child Left Behind Act* in 2001, a reauthorization of the *Elementary & Secondary Education Act*. Each had its supporters and its critics.

In 1993, President Clinton signed the Goals 2000, Educate America Act, which established eight national educational goals. The *Advocating for the Child* feature lists the goals.

The first goal—*every child will enter school ready to learn*—had the most relevance to early childhood education. The intent was to address issues related to children's health and well-being prior to school entrance. Aimed at adequately meeting the needs of all children, this legislation was lofty, perhaps a bit too lofty for available resources.

This legislation resulted in the development of standards for children's achievement and performance. Supporters felt that the strength of this legislation was that children would demonstrate what they could do rather than measure achievement

Advocating for the Child

Legislation Enacted to Support Children with Disabilities

While federal legislation during the era of The Great Society focused primarily on families and children living in poverty, subsequent legislation primarily addressed the needs of children with disabilities.

Education for All Handicapped Children Act, 1975

This landmark legislative act mandated free and appropriate education for all children ages 3–21 in the least restrictive environment. Federal grants to provide preschools for children with disabilities were available.

Education of the Handicapped Act Amendments, 1986

With this legislation, programs were extended to children birth to age 2 for comprehensive early intervention.

Family Support Act, 1988

This act came under the Social Security Act and had two child care assistance provisions. (1) **Aid to Families with Dependent Children** (AFDC) provided child care assistance to low-income families where a parent was employed or enrolled in job training. (2) **Transitional Child Care** (TCC) provided financial assistance to families transitioning from AFDC to independence. In 1990, an **At-Risk Child Care** program was added to support children at risk of abuse or neglect.

Americans with Disabilities Act, 1990

This act affirmed the civil rights of persons with disabilities by mandating public services to modify equipment and make accommodations for persons with disabilities. Public schools and child care centers must also comply. It also protected a young child with a disability from being turned away from a child care center.

Individuals with Disabilities Act (IDEA), 1990

This initiative changed the name of the Education of the Handicapped Act. It expanded services for persons with disabilities. Later amendments expanded accountability for children with disabilities and expanded the application of the label *developmental delay*.

Child Care and Development Block Grants, 1990

The grants enacted by this legislation were designed to support child care for children at risk of abuse or neglect. It also served families who did not qualify for AFDC or Head Start but were struggling to make ends meet.

based on narrow information from a multiple-choice test. On the other hand, critics suggested that the performance standards and assessment as articulated did not adequately embrace individual and cultural differences. Critics also noted that resources were too limited to adequately address the goals.

In 2001, President George W. Bush signed the No Child Left Behind Act (NCLB). This law greatly expanded the federal role in matters related to public schools, particularly accountability. The expectation of NCLB was that individual schools would demonstrate *adequate yearly progress* (AYP) (Chapter 2) and employ only highly qualified teachers. Schools consistently not making AYP would be sanctioned and parents would have the option to move their children to other schools.

Supporters of this legislation contended that high-stakes tests and expectations for meeting yearly progress would further hold teachers and school districts accountable for student achievement. Formalizing accountability by requiring AYP, supporters of NCLB felt it less likely that children's needs would be overlooked, causing them to fall through the cracks.

On the other hand, critics felt that teaching quality and student achievement were inappropriately equated with test scores; this equating was simplistic and ignored the broader concept of accountability (Cochran-Smith, 2003). Critics felt that if teachers were accountable for meeting the unique needs of individual children, they needed resources and flexibility to accommodate the needs of individual children. However, tension over accountability as measured by children's test scores distracted teachers from focusing on individual needs. Critics also noted that parents whose children attended failing schools would not be able to choose a more desirable school if they lived in communities with only one school or where only a few of several schools met AYP.

Paul Conklin/Photo Edit.

⟨ The History of Bilingual Education

Imagine yourself living in a society where you did not speak the native language. Imagine yourself trying to buy food, obtain a drivers license, or get a job. For most of us, that is a frightening thought. Contemporary issues related to bilingual education are discussed in Chapter 10; here, we provide its historical context, particularly as it relates to governance (see the Advocating for the Child feature on page 59).

Advocating for the Child

Goals 2000, Educate America Act

By the year 2000:

- All children in America will start school ready to learn.

- The high school graduation rate will increase to at least 90%.

- All students will leave grades 4, 8, and 12 having demonstrated competency over challenging subject matter including English, mathematics, science, foreign languages, civics and government, economics, arts, history, and geography, and every school in America will ensure that all students learn to use their minds well, so they may be prepared for responsible citizenship, further learning, and productive employment in our nation's modern economy.

- The nation's teaching force will have access to programs for the continued improvement of their professional skills and the opportunity to acquire the knowledge and skills needed to instruct and prepare all American students for the next century.

- United States students will be first in the world in mathematics and science achievement.

- Every adult American will be literate and will possess the knowledge and skills necessary to compete in a global economy and exercise the rights and responsibilities of citizenship.

- Every school in the United States will be free of drugs, violence, and the unauthorized presence of firearms and alcohol and will offer a disciplined environment conducive to learning.

- Every school will promote partnerships that will increase parental involvement and participation in promoting the social, emotional, and academic growth of children.

Dating back to ancient times, hundreds of languages were spoken among the indigenous people living in what is now the United States. When the first generations of European immigrants came to the United States, they tended to settle in enclaves with common languages and cultural practices. While some states offered bilingual instruction, it was commonly accepted that children would assimilate into the mainstream, which included learning to speak English (Ovando, 2003).

During the industrial era, some states adopted English-only school laws. These laws evolved from the goal to acculturate Native Americans into the ways of mainstream America. In 1890, the Immigration Restriction League was founded; it proposed English literacy tests for immigrants (Ovando, 2003). On June 29, 1906, the federal Naturalization Act was passed; it established uniform procedures for naturalization and made knowledge of English language a requirement for naturalization. By 1923, 34 states mandated English-only instruction in their schools. However, the tide turned during the era of civil rights and the implementation of the Civil Rights Act in 1964 (see *Advocating for the Child*). Even as the 21st century dawned, debate continued about immigration and meeting the learning needs of English language learners in our nation's schools.

The Relationship of Church and State

Think back to your own experiences in school. If you attended public school, how was religion addressed? Did you study religions from a historical perspective? Did you practice religion in any way? Was there ever a controversy over the separation of church and state in your school district or state? Is it constitutional to study about religion in public schools? Should study of religion be included in public schools?

We discussed in Chapter 2 that the primary reason for schools in colonial times was to teach young children to read the Bible and the laws of the state. Initially, there was no separation of church and state; in fact, schools served as a socializing agent for churches. Over time, however, the issue of separation of church and state became more important, due primarily to the great diversity of religions in the United States. In other words, anytime a religious group, Protestants, for example, wanted to integrate religious teaching into public school curriculum, another group spoke up in protest. In our diverse nation, there was great need to recognize many religious traditions as well as those who did not adhere to any religion. Many, many decades after the Pilgrims' arrival, separation of church and state was legislated, but it took even more time before the legislation was acknowledged in individual states.

Following is a chronological overview of policy related to separation of church and state. It is organized by the same time periods presented in Chapter 2.

Colonial Era

In the 17th century, each of the colonies had its own religious orientation. Massachusetts and Connecticut had state-supported Congregational churches, while Virginia had the Church of England, and so on. There were no laws mandating separation of church and state. Although each group—Congregationalists, Presbyterians, Episcopalians, etc.—felt their church would make an ideal national church, there was no majority strong enough for one religion to become dominant (Fraser, 1999). Eventually, the notion that no one wanted the religion of others forced upon them ignited sentiments for separation of church and state. In 1791, the first

Advocating for the Child

Late Twentieth Century Legislation Related to Bilingual Education

On the heels of the civil rights movement, designed to rid America of discrimination based on ethnicity, court cases and federal policy shifted the tide for bilingual education.

Immigration Act, 1965

Spurred by the civil rights movement and signed into law by President Lyndon Johnson, this act changed the method by which immigrants would be admitted to the United States. It allowed for immigration of more people, including separate quotas for refugees.

Bilingual Education Act, 1968

This act provided supplemental funding to assist school districts in meeting the special education needs of large numbers of children who were English language learners.

Lau v. Nichols, 1974

This lawsuit was brought against the San Francisco School District by a group of Chinese-speaking students who said that instruction only in English denied them meaningful educational opportunities. The case resulted in a ruling that equal treatment of English-speaking and non-English-speaking children was inequitable.

Lau Remedies, 1975

This act grew out of the *Lau v. Nichols* court case and provided the following:

- Guidelines for schools to determine the language proficiency of language-minority students.
- Specific pedagogical strategies for English language learners.
- Defined professional standards for bilingual teachers.
- Requirements for school districts to provide evidence of effective education for language-minority students (Ovando, 2003).

Civil Rights Language Minority Regulations, 1980

This legislation required that bilingual instruction be provided by qualified instructors.

Castaneda v. Pickard, 1981

This case resulted in more specific guidelines to measure whether schools are in compliance with the Lau Remedies. In general, the guidelines called for use of appropriate instructional strategies, and sufficient staff to meet the needs, and schools were asked to provide evidence of effective instruction (assessment results).

amendment established that "Congress shall make no law respecting an establishment of religion, or prohibiting the free exercise thereof. . . ." However, the matter was far from settled in public schools.

Industrial Era

In the period following the American Revolution, schools, religion, and good government were inextricably linked in the minds of many (Fraser, 1999). The Northwest Ordinance of 1787 noted, "religion, morality, and knowledge being necessary to good government and the happiness of mankind, schools and the means of education shall forever be encouraged" (Fraser, 1999, p. 23). States consisted of clusters of like-minded people who supported and controlled churches and schools, and it took until the mid-19th century for the constitutional separation of church and state to be fully acknowledged in the individual states.

Massachusetts was one of the last states to end religious schools. A Unitarian himself, Secretary of Education Horace Mann (Chapter 2) was a supporter of religious education in the common schools, but he said it should be general and tolerant. He noted that a goal of schooling was to lead children to think and make decisions about how they would vote and he saw decisions about religion as no different. Therefore, in Massachusetts, children listened to Bible readings in school but teachers were not allowed to make interpretive comments. In other words, they would read the Bible but there would be no discussion. Mann believed any interpretation of the Bible should done in Sunday school. The core of Christianity was taught in schools but the details were left to churches.

As the number of common schools increased in the Midwest, many citizens wanted texts to be handbooks of common morality and Protestant virtues. They wanted them to reflect white middle-class Protestant morality so they could be used to affirm Protestant dominance.

History of Roman Catholic Schools

Many Roman Catholics immigrated from England to the colonies during the 16th and 17th centuries to escape persecution and economic troubles; they settled in Maryland. They were few in number at first, but by 1850 they were the largest single religious denomination in the nation (Fraser, 1999). This had huge implications for schools.

The common schools were steeped in the Protestant ideals. Catholics were allowed into the common schools, but they had to learn Protestant values. In New York City particularly, the conflict between the immigrant Catholics and nativists grew. With Catholics making up only about 2% of the population in New York, they opened a school in St. Peter's Church (Fraser, 1999). In 1806, the parish applied for and received a portion of state school funds. As time passed, the Catholic population grew and another school was opened.

Also in 1806, the Free School Society was founded by a group of elite businessmen representing several Protestant orientations. The goal of the Free School Society was to provide schools for the city's poor children that were unaffiliated with a particular religion. Their goal was to provide education to children of the poor equal to that of affluent children (a challenging goal still today). Within the next 20 years, the group wanted to become the only common school, and thus needed funds being used by the religious schools (Fraser, 1999).

Being the city's elite, the leadership of the Free School Society was well connected to the legislature and they persuaded the lawmakers to give all public school funds to the Free School Society. In 1825, the Free School Society was renamed the Public School Society, and all funds were cut off for sectarian schools (Fraser, 1999). The impact on the Catholics was especially profound because most of the Catholic immigrants were among the poorest families in New York City. They did not have funds to support their schools.

While more affluent Catholic children continued in the sectarian schools, many others had to attend the free public schools, which still espoused Protestant values and doctrine. When Governor Seward proposed reconsideration of the 1825 decision, the Public School Society began negotiating, offering to remove offensive textbooks and materials. The result of this newest conflict was adherence to separation of church and state; the Public School Society was to become nonsectarian in their teaching. However, conflict remained as Catholics continued to find anti-Catholic sentiment in instructional materials.

The Progressive Era

Charles Darwin upset many Christians when he posed his scientific theory of evolution in 1859. Christians believed in creationism and not evolution, and the issue

John Scopes. Hulton Archive/Getty Images.

of *creationism vs. evolution* became a source of great debate that continues in some areas of our nation today. By the late 19th and early 20th centuries, tension had escalated between theological modernists and fundamentalists. The theological modernists, who sought to understand the Bible in the context it was written yet apply it to modern life, accepted the theory of evolution. On the other hand, fundamentalists interpreted the Bible literally and insisted on the infallibility of God's word (Fraser, 1999). They believed in creationism.

During the progressive era, many continued to advocate for religious neutrality in public schools and for no government support for Catholic schools. At odds with religious neutrality, many states passed antievolution legislation forbidding the teaching of the theory of evolution. The 1925 Tennessee trial of John Scopes, the high school biology teacher who taught the theory of evolution, gave fuel to this movement.

John Scopes was convinced by the American Civil Liberties Union (ACLU) to be a test case for the creationism vs. evolution debate. The goal of the ACLU was more than protection of academic freedom; it was to preserve personal liberty as well (Fraser, 1999). The trial drew much attention, and in the end John Scopes was found guilty. The state of Tennessee overturned the conviction on a technicality, perhaps so that the ACLU could not have its day in front of the Supreme Court.

The Twentieth Century

During the decades following the Scopes trial, battles over the relationship between church and state gradually moved from the state to the federal level, owing largely to Protestant intolerance. For example, the Klu Klux Klan was advocating loudly for white, Protestant supremacy.

As time passed, the U.S. Supreme Court began hearing more and more cases related to the issue of separation of church and state, and they eventually determined that the First Amendment did apply to local as well as federal decisions. In the 1948 case of *McCollum v. Board of Education*, the Supreme Court ruled against programs that allowed school children to attend religious instruction during the regular school day. In the 1962 case of *Engel v. Vitale*, the Supreme Court rendered a decision prohibiting prayer in public schools. In the case of *Abington School District v. Schempp* in 1963, the Supreme Court decision ended Bible reading in school.

Debate related to the relationship between church and state continued for the remainder of the 20th century. One particularly prominent issue was distribution of religious literature in public schools. In general, courts allowed such distribution as a matter of freedom of speech but permitted schools to ban the distribution if it became disruptive. The issue of the constitutionality of release time religious instruction programs made its way back into the courts during this era. While the Supreme Court ruled that they were constitutional, schools were under no obligation to create such programs, were required to leave the door open for all religions to participate, and were not allowed to penalize nonparticipants in any way (Haynes & Thomas, 1998).

The essence of the debate can be summed in the words *freedom of* and *freedom from*. Ideally, all children in public schools will have to right to self-expression and to practice their religious traditions—*freedom of*. On the other hand, children will be protected from indoctrination by others in public institutions—*freedom from*.

Separation of Church and State Today

Within the debate about the separation of church and state, some argue that religion should be completely absent from public schools. Others note that complete absence is a blatant misrepresentation of history and culture (Marty & Moore, 2000). Supporting the absence of religion seems harmless; yet attitudes and values with regard to religion, whether one chooses to practice or not, are at the core of human existence. To ignore them might be likened to trying to ignore an individual's gender or skin color. Furthermore, young children talk about their family's religious beliefs and practices or decision not to practice religion, and early childhood educators must understand how to respond in ways that neither promote nor reject any family's values.

 ## My Developing Professional View

> We have come through many decades of legislation designed to help early childhood educators better meet the cultural and learning needs of children. What is your view of early childhood educators' responsibility for being accountable for the growth and development of young children in their classrooms?

Because understanding religious attitudes, beliefs, and values is critical to understanding the human existence, there is a place for teaching about religion (as opposed to proselytizing) in the public schools; and, it is constitutional. In other words, it is inappropriate to celebrate religion in the public schools, but learning about religion is appropriate and necessary. Even young children can learn about the values and beliefs of others, the origin of practices, and so on. However, any discussion of religion is often seen as off limits by educators who struggle to identify a constitutionally permissible way to teach about religion as an aspect of culture. Specific strategies for teaching about religion to young children are discussed in Chapter 7.

Individual Behaviors. Guidance for what is acceptable and unacceptable behavior in public care and education related to separation of church and state comes from interpretation of the First Amendment via court cases. Courts have found in favor of allowing children in public schools to practice their religion as long as it is not disruptive to the functioning of the educational setting. For example, a quiet personal prayer is allowed; prayer over the intercom system is not.

Educators and staff, on the other hand, are more restricted than children. Because they are in a position of authority in a public setting that does not promote a particular religion, they must practice more restraint. Educators and staff cannot lead children in prayer. They cannot display bold religious icons, even in their personal space. For example, wearing a small cross around your neck is acceptable but keeping a large figurine of Jesus on your desk is not appropriate.

SUMMARY

In this chapter, we have examined governance of early education and care over time. As a society that has grown from a small group of immigrants during the colonial era to hundreds of millions of people today, the United States has enacted policy and legislation that have attempted, over time, to meet the needs of all young children. Social and political circumstances have highly influenced policy and legislation.

We have examined the influence of the social–political environment on policy and legislation affecting early childhood education. From the WPA programs to policies to support children with disabilities, policy and legislation have tried to address the diverse needs of young children and their families. Policy to address the needs of English language learners has come about. Legislation related to the separation of church and state has also flowed with the tide of the political environment. Our U.S. society has evolved from colonial days when schools were a socializing agent for churches to the 21st century when great religious diversity requires objectivity in public care and education to value all families' religious preferences as well as those who do not adhere to any religion.

⟩ ENRICHMENT ACTIVITIES

Individual Activities

1. Through your local legislator or the website for your state government, learn about the rules and regulations for child care in your state.

Cooperative Activity

2. Each group member will review issues of your local newspaper over a few weeks' time paying attention to articles having to do with state or federal policy. (Libraries have back copies.) For example, you might find articles about NCLB, your state's assessment policy (student achievement), or an issue related to separation of church and state. Review the articles together. What policy related issues are currently in the news? What can you learn about public opinion about the policy? What can you learn about early childhood educators' opinion of the policy?

Advocacy Activity

3. Access the website for the Children's Defense Fund, a national group that advocates on behalf of young children, particularly as it relates to federal legislation. It can be found at (http://www.childrensdefense.org/). Find out what their current agenda is and research and develop a thoughtful position on an issue of interest you. Share your position with the class and others.

⟩ FOR FURTHER READING

Children's Defense Fund. [Annual editions]. *Yearbook: The state of America's children*. Washington, DC: Author

Fraser, J. W. (1999). *Between church and state: Religion and public education in a multicultural America*. New York: St. Martin's Griffin.

Haynes, C. C., & Thomas, O. (Eds.). (1998). *Finding common ground: A First Amendment guide to religion and public education*. Nashville, TN: First Amendment Center.

Marty, M. E., with Moore, J. (2000). *Education, religion, and the common good*. San Francisco, CA: Jossey-Bass.

Professional Development Resources

CHILDREN NOW

1212 Broadway, 5th Floor
Oakland, CA 94612
http://www.childrennow.org/

STATE GOVERNMENTS
http://www.statelocalgov.net/

THE FIRST AMENDMENT CENTER

1207 18th Avenue South
Nashville, TN 37212
http://www.freedomforum.org/

SELF-ASSESSMENT

1. Explain the economic and political influences behind the centralization of authority for public schools.

2. Identify some social, economic, and political factors of the 20th and 21st centuries that led to increased federal legislation affecting young children and children with disabilities.

3. Generally explain the NCLB act.

4. Explain the role of early childhood educators regarding separation of church and state.

Scenario

You are a kindergarten teacher who does many activities related to mainstream holiday themes, particularly Christmas and Easter. A parent comes to you to complain, noting that he and his family are atheists. Take the perspective of Horace Mann and respond to this parent.

REFERENCES

Bok, M. (1992). *Civil rights and the social programs of the 1960s: The social justice functions of social policy*. Westport, CT: Praeger Publishers.

Cochran-Smith, M. (2003). The unforgiving complexity of teaching: Avoiding simplicity in the age of accountability. *Journal of Teacher Education, 54*(1), 3–5.

Fraser, J. W. (1999). *Between church and state: Religion and public education in a multicultural America*. New York: St. Martin's Griffin.

Haynes, C. C., & Thomas, O. (Eds.). (1998). Finding common ground: A First Amendment guide to religion and public education. Nashville, TN: First Amendment Center.

Hobsbawm, E. J. (1987). *The age of empire, 1875–1914*. New York: Pantheon Books.

Marty, M. E., with Moore, J. (2000). *Education, religion, and the common good*. San Francisco, CA: Jossey-Bass.

National Commission on Excellence in Education. (1984). *A nation at risk*. Cambridge, MA: USA Research.

Osborn, D. K. (1975). *Early childhood education in the historical perspective* (3rd ed.). Athens, GA: Daye Press.

Ovando, C. J. (2003). Bilingual education in the United States: Historical development and current issues. *Bilingual Research Journal, 27*(1), 1.

Sergiovanni, T. J., Burlingame, M., Coombs, F. D., & Thurston, P. W. (1980). *Educational governance and administration*. Englewood Cliffs, NJ: Prentice-Hall.

Snauwaert, D. T. (1993). *Democracy, education, and governance: A developmental conception*. Albany, NY: State University of New York Press.

Weintraub, F. J., & Ballard, J. (1982). Introduction: Bridging the decades. In J. Ballard, B. A. Ramirez, & F. J. Weintraub (Eds.), *Special education in America: Its legal and governmental foundations*, pp. 1–9. Reston, VA: Council for Exceptional Children.

The Role of Early Childhood Educators in Children's Lives

4

Early childhood educators are professionally prepared to work with children. The role of early childhood educators is to understand the nature of young children, their developmental needs, the social environments in which they are living, and the characteristics of developmentally and culturally appropriate curriculum and instruction. High-quality early childhood educators maintain a continuous agenda for professional development in order to remain current in knowledge about development and research-based appropriate practices. Furthermore, high-quality early childhood educators serve as advocates for young children and their families.

This first chapter in Part 2 addresses information important for any early childhood educator who works with children from birth to age 8. Subsequent chapters in this part of the text are specific to the age of children with whom you are working. The chapter has three general sections: (1) Preparing to Be an Early Childhood Educator, (2) Appropriate Practices, and (3) Advocacy.

After reading this chapter, you will understand:

▶ Professional preparation requirements and professional development opportunities for early childhood educators.

▶ Contemporary philosophies of learning and development for young children.

▶ Characteristics of developmentally appropriate practices for young children.

▶ Characteristics of culturally appropriate practices for young children.

▶ The value of play.

▶ Characteristics of an integrated curriculum.

▶ Strategies for advocating on behalf of young children.

⟨ Preparing to Be an Early Childhood Educator

As a future early childhood educator, you will find many career opportunities available to you. The professional preparation you will need depends on the job. Oversight for credentialing early childhood educators is provided by individual states, so requirements vary somewhat across the nation. Colleges and universities offer associate, bachelor, and graduate degree programs or emphasis areas in elementary and early childhood education. Within postsecondary institutions, programs may be found in various colleges. Some examples of these colleges are education, psychology, family life, and human ecology.

Child Care and Pre-K Programs

While requirements vary from state to state, head teachers and child care center directors are typically required to have an associate's degree or course work that meets state licensure requirements. Teachers in Head Start are required to hold a bachelor's degree. Some course work may be required for teachers and their assistants who work under the supervision of a qualified director or head teacher.

Child Development Associate Credential. The Child Development Associate (CDA) certificate can be earned through the CDA National Credentialing Program, sponsored by the Council for Early Childhood Professional Recognition. To be eligible for a CDA credential, you must have a high school diploma or equivalent and be at least 18 years old. To obtain the CDA credential, you must take 120 hours of formal training from an accredited agency and demonstrate knowledge of child development and best professional practice in settings for young children.

National Board Certification. This certification is available for educators of children age 3 through grade 12. The Early Childhood/Generalist certification is appropriate for early childhood teachers of children age 3 through grade 3. You can voluntarily earn this certification, which lasts for 10 years, but it does not take the place of any state certification requirements. To complete this certification, you engage in reflection and self-assessment related to rigorous standards, and develop a portfolio that reflects your competence as teacher. Your performance is assessed against the standards.

Grades K–3

A minimum of a bachelor's degree is required to teach grades K–3 in public and private schools (private school requirements vary). State requirements vary with regard to certification to teach kindergarten; some states mandate early childhood licensure or certification. Upon completion of your degree requirements from your institution, you apply through the state office of education for teacher licensure or certification. Most states complete background checks prior to granting licensure or certification and many require teachers to pass a competency exam.

The requirement for teachers to pass a competency exam is becoming common among states because the No Child Left Behind (NCLB) legislation calls for highly qualified teachers. In order to receive federal NCLB funds, states must submit a plan for identifying highly qualified teachers. When the plan is approved, funds are provided. For example, many states are adopting the *Praxis 2 Test, Principles of Learning and Teaching*, as a means or partial means of identifying both qualified and highly qualified teachers.

Graduate Degrees. Many colleges and universities offer master's and doctoral degrees in early childhood education or related fields (family and human development, for example). Earning a graduate degree opens the door for opportunities to be a teacher leader in early childhood settings and to teach in postsecondary settings.

Professional Development

The field of early childhood education is constantly changing because, through research and experience, we continue to learn more about:

▶ How young children develop and learn.

▶ Practice in early childhood settings that is developmentally and culturally responsive.

▶ The impact of public policy.

It is the responsibility of all early childhood educators to remain current in all aspects of early childhood education—development, culture, curriculum and instruction, and public policy. Following are some strategies for engaging in professional development.

Journaling. Any professional development plan must have goals, and one way to establish goals that are appropriate for you is to write regularly in a journal. However, merely writing is not enough. It is critical that you think reflectively and focus on aspects of your job that you find challenging. Based on this self-assessment, you can set personal goals for improving your practice and investigate resources for addressing them.

Professional Organizations. There are several national and state organizations that focus on young children. (A partial list is included at the end of this chapter.) As a member of a professional organization, you will receive current information relevant to you as an early childhood professional. Many professional organizations publish journals and host conferences where early childhood professionals come together to learn from each other. Organizations such as the *National Association for the Education of Young Children (NAEYC)* and the *Association for Childhood Education International (ACEI)* have local affiliates and you can become an active member. If you join the *Children's Defense Fund* you will regularly receive information on national policy that affects families and children.

Reading. Information about the latest research-based knowledge of culturally and developmentally appropriate practice, the impact of public policy, and the actions of policy makers are published in various books and journals. You can find these books and journals in academic libraries. You can subscribe to the journals or receive them by joining a professional organization (NAEYC, for example). The most reliable information is found in refereed journals, which are publications that print only articles deemed by early childhood scholars to be accurate, current, and research-based. Information found in magazines may or may not accurately reflect high-quality scholarly work.

Workshops. School districts and local affiliates of professional organizations sometimes offer workshops and in-service experiences for little or no cost. You can usually find out about such offerings by contacting your local school district's administrative office.

College and University Courses. Courses offered through accredited colleges and universities have endured the scrutiny of an accreditation team and are the most reliable in terms of offering accurate, research-based, up-to-date content. Ask about accreditation of the program in which you are currently enrolled.

Ellen Senisi.

⟩ Philosophies of Learning

Whether early childhood educators articulate a philosophical approach or not, they have beliefs about how children learn and develop, and those beliefs are reflected in their practice. Grounded in the work of earlier scholars, several philosophies of learning are embraced by contemporary early childhood educators. Some early childhood educators adhere to a single philosophy, whereas others take an eclectic philosophical approach to working with young children.

Ellen Senisi.

Following is a discussion of the most prominent contemporary philosophies of learning and development. Particular philosophies tend to emphasize the role of either nature or nurture over the other. In other words, the impacts of children's innate characteristics (nature) and environmental factors (nurture) on their development are emphasized differently within the philosophies. As you read about them, be thinking about your own developing philosophy. Reflect on your past experiences and learning as you think about your philosophy of learning. What kinds of experiences helped you learn? From your own experience, what do you think about the impact of nature and nurture on development?

The *Focus on History* reminds you of the historical roots of the theories that were introduced in Chapter 2. It also briefly characterizes each.

Focus on History

Historical Roots of Learning Theories

Theory	Historical Roots	Major Premise
Brain-based development	Ancient doctors; emergence of technology enhanced study (e.g., magnetic resonance in imaging)	Sections of the brain control different functions (e.g., language, movement); theory highlights how brain development and function relate to learning. Emphasis on interaction of Nature and Nurture
Constructivism	Piaget—Schema theory	Children learn as they actively engage in tasks and develop schema for how things are; meaning is constructed from experience with objects and people. Emphasis on Nurture
Behaviorism	Skinner—Reinforcement Bandura—Social learning theory	Children are born as empty vessels and learn as their behaviors are reinforced by the environment; Social learning theory suggests that significant others in the lives of children teach by modeling. Emphasis on Nurture
Maturation	Gesell	Individual children are on a developmental pathway which should not be accelerated. Emphasis on Nature

⟩ Brain-Based Development

New technologies have enhanced the ability of scientists to research the brain. While there is still much that is not known, some generalizations about brain development can be made (Bergen & Coscia, 2001). In general, we know that brain development during the early years (Bergen & Coscia, 2001):

▶ Is critical to children's knowledge construction.

▶ Is the result of the interaction of genes and the environment.

▶ Influences learning due to complex interactions among the modular components of the brain.

▶ Allows for multiple and diverse experiences (or lack of experiences) to influence its development due to the brain's plasticity.

Neurons in our brains are responsible for communication between our brains and our bodies, and we have around 100 billion of them at birth (Shore, 1997). Brain synapses are roadways between the neurons that carry messages to our bodies. Scientists have learned that, beginning at birth, our brains overproduce synapses. In fact, rapid development of synapses beginning at birth continues through the early years. Through experience, humans use some neurons more than others and, eventually, the brain prunes away synapses between unused neurons. You've probably noticed that talent runs in families. In a musical family, for example, it is likely that children have many experiences listening to music, singing, exploring musical instruments, and so on. Children in such a family are likely to develop musically. The process of pruning is part of normal development. Figure 4.1 exemplifies this process.

This has some implications for early childhood educators. First, there appear to be some sensitive periods for development. For example, the first 3 years of life are a sensitive period for language development, so it is an important time for rich language experiences. A teacher of 3-year-olds plans many language experiences including story reading and telling, modeling language in context, sociodramatic play, and providing many small group activities where children talk and interact with adults and peers.

Many diverse experiences are needed to support brain development and should be part of the early childhood environment. This includes a balance of language activities, creative expression (e.g., paint, clay, movement), social interaction, constructive activities (e.g., blocks, Legos, woodworking), physical activity, and experiences in the community (e.g., field trips, classroom visitors). Brain development is influenced by physical conditions such as nutrition and the presence or absence of environmental toxins and disease. Early childhood educators are important advocates for improvement of environmental conditions for young children (Bergen & Coscia, 2001).

Brain-based philosophy focuses on the physical aspects of the brain, and findings can be generally applied to all humans. However, we must avoid the tendency to assume that all children are alike. Each child has unique prior experiences and individual patterns of growth.

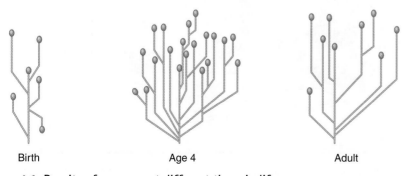

Birth   Age 4   Adult

Figure 4.1 Density of synapses at different times in life.

Multiple Intelligences

Howard Gardner (Gardner, 1991) identified various ways that human intelligence is manifest. Figure 4.2 describes the nine intelligences identified by Gardner, who believed that we all have each of these intelligences to a varied extent; in individuals, however, some are more prominent than others. Gardner's theory is based on

Verbal/Linguistic children have strengths in speaking, writing, reading, and listening. Young verbal/linguistic children like stories, listening centers, puppet shows, dramatic play, reading, etc.

Visual/Spatial children learn best with visual stimuli. Young visual/spatial children like graphs, maps, illustrations, art, puzzles, constructive play (e.g., blocks, Legos), puppet shows, etc.

Mathematical/Logical children have an aptitude for numbers and problem solving. Young mathematical/logical children like board games, number activities, constructive play, etc.

Musical/Rhythmic children learn songs and rhythms. Young musical/rhythmic children enjoy activities involving music, movement, rhyme, chants, etc.

Bodily/Kinesthetic children learn best through movement. Young bodily/kinesthetic children enjoy activities where they can move around and manipulate objects. These might include hands-on inquiry, dramatic play, music, constructive play, etc.

Intrapersonal children have a clear picture of themselves and their ideas. Young intrapersonal children may appear sensitive but will enjoy talking about their ideas, individual projects, etc.

Interpersonal children enjoy others. Young interpersonal children appreciate small group activities, cooperative learning, dramatic play, group games, etc.

Naturalist children enjoy the outdoors and appreciate living things. Young naturalist children will be drawn to activities like collecting things from the environment (e.g., leaves in fall, rocks) and sorting or classifying them, caring for a class pet, etc.

Existentialist children think about being human in the world. Young existentialist children are inquisitive and ask questions about their world. They enjoy scientific inquiry, activities that involve exploration, etc.

Figure 4.2 **Gardner's multiple intelligences.**

the idea that a person's intelligence is not fixed and is affected by environment, cultural influences, and biological factors. This has implications for teachers to acknowledge children's ways of knowing, to capitalize on their strengths, and to develop their weaknesses by using a variety of instructional strategies.

Children whose prominent intelligences are most aligned with traditional expectations in care and educational settings are *verbal/linguistic* and *mathematical/logical*. Typically, these children have experienced the most success in care and educational settings because they tend to excel at linguistic and mathematical tasks. *Interpersonal* children have often been viewed as too talkative while *intrapersonal* children might be labeled as shy. The strengths of *musical/rhythmic* and *naturalist* children are not always valued as much as the strengths of verbal/linguistic and mathematical/logical children.

Think about which intelligences are your strongest. What implications does that have for you as a learner? The *Window into the Classroom* exemplifies how two teachers structured learning environments that acknowledged children's individual strengths. These teachers provided opportunities for children to express their own interests and abilities as well as to learn from others.

Window into the Classroom

First Graders

Members of Marcus' first-grade class are working on a cooperative project as part of their integrated unit on mammals. The children are working in cooperative groups based on their interest in animals from various habitats including jungles, farms, deserts, mountains, water, and human homes. Whole class activities include reading, listening to guest speakers, note taking, and viewing pictures.

Marcus assists the cooperative groups of children as they decide how they will investigate the topic of mammals from their chosen habitat. Each group has to decide what task each child will perform as all participate in the research and presentation, bringing their strengths to the project while learning from the others.

Juan, Marcia, and David are exploring farm mammals. Juan's strengths are intrapersonal and interpersonal; he chooses to conduct an interview with the farmer who came to visit the class. Marcia is visua/spatial and naturalist; she observed farm animals in their habitat as her part of the research. David is verba/linguistic and musica/rhythmic; he sought out nonfiction books and poems about farm animals.

With the research portion of the project completed, the students now must share what they have learned. With the assistance of classroom volunteers, Marcia (visua/spatial and naturalist) is making a chart showing common farm animals and their contribution to the farm industry. David (verba/linguistic and musica/rhythmic) is writing captions for Marcia's chart and a short poem to explain it. Juan (intrapersonal and interpersonal) is making notes so he can present their findings to the class.

Three-Year-Olds

Lucy is the head teacher for 3-year-olds in a child care center located in a large city. It is late September, signs of fall are evident, and the children are learning about seasonal changes. Lucy has been reading stories to the children about fall, and they have discussed their personal experiences such as finding it necessary to wear a sweater or jacket to school now.

Today, Lucy, her assistant teacher, and ten 3-year-olds are taking a walk to observe the signs of fall. As they walk along, Lucy points out leaves on the ground, and they notice that the abundance of summer flowers is no longer in bloom. The children and their teachers spend several minutes observing chipmunks gathering the nuts they had left out for them.

Robert (naturalist) is fascinated by the leaves and picks up several. He notices, "This one is orange-ish and this one is red." Several other children begin picking leaves and talking about their color. Grace (existentialist) wonders, "Why the chipmunks are taking the nuts to their homes," instead of eating them. This gave Lucy the opportunity to explain that they are storing food for the cold, snowy months ahead.

The children returned to their room, discussed their observations, and then went to a small group activity of their choice. At the end of the day, the children came together to share what they had been doing; some had continued to think about characteristics of fall. Michael (verba/linguistic) shared a story he had written (via pictures). Robert (naturalist) showed how he had glued his leaves on a large piece of paper, grouped by color. Isabelle and Teresa (visua/spatial) shared the pictures about fall they had painted.

Constructivism

Grounded primarily in Piaget's theory (Chapter 2), the view of a constructivist early childhood educator is that children are developing mental schema about their world as they interact with objects and people. As they interact, they bring subjective meaning to new experiences based on their own unique prior experiences. Children assimilate new information into existing schema; or, they refine the existing schema, through accommodation, to include the new experience. Early childhood educators build on what children can do rather than what they cannot do and provide active experiences to enhance learning and correct misconceptions.

High-quality constructivist early childhood settings include small group experiences that enable children to interact with each other and with a wide variety of materials. These activities support their developing understanding (constructions) of their world. For example, at a writing center in kindergarten, children talk about what they are writing (perhaps written in the form of lines and circles or strings of letters), and read their messages to each other. Three-year-olds playing at the block center discuss the characteristics of the blocks (e.g., "I need a long one") and what they can do (e.g., "You need a long one to hold that up").

Young children manipulate objects to learn about them and what they do. For example, an infant learns that a ball rolls when it is dropped but a block does not, water and sand run through your fingers, a pillow is soft and a rock is hard.

As children are developmentally ready, they receive explicit skills instruction that is aligned with their developmental stages (e.g., procedures for putting away materials for 2-year-olds, phonics for 5-year-olds). Then, children are given many opportunities to use the skills in active learning experiences. For example, 2-year-olds participate in cleanup when it is time to go home. Six-year-olds learn the conventions of writing as they create stories.

Constructivist early childhood educators must carefully maintain continuity among learning experiences and provide systematic skills instruction as children are ready for it (of particular importance in kindergarten and the primary grades). Children's development must be continuously and systematically assessed so that skills instruction and activities can be planned to build on their existing knowledge.

Behaviorism

Grounded in the work of Skinner (Chapter 2), behaviorists believe that children's behaviors (e.g., acquisition of language, learning to read, etc.) are reinforced by the environment. Behaviorists teach by their model, reinforce desirable behavior, and avoid reinforcing undesirable behavior. Reinforcement takes many forms, including approving comments and smiles, pleasure inherent in the task, and stickers or extra free time. Effective reinforcements will vary among children. If you ground your teaching in this philosophy, you will need to be certain you identify something that is actually reinforcing to the particular child. You will also want to refrain from using extrinsic reinforcements if the child is already intrinsically motivated to do the task. The goal of behaviorist educators is that children will eventually become self-governing.

Early childhood educators who ground their practice in this philosophy carefully determine what is reinforcing for individual children so they can provide incentives that appeal to each child. They are also careful not to reinforce behaviors unintentionally. For example, writing a child's name on the board for not completing her work may actually reinforce noncompletion of work if her goal is to gain attention (negative attention is still attention). In other words, if she likes the attention she gets when her name is written on the board, she will continue noncompletion of work to sustain the attention.

Behaviorist early childhood educators must be cautious not to be overly controlling or to overuse rigid instructional strategies and extrinsic incentives. If this happens, children may be denied opportunities to think creatively and problem solve independently. Behaviorists must be cautious not to use the principles to control children's behavior; rather, they must use them to teach.

Maturation

Grounded in the work of Gesell (Chapter 2), maturationists believe that children have a predetermined developmental clock that is not particularly influenced by the environment. According to this philosophy, strategies to excel in learning cannot and should not be used. Children who lag behind their age-mates simply need the gift of time. The work of maturationists has resulted in normative charts that identify general benchmarks for children's typical development. Such charts are very useful as long as early childhood professionals acknowledge the great variation in typically developing children and view the benchmarks as the norms they are. A group of children of any age will demonstrate variance in patterns and timing of their growth and development.

Maturationist principles are reflected in concepts such as *readiness, academic redshirting*, and *retention*, discussed in more detail in Chapter 6. The term readiness implies there are requisite skills and knowledge that children must have prior to school entrance. If they do not have those skills, they are not ready to enter school. Academic redshirting is taken from the practice in high-school and college sports when players are held from competition until they are more developed. For children entering kindergarten, it refers to the practice of holding them out of school for a year until they are more developed. Retention in kindergarten has been commonly practiced for children whose skills do not meet expectation for entry into first grade. The *Advocating for the Child* provides an overview of the political influences on the practice of retention.

Early childhood educators who ascribe to maturationism must be cautious about mistaking a developmental delay for immaturity. In the case of a developmental delay, early intervention is critically important, and merely providing time

Advocating for the Child

Grade retention has a longer, more documented history than does the practice of *academic redshirting*, dating back to post-Civil War, urban schools. For ease of instruction, children were organized into homogeneous groups. Age was a primary factor in determining groups but academic achievement was also considered. That is, children were organized into grades by age, but if they did not achieve adequately, they were retained (Johnson et al., 1990). Since that time, the practice of retention has ebbed and flowed with the political tide of our nation.

At first, the practice was used to address the needs of "slow learners." From the 1930s until the 1960s, "social promotion" was the common practice. Then, following the Soviet Union's successful launching in 1957 of Sputnik, the first earth satellite ever launched, the political tide changed. Fearing the power of the Soviet Union and potential spread of communism, the U.S. government felt pressure to be competitive, and academic achievement, particularly in math and science, became an educational focus. The federal government began providing funding opportunities for math and science education and educational achievement was scrutinized.

In the 1960s, the political tide again shifted as the downward trend of standardized achievement test scores was evident. Critics pointed to the practice of social promotion as the culprit, and the next decades saw increased public demand for accountability and the establishment of graduation standards (Johnson et al., 1990). Those who did not meet the standards were retained. Supporters of retention suggest that retention in the early grades is much more beneficial than later (Mantzicopoulos & Morrison, 1992); thus, the practice has traditionally been more common in kindergarten and first grade.

Today, the bulk of research on retention and social promotion find them to be ineffective practices and not in children's best interest.

for the child to mature would delay access to early intervention. Furthermore, there is no compelling evidence that either academic redshirting or retention provides long-term achievement gains, and immediate gains tend to diminish by grade 3 (Graue, 2001; Graue & DiPerna, 2000; Johnson, Merrell, & Stover, 1990; Marshall, 2003).

Now that you have read about some philosophies of learning, think back to your own early education. Do any of your past teachers align with any of these philosophies?

Appropriate Practices

We have learned from research that children learn best in a learner-centered environment (Bradford, Brown, & Cocking, 1999). Regardless of your philosophy of learning, you probably agree that practice in early care and education settings should be learner-centered or aligned with the developmental and cultural characteristics of the children they serve. The early childhood community refers to this as developmentally appropriate practice (DAP).

Developmentally Appropriate Practice

The principles of DAP resulted from early childhood educators' understanding of how children learn and develop (Bredekamp & Copple, 1997). In 1987, the National Association for the Education of Young Children created guidelines for developmentally appropriate practice and revised them in 1997. The principles of DAP continue to inform the practice of high-quality early childhood educators today.

Developmentally appropriate practice varies based on the developmental level, cultural background, and learning needs of individual children and looks different across age groups of young children (e.g., toddlers, primary grade children). The specific principles of DAP are listed in the *Theory into Practice* feature. As early childhood educators implement DAP, they consider the following (Bredekamp & Copple, 1997).

What is known about child development and learning or general age-related predictions that suggest safe, interesting, and supportive activities for young children. For example, we know that infants manipulate and mouth objects to learn about them and what they will do, so they need many varied and safe objects to explore. First graders can learn mathematical operations but, as concert operational thinkers (Chapter 2), they need objects to manipulate to understand concepts (e.g., addition, subtraction).

What is known about individual children in the group so that activities can be adjusted to meet the needs of each child. For example, 3-year-old Emily is very reluctant to join activities with many children present so she is encouraged to play and interact in groups or two or three. In Ms. Perry's first-grade class, children read in books that are on their individual reading levels.

Knowledge of the social or cultural contexts in which children live so that learning experiences can be relevant and meaningful for each child. For example, 2-year-olds in Kansas listen to stories about farm animals and pets that they have the opportunity to observe, but not whales or penguins that they may have never seen. Children see pictures of people who look like them (e.g., skin color, facial features) in their early childhood environment.

Culturally Relevant Practice

Cultural diversity takes many forms including differences in ethnicity, language, religion, ability, class, sexual orientation, and gender. Many have dismissed the *assimilation* or *melting pot theory* which acknowledges a uniform society where the norms of the mainstream culture are primarily valued. In this view, all citizens are expected to conform to mainstream values and adopt mainstream attitudes. A more inclusive approach is to celebrate differences and view them as something that enriches our society. A *stew pot*, rather than a melting pot, is a metaphor that highlights the richness of a diverse society. The rich and enjoyable flavor of the stew is the result of the many different ingredients, easily distinguishable from each other, that are blended to create it.

Early childhood settings are experiencing increasing diversity related to language, culture, and ability. Educators of young children must be able to develop appropriate curriculum and instructional strategies to meet diverse cultural needs. Culturally relevant practice addresses three primary dimensions: the classroom environment, instructional strategies and curriculum development, and interactions with parents. Although these dimensions are more fully developed in subsequent chapters, some general principles of culturally relevant practice are as follows:

▶ Children have opportunities to read, write, speak, and listen in their native language as well as in English.

▶ Early childhood educators work to become knowledgeable about each child's background of experiences and aware of each child's interests and abilities.

▶ The environment includes pictures, books, and other artifacts that reflect multiple cultures and ways of living. These might include faces of many colors, people depicted in nontraditional roles (e.g., female firefighter, male nurse), nonmainstream food boxes in dramatic play, and people of various abilities (e.g., depicted in wheelchairs, with hearing aids, with Down syndrome) engaged in productive activities.

▶ Cooperative activities are used and competitive activities are nonexistent (infant, toddler, preschool, kindergarten settings) or limited primarily to team competition (primary grades).

▶ Early childhood educators openly and immediately mediate conflict in supportive ways.

▶ Curricular topics reflect a variety of cultures (e.g., stories, music, and art from various cultures are explored; the nature of tools to enhance sight, mobility, etc., are explored).

▶ Parents are involved in their children's learning experiences in ways that are comfortable for them.

▶ Speakers of the family's native languages are present as often as possible.

▶ Parents and community members from a variety of cultures are invited to share their cultures with the children.

The Value of Play

Play is an activity in which children across cultures enthusiastically engage. There are many types of play, and play behavior varies according to children's developmental stages and cultural backgrounds. An activity is considered to be play (Monighan-Nourot, Scales, Van Hoorn, & Almy, 1987) if:

▶ It is intrinsically motivated.

▶ Children are actively engaged.

▶ Children's attention is focused on the process, not a product.

Theory into Practice

Based on empirical research, the following principles have been set forth by the National Association for the Education of Young Children to guide practice in classrooms and other settings serving children birth to age 8.

1. Domains of children's development—physical, social, emotional, and cognitive—are closely related. Development in one domain influences and is influenced by development in other domains.

2. Development occurs in a relatively orderly sequence, with later abilities, skills, and knowledge building on those already acquired.

3. Development proceeds at varying rates from child to child as well as unevenly within different areas of each child's functioning.

4. Early experiences have both cumulative and delayed effects on individual children's development. Optimal periods exist for certain types of development and learning.

5. Development proceeds in predictable directions toward greater complexity, organization, and internalization.

6. Development and learning occur in and are influenced by multiple social and cultural contexts.

7. Children are active learners, drawing on direct physical and social experiences as well as culturally transmitted knowledge to construct their own understandings of the world around them.

8. Development and learning result from interaction of biological maturation and the environment, which includes both the physical and social worlds in which children live.

9. Play is an important vehicle for children's social, emotional, and cognitive development, as well as a reflection of their development.

10. Development advances when children have opportunities to practice newly acquired skills as well as when they experience a challenge just beyond the level of their present mastery.

11. Children demonstrate different modes of knowing and learning and different ways of representing what they know.

12. Children develop and learn best in the context of a community where they are safe and valued, their physical needs are met, and they feel psychologically secure.

Source: Bredekamp, S., & Copple, C. (Eds.). (1997). *Developmentally appropriate practice in early childhood programs* (revised ed.) pp, 10–15. Washington, DC: National Association for the Education of Young Children.

▶ The behavior is nonliteral.

▶ The activity is not bound by external rules.

Play is fundamental to development (Van Hoorn, Scales, Nourot, & Alward, 1999) and early childhood settings should offer many play opportunities. In play, children demonstrate skills they have not yet mastered in reality. For example, a

5-year-old might sit very still in a pretend role where she is hiding from a villain, but that same 5-year-old might have a difficult time sitting to complete a work sheet. She might spend 30 minutes making a block construction but be unable to spend 10 minutes writing the letters of the alphabet.

Scholars do not agree on how culture is manifest in children's play; yet, they agree that children everywhere play. Culture influences play in that the play reflects the tools (toys) and the customs, beliefs, and institutions (play settings) of the culture (Frost, Wortham, & Reifel, 2001). Observing children playing is like looking through a window into how they view their world. The *Focus on Diversity* is an example of the influence of culture as it relates to ethnicity on children's play.

Play and Social–Emotional Development

Parten (1932) identified different types of play behavior, including the following:

▶ Unoccupied behavior

▶ Onlooker behavior

▶ Solitary play

▶ Parallel play

▶ Associative play

▶ Cooperative play

To some degree, these play types are developmental. For example, 2-year-olds are typically not socially developed enough to engage in cooperative play or even associative play. You will usually see typically developing 2-year-olds in solitary or parallel play. You can observe 4-year-olds in cooperative play at times and solitary play at other times, and children of any age in unoccupied and onlooker behavior.

Focus on Diversity

Following is the dialogue as 4-year-olds Kim, Terry, and Angela negotiate the script for their housekeeping play. Kim is an English-speaking, female Japanese-American whose parents immigrated to the United States just before she was born. Terry, a male, and Angela, a female, are both of European descent and their families have lived in this country for several generations.

   Angela: *Let's pretend this is my house and I'm the mother.*
      Kim: *Why can't I be the mother?*
   Angela: *'Cause I wanna be the mother.*
      Kim: *Well, I'm gonna be the mother at a different house then.*
   Angela: *Okay. Let's be friends with our babies.*
[Kim picks up a doll and holds it like a baby.]
    Terry: *I'm gonna be the dad.*
   Angela: *But the dad went to work; you be my baby. I can push you in the stroller.*
    Terry: *Okay.*
      Kim: *No, Terry should be the dad; you [Angela] should be the baby.*

This brief episode reflects the influence of culture on the children's sociodramatic play. Based on research (Frost et al., 2001), girls in both Japanese and American cultures are more likely than boys to define roles, particularly in relation to kinship. Furthermore, girls in both cultures value the role of mother as an authority and Japanese girls are more likely than American girls to argue for playing the role of mother. Unlike American boys, Japanese boys are not likely to volunteer for the role of baby, which may be reflected in Kim's suggestion that Terry take the role of father.

The *unoccupied child* attends to anything of interest while the *onlooker* is watching other children play. During *solitary play*, children play alone with objects that are not being used by other players. The *parallel player* plays independently among other children. During *associative play*, children are engaged in similar activities and they share materials; however, their play has no common goal and is not formally organized by the players. During *cooperative play*, children verbally agree upon play scripts or they cooperatively create a product or achieve a goal. They discuss and negotiate how they will play, what materials they will use, and so on.

Sociodramatic play is the most advanced form of social play. As you can tell by its name, sociodramatic play involves more than one child. It is social. During sociodramatic play, children negotiate the play context, theme, and roles. For example, if they decide to play veterinarian, they must decide who will be the veterinarian, the pet, and the pet owner. They will have to decide why the pet has to go to the veterinarian and what the diagnosis will be and so on. You have probably heard young children at play saying, "Let's pretend. . . ."

Play and Cognitive Development

Cognitive development is supported as children observe, interact, and talk while engaging in various types of play. Social interaction supports conceptual understanding and language development. For example, Maria used a pretend credit card to pay for her meal during restaurant play. Her co-player Emily had never seen a credit card before and was introduced to them in the context of their play. Credit cards began to appear in her play later.

Classification and Conservation. Children learn about objects as they manipulate them and this helps their reasoning ability to mature. For example, very young children can pay attention to only one attribute of objects at a time—shape or color, for example. A child classifying a set of objects based on shape may switch during the process to focus on color, but he initially focuses on only one attribute. As children mature and have many experiences playing with objects, they become able to focus on both shape and color.

Play helps children learn to conserve mass and volume. Through experiences handling objects, they eventually understand that the amount of clay stays the same even though the shape is changed or that the amount of water is constant regardless of the container it is in.

Symbolic Thinking. In Chapter 2, we discussed Vygotsky's theory about how children develop as symbolic thinkers. A play environment rich with some realistic (e.g., toy kitchen, dishes, chairs, etc.) and some neutral props (e.g., paper towel roll, block) supports children's development of symbolic thinking. The realistic props give them content for their play. For example, toy kitchen appliances, dishes, and chairs will create house play, a familiar environment for young children. The neutral toys will be assigned meaning. For example, the paper towel roll might become a telescope and watching for the space shuttle becomes part of the play. A block might become the mailbox and letter writing (or bill writing!) becomes part of the play.

⸱ Your Role in Supporting Children's Play

There are many ways that adults can support children's play. As you support children during play, you expand their learning opportunities.

Support from Outside the Play

Adults can support children's play without getting directly involved by providing appropriate materials, play environments, and suggestions.

Play Materials. We have already discussed providing a balance of realistic and neutral play props to enrich play content and invite symbolic thinking. When you select play materials for sociodramatic play, be sure they are familiar enough that children will know how to play with them. For example, children will know how to play grocery store or McDonald's but will probably not know how to play bat scientist or space station. Many early childhood educators use children's literature to teach them about things they have not experienced and then structure a dramatic play area on the theme. For example, if you read books about bats and people who study them, your dramatic play center might be a bat cave.

With the appropriate materials, children will create elaborate constructions with blocks or Legos. You need to be sure there are enough materials for children to share and to complete elaborate constructions.

Play Environments. The play environment should be free of hazards and spacious enough that children can develop the play scenario. Time is also an important factor; children need at least 30 minutes (Christie & Wardle, 1992) to negotiate (e.g., sociodramatic play roles or use of constructive materials) and then carry out the play.

Suggestions. From a position outside of the play, you can make suggestions to redirect or extend it. For example, saying, "Let's pretend the doorbell rings and it's the mail carrier with a special envelope," enables you to introduce a literacy experience into the play (Dever & Wishon, 1995). The introduction of a new prop, a letter for example, might also extend the play.

Support from Inside the Play

As long as you do not take control of the play, young children will usually welcome you as a player. You can enter the play to provide new information, redirect it, or just to have fun. If play becomes too aggressive, for example, you can redirect it to be less aggressive, a strategy discussed more fully in Chapter 8. You can enter the play to model a role that might be unfamiliar to the children, a bat scientist, for example.

Curriculum Development

When teachers of young children make decisions about curriculum and instruction, they consider the developmental stages, abilities, interests, and cultural backgrounds of their learners. The NAEYC (Bredekamp & Copple, 1997) provides the following general guidelines for curriculum development for young children. Developmentally appropriate curriculum:

▶ Provides for all areas of a child's development: physical, emotional, social, linguistic, aesthetic, and cognitive.

▶ Includes a broad range of content across disciplines that is socially relevant, intellectually engaging, and personally meaningful to children.

▶ Builds upon what children already know and are able to do (activating prior knowledge) to consolidate their learning and to foster their acquisition of new concepts and skills.

▶ Frequently integrates across traditional subject-matter divisions to help children make meaningful connections and provides opportunities for rich conceptual development; focusing on one subject is also a valid strategy at times.

Laura Dwight Photography.

David Young-Wolff/PhotoEdit.

▶ Promotes the development of knowledge and understanding, processes and skills, as well as the dispositions to use and apply skills, and to go on learning.

▶ Has intellectual integrity, reflecting the key concepts and tools of inquiry of recognized disciplines in ways that are accessible and achievable for young children ages 3 through 8 (e.g., problem solving, science experiments, collecting and analyzing data, writing, performing).

▶ Provides opportunities to support children's home culture and language while also developing all children's abilities to participate in the shared community of the program and classroom.

▶ Addresses goals that are realistic and attainable for most children in the classroom.

▶ Physically and philosophically integrates technology in the classroom curriculum and teaching, when appropriate. (p. 20)

Infants and Toddlers

In developmentally appropriate programs, infants and toddlers enjoy manipulating objects and interacting with adults and children in small groups as they learn about their world. Through their senses, they learn the properties of objects and what the objects will do. For example, they learn that a ball bounces, blocks can be stacked, sand falls through fingers, and so on. Language develops as they interact with peers and adults. Listening to and talking about stories on an adult's lap or in small groups helps children develop language and learn about their world.

Children Ages 3–8

In developmentally appropriate programs, children are actively engaged in exploration of their social and physical world and are explicitly taught skills needed for learning. Learning time is spent using children's developing skills (e.g., reading, writing, listening, speaking, observing, classifying, counting) in context as they learn about the world around them. For example, 3-year-olds learn sequencing when they are taught the procedure for putting away their materials. Attention is drawn to the letters in their names as their cubbies are labeled. Six-year-olds learn how to use end marks correctly in the context of their own writing.

Integrated Curriculum

On the basis of the NAEYC guidelines, early childhood educators in pre-kindergarten through the primary grades use the integrated approach to teaching content. The integrated curriculum engages children in meaningful learning experiences by

▶ Bringing together content learning and process skills so that children are using their developing skills to learn about their world.

▶ Addressing substantial, interesting questions about the real world.

▶ Providing opportunities for in-depth exploration.

A truly integrated curriculum goes beyond merely imposing a theme on a series of activities; it integrates the curriculum in a way that helps children learn about an interesting topic. It connects to what they already know and builds their understanding. Planning is focused on the questions: What do children need to know about their world? What interests them? Teachers capitalize on opportunities to teach skills in the context of the unit.

The *Window into the Classroom* exemplifies a content unit of study spurred by second-grade students' interests and guided by the teacher.

Teachers guide children's exploration of topics of study. Particular topics and the level and type of teacher involvement depend of the age of the children. For example, preschool children focus on animals from their environment because it is difficult for them to think about animals they have never seen.

Window into the Classroom

Maria is a second-grade teacher who considers the developmental and cultural characteristics of children in her class when she plans curriculum. She knows that young children learn best when the topic of study is interesting and relevant to them. She also knows that they are more likely to develop skills if the skills are taught and then used in a meaningful context for a known purpose.

On this particular Monday morning, Maria arrived at school and noticed that the hermit crab she received in the mail last Friday seemed not to have moved since she put it in the terrarium. She was suspicious that the hermit crab had died. However, being unsure about the condition of the hermit crab, she invited the children to wonder with her about the condition of the animal, which excited them to learn about hermit crabs.

They immediately generated a list of questions they had about hermit crabs, including these:

- How much do hermit crabs sleep? Do they move around a lot?

- What do they eat? How much do they eat? How often do they eat?

- Are there boy hermit crabs and girl hermit crabs? Do hermit crabs live in families? Who takes care of the babies?

- Where do hermit crabs live?

- Do hermit crabs bite? Are they dangerous?

The children were formed into groups based on common interests to answer the questions. Each group had a set of questions to answer. To begin seeking answers to their questions, a representative of each group went to the library to enlist the help of the media specialist in finding books about hermit crabs. Some of the books were used for read alouds with the entire class and others were read in the groups where children took notes about information relevant to their questions and interests.

Two children learned from the media specialist that a biology teacher at a local high school was an expert on hermit crabs. The children called her and invited her to their class as a guest speaker. The biology teacher indicated that she got out of school at 2:20 and queried whether that would allow enough time for her to speak to the class. In order to answer that question, Maria assisted the children in doing the math.

Second grade gets out 1 hour after the high school. The high school teacher estimated that it would take her 20 minutes to get out of her building and arrive at their classroom. Allowing 5 minutes at the end of the day to prepare to go home, the children called her back to let her know that she would have 35 minutes to talk to them about hermit crabs.

In this unit, the children used their developing skills to learn more about their world by finding answers to their questions. They also discovered that the hermit crab was not dead; rather, it was a type of crab that is nocturnal.

Children in the primary grades will initially focus on animals with which they are familiar but can build to the study of less familiar animals. In preschool and kindergarten, teachers identify books and read them to the children; in the primary grades, children will select and read books more independently.

There are several ways to approach the development of an integrated unit of study but, in general, planning involves the generation of important questions, an investigation of the topic using multiple strategies, and activities so children can share their new learning. The *Window into the Classroom* provides an example of an integrated unit of study with 4-year-olds.

Window into the Classroom

Janette works with 4-year-olds in the local Head Start program. She plans learning experiences that are active and interesting and relevant to the lives of the children. She plans curriculum around topics that she knows are typically interesting to 4-year-olds, but she also pays careful attention to the interests of particular children in her class.

Recently, Darcy brought a picture of the new kitty her mother gave her. Darcy told the children about her new pet and then Janette posted the picture on the bulletin board for everyone to see. Janette noticed the *pet* theme in subsequent conversations and in the children's dramatic play. The children were interested and Janette capitalized on that by planning a unit to learn about pets.

Janette asked the children to draw a picture of a pet they have or would like to have. When they were finished, the children then came together in a small circle and shared their pictures. Janette encouraged them to use descriptive language as they talked about their favorite pets. To create a large graph (organizing data) of their favorite pets, each child placed a Post-it under a picture of his/her favorite pet. The children noticed that cats were the favorite pet, followed by dogs, and gerbils came in third.

To investigate the world of pets, Janette found several picture books about pets that she read to the children. After reading *Your First Goldfish* (Gilbert, 1991), she purchased some goldfish for the classroom. Each day, the children took turns feeding the goldfish the appropriate amount of food.

To further investigate the care of pets, Janette invited a local veterinarian to talk to the children about care of pets. She asked the veterinarian to focus on pets the children had indicated were their favorites. After reading several picture books about veterinarians, she turned the dramatic play center into a veterinarian's office.

To culminate the study of pets, the children shared their new learning through stories. Each child dictated a pet story to Janette or to her assistant. The teachers encouraged the children to recall what they had learned as they dictated their stories.

Advocacy

Of course young children do not have the maturity, skills, and knowledge to advocate for their rights and needs, and many of their parents lack the resources, skills, and knowledge to advocate on their behalf. In fact, in many circumstances, parents would have to have studied early childhood education to be strong advocates. They may not have the background knowledge to know the importance of advocacy in a particular situation. For example, we have just learned something about the value of play. What if the school district had a policy disallowing play in kindergarten? Do you think most parents, if they had never been students of early childhood education, would have the requisite knowledge to advocate for the inclusion of play in kindergarten?

Policy decisions and resource allocations are made at government and administrative levels where expertise in early childhood education is not required. Policy makers are well-intended but, like many parents, do not always have the background knowledge to make good policy decisions. As early childhood educators, we are well-positioned to advocate on behalf of young children and their families. We understand the needs of young children and how to address them and the impact of national and state policy on the lives of children and their families.

Advocacy can take the form of *personal*, *public policy*, or *private sector* (Robinson & Stark, 2002). You can participate in advocacy in ways in which you feel comfortable, but it is the responsibility of all early childhood educators to participate in advocacy in some way.

Personal. Advocacy of a personal nature is about sharing your views with others for the purpose of raising awareness about an issue (Robinson & Stark, 2002). It may take the form of private spontaneous conversations, planned presentations to small groups to which you belong (e.g., a book club, church group), educating parents in your early childhood setting, or writing an op-ed or letter to the editor in your local paper. For example, if a local mall had violent video games easily accessible to children, you might write to the mall administrators and ask to have the games removed from easy access. You might educate the parents of children in your class about problems related to violent games.

Public Policy Advocacy. Early childhood educators who engage in public policy advocacy challenge school boards, governing boards, and local, state, and national policy makers to create policy that is responsive to the needs of large numbers of children and their families (Robinson & Stark, 2002). Policies might affect child care licensure, teacher certification or licensure, waste disposal, or standardized testing of young children, to name only a few. For example, if your state is thinking about dropping special requirements for licensure of early childhood professionals, you might write to your state superintendent or legislators to present an argument against doing that.

Private-Sector Advocacy. In private-sector advocacy, early childhood educators advocate for private-sector policies and practices that support children and families. You might educate a local business about family-friendly work policies, job sharing, for example. You might invite the business to support your center or school by donating materials or time. As a private-sector advocate you might challenge computer software companies and toy manufacturers to develop nonviolent toys and games (Robinson & Stark, 2002).

Watch your local paper for the next several days. Are there issues in your community right now about which you could advocate?

 My Developing Professional View

> This chapter talks about developmentally appropriate practice and the value of play. Can you make a connection between the two? How might you defend developmentally appropriate practice and play in your classroom?

SUMMARY

In this chapter, we have discussed the multiple aspects of the role of early childhood educators. Foremost, early childhood educators must have sufficient professional preparation to understand the nature of young children, their developmental needs, and the social environments in which they are living. On the basis of this understanding, early childhood educators create developmentally and culturally appropriate curriculum. This curriculum integrates the disciplines while children learn interesting, relevant content about their world. High-quality early childhood educators acknowledge the value of play and give it a prominent place in the curriculum.

The role of early childhood educators also includes a continuous agenda for professional development to remain knowledgeable about child development and research-based practices. Finally, the role of early childhood educators is to advocate on behalf of young children and their families.

⟩ ENRICHMENT ACTIVITIES

Individual Activities

1. The integrated approach to curriculum development is encouraged because it is the approach that best reflects the world in which young children live. To reflect on that from your perspective, identify two tasks you have completed in the past week. Then, identify the skills and content knowledge you needed to complete the tasks. Finally, identify the various academic disciplines of the skills and knowledge you used.

2. Access the website for your state's office of education to determine how your state defines highly qualified teachers.

3. Research the origin and evolution of an early childhood organization other than NAEYC (outlined on page 71) to determine the social and political factors that influenced the origin and evolution of that organization. (A partial list of organizations can be found under *Professional Development Resources* on p. 89.)

4. Based on your experiences to date, begin articulating your philosophy of education. Be sure you reflect on your experiences as a learner as well as content you have learned in your education program.

Cooperative Activity

5. Within your cooperative group, identify a topic for an integrated curriculum unit for a particular age group of children. Identify the various subtopics your unit will address. Each group member is to identify at least five children's books, focused on one of the subtopics that are appropriate for the age group and that will advance their understanding of the content. Bring your findings together and develop an annotated bibliography of children's books for the unit.

Advocacy Activity

6. Develop a presentation for an audience of teachers that outlines a rationale for, and examples of, developmentally appropriate practice.

FOR FURTHER READING

Advocacy

Lewis, J., Jongsam, K., & Berger, A. (Eds.). (2004) *On the frontline: Advocating effectively for your classroom, your school, your profession.* Newark, DE: International Reading Association IRA.

Robinson, A., & Stark, D. R. (2002). *Advocates in action: Making a difference for young children.* Washington, DC: National Association for the Education of Young Children.

Integrated Curriculum

Cooper, J., & Dever, M. T. (2001). Socio-dramatic play as a vehicle for curriculum integration in first grade. *Young Children, 56*(3), 58–63.

Dever, M. T., Barta, J. J., & Falconer, R. (1999). Project Boxes: A curriculum development innovation for achieving developmentally appropriate practice in the primary grades. *The NALS Journal, 23*(1), 16–20.

Hannon, J. (2006). Lessons from Ana. *Rethinking Schools, 20*(4), 47.

Helm, J. H., & Katz, L. (2001). *Young investigators: The project approach in the early years.* New York: Teachers College Press, and Washington, DC: National Association for the Education of Young Children, published simultaneously.

Helm, J., Huebner, A., & Long, B. (2000). Quiltmaking: A perfect project for preschool and primary. *Young Children, 55*(3), 44–49.

Katz, L. G. (1994). *The project approach.* Champaign, IL: ERIC Clearinghouse on Elementary and Early Childhood Education.

Learning Theories

Bergen, D., & Coscia, J. (2001). *Brain research and childhood education: Implications for educators.* Olney, MD: Association for Childhood Education International.

Carlisle, A. (2001). Using the multiple intelligences theory to assess early childhood curricula. *Young Children, 56*(6), 77–83.

Gallagher, K. C. (2005). Brain research and early childhood development: A primer for developmentally appropriate practice. *Young Children, 60*(4), 12–20.

Play

Klein, T.P., Wirth, D., & Linas, K. (2003). Play: Children's context for development. *Young Children, 58*(3), 38–45.

Koralek, D. (Ed.). (2004). *Spotlight on young children and PLAY.* Washington, DC: National Association for the Education of Young Children.

Elkind, D. (2003). Thanks for the memory: The lasting value of true play. *Young Children, 58*(3), 46–50.

Roskos, K., & Christie, J. (2001). On not pushing too hard: A few cautionary remarks about linking play and literacy. *Young Children, 56*(3), 64–66.

Stegelin, D. A. (2005). Making the case of play policy: Research-based reasons to support play-based environments. *Young Children, 60*(2), 76–85.

Vygotsky, L. S. (1966). Play and its role in the mental development of the child. *Soviet Psychology, 12*, 62–76.

Professional Development Resources

ASSOCIATION FOR CHILDHOOD EDUCATION INTERNATIONAL

The Olney Professional Building
17904 Georgia Avenue, Suite 215
Olney, MD 20832
http://www.acei.org/

CHILDREN'S DEFENSE FUND

25 E Street NW
Washington, DC 20001
http://www.childrensdefense.org/

COUNCIL FOR EARLY CHILDHOOD PROFESSIONAL RECOGNITION

2460 16th Street NW
Washington, DC 20009-3575
http://www.cdacouncil.org/

NATIONAL ASSOCIATION FOR THE EDUCATION OF YOUNG CHILDREN

1509 16th Street NW
Washington, DC 20036-1426
http://www.naeyc.org/

NATIONAL ASSOCIATION FOR FAMILY CHILD CARE

5202 Pinemont Drive
Salt Lake City, UT 84123
http://www.nafcc.org/

STAND FOR CHILDREN

1420 Columbia Road NW, 3rd Floor
Washington, DC 20009
http://www.stand.org/

ZERO TO THREE: NATIONAL CENTER FOR INFANTS, TODDLERS, AND FAMILIES

2000 M Street NW, Suite 200
Washington, DC 20036
http://www.zerotothree.org/

SELF-ASSESSMENT

1. Explain the philosophy of early childhood education with which you are most aligned, giving reasons for your choice, and identify two or three characteristics of a classroom that would reflect that philosophy.

2. Explain why play is important in an early childhood setting. Write a newsletter for an early childhood setting (infant, toddler, pre-K, K, primary) to educate parents about why you include play in your curriculum.

3. Define developmentally appropriate practice and culturally appropriate practices for young children. Identify at least three ways in which those considerations will impact your early childhood environment.

4. Some methods for developing curriculum were discussed in this chapter. How are they similar? How are they different?

5. Explain why advocacy is important for early childhood educators. Provide an example of advocacy for young children.

Scenario

You are the teacher in a preschool class of 4-year-olds turning 5 who will be going to kindergarten next year. Aware of the value of play, you have built ample time for various kinds of play into your curriculum. One day as parents are dropping their children off at preschool, a father asks to speak to you. "My son comes home most days and talks about playing restaurant and veterinarian and things like that. He doesn't seem to talk about anything he's learned. Do you think is it such a good idea to spend so much time playing at school? Don't you think the children should be learning so they'll be ready for kindergarten?" Write a brief rationale for your inclusion of sociodramatic play in your curriculum.

REFERENCES

Bergen, D., & Coscia, J. (2001). *Brain research and childhood education: Implications for educators*. Olney, MD: Association for Childhood Education International.

Branford, J. D., Brown, A. L., & Cocking, R.R. (Eds.). (1999). *How people learn: Brain, mind, experience, and school*. Washington, DC: National Academy Press.

Bredekamp, S., & Copple, C. (Eds.). (1997). *Developmentally appropriate practice in early childhood programs* (revised ed.). Washington, DC: National Association for the Education of Young Children.

Christie, J. F., & Wardle, F. (1992). How much time is needed for play? *Young Children, 47*(3), 28–32.

Dever, M. T., & Wishon, P. M. (1995). Play as a context for literacy learning: A qualitative analysis. *Early Child Development and Care, 113*, 31–43.

Frost, J. L., Wortham, S.C., & Reifel, S. (2001). *Play and child development*. Upper Saddle River, NJ: Prentice-Hall.

Gardner, H. (1991). *To open minds*. New York: Basic Books.

Gilbert, M. (1991). *Your first goldfish*. Neptune, NJ: TFH Publications.

Graue, E. (2001). Research in review: What's going on in the children's garden? Kindergarten today. *Young Children, 56*(3), 67–73.

Graue, M. E., & DiPerna, J. (2000). Redshirting and early retention: Who gets the "gift of time" and what are its outcomes? *American Educational Research Journal, 37*(2), 509–534.

Johnson, E. R., Merrell, K. W., & Stover, L. (1990, October). The effects of early grade retention on the academic achievement of fourth-grade students. *Psychology in the Schools, 27*, 333–338.

Mantzicopoulos, P., & Morrison, D. (1992). Kindergarten retention: Academic and behavioral outcomes through the end of second grade. *American Educational Research Journal, 29*(1), 182–198.

Marshall, H. H. (2003). Opportunity deferred or opportunity taken? An updated look at delaying kindergarten entry. *Young Children, 8*(5), 84–93.

Monighan-Nourot, P., Scales, B., Van Hoorn, J., with Almy, M. (1987). *Looking at children's play: A bridge between theory and practice*. New York: Teachers College Press.

Parten, M. B. (1932). Social participation among preschool children. *Journal of Abnormal and Social Psychology, 27*, 243–269.

Robinson, A., & Stark, D. R. (2002). *Advocates in action: Making a difference for young children*. Washington, DC: National Association for the Education of Young Children.

Shore, R. (1997). *Rethinking the brain: New insights into early development*. New York: Families and Work Institute.

Van Hoorn, J., Scales, B., Nourot, P. M., & Alward, K. R. (1999). *Play at the center of the curriculum* (2nd ed.). Upper Saddle River, NJ: Prentice-Hall.

Vygotsky, L. S. (1978) *Mind in society*. Cambridge MA: Harvard University Press.

Infants and Toddlers

5

Did you experience regular out of home child care as an infant or toddler? Did your parents? Did your grandparents? The further back you go in your family history, the more likely it is that the children had a parent who cared for the children at home.

World War II heralded increasing numbers of mothers in the workforce (Chapter 2), a phenomenon that continued for decades. According to the Children's Defense Fund (2001), 67% of mothers worked outside of the home in the year 2000. Today, more infants and toddlers are experiencing out of home care, part- or full-time. In order to provide high-quality care settings for infants and toddlers, it is critical that early childhood educators understand their unique development characteristics and needs.

This chapter begins with an overview of the developmental nature of infants and toddlers, including language, cognitive, social/emotional, and physical development. Issues related to attachment are discussed. Programs for infants and toddlers are described including characteristics of antibias settings.

After reading this chapter, you will understand:

▶ The developmental nature of infants and toddlers and characteristics of high-quality early childhood educators.

▶ Theories of language acquisition.

▶ The stages of language development.

▶ Issues related to attachment.

▶ The importance of early intervention.

▶ Characteristics of infant/toddler play.

▶ Examples of programs for infants and toddlers.

▶ Characteristics of antibias environments for infants and toddlers.

Developmental Characteristics of Infants and Toddlers

From the moment of conception, humans embark on a developmental path. The cognitive, social–emotional, and physical domains develop concurrently and in concert. High-quality early childhood educators understand the developmental continuum on which infants and toddlers are growing and respond to them in ways that support that growth.

Table 5.1 generally characterizes the development of infants and suggests ways early childhood educators support their growth and development. Table 5.2 characterizes toddlers and supportive behaviors of early childhood educators.

Language Development

Montessori noted the first 3 years of life as a sensitive period for acquiring language. From birth to age 3, young children's language develops from crying to communicate their needs to an expressive vocabulary of as many as 200 words. It is indeed a marvelous feat!

Theories of Language Acquisition

Here we address two primary theories of language acquisition. The *behaviorist theory of language acquisition* was postulated by Skinner (1957), and Chomsky (2002) has been a major proponent of the *nativist theory of language acquisition*. Both theories suggest that the basics of language come from others in the environment, but they differ at that point.

Behaviorist Theory of Language Acquisition. Behaviorists explain language acquisition with the theory of reinforcement. Skinner (1957) proposed, "The parent sets up a repertoire of responses in the child by reinforcing the many instances of a response" (p. 29). He further argued that the parent or literate other shapes the development of language by reinforcing approximations of the correct response. At first, any utterance resembling the correct response is reinforced, but eventually parents insist on a closer approximation until the child uses conventional language. There is no stimulus to evoke a response; rather, the parent waits for a given response to occur and then reinforces it (Skinner, 1957). For example, when a child says, "I want juice," the parent responds by providing juice.

Nativist Theory of Language Acquisition. Grounded in brain-based development theory, those ascribing to the nativist theory of language acquisition agree that language acquisition is both innate and hereditary. Adherents to this theory concede that while reinforcement has some influence on language acquisition, the

Table 5.1   Portrait of Infants and Their Caregivers

What Infants Do	What Early Childhood Educators Do
Cognitive and Language Development	
Birth to 4 Months	
Cry as the first production of language.	Talk with infants during play, holding, diapering, and feeding about what is happening and what is in the infant's immediate environment.
Begin to explore noise making with coos, babbles, and screeches (e.g., "aaaaaaaaaaa").	
Grasp objects and explore with hands and feet.	Listen and respond to infants' cries and other cues.
	Provide safe objects for exploration.
4–8 Months	
Babbling contains both vowel and consonant sounds.	Interact frequently with infant.
Begin to use sounds as a means of communication as well as exploration of noise (e.g., "gagagaga").	Read to infant regularly, in English and in the infant's native language.
Begin to engage in dialogue.	Engage in dialogue with the infant by speaking and then listening to the infant's communication.
Smile socially and observe own hands and feet.	
Grasp and manipulate objects.	
Anticipate being picked up or fed.	
Understand many words.	
Use sign language to communicate needs (e.g., done, more).	
8–15 Months	
First words emerge as single-word utterances and are somewhat unintelligible (e.g., "kiko" for kitty cat).	Respond to utterances by repeating and expanding the infant's words (e.g., "Yes, that is a kitty cat").
Look for an object when it disappears (object permanence).	
Point to own and another's body parts.	
Social–Emotional	
Birth to 4 Months	
Develop (or not) trust through interactions with caregivers.	Communicate daily with parents to learn about infants in their care and to learn the cues of individual infants.
Begin to attach to multiple caregivers.	
Recognize primary caregivers but are not typically anxious around unfamiliar people.	Respond in warm and nurturing ways to infants' cries and other cues.
Function best with a consistent primary caregiver in the early childhood setting.	A primary caregiver gets to know each infant well.
	Focus on and encourage accomplishments.
4–8 Months	
Begin to demonstrate preference for primary caregivers and anxiety around strangers.	Hold and talk to infant warmly when the infant becomes anxious.

Table 5.1	*(Continued)*

8–15 Months

Show affection to familiar people.

Demonstrate anger (e.g., toy is taken away).

Show pleasure in accomplishments.

Physical

Birth to 4 Months

Mouth hands and objects.	Provide many objects that can be safely handled.
Grasp objects.	Position infants so they can make eye contact and observe their environment.
Hold head up.	
Follow movement with eyes.	

4–8 Months

Sit up.	Provide a spoon and encourage the infant to feed him/herself.
Hold a bottle.	
Grasp tools (e.g., spoon).	
Pick up food with fingers and put in mouth.	

8–15 Months

Pull self up and crawl (8–12 months).	Provide crayons and other tools, clay, etc.
Walk (10–14 months).	Allow infant to assist with dressing.
Assist with dressing (e.g., put arm in sleeve).	
Grasp a crayon and create marks.	

Source: Bredekamp & Copple (1997)

Michael Newman/PhotoEdit.

process is more complex than that (Chomsky, 2002). Chomsky suggested that acquisition of language is unique to humans because we have a *faculty of language* (FL) or *language acquisition device* (LAD). He said few would argue "that a child can somehow distinguish linguistic materials from the rest of the confusion around it, hence postulating the existence of FL (=LAD)" (p. 86). Nativists suggest that language develops through experience and maturation, stabilizing at various stages (Chomsky, 2002).

Some nativists believe that the tendency of toddlers to overgeneralize the rules of language is evidence of the accuracy of their theory. For example, adults do not model the word *taked* instead of *took*; rather, the toddler creates the word by generalizing the rule for making present tense verbs into past tense. Children also create words or phrases that

Table 5.2 Portrait of Toddlers and Their Caregivers

What Toddlers Do	What Early Childhood Educators Do
Cognitive and Language	
15–24 Months	
Enjoy frequent reading periods with books that have interesting characters and plots, and predictable language.	Read regularly to individual and small groups of toddlers and comment on the pictures.
Point to pictures and name them.	Read in English and in the child's native language if possible.
Speak in two word utterances (telegraphic speech). Bilingual toddlers may switch between two languages.	Provide a variety of board books for toddlers to handle.
Name familiar objects in books and in the environment.	Communicate with parents to learn what utterances mean so they can respond appropriately to unintelligible language.
View the world only from own point of view (egocentrism).	Model conventional speech rather than correcting unconventional speech.
Stack and nest objects.	Provide many objects to explore and provide social interactions for toddlers that support their learning.
24–30 Months	
Overgeneralize the rules of language (e.g., "goed" instead of "went," "taked" instead of "took").	Alternate quiet and active periods of activity.
Develop an expressive vocabulary of 200 words or more.	
Use adjectives and demonstrate beginning knowledge of grammatical constructions (e.g., use of prepositions, plurals).	
May listen to stories for extended periods.	
Social–Emotional	
15–24 Months	
Assert own desires.	Redirect problematic behaviors.
Take objects from another. Fuss when objects are taken from him/her.	Respond with positive language showing toddlers what they can do, rather than what they cannot (e.g., "You can bang the stick on the drum").
Want immediate gratification.	Provide multiples of the same toy to avoid conflicts.
Respond well to routines.	Provide routines for eating, sleeping, and toileting and flexible periods of quiet and active experiences.
Have difficulty separating from primary caregivers.	
24–30 Months	
May separate from primary caregiver more easily.	Follow children's interests.
Beginning to enjoy being around peers.	Are reassuring to toddlers experiencing separation anxiety.
Begin to delay gratification.	

Table 5.2	(Continued)

Physical

15–24 Months

Scribble with crayons and markers.	Watch toddlers carefully to keep them safe.
Go up and down stairs on bottom or knees at first.	Encourage motor activity that is safe.
Walk and run.	Help toddlers manage stairs.
Climb onto furniture.	Play ball and engage in other gross motor activities.
Manipulate clay.	

24–30 Months

Walk up and down stairs.

Jump.

Kick a ball.

Pedal a small tricycle.

Source: Bredekamp & Copple (1997)

they have never heard others use. For example, as Sophie and Isabelle pretended to be dogs, Molly took the role of the dog owner, and asked her grandma to be "the dog taker," her expression for dogcatcher. Referring to his birthday last year, Xavier created the term "yesteryear."

Stages of Language Development

Receptive language, the process of understanding language, begins long before infants can talk. They are capable of perceiving the sounds of speech, even in the first months of life, and they learn to respond to speech before they can produce it. For example, if you picked up an infant who was busy playing with blocks and said, "It's nap time now," you might encounter some rebellion. While the infants cannot say, "I don't want to take a nap," they can show you that they do not want to take a nap by fussing, pulling away, or some other behavior.

Expressive language refers to language that is produced. Psycholinguists agree that language develops in predictable patterns described below.

- ▶ *Crying* is infants' first means of communication. Through crying, they communicate their needs by varying pitch, intonation, and pauses. Parents and caregivers learn to understand what infants' various crying behaviors mean (e.g., tired, hungry).

- ▶ *Babbling* emerges in the first months of life. Infants often produce babbling sounds just for the pleasure of it. The sounds begin with strings of vowels, then consonants, and eventually strings of consonant–vowel sounds such as the well-known *mamamamama*. Eventually, the sounds are shortened—*mama*—and begin to resemble adult speech.

- ▶ *Holophrasic speech*, single-word utterances, appears late in the first year of life. Single words are used for identification (e.g., doggie, nose) and for social interaction (e.g., bye-bye).

► *Telegraphic speech*, a combination of two words, emerges during the second year of life. Often the words are a noun and a verb such as *baby cry* or *doggy bark*. The term *telegraphic* is taken from the archaic telegraph system used long ago to transmit messages. Because one paid by the word, it was necessary to conserve on the number of words used. Most psycholinguists believe that, when telegraphic speech emerges, it is a sign that toddlers are applying the rules of their language. For example, they put words in the correct order such as *doggy bark* rather than *bark doggy*.

► *Vocabulary development* continues, and by age 2 children have about a 200-word vocabulary. In addition, their sentences expand as they learn to use adjectives, adverbs, and compound sentences. There is further evidence that toddlers are applying the rules of language by their tendency to *overgeneralize* or misapply the rules. For example, they misapply the rule that adding *s* makes a word plural when they say *mouses*.

► *Grammar and syntax develop*. As children learn vocabulary, they also learn how to put words together to communicate their thoughts. Consistent patterns are evident as young children learn appropriate word order, how to use prepositions, how to create plurals, and so on.

Bob Daemmrich/The Image Works.

Private Speech. It is not unusual to observe toddlers in what Vygotsky (1962) referred to as private speech, or talking out loud with no intended audience. Vygotsky suggested that private speech comes from the culture as children repeat what others have said to them in an attempt to internalize ideas or to achieve self-control. That is, private speech helps them think about what they are doing. For example, the toddler putting away blocks might be heard saying, "Big blocks here and small blocks here," perhaps a repeat of something an adult said.

Signing. Next time you are in a conversation, pay attention to the nonverbal communication. For example, do you extend your thumb and pinky and put them to your ear when you refer to a phone conversation? Do you spread your arms when you want to indicate something is wide? Parents and early childhood educators have found that infants, too, can learn sign language as a means of communicating their needs before they learn to talk. For example, they learn the signs for *more* and *done* to communicate their needs at mealtime.

Reading to Infants and Toddlers

Parents and early childhood educators should begin reading to infants at the moment of birth. (Many parents read during pregnancy as well.) Early reading experiences support infants' developing receptive language and expressive language; warm contact during reading also supports healthy social–emotional development. Frequent and regular reading is just a good habit for adults to develop with children.

There are many picture book titles that are manufactured in the form of sturdy board books designed to withstand mouthing and handling by infants and toddlers. The stories are short and have colorful illustrations to hold their attention. Many are written in rhyme to support their developing phonemic awareness (awareness of the distinct sounds in a speech stream). Enjoying these books during lap and small group reading periods provides feelings of closeness and warmth for infants and toddlers.

Ellen B. Senisi/The Image Works.

Language Is Cultural

Language development is both biological and cultural. The cultural aspects of language development are addressed more fully in Chapter 10, but it should be noted here that the way in which language develops reflects the values and models of the home culture. The language children produce mirrors the native language, dialect, and slang used in the home. Suffice it to say, healthy language development relies on interaction between the child and more literate others.

Delayed Language Development

Although they have unique timing and patterns in their language development, typically developing children go through predictable stages of language development. Some children have delayed language development or development that lags so far behind benchmarks that it is clear the child is not progressing adequately. For example, a 2-year-old in the holophasic stage of language may be language delayed. Some language delays can be explained as in the case of hearing impairment or Down syndrome. If you suspect a language delay, refer the infant or toddler for language diagnostic testing so that early intervention can be implemented if necessary.

Hearing Impairment. Initially, partial- and non-hearing infants vocalize in much the same way as hearing infants, but by age 6 months vocalizations decrease and do not progress on the typical developmental continuum (Petitto & Marentette, 1991). However, partial- and non-hearing infants and toddlers can learn sign language just as hearing infants and toddlers learn oral language. In fact, infants and toddlers have been known to create their own sign language. Just as hearing infants babble orally, partial- and non-hearing infants babble in sign language.

Whether hearing or not, the infant and toddler years are a sensitive period for language acquisition. This means that early intervention is critical for children who are not developing language. Examples of ways to mediate language acquisition include teaching sign language and providing cochlear implants.

Down Syndrome. Children with Down syndrome will demonstrate delayed language. Sometime during the first year, infants with Down syndrome experience disruption in language development. Furthermore, they tend to have difficulty with communication in general, paying less attention to adults when they talk, initiating fewer conversations, and providing briefer and fewer responses when they do speak. Lack of verbal or social interaction further impacts language development. Early intervention is very important for children with Down syndrome.

Language Delays. Some children develop language at a slower rate than typically developing children. However, the term delay should not be misunderstood; children with language delays do not always catch up with their peers.

There are various explanations for language delays, including poverty, stress, minimal brain dysfunction (minor brain impairment), and poor health. Although early intervention prior to entrance to formal schooling is necessary, no single intervention will work for all children with language delays. Interventions must be developed based on reasons for the language delay. This topic is developed more fully in Chapter 11.

David Young-Wolff/PhotoEdit.   Lauren Shear/Photo Researchers.

Cognitive Development

In Chapter 2, we discussed Piaget's stages of cognitive development. Recognizing individual patterns and timing of development, he noted that children are in the *sensorimotor stage* for roughly the first 2 $1/2$ years of life. This is a time when children learn through their senses. Following are stages of cognitive development that occur during the sensorimotor stage.

Stage I, Birth Reflexes. This stage spans the first month of life (Piaget, 1952). Infants engage in reflexive or automatic actions including sucking, grasping, crying, and swallowing. The reflexes are modified as the infant exercises them. For example, infants become proficient enough to grasp objects of different shapes and hang on to them.

Stage II, Primary Circular Reactions. The 1- to 4-month-old infant purposefully engages in activities that were previously reflexive (Lavatelli, 1970). Infants at this stage intentionally grasp objects because they are interesting. The circular aspect refers to infants' desire to repeat newly discovered experiences.

Stage III, Secondary Circular Reactions. This stage spans approximately 4–8 months and is characterized by the intellectual hallmark known as *object permanence* (Piaget, 1952). That is, the infant now knows that objects exist even though they cannot be seen. If you hide an object from an infant in this stage of development, she is likely to search for it. At this stage, infants show increasing purposefulness in their actions and they respond to others in their environment. Actions are repeated for the sheer pleasure of repeating them.

Stage IV, Coordination of Secondary Schemes. The hallmark of this stage, which spans 8–12 months, is the occurrence of *first intentional behaviors* (Piaget, 1952). Behaviors during this stage include intentionally pushing an obstacle aside and actively searching for interesting objects. For example, an infant will search for that favorite stuffed toy at bedtime.

Stage V, Tertiary Circular Reactions. From 12 to 18 months, infants now experiment with actions. They repeat actions and try new ones to see what will happen. They also demonstrate goal-oriented behavior (Lavatelli, 1970). For example, a toddler might intentionally bang a stick on a drum or cover a doll with a blanket. Because children become mobile during this time period, their repertoire of activities is expanded.

Stage VI, Symbolic Representation. From 18 months on, children have the ability to think symbolically. This enables them to remember things, pretend, and problem solve because they can hold mental images of things in their minds (Piaget, 1952). Recall from Chapter 4 that language is the first evidence of children's symbolic thinking. Initially, children mentally represent things through words. As they grow and develop, symbolic thinking appears in their play when they use objects to represent something else. Finally, children acquire and use the socially defined, abstract symbols of printed language as they become readers and writers (Vygotsky, 1978).

Egocentrism

Egocentrism is a cognitive state where infants and toddlers do not have the ability to take the perspective of others. It should not be confused with the social state of self-centeredness or selfishness; infants and toddlers literally do not take another's point of view. To exemplify, following is a phone conversation between $2\frac{1}{2}$-year-old Isabelle and her Grandma:

   I: Grandma, I went to the stock show wif my daddy.
   G: You did! What did you see?
   I: I sawed pigs and horsies.
   G: What else did you see?
   I: The horsies were gall-uping like this.

At this point, Grandma got a picture in her mind of Isabelle imitating galloping horses. From Isabelle's perspective, her imitation served to communicate meaning. She did not have the mental ability to take Grandma's perspective and realize that Grandma could not see her referent for "like this."

Reasoning

There are other cognitive capabilities that have not yet developed for infants and toddlers. These include cause and effect relationships, conservation of volume and number, and focusing on more than one characteristic of an object at a time. High-quality early childhood educators provide many experiences with objects to support development in these areas.

Physical Development

The period from birth to age 2 is one of rapid physical development. By age 2, children may be four times heavier and a foot or more taller than at birth. During the infant and toddler stages, their heads are disproportionately large.

Neuroscientists have found that, at birth, infants have 100 billion neurons (transmit and store information) in their brains. If the brain is well stimulated and nourished, these neurons can produce as many as 15,000 synapses or connections among the nerve cells. Synapses that are regularly used become permanent; those infrequently used undergo pruning and go away. Rapid pruning begins by age 8 or 9. As nerve cells develop, they acquire a lipid substance that forms a protective shield around them which contributes to more accurate and rapid transmission of neural impulses (Bergen & Coscia, 2001). Infants' and toddlers' rapid changes in motor activity—sitting, crawling, standing, walking—are evidence of this. Between the ages of 18 months and 3 years, young children master many physical skills including kicking a ball, standing on one foot, walking on tiptoe, hopping, and walking up and down stairs.

Fine Motor Development. Fine motor skills develop from the basic grasping reflex of the newborn to intentionally drawing familiar shapes. When toddlers first use drawing and writing tools, they usually grasp them in their fists and make back and forth movements across the paper. As they mature, they learn to hold tools between their fingers and thumb and their sweeping marks become circles, sticks, and other familiar shapes. Figure 5.1 depicts a drawing of dinosaurs, created by a $2\frac{1}{2}$-year-old. Notice that it has some sweeping marks along with several circles and sticks.

Pixtal/SUPERSTOCK.

Figure 5.1 Dinosaur drawing by a 2 $\frac{1}{2}$-year-old.

Toileting. Typically between the ages of 2 and 3 years, young children learn toileting. Toileting is a social expectation that is governed in part by physical development. That is, children must be developed enough to feel the full bladder or bowel and be able to assert control over the reflex. Thus, toddlers must be mature enough to know they need to use the toilet and then learn to do so. This process requires well-established routines and careful communication between parents and early childhood educators so that children see toileting as positive and not a source of conflict.

Social–Emotional Development

At birth, infants understand only their own needs and whether or not they are met. As they mature, they become increasingly aware of those around them and engage in interactions with them, first by smiling and gazing. Within a few months, they will engage in conversation with others. The conversations are not conventional in the sense that the infants use words, but there is an exchange. They babble and emit single-vowel utterances as their part of the conversation.

Impulse Control

By the age of 1 year, most infants are mobile; yet they do not have impulse control or the ability to delay gratification. Coupling mobility with lack of impulse control makes them a danger to themselves because they are interested in most things and set out to explore them. It is important to monitor infants' activities carefully, a phenomenon discussed more fully in Chapter 8.

Attachment

Erikson (1963) highlighted the critical importance of developing trust during infancy. This sense of trust is manifest in *attachment*, or contact that leads to an emotional bond (Bowlby, 1969). About 70% of American infants attach securely to mother or a primary caregiver, while 30% do not (Trawick-Smith, 1997). Infants need a physically and psychologically safe, predictable environment in order to securely attach to primary caregivers. They will attach to more than one primary caregiver, particularly if there are several caregivers living in the home or several with whom they spend time regularly.

Jose Luis Pelaez/Blend Images/Getty Images, Inc.

Ainsworth, Blehar, Waters, and Wall (1978) identified three types of attachment: *secure, insecure ambivalent*, and *insecure avoidant*.

▶ *Secure attachment* characterizes infants who approach a new environment happily when in the company of the primary caregiver. These infants will cry when the primary caregiver leaves but will readily go to her when she returns. By 6–8 months, most securely attached infants will demonstrate *separation anxiety* by becoming distressed when left by the primary caregiver. They also experience *stranger anxiety*, or anxiety when an unfamiliar person takes the infant from the primary caregiver. Although infants and toddlers demonstrate separation and stranger anxiety to different degrees, trust develops when they positively experience separation and strangers. Eventually, they accept new people more easily.

▶ *Insecure ambivalent* infants cry when they are left by the primary caregiver. Upon the return of the primary caregiver, they alternate between anxious clinging and rejection of the primary caregiver.

▶ *Insecure avoidant* infants often do not cry when left by the primary caregiver and do not go to her when she returns.

There are at least two possible causes for insecure attachment: extensive maternal separation and negative maternal attitude (Karen, 1994). Extensive maternal separation happens in cases where the mother is incarcerated or she has a lengthy illness. Extensive maternal separation used to happen decades ago when parents were not permitted to sleep in the room with their hospitalized infant.

Mothers who have mental illness or engage in drug use often have negative maternal attitudes. Women who are themselves victims of abuse may find the challenges of child raising overwhelming and develop negative maternal attitudes.

Your role as an early childhood educator is to support healthy attachment by getting to know individual infants, responding to their needs, and providing a stimulating and nurturing environment. Seek out early interventions for insecurely attached infants.

Cultural Considerations. Different personal qualities are valued across cultures. For example, in families where independence is nurtured at an early age, infants and toddlers may separate easily and even ignore the primary caregiver upon return. In families where infants and toddlers are seldom apart from the primary caregiver, separation will be more difficult. As an early childhood educator, you must become familiar with the family values and practices of infants in your care.

Temperament

Infants' personalities become apparent within the first months of life, when babies are characterized as easy, fussy, mellow, and so on. Although the environment influences how the temperament will develop, infants are born with basic temperaments that influence their social interactions. As an adult working with infants, you can help them develop in positive ways.

Adults working with infants learn to how to respond to differences in temperament. For example, when an infant appears to be fearful, you are reassuring and comforting. If an infant is very active, you introduce quiet activities (e.g., book reading, singing) for brief periods.

Photodisc/Getty Images, Inc.

⟩ Play

Infant play behaviors are spontaneous, and they are bound by their perceptions of the immediate environment (Vygotsky, 1966). Infants explore objects in isolation and in accordance with the physical characteristics of the object (Chapter 4). That is, soft objects are chewed, noise is made with objects designed for that purpose, and so on. Toward the beginning of the second year of life, objects may be combined but are still used only for their intended purpose. For example, the infant or toddler might place a blanket on a pillow and pretend to sleep or pretend to eat with an empty spoon and plate.

Early play is characterized by actions that are repeated simply for the pleasure of performing them (Piaget & Inhelder, 1969). For example, the infant might discover that hitting an object causes it to swing. Repetition of this behavior serves as a source of pleasure for the infant.

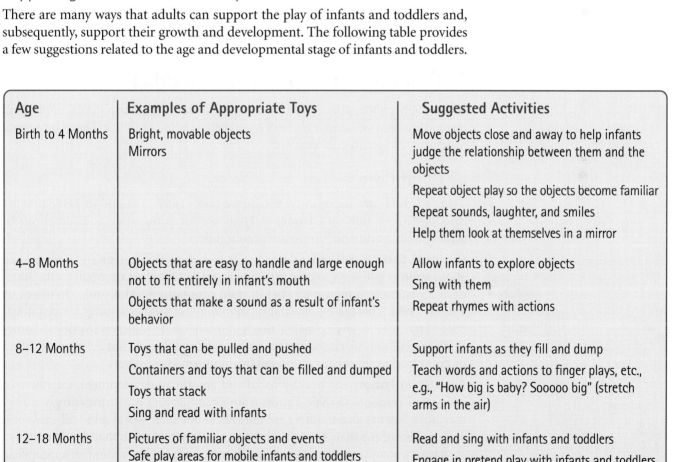

Play behaviors become more extended and mature throughout infancy and toddlerhood. The simple clapping of hands observable in a 6-month-old infant evolves into simple pretend play where toddlers play out real-life scenarios, particularly when it is supported by an adult. The *Focus on Children* chronicles toddler play about the familiar activity of having a picnic in the park.

Supporting Infant and Toddler Play

There are many ways that adults can support the play of infants and toddlers and, subsequently, support their growth and development. The following table provides a few suggestions related to the age and developmental stage of infants and toddlers.

Age	Examples of Appropriate Toys	Suggested Activities
Birth to 4 Months	Bright, movable objects Mirrors	Move objects close and away to help infants judge the relationship between them and the objects Repeat object play so the objects become familiar Repeat sounds, laughter, and smiles Help them look at themselves in a mirror
4–8 Months	Objects that are easy to handle and large enough not to fit entirely in infant's mouth Objects that make a sound as a result of infant's behavior	Allow infants to explore objects Sing with them Repeat rhymes with actions
8–12 Months	Toys that can be pulled and pushed Containers and toys that can be filled and dumped Toys that stack Sing and read with infants	Support infants as they fill and dump Teach words and actions to finger plays, etc., e.g., "How big is baby? Sooooo big" (stretch arms in the air)
12–18 Months	Pictures of familiar objects and events Safe play areas for mobile infants and toddlers Realistic toys, e.g., cups and dishes, trucks, cars, dolls, stuffed animals	Read and sing with infants and toddlers Engage in pretend play with infants and toddlers Put words with actions to support language development

Source: Adapted from Sawyers, J. K., & Rogers, C. S. (2004). Helping babies play. In D. Koralek (Ed.), *Spotlight on young children and PLAY* (pp. 42–43). Washington, DC: National Association for the Education of Young Children.

Focus on Children

Isabelle, 2 $\frac{1}{2}$, is busy gathering up her dolls and carrying them into the living room. She has an interesting mixture of baby dolls and princess dolls. Next, she lines her dolls up against the couch and begins covering them with blankets.

Mother: *What are you doing?*

Isabelle: *My babies are going to sleep.*

Mother: *Oh. When they wake up, do you think they would like to go on a picnic in the park?*

Isabelle: *Ummm, ya.*

[At this point, Isabelle uncovers her dolls and goes to her play kitchen to get utensils and dishes.]

Mother: *Do you need a blanket to sit on for your picnic?*

Isabelle: *Oh ya, I need a blanket.*

[Isabelle grabbed the blanket she had just taken off of the dolls and proceeded to arrange her utensils on it. Then the play began.]

Isabelle: *Here, baby, do you want some foods? Princess Fiona, do you want to drink?*

With a bit of dialogue, Isabelle continues her play by holding a spoon or a cup to the dolls' mouths. The duration of this episode was just over a minute.

Isabelle is engaged in early pretend play. That is, she can pretend but is still bound by the function of objects (e.g., cups are for drinking, spoons are for eating) as well as her own personal experience. She has been on picnics before and knows what one does on a picnic. From experience, she knows how to use cups and spoons.

Isabelle's mother assisted her play by making suggestions for extending it. This wise mother suggested activities familiar to Isabelle which supported her as she created content for her play.

Programs for Infants and Toddlers

Increasingly, children are in part- or full-time child care. Some parents simply want a part-time, out of home experience for their infant or toddler. There are several programs for infants and toddlers.

Child Care

Types of child care including *family home care, center care,* and *in-home care* are discussed more fully in Chapter 6. Here, we focus on some considerations to achieve high-quality care for infants and toddlers.

Qualified Early Childhood Educators. It is critical that caregivers are educated about appropriate ways to care for infants and toddlers, yet over half of the states do not require training for all staff in child care settings (Holcomb, Dreisback, & Hutter, 1999). This can be devastating in infant and toddler settings where knowledge of the unique developmental needs of infants and toddlers is so critical. Something as basic as understanding that infants and toddlers do not delay gratification or know how to share can be ignored by uninformed caregivers.

Adult/Child Ratios. For healthy social and emotional development, infants need immediate response to their distress from a familiar and nurturing caregiver. Furthermore, infants and toddlers are curious about their world and will explore it with no regard for their safety or the safety of others. Add to that the demands of structuring an optimal learning environment, discussed earlier, and an appropriate adult/child ratio is important.

It is ideal for healthy attachment if each infant has a primary caregiver assigned to him/her. Experts recommend three or four infants per adult and four to six toddlers per adult (Holcomb et al., 1999). Sadly, less than half of the states currently meet the recommended standard, owing largely to the high cost encountered when adult/child ratios are decreased.

Environments. Toys and other materials must be developmentally appropriate and physically safe. Infants and toddlers put toys in their mouths, swing them, throw them, and so on with no regard for safety. There also needs to be a sufficient amount and variation of toys to avoid conflict and to promote development.

Infants and toddlers need spaces to be mobile and quiet, for feeding, and for sleeping. Space for diapering is also needed. These spaces need to be sufficient such that ample high chairs, cribs, changing tables, etc. are available. Consideration must also be given to toddlers who may be learning toileting.

Reggio Emilia

Recall from Chapter 2, Reggio Emilia is the name of a small town in Italy, the first home of Reggio Emilia schools. Today, Reggio Emilia schools serve children from birth to age 6. Reggio Emilia schools for children ages 3–6 are discussed in Chapter 6; here, we briefly discuss schools for infants and toddlers.

The Reggio Emilia curriculum unfolds as children express interests. These interests then guide exploration of the social and physical world. In settings for infants and toddlers, early childhood educators learn to recognize moments that can potentially evolve into projects appropriate for young children of that age. The *Window into the Classroom* exemplifies how such a project might work.

Window into the Classroom

Infants and toddlers learn about what things do through active exploration. In this Reggio Emilia setting, early childhood educator Mia supported Jeff (20 months) and Jamaica (23 months) in the *painting project*.

Mia was with Jeff at the painting table where there were several large sheets of paper and six tubs of paint, each a different color. Each tub had a lid with a hole in it for a paintbrush. Mia was talking with Jeff as he stroked his paintbrush across the paper. "Now try this brush to see what color is in the tub," Mia said. At her direction, Jeff tried the various colors of paint. Eventually the interaction caught the attention of Jamaica.

Jamaica joined the play by painting round figures on the paper. "See Jeff," Jamaica commented, pointing to her picture. At this point, Mia introduced some rubber stamps of various shapes—circle, triangle, square, moon, star. As she held up the moon stamp, Mia said, "What can you do with this shape if you paint the bottom of it?"

"Ohhhhhhh," squealed Jamaica as she took the shape, covered the bottom with red paint and pressed it on the paper. "Look," said Mia, "you made a moon on your paper." Jeff watched Mia and Jamaica but continued to paint on his paper with his brush. Jamaica delighted in painting and stamping with each of the stamps.

The painting table was a favorite for both Jeff and Jamaica. Both were learning about the properties of paint and what they could do with it. Eventually, Jeff tried painting the stamps and stamping them on his paper.

After a few days of painting and stamping, Mia and Jeff were again at the paint table. This time, however, instead of picking up stamps, Jeff, looking pensive, took the green paintbrush and began painting his hand. He then placed his hand on the paper and lifted it, to reveal a handprint. "See," he squealed delightfully. "Jeff," Mia declared, "you have used paint to make a print of your hand." The next day, Jeff experimented with painting his finger tips and making fingerprints.

Fully engaged in play with paint, Jeff and Jamaica were learning about what one can do with paint. Scaffolded by Mia, they discovered that they could cover objects with paint to leave an imprint on paper. Jeff subsequently tested his theory by painting his hand and fingertips to make imprints on the paper. Mia supported his inquiry by gently offering new materials, making suggestions, and putting language with what the children were doing.

Early Head Start

Initially, Head Start served children for 1 year before they entered school. Since that time, new brain research suggests that critical developmental periods occur long before age 4. In fact, we have accumulated knowledge about the critical importance of good prenatal habits, health care, and environments that support growth and development. In light of emerging research, Early Head Start came about in 1995 as part of the Head Start Reauthorization Act. It is focused on working with mothers and their infants and toddlers, and it is overseen by the states that fund it with federal contracts.

Early Head Start programs are home-based. The program emphasizes health care, nutrition, parent education, literacy, and appropriate learning experiences for infants and toddlers. Mothers are taught parenting skills and good health practices. They have opportunities to develop their literacy and other academic skills. They also learn the importance of practices such as reading to their children.

The U.S. Department of Health and Human Services reports that Early Head Start has led to better parenting and fewer cognitive, language, and behavior problems for children later in life (HHS News, 2002). Furthermore, research suggests that, when compared to children who did not experience Early Head Start, children who did displayed higher emotional engagement with a parent, sustained attention with play objects longer, and were less aggressive (Love, Kisker, & Ross, 2005). Early Head Start parents were more emotionally supportive, talked and read with their children more, and were less likely to spank their children. The most positive impact resulted from a blend of home-visiting and center-based services where performance standards were implemented early (Love et al., 2005).

Montessori

Maria Montessori believed that the first 3 years of life are critical to healthy growth and development. What happens during those years sets the trajectory for a lifetime (Hainstock, 1986). Recall from Chapter 2 that one of Montessori's principles was respect for the child. This principle is clearly reflected in Montessori early childhood settings for infants and toddlers.

Infants. Infants need to feel secure and safe in their environment. Typically, before a parent leaves an infant in a Montessori setting, continuity between home and the early childhood setting is established when the infant and parent come to the Montessori setting for a lengthy visit. During the visit, the teacher and parent observe each other and the infant's responses. The teacher begins learning how the parent responds to the infant's cues, and the parent can observe the teacher's interactions with the infant.

This initial visit helps the infant transition into the Montessori setting from the nurturing arms of a parent. When the infant is left, the teacher observes the infant, structures appropriate activities, and again observes the infant's response. In Montessori centers, infants enjoy routines, a calm environment, and limited materials to avoid overstimulation.

Toddlers. In some ways, the Montessori environment for toddlers resembles the preschool environment, discussed in more detail in Chapter 6. It has areas for

Ellen B. Senisi/The Image Works.

sensory learning, art, and language development. As with infants, the materials in the environment are sparse so that toddlers do not become overstimulated (Hainstock, 1986).

Toddlers have many self-correcting materials designed to help them build concrete patterns of order in their minds. For example, they nest objects or order them from shortest to longest. They are also free to explore the materials (Hainstock, 1986). Materials in the Montessori schools for toddlers are arranged so that children learn a sequence of activities whereby they take the materials off the shelf, play with them, and then put them back. They may not do all of the activities at first, but with the supportive guidance of the teacher, toddlers learn to complete all of the activities.

In Montessori settings, toddlers enjoy routines. Teachers communicate respectfully with them, pointing out what they are permitted and able to do rather than what they are not permitted or not capable to do.

Creating an Antibias Environment

There is one group in our society that does not demonstrate prejudiced attitudes; that group is infants. This suggests that prejudice (attitude) and discrimination (behavior) are learned. Children as young as 2 years old notice differences, differentiating between boys and girls, skin colors, clothing, and so on. If healthy attitudes about differences are nurtured in infant and toddler years, a trajectory for children to learn tolerance and understanding is set.

Acceptance. The antibias curriculum in infant and toddler settings begins with each individual child feeling accepted. All children in the environment, regardless of ethnicity, religion, social class, ability, or gender, must experience the same responsive and nurturing care from caregivers. Antibias attitudes begin when individuals feel accepted and valued through personal experience.

Infants and toddlers are fortunate if they are able to participate in groups that are diverse in terms of ethnicity, religion, social class, ability, and gender. Children

Focus on Diversity

For the past several decades, the number of children living in poverty has been increasing. In America, a baby is born into poverty every 44 seconds; a baby is born without health insurance every minute; and a baby is born at low birth weight every 2 minutes (Children's Defense Fund, 2001).

Being born into poverty can have lasting effects. Conditions relating to health care, parenting, and living environments influence children's development. If they do not have appropriate health care and a stimulating living environment, children who live in poverty during infancy may have difficulty with school-related cognitive tasks later. The limited resources for families living in poverty place young children at great risk.

Research (Children's Defense Fund, 2001) suggests the following:

- Every tax dollar invested in high-quality early childhood programs for children living in poverty saves $7.00.
- Every tax dollar invested in diphtheria, tetanus, and whooping cough immunizations saves $23.00.
- Every tax dollar spent on the Women, Infants, and Children (WIC) nutritional programs saves $3.07 during an infant's first year.
- Every year a child lives in poverty costs $9,000 in lost future productivity over the child's working life. (p. xvii)

who are different in some ways can listen to stories or build with blocks alongside each other. Through these positive activities, they learn to understand and accept difference.

Toddlers are becoming aware of differences in physical appearance. They notice different skin and hair colors and people using wheelchairs or other types of physical aids. In the midst of diapering and toilet learning, they will notice genital differences, too. Your role as an early childhood educator is to acknowledge children's questions and comments in accepting ways. For example, responding to a 2-year-old's comment about skin color, you might say, "Yes, his skin is brown. Yours is tan and Jeremy's is light brown. There are many different skin colors in our group."

Early childhood educators should feel comfortable using appropriate language regarding genitals. "David has a penis and you have a vagina." Derman-Sparks (1989) made the following comments regarding children's comments about genitals. (1) Do not make fun of children's comments about genitals. (2) Do not reprimand children for asking about genitals. (3) Brief responses to children's comments do not constitute sex education; you are responding to children's developmental task of learning about their bodies (p. 22).

Materials. As with older children, learning materials should reflect our nation's diversity. For example, infants like to focus on faces. Have faces of many colors present among caregivers, in books, and on the walls.

Poverty. We often think of prejudice relative to ethnicity, forgetting that many factors give rise to prejudice. One often overlooked factor is social–economic status (SES). Teachers are seldom encouraged to reflect on ways that SES bias affects them. They are educated about racism or sexism but seldom about classism (Davidson & Schniedewind, 1996).

Many infants are born into poverty, a condition which correlates to some delays in development. For example, parents in low SES families tend to have fewer sustained conversations with their young children than those from higher SES families (Hoff, 2003; Hoff-Ginsberg & Tardif, 1995). Sustained and frequent conversations

My Developing Professional View

Considering the nature of infants and toddlers and the descriptions of infant and toddler programs presented in this chapter, what are the four or five most important considerations when structuring an optimal curriculum for infants and toddlers?

Focus on History

In the late 1960s, Senator Robert Kennedy took a trip to the Mississippi Delta and was outraged by the conditions he encountered. The bloated bellies of hungry children gave him impetus to direct political change that would affect the lives of children living in poverty. Senator Kennedy:

• Encouraged doctors to provide services to children in poor communities and to document hunger they observed.

• Convinced the Agriculture secretary to reduce barriers to acquiring food stamps.

• Encouraged *60 Minutes* on CBS to bring attention to the poverty in Mississippi by airing a documentary.

• Encouraged fellow senators to hold hearings to make the issue of poverty more visible.

During the subsequent Nixon administration, child and family nutrition programs were expanded, leading to near eradication of child hunger. During the Reagan administration, however, tax breaks for some, coupled with the cost of military buildup took its toll on programs for children and families. More recently, tax cuts implemented by the G. W. Bush administration further widened the gap between the rich and poor.

Source: Children's Defense Fund. (2001). *Yearbook 2001: The state of America's children.* Washington, DC: Children's Defense Fund.

support language development which, in turn, supports children's development as readers and writers. Children of poverty need healthy, nurturing early childhood environments if they are to develop at a rate comparable to children from higher SES. The *Focus on Diversity* highlights the elements of this issue, and the *Focus on History* provides some historical background.

Summary

The focus of this chapter is infants and toddlers. Infants and toddlers have unique developmental needs for healthy growth and development. Of particular concern during infant and toddler years is language development and the development of a healthy sense of trust. Early childhood educators working in settings for infants and toddlers must be educated about the developmental characteristics and needs of children in their care. They can mediate early intervention for infants and toddlers who need it.

There are several programs for infants and toddlers. Early childhood educators in high-quality programs acknowledge the sensitive periods for developing language, trust, and a positive sense of self. They acknowledge the value of play to children's social, emotional, physical, and cognitive development. They learn how to scaffold play and how to follow the interests of children in their care.

Prejudice is learned. Thus, from the moment of birth, children need opportunities to feel accepted and valued and to learn tolerance and acceptance. Attitudes toward children living in poverty are often not addressed in teacher education programs. High-quality early childhood educators address personal bias and support all children in their care.

⸘ Enrichment Activities

Individual Activities

1. Observe an infant or toddler in an early childhood setting for 1–2 hours. Record as accurately as you can what you observe. Using Tables 5.1 and 5.2 in this chapter as resources, describe the developmental nature of the young child.

2. Access the website for your state government to determine what programs your state has for infants and toddlers who may not otherwise have access to proper health care (e.g., Early Head Start, CHIPS).

Cooperative Activity

3. Have each member of your cooperative group interview an early childhood educator in an infant or toddler setting to find out what s/he learns by observing the infants or toddlers at play. Also determine how the early childhood educator supports the play (e.g., describing, providing materials). Discuss your findings in your group to determine if there are any patterns in the behaviors of the early childhood educators each of you interviewed.

Advocacy Activity

4. Access the website for the National Child Care Information Center at http://www.nccic.org/ or your state government website to determine child care regulations for infants and toddlers in your state. Based on what you know, are the regulations adequate (e.g., appropriate adult/child ratio, trained staff)? Review some other states to see how your state compares to others. Decide how infant and toddler care might be improved in your state and then email or write a letter to your local legislature advocating for more rigorous standards.

} FOR FURTHER READING

Attachment

Elliot, D. (2003). Challenging our assumptions: Helping a baby adjust to center care. *Young Children, 58*(4), 22–28.

Honig, A. S. (2002). *Secure relationships: Nurturing infant/toddler attachment in early care settings.* Washington, DC: National Association for the Education of Young Children.

Raikes, H. (1996). A secure base for babies: Applying attachment concepts to the infant care setting. *Young Children, 51*(5), 59–67.

Watson, M. (2003). Attachment theory and challenging behaviors: Reconstructing the nature of relationships. *Young Children, 58*(4), 12–20.

Infants and Toddlers

Derman-Sparks, L., & A.B.C. Task Force. (1989). *Anti-bias curriculum: Tools for empowering young children.* Washington, DC: National Association for the Education of Young Children.

Geist, E. (2003). Infants and toddlers exploring mathematics. *Young Children, 58*(1), 10–12.

Lobman, C. (2003). The bugs are coming! Improvisation and early childhood teaching. *Young Children, 58*(3), 18–23.

Rofrano, F. (2002). A reflection on caring as infant curriculum. *Young Children, 57*(1), 49–51.

Szanton, E. S. (2001). Viewpoint: For America's infants and toddlers, are important values threatened by our zeal to "teach"? *Young Children, 56*(1), 15–21.

Williamson, S. (2006). Challenge or strength? Caring for infants and toddlers in mixed-age groups in family child care. *Young Children, 61*(4), 40–44.

Professional Development Resources

AMERICAN MONTESSORI SOCIETY

175 Fifth Avenue
New York, NY 10010

HEAD START BUREAU

Department of Health and Human Services
330 C Street SW
Room 2018
Washington, DC 20201
http://www.acf.hhs.gov/programs/hsb/

NATIONAL ASSOCIATION FOR THE EDUCATION OF YOUNG CHILDREN

1509 16th Street NW
Washington, DC 20036-1426
http://www.naeyc.org/

NATIONAL ASSOCIATION OF CHILD CARE RESOURCE AND REFERRAL AGENCIES

3101 Wilson Boulevard
Suite 350
Arlington, VA 22201
http://www.naccrra.org/

RESOURCES FOR INFANT EDUCARERS

1550 Murray Circle
Los Angeles, CA 90026
http://www.rie.org/

} SELF-ASSESSMENT

1. Compare and contrast the behaviorist and nativist theories of language development.

2. Discuss the developmental characteristics of infants. Discuss the developmental characteristics of toddlers.

3. Define the term egocentric. Give an example of egocentric behavior one might observe in a toddler.

4. Describe an antibias environment in an infant or toddler setting.

Scenario

Your friend has just been hired as a caregiver in an infant and toddler setting. She knows that the early years are critical for language development but is concerned that she may not know enough about how to support language development in infants and toddlers. Write some guidelines to help her provide excellent support for the language development of the infants and toddlers in her care.

REFERENCES

Ainsworth, M. D. S., Blehar, M. C., Waters, E., & Wall, S. (1978). *Patterns of attachment.* Hillsdale, NJ: Lawrence Erlbaum Associates.

Bergen, D., & Coscia, J. (2001). *Brain research and childhood education: Implications for educators.* Olney, MD: Association for Childhood Education International.

Bowlby, J. (1969). *Attachment and loss: (Vol. 2: Separation, anxiety, and anger).* New York: Basic Books.

Bredekamp, S., & Copple, C. (Eds.). (1997). *Developmentally appropriate practice in early childhood programs (revised ed.).* Washington, DC: National Association for the Education of Young Children.

Children's Defense Fund. (2001). *Yearbook 2001: The state of America's children.* Washington, DC: Children's Defense Fund.

Chomsky, N. (2002). *On nature and language.* New York: Cambridge University Press.

Davidson, E., & Schniedewind, N. (1996). Class differences: Economic inequality in the classrooms. In D. A. Byrnes & G. Kiger (Eds.), *Common bonds.* (pp. 49–63). Wheaton, MD: Association for Childhood Education International.

Derman-Sparks, L., & A.B.C. Task Force. (1989). *Anti-bias curriculum: Tools for empowering young children.* Washington, DC: National Association for the Education of Young Children.

Erikson, E. (1963). *Childhood and society* (2nd ed.). New York: Norton.

Hainstock, E. (1986). *The essential Montessori* (updated ed.). New York: New American Library.

Hoff, E. (2003). Causes and consequences of SES-related differences in parent-to-child speech. In M. H. Bornstein & R. H. Bradley (Eds.), *Socioeconomic status, parenting and child development* (pp. 147–160). Mahwah, NJ: Lawrence Erlbaum Associates.

Hoff-Ginsberg, E., & Tardif, T. (1995). Socioeconomic status and parenting. In M. H. Bornstein (Ed.), *Handbook of parenting, biology and ecology of parenting* (Vol. 2, pp. 161–188). Mahwah, NJ: Lawrence Erlbaum Associates.

Holcomb, B., Dreisbach, S., & Hutter, S. (1999, July/August). How does your state rate? *Working Mother, 8,* 25–26, 30–32, 34, 36, 38, 40.

HSS News. (2002, June). Study shows positive results from Early Head Start program. U.S. Department of Health and Human Services, Washington, DC.

Karen, R. (1994). *Becoming attached: Unfolding the mystery of the infant–mother bond and its impact on later life.* New York: Warner Books.

Lavatelli, C. S. (1970). *Piaget's theory applied to an early childhood curriculum.* Boston: A Center for Media Development.

Love, J. M., Kisker, E. E., & Ross, C. (2005). The effectiveness of Early Head Start for 3-year-old children and their parents: Lessons from policy and programs. *Developmental Psychology, 41*(6), 885–901.

Newport, E. L. (1977). Mother, I'd rather do it myself: Some effects and non-effects on maternal speech style. In C.E. Snow & C.A. Ferguson (Eds.), *Talking to children* (pp. 112–129). Cambridge, England: Cambridge University Press.

Petitto, L. A., & Marentette, P. F. (1991). Babbling in the manual mode: Evidence for the ontogeny of language. *Science, 251,* 1493–1496.

Piaget, J. (1952). *The origins of intelligence in children.* New York: International University Press.

Piaget, J., & Inhelder, B. (1969). *The psychology of the child.* New York: Basic Books.

Sawyers, J. K., & Rogers, C. S. (2004). Helping babies play. In D. Koralek (Ed.), *Spotlight on young children and PLAY* (pp. 42–43). Washington, DC: National Association for the Education of Young Children.

Skinner, B. F. (1957). *Verbal behavior.* Englewood Cliffs, NJ: Prentice-Hall.

Trawick-Smith, F. (1997). *Early childhood development: A multicultural perspective.* Upper Saddle River, NJ: Prentice-Hall.

Vygotsky, L. S. (1962). *Thought and language.* Cambridge, MA: MIT Press.

Vygotsky, L. S. (1966). Play and its role in the mental development of the child. *Soviet Psychology, 12,* 62–76.

Vygotsky, L. S. (1978). *Mind in society.* Cambridge, MA: Harvard University Press.

Preschool and Kindergarten

6

Did you attend preschool before you were old enough for public school? Did you attend kindergarten? Do you have any memories of those early educational experiences? If you attended kindergarten, did your friends attend as well? If you attended kindergarten, do you know that it is most likely you were not required to attend kindergarten?

Early childhood educators provide developmentally and culturally appropriate programs for young children. This chapter has three parts and focuses on children age 3 to 5 years old. We begin with an overview of the nature of young children ages 3–5. Developmentally and culturally appropriate curriculum, appropriate teacher behaviors, and antibias teaching in early childhood programs serving that age range are examined. The second part describes types of child care and addresses issues related to quality child care. The final part examines issues related to kindergarten.

After reading this chapter, you will understand:

▶ The developmental nature of children 3 to 5 years old as it relates to learning.

▶ Considerations for working with children 3 to 5 years old.

▶ Characteristics of contemporary programs for 3- to 5-year-olds.

▶ Types of child care settings.

▶ Characteristics of quality child care.

▶ Strategies for teaching antibias attitudes to 3- to 5-year-olds.

▶ Issues related to kindergarten.

Developmentally and Culturally Appropriate Programs for Three- to Five-Year-Olds

Three to 5-year-olds are served in preschool, kindergarten, and child care programs. They are considered as a group here because of their developmental similarities. Most are in what Piaget called the "preoperational stage" of thinking (Chapter 2). By age 3, children have grown beyond toddlers in social, emotional, cognitive, language, and physical development; yet, most 5-year-olds have not yet made the cognitive shift that typically happens sometime between ages 5 and 7.

Following is an overview of the developmental norms related to learning of 3- to 5-year-olds that must be considered by early childhood educators who work with this age group. It is important to consider that children demonstrate significant growth during these years, and that they have individual time clocks for their growth. If you can, go to an early childhood setting or watch a group of 3- to 5-years-olds in your neighborhood. What differences can you note among them? What similarities do you see?

Although the primary focus of this text is not on curriculum and instruction, it is important to gain a basic understanding of appropriate learning environments for 3- to 5-year-olds. Table 6.1 aligns what we know about children's development with developmentally appropriate teacher behaviors.

Language Development

Expanding Vocabulary. Three- to 5-year-olds are rapidly developing language. Between ages 3 and 5, children's vocabularies will expand from approximately 2,000 to 8,000 words. During this time, most children perfect the sounds of speech with the exception of a few difficult ones (e.g., *l* and *th*) (Bredekamp & Copple, 1997). While children in this age group are rapidly developing conventional speech, they tend to overgeneralize speech conventions as they learn new words. For example, have you ever heard a child say *goed* rather than *went*? Children of this age will inappropriately apply the *add "ed" to indicate past tense* rule such that they might say *goed* instead of *went* and *runned* instead of *ran*. Many children outgrow this tendency by age 5.

Language and Social Interaction. Three- to 5-year-olds are learning to use language more effectively to meet their social needs. During this time children's ability to listen to others without interrupting, to use nonverbal communication, and to use an expressive voice tone and inflection matures. Because they are somewhat egocentric in their language use, they make ambiguous statements at times. For example, a child of this age might say, "I wanna go there" with no referent for *there*. From her perspective, she knows where *there* is, but it does not occur to her that you do not know.

Literacy. Young children who, beginning in infancy have had regular and frequent literacy experiences (e.g., reading and storytelling, conversations with others) will begin demonstrating some print literacy skills in their native language during this period. Many will engage in nonconventional writing. Writing appears on a developmental continuum as children represent their thoughts via pictures, scribbling, strings of familiar letters, and eventually invented spelling. At the level of invented spelling, young children are using their knowledge of letter sounds as they create words. They now have graphophonemic awareness, which means they can match letters with their sounds.

During this period, many children begin developing phonemic awareness. This means they can reflect on units of spoken language that are smaller than syllables. For example, children who know that the words *hat*, *cat*, and *rat* sound a bit

Table 6.1	Appropriate Behaviors for Early Childhood Educators Working with Children 3- to 5 Years Old

What 3-to 5-Year-Old Children Do		What Early Childhood Educators Do
Language	Overgeneralize language rules. Vocabulary is rapidly expanding. Print literacy may begin emerging. Are developing conceptual understanding.	Model conventional language and expand vocabulary by using words in context. Provide many experiences with books, songs, finger plays, poems, and other literacy materials. Provide many opportunities for social interaction to give children opportunities to expand language. Provide interesting, relevant topics of study.
Cognitive	Learn by doing. Generally view the world from their unique point of view but are beginning to take the perspective of others. Overgeneralize conceptual understanding. Are developing symbolic thought. Memory is not fully developed.	Provide hands-on, minds-on activities with fluid and solid materials. Provide opportunities to see another's point of view through stories and careful monitoring of social interactions. Provide topics of study that reflect their immediate world. Provide opportunities for constructive and pretend play. Engage them in memory games and classroom jobs that use their memories at an appropriate level.
Social/ Emotional	Begin to develop true friendships. They function best in small groups. Overestimate both capabilities and failures. Have a fragile self-concept.	Provide many small group activities where children can learn social skills as they interact with peers. Mediate conflicts and teach socially appropriate behavior. Avoid competitive games. Use small cooperative groups. Give them meaningful tasks that are challenging yet within their abilities to be successful. Capitalize on what children can do rather than what they cannot do.
Physical	Have not yet developed precise control of hand muscles. Can sit only for brief periods of time.	Provide fine motor activities like painting and molding with clay. Avoid tedious activities like writing unless children show readiness and desire. Limit sitting to short periods of time. Alternate active and quiet activities.

Adapted from Bredekamp, S., & Copple, C. (Eds). (1997). *Developmentally appropriate practice in early childhood programs* (revised ed.). Washington, DC: National Association for the Education of Young Children.

different are demonstrating phonemic awareness. Acquisition of phonemic awareness is purely auditory and should not be confused with graphophonemic awareness. By the time children enter kindergarten, it is not unusual for many of them to have developed awareness of print conventions:

▶ Knowledge that print rather than pictures carries the message in books.

▶ The ability to identify the front and back of a book.

▶ The ability to recognize and even write their names.

▶ Letter/sound knowledge or graphophonemic awareness.

Activities that optimally support oral and print literacy development include opportunities to use language in context, to listen to stories, to examine books independently, and to enjoy songs, poems, and finger plays.

Cognitive Development

Learn by Doing. Three- to 5-year-old children learn and operate from personal experiences. They learn by doing and need many active experiences with objects and people in order to develop skills and learn about their world. For example, they will understand the word *rough* as it relates to a surface because they can experience a surface by touching it. However, the word *rough* used more abstractly to refer to a "rough day" may not be understood by children of this age. Thus, activities that optimally support development provide opportunities for children to manipulate objects and think about what they are doing. Early childhood educators provide guidance during these activities by talking with them.

Symbolic Thinking. Three- to 5-year-olds are developing as abstract thinkers. As we discussed in Chapter 4, symbolic thought, or the ability to mentally represent things, is manifest in their language and their play. You might wish to visit an early childhood setting and compare the language skills and the sociodramatic play of a 3-year-old and a 5-year-old. Try to describe the differences between their use of words and their symbolic representations during play.

Egocentrism. Until the last part of the 20th century, early childhood scholars viewed 3- to 5-year-old children as quite egocentric. More recently, scholars have noted that, while 3- to 5-year-old children still view the world from their own point of view, they are increasingly able to take the perspective of others. For example, Borke (1975) found that when 3-year-olds were asked to show rather than draw what a doll was looking at, they could take the doll's perspective. In other words, the lesser demands of the response, show rather than draw, enabled them to demonstrate perspective taking.

Early childhood educators can support children's developing perspective taking skills. Mediating conflict in supportive ways and inviting children to share their various perspectives supports their developing ability to acknowledge the point of view of others. Discussions around stories and picture books also provide opportunities for children to take the perspective of another.

Information Processing. Think back to your childhood days. Do you have more detailed memories of your school years or your preschool years? You most likely answered with your school years. This is because the capacity to store and retrieve information is not fully developed in 3- to 5-year olds. Children of this age can generally retain two to three chunks of information in their short-term memories. However, they do not have well-developed strategies for transferring information to long-term memory and

Laura Dwight Photography.

storing it so that it can be retained. Isabelle exemplified this during our visit to her preschool. We could not help but notice her excitement as she brought in the snack for the day. "It's grapes and watermelon and cheese!" she proudly announced. Two hours later, story time was ending and the teacher asked Isabelle, "What did you bring for our snack today?" Isabelle answered, "Uhmmm, wait, I gotta go look."

Reasoning. Over the years from age 3 to age 5, children's reasoning abilities mature. At age 3, children reason from the particular to the particular (my dog is friendly, so yours must be too), overgeneralize concepts (all four legged, furry animals are dogs), and create illogical relationships (my mom's car is bigger than my dad's so it must be faster) (Bredekamp & Copple, 1997). By age 5, children's thinking has become more logical. For example, 5-year-olds will look beyond merely four-legged and furry to differentiate between dogs, cats, horses, cows, or any animals they have experienced.

Elizabeth Crews.

The ability for children in this age group to conserve volume and mass is limited. Try giving a preschool age child some clay and ask him to roll it into a ball. Then ask him to flatten it into a pancake, and ask if there is more clay now. If he is not yet able to conserve mass, he will say there is more clay now. Try the same experiment by asking the child to pour water from a short glass into a tall glass. If he does not conserve volume, he will say there is more water when it is poured into the tall glass.

Children learn to conserve volume and mass through many experiences with fluid materials. Some children have more experiences than others, and researchers (Price-Williams, Gordon, & Ramirez, 1969) found this has implications related to children's ability to conserve. Returning to the clay example, young children in Mexico who lived in pottery-making families were better able to conserve mass than a group of children who did not live in pottery-making families. Perhaps this is because they observed their parents working with clay and estimating amounts of clay for different sized pots. It may also be that these parents notice quantity and emphasize estimation of quantity in their daily lives (Trawick-Smith, 1997).

Social–Emotional Development

Friendships. Three- to 5-year-old children increasingly enjoy interaction with peers and are capable of developing ongoing friendships. They are learning the *give and take* nature of true friendship, and are learning to share and wait for a turn.

They will reject friends, too. Three-year-olds often reject peers with physical aggression, but by age 5, children's language has developed to a level that they are more able to address conflicts with words. For example, a 5-year-old may threaten to end a friendship or leave another out of an activity. You have probably heard a child say, "You can't come to my birthday party," or "I won't be your friend anymore."

Cooperative. Children of this age are developing a strong sense of cooperation. They enjoy group games and activities. They enjoy dramatic play and can often be heard negotiating roles and scenarios for their play.

Generalize Capabilities. Children age 3 to 5 years old are developing so rapidly that they often can do something today that they could not do yesterday. On this basis, children see themselves as highly capable and tend to overgeneralize their capabilities. If they are successful at something, they become confident that they will always be successful at the particular task. Similarly, if they are unsuccessful at something, they may become easily discouraged about their capability. For example, when a child successfully kicks the soccer ball to the appropriate teammate, she begins building a sense of competence as a soccer player. Conversely, if she runs to kick it and misses, she may decide that she will never be a good soccer player. Considering this, competitive games where children are identified as *winners* and *losers* should be avoided for young children of this age.

As early childhood educators, we must be cautious not to have expectations for children that are beyond their developmental levels. If they do not meet the expectations, they may decide they will never measure up. This is accomplished by focusing on what individual children can do and building learning experiences from there.

Physical Development

Gross Motor Development. Children age 3 to 5 years old have lots of energy and need to be active. They enjoy active games and opportunities to use their developing gross motor skills. They can jump, climb, run, and walk forward and backward and, by age 5, most can skip. They enjoy jumping over and crawling under things. Activities that require the child to sit for a length of time should be relevant, meaningful, interesting, and brief.

Fine Motor Development. While children's fine motor skills are developing, tedious tasks like writing and cutting on the lines are difficult, even for many 5-year-olds. However, their muscles will continue to develop as they use them to paint, mold with clay, use constructive materials (e.g., Duplos, Legos, blocks), and so on. In addition, their binocular vision is still developing, so seeing things at a distance will be tedious and difficult.

Symbolic Play. We discussed children's play in Chapter 4 and highlighted its significant contribution to development. Recall that prior to age 3, symbolic representations used in play are fairly realistic because young children cannot stretch their thinking to represent reality with unrealistic objects. Around the age of 3, pretend or symbolic play becomes richer and more elaborate as children begin to use unrealistic objects to represent reality (Piaget, 1962). For example, a child might use a cardboard box as a bed or a paper towel roll as a hairbrush.

During the period from age 3 to 5 years, symbolic play (observed in dramatic play) gradually matures, to peak around age 6. Children become increasingly proficient at creating coherent themes and sharing the symbolic meaning of objects. By age 5, they can be observed carrying out fairly complex and lengthy playtime episodes.

⟩ Programs for Three- to Five-Year-Olds

Recall from previous chapters that there was an increase in preschool and kindergarten programs during the last half of the 20th century. There were three primary reasons for this shift:

1. There was an increase in the number of mothers in the workforce.

2. Preschool and kindergarten programs were viewed by many early childhood scholars and educators, as well as politicians, as a means of closing the achievement gap between children living in poverty and those from middle- and upper-class families.

3. With the focus on accountability that began in the 1970s, preschool and kindergarten were viewed as a way to give children an early start on school.

Some states now offer voluntary public prekindergarten education for all 4-year-olds. For example, in 2002, the state of Florida passed a constitutional amendment to create voluntary universal prekindergarten programs, and since the fall of 2005, 4-year-olds in Florida have had the option of attending those programs.

Several prekindergarten programs, or curriculum models, exist today. These models primarily serve prekindergarten children ages 3–5 years although some continue through the primary grades and even into middle school. Typically, kindergarten is part of formal schooling, but in some programs, Waldorf, Montessori, and High/Scope, for example, children can attend kindergarten where they attended preschool.

Table 6.2 provides a brief overview of some programs and their major emphases. As you read about these programs, look for any common elements among them. For example, is play valued? In what ways do their characteristics reflect what we know about young children and their development?

Head Start

Established in 1965, Head Start has a long history as a comprehensive, federally funded preschool program serving children living in poverty. It is the only national program of its type. Focused on the whole child, Head Start programs today provide a comprehensive early experience that addresses early education, parent and community involvement, and health care for 3- to 5-year-olds. Head Start agencies provide services in the areas of education, early childhood development, health care, dental care, nutrition, and mental health. It is intended to, literally, give young children a "head start" on

Table 6.2	Programs for 3- to 5-Year-Olds	
Program	**Philosophical Approach**	**Major Emphases**
Head Start	Eclectic	Address the needs of the whole child Multicultural education Address family needs and services Collaboration with the community
High/Scope	Constructivism	Engage children in active learning experiences Balance child-directed activities with teacher-directed activities Plan–do–review
Bank Street	Constructivism	Active learning Integrated curriculum Social competence
Reggio Emilia	Constructivism	Children's interests guide curriculum development Art is paramount in the curriculum Children and adults are co-learners
Waldorf	Maturationism	Childhood should not be rushed Mixed-age groups Homelike atmosphere Multisensory curriculum
Montessori	Brain-based Development	Prepared environment Self-correcting materials Follow children's interests Sensory stimulation Independent activity

school readiness. Head Start is overseen by the Head Start Bureau, the Administration for Children and Families, U.S. Department of Health and Human Services. It is administered at the local level so that diverse community needs can be met.

Long-term evaluations of Head Start suggest that the program helps close the achievement gap between children living in poverty and their more advantaged peers (Children's Defense Fund, 2005). The *Focus on Children* highlights the research base on the importance of such programs for children living in poverty.

There are eligibility requirements for Head Start programs. At least 90% of families served by Head Start must be living at or below the federal poverty level. In 2005, that meant that a family of three living on $16,090 annual income or less was eligible. Moreover, at least 10% of the slots must go first to children with disabilities (Children's Defense Fund, 2005).

All Head Start programs must comply with federal performance standards which are intended to:

▶ Provide young children with health and developmental screenings.

▶ Provide nutritious meals and information for families about nutrition.

▶ Provide developmentally appropriate learning experiences.

▶ Strengthen families as nurturers of young children.

▶ Connect families to services in the community.

▶ Involve parents in decision making.

Multiculturalism is a major focus of the performance standards for Head Start classrooms. Considerations related to respect for gender, religious, class, ethnic, and language diversity are key to curriculum planning and preparing the learning environment. Head Start teachers and staff are expected to model and teach respect for difference.

Focus on Children

Owing to limited family resources, young children living in poverty have different life experiences than their more affluent counterparts. For example, low-income families may not have the financial resources to acquire newspapers, books, and magazines. In general, low-income parents are less educated than middle- and upper-income parents and may not value reading as a worthwhile activity. They are less likely to engage their children in language-rich conversations and are unable to provide many experiences through travel. Parental work schedules and limited resources may make participation in community events challenging. Although children from low-income families may have many practical skills when they enter school, they usually have less developed prereading skills and academic abilities than their more affluent peers.

Although scholars are not in complete agreement about the benefits of preschool programs to later reading achievement for children living in poverty, some general, research-based statements can be made.

• Participation in quality preschool programs leads to increased cognitive abilities and later reading achievement.

• As reading achievement persists, gains in math and language achievement are also present.

• Persistent gains in later reading achievement are not accompanied by persistent gains in cognitive abilities and IQ.

• Early gains in cognitive abilities may be manifest in many ways due to their effect on motivation, expectations, opportunities to learn, school behavior, and achievement.

• Most child care programs have relatively small effects.

• Highly intensive, full-day, year-round preschool education has the greatest long-term impact on cognitive and academic gains for children living in poverty.

• Lesser funded programs have less impact on later reading achievement than do better funded programs.

Source: Barnett, W. S. (2001). Preschool education for economically disadvantaged children: Effects on reading achievement and related outcomes. In S. B. Neuman & D. K. Dickinson (Eds.), *Handbook of early literacy research.* New York: Guilford Press.

In order to address the cycle of poverty, parent involvement and services for families are components of Head Start programs. Through home visits and other educational activities, parents become educated on how to support their children's growth and development in the home. They are encouraged to volunteer in their child's Head Start classroom. They are also provided with information on available community services, including language and health services, adult education, crisis intervention, and job training.

Health care is a component of Head Start programs. Children are screened for visual, hearing, and language delay, and nutritious meals are provided, often breakfast and lunch. Children receive immunizations, and their dental and mental health care needs are addressed. The *Window into the Classroom* takes you into a Head Start classroom.

High/Scope

In Chapter 2, we discussed the origin of the High/Scope approach to early childhood education. Following the War on Poverty in the 1960s, the High/Scope Educational Research Foundation was founded in 1970 by David P. Weikart to address the needs of preschool children living in poverty. Since its inception, it has been researched and found to support children's long-term achievement gains. It has been expanded to include programs for infants, toddlers, kindergarteners, and primary grade children, and is used throughout the United States and other countries.

Window into the Classroom

As we enter the Head Start classroom of 4- and 5-year-olds, we are welcomed by the director, Jan. Looking around the room, we notice many activities, each overseen by an adult. Some of the adults in the room are volunteers (parents and community members), whereas others are Head Start teachers.

One small group of children has just finished listening to a dentist talk about good dental hygiene. After they swish fluoride in their mouths (a regular activity), each is given a toothbrush to take home. Another group is listening to a story being read in Spanish. The third group is manipulating objects of various textures and their teacher is helping them use descriptive words as they talk about them. Yet another teacher is talking with a parent about bus schedules and encouraging her to use the bus service to take her children to story time at the library and to check out books.

Each of these activities reflects Head Start goals. Children receive education and experiences related to good health and hygiene. They enjoy developmentally appropriate learning experiences, and parents are educated about appropriate learning experiences. Parents also learn about community resources and how to access them.

Jan talked about her Head Start program. In terms of families, Jan explained that her program serves families in various circumstances. Some are temporarily poor because their parents are in school, some have immigrated to the United States to find a better life for their families, while others are part of intergenerational poverty and have not been able to break the cycle. Needs among these families vary. Some parents struggle to balance the responsibilities of school, work, and children. Others may be challenged by language differences or by inadequate job skills. Some may have difficulty trusting others and may not be open to new ideas. Jan explained, "We are very sensitive to the needs of families. We try to connect parents with employment and educational opportunities."

Jan also expressed sensitivity to the children's needs. "We do not use *sharing time* as a language and socialization activity. We feel that bringing toys puts undue pressure on families and children to buy and have toys. I don't even think sharing time accomplishes its intended goal which is language development; it becomes a boring conversation with the teacher and child." Jan notes that they prefer *show and teach* or *author's chair* as opportunities for children to share in front of the group. "This gives children the opportunity to describe and show to their peers a new skill they have learned or to share a story they have created."

In addition to the culture of low-income, Head Start children represent various ethnic cultures. Jan noted, "We let the parents take the lead in that we ask them what they would appreciate to represent their culture in our environment and lessons. We have parents help us label items in our room in their home language."

Key Experiences. Activities and curriculum in High/Scope programs reflect an active learning philosophy grounded in the constructivist theory. Active engagement and social interaction are important. Active learning in High/Scope programs focuses on key experiences that address social–emotional, physical, and cognitive development. The categories of key experiences (Hohmann & Weikart, 1995) are

- ▶ Creative representation
- ▶ Language and literacy
- ▶ Initiative and social relations
- ▶ Movement
- ▶ Music
- ▶ Classification
- ▶ Number
- ▶ Seriation
- ▶ Space
- ▶ Time

Child-Directed Activities. A fundamental characteristic of High/Scope programs is child-directed activities where children are organized in small groups to interact with people and materials. Early childhood educators are central to the child-directed learning environment because they facilitate learning by arranging interest areas, providing hands-on activities, and talking with children to extend their thinking. For example, children at a block center decide what they wish to construct and how they will construct it. Educators facilitate the process by providing enough materials to invite creative thinking, helping the children negotiate the task, and posing open-ended questions like, "What do you think might happen if you used the big blocks instead of the small ones?"

Many child-directed activities in High/Scope programs follow a process developed by the founders of High/Scope, called *plan–do–review*. Teachers use each phase of the plan–do–review process to observe and assess children in terms of a particular key experience.(Hohmann, Banet, & Weikart, 1979):

- ▶ Planning time. Children decide what they will do and share their idea with a teacher who helps them elaborate the idea. The teacher records the plan and helps the children get started.

Laura Dwight Photography.

▶ Work time. Children carry out the plan as teachers move among them, assisting and supporting their activities.

▶ Recall time. Children meet in small groups with a teacher to recall or reflect on what they did.

Teacher-Directed Activities. Teachers guide activities during circle time and outdoor play. During circle time, teachers lead children in songs and movement, and help them share special news they might have (e.g., a new sister). Outdoor play incorporates large muscle activities. Assessment through observation and related to key experiences is ongoing.

Bank Street

In Chapter 2, we introduced Lucy Sprague Mitchell, a follower of John Dewey, who founded the Bureau of Educational Experiments. Today, it is Bank Street College of Education, home of the Family Center which provides special education and child care for children 6 months to 4 years of age. It also houses the School for Children which functions as a laboratory school for children ages 3 to 13. Bank Street College of Education provides information on best practices for teaching children by implementing projects to address contemporary needs of children and families.

The Bank Street philosophy reflects the work of Dewey and Mitchell, who promoted learning through direct experience with a positive sense of self being the paramount goal. The general goal of Bank Street School for Children is to help children develop individually, socially, and creatively.

Programs at Bank Street School for Children acknowledge the developmental continuum of children's growth. Early childhood educators support children's growth by working as facilitators of learning; they guide hands-on activities and support dialogue and discussion (Bank Street College of Education, 2003).

Curriculum at Bank Street is based primarily on activities of daily living. For example, children enjoy dramatic play around familiar themes like house or restaurant. They choose from activities that provide opportunities to explore materials and interact with others. Through the integrated curriculum children enjoy songs, art, and stories as they examine social systems (Bank Street College of Education, 2003).

Reggio Emilia

We discussed Reggio Emilia schools for infants and toddlers in Chapter 5 and turn now to schools for children ages 3 to 6. Grounded in constructivist philosophy, Reggio Emilia schools acknowledge that children must reconstruct or rediscover their own truth through interesting activities. The Reggio philosophy embraces Dewey's theory that children learn through their experiences as they continually reconstruct them, and Vygotsky's concept of the zone of proximal development which states that social interaction supports individual growth (Rankin, 2004). Reggio educators view children as curious constructors of knowledge who learn best when they are actively engaged with materials, their environment, other children, and adults. The general characteristics of Reggio schools are as follows:

▶ Parents are involved in their child's learning.

▶ Children and teachers collaboratively engage in inquiry projects as they learn about their world.

▶ The curriculum is emergent.

▶ Creativity, especially through art, is prominent.

▶ Children are encouraged to express their ideas and feelings.

▶ The entire community is the classroom.

▶ Teachers usually stay with the same group of children for 3 years.

▶ Teachers work as co-teachers.

In Reggio schools, children are viewed as competent beings who bring knowledge and skills to learning activities. Two early childhood educators work as co-teachers in a classroom of 25 children. They serve as collaborators rather than leaders as they engage with the children in inquiry projects that epitomize the integrated curriculum. As projects develop, adults and children continually exchange ideas (Hendrick, 2004).

The mutuality of roles between teachers and children should not be misunderstood. Teachers do not merely wait for children to express interest and then follow along. The curriculum is initiated from children's interests and teachers brainstorm possible ways to investigate topics of interest. The various possibilities are proposed to children, discussed, modified, and subsequently discarded or pursued (Hendrick, 2004). The inquiry that follows will include many materials (including books), excursions, and social interaction. For example, children might draw their ideas, listen to relevant stories, visit the real thing, observe closely, and discuss their observations. Then, they return to the predrawing and compare their initial idea to their findings (Hendrick, 2004). Teachers document children's thinking with observational notes, photographs, and children's work.

Reggio Emilia schools place great emphasis on art. An *atelierista*, a person trained in the arts, is a member of the staff who teaches artistic techniques in the context of children's projects.

Waldorf

Grounded in the ideas of Rudolf Steiner (Chapter 2), the Waldorf schools can be found worldwide. Waldorf schools reflect the maturationist theory of child development. Like Steiner, Waldorf early childhood educators believe that childhood should be highly valued and not rushed. Waldorf schools have a homelike feeling where children are configured in mixed-age groups and stay with the same teacher throughout their experience. The Waldorf school curriculum is multisensory and children's individual needs, strengths, and interests are acknowledged. The learning environment is structured to meet the learners at their developmental levels.

PhotoDisc/Getty Images, Inc.

Characteristics of Waldorf preschools and kindergartens are as follows:

▶ Indoor and outdoor play.

▶ Crafts, stories, and songs.

▶ A de-emphasis on academics in prekindergarten and kindergarten.

▶ Learning happens during routine tasks such as cooking where teachers model and children assist.

In early childhood, play is at the heart of the curriculum as children think creatively, negotiate, and problem solve in the context of their play. Many play materials come from the natural environment (e.g., wood pieces, seashells). Children also enjoy nature walks, movement activities, and creative expression with art media. The language arts curriculum includes reading and storytelling, puppets, songs, and poems.

Montessori

In 1960, the American Montessori Society (AMS) was started by Dr. Nancy Mc-Cromick Rambusch at the Whitby School in Greenwich, Connecticut. Its mission was to promote the Montessori philosophy in the context of American life. This group initiated a teacher education program at Xavier University in Ohio where teacher candidates went to learn Montessori principles and practices. Montessori teacher education programs have grown over the past years.

Contemporary American Montessori schools are grounded in the theory and beliefs of Maria Montessori and reflect the principles she set forth (Chapter 2). Montessori's philosophy is primarily aligned with the brain-based development theory of learning. Most Montessori schools serve children ages 3–5. However, there are programs that serve toddlers as well as children ages 6–9 and 9–12.

Window into the Classroom

Ginny has been a Montessori teacher for over 20 years. She earned a bachelor's degree in elementary education and then completed a Montessori training program that involved an intensive summer session followed by a 1-year internship with a certified Montessori teacher. Activities in Ginny's school reflect Maria Montessori's view of development and the early childhood educator's role in meeting the developmental needs of children. In Ginny's school, teachers observe children so they can prepare an environment that stimulates their development, children work at their own pace with sensory materials, and early childhood educators follow the lead of the children.

Today, there are two head teachers and two assistants, in addition to Ginny, with a mixed age group of 17 children (2 $\frac{1}{2}$ to 5 years old). The children are engaged in free choice time. Three young girls are building with blocks, each with a rug for her construction. Another is at the computer while another is working with lacing cards. One teacher is playing Concentration on the floor with a group and several boys are cutting shapes and decorating them. Three children are looking at books inside a tepee. As they feel inclined, children leave their activity for the snack table to enjoy oranges, carrots, and a cookie. During free choice, early childhood educators frequently pick up clipboards to record observational information.

There is a large picture on the wall of Native Americans featured in indigenous dress reflecting various geographical locations across the nation. The choice of a tepee for the reading center also reflects this theme. The theme was chosen when the children raised questions concerning Native Americans after hearing about them in stories related to Columbus Day and Thanksgiving. Consistent with Montessori principles, Ginny supported their development by following the interest of the children. She gathered resources for them to learn more about Native Americans.

Following an hour of free choice play, the children meet in a large group on the floor where they have language and movement activities for about 15 minutes. Other large group activities include exploration projects (examining leaves in the fall, for example) and outdoor play. Large group activities are much shorter than free choice time where children select their activity and advance at a pace that is comfortable for them.

Montessori educators believe:

▶ Children should be actively engaged in spontaneous activity.

▶ Children need freedom of choice.

▶ Children are sensitive to sensory stimulation.

▶ The children's needs dictate the learning experiences provided.

Through careful observation, teachers prepare an environment that captures children's interest, stimulates their senses, and actively engages them with appealing materials. Tactile and didactic materials are used to support motor, sensory, and language development. The materials are sequenced according to complexity and support children's independence because they are self correcting. For example, if the *brown stairs* are not arranged in proper order, they do not look like stairs. Table 6.3 describes selected Montessori materials for preschool and kindergarten age children designed to support learning through the senses and development of their independence as learners. Traditionally, play was less prominent in Montessori schools than in others we have discussed; however, today, you will see children enjoying sociodramatic play in a Montessori school.

In Montessori schools, children are encouraged to move at their own pace as they choose activities. The educator's role is to unobtrusively guide learning by preparing the environment and then observing children in it. The educators' work is cyclical as they observe children, prepare an environment that meets their developmental needs, introduce the materials, and again observe children as they interact with them.

Initially, Montessori schools functioned in isolation from other early childhood programs, but today they are much more aligned. In 2002, the American Montessori Society and the National Association for the Education of Young Children completed negotiations for joint accreditation of early childhood programs. This collaborative effort situates Montessori schools more noticeably within the broader early childhood community. The *Window into the Classroom* takes you into a classroom that reflects a typical day in a contemporary Montessori school.

Table 6.3	Examples of Montessori Materials That Stimulate the Senses

Name	Description
Brown stairs	Ten wooden blocks differ in thickness so that when arranged in a row, they resemble a stairway. Children develop visual discrimination skills.
Red rods	Ten red rods vary in length with each being 1 centimeter longer than the last. Children develop visual discrimination skills.
Smelling jars	Jars made of nontransparent glass are filled with materials. Children cannot see into the jars but match jars with like substances by using the sense of smell.
Fabric box	Children use their sense of touch to pair fabrics that feel alike.
Cylinder blocks	These blocks progress in diameter and height for visual discrimination and have knobs on the top to develop the pencil grip.
Knobless cylinders	Children progress from the cylinders with knobs to those without.

Teaching Antibias Attitudes

It is important to begin teaching antibias attitudes when children are young. Because children 3 to 5 years old understand their world from their direct experiences, antibias teaching is best integrated into children's daily activities.

Similarities and Differences. Children have many similarities and differences in their appearance, interests, strengths, talents, daily activities, and family practices. By age 3, they have begun to notice similarities and differences among people. High-quality early childhood educators help children see that differences enrich our human existence.

Using children's personal experiences as a point of reference, early childhood educators facilitate discussions that assist children to learn about others and how people are alike and different. Children recognize differences by talking about such things as skin color, hair color, strengths, talents, and so on. Actual photos of the children and their families will support discussion of similarities and differences.

Classroom Environment. Play props, wall displays, and classroom guests that reflect diversity across gender, class, ability, ethnicity, and religion help young children learn about and value difference. For example, include faces of many shapes and colors on bulletin boards. Depict people in wheelchairs, wearing glasses, skullcaps, or veils, engaged in productive activities. Include dolls with various skin colors in the dramatic play center. This is particularly important in classrooms with homogeneous groups of children who may not experience diversity in their daily lives.

Crayons and paint of various shades of flesh tones can be purchased with such appealing names as "peach," "mahogany," and "cinnamon." Tempera paint and play dough can be mixed to represent many skin colors. Help children match the colors to their individual skin colors as they are doing art projects.

Excluding Others. Children must learn that it is unacceptable for them to exclude others based on gender, ethnicity, religion, ability, or class. When this happens, early childhood educators must intervene immediately. Derman-Sparks (1989) suggests the following:

- ▶ *Comfort or support the targeted child.* Help the target child verbalize his feelings to the discriminator rather than accept being a victim (e.g., "I don't like it when you won't let me play").

- ▶ *Determine the real reason for the conflict.* The discriminator may have had a reason not related to the child's identity for excluding (e.g., she wanted to be the fire chief and the victim already had the appropriate hat). Help the child realize why she excluded another and what she could do instead (e.g., take turns being the fire chief, have two fire chiefs).

- ▶ Multiple incidents may indicate children are being excluded because of prejudice. In this case, children need to learn that exclusion is unacceptable. Children must know that, "In this classroom, it is not okay to refuse to play with someone because he has a brace" (is black, is a boy, etc.). Talk with the excluder's family and enlist their cooperation.

Sometimes what is valued in the early childhood setting is inconsistent with a particular family's values (as evidenced by the child's behavior). For example, some parents may not allow their child to play with a child of color or with a child with a disability. As a teacher, you should respond in two ways. One, gently try to educate parents to be more tolerant. Often bigotry is the result of miseducation and limited experience with those who are different. Second, explain to parents that your central focus is on creating a safe, nurturing early childhood environment, not changing their family values.

Literature. There are many children's books on the market, appropriate for children 3 to 5 years old, that depict the human existence in various ways. They can be used to generate discussion to raise children's awareness of similarities and differences. For example, *Families Are Different* by Pellegrini depicts an interracial family.

As with toddlers (Chapter 5), early childhood educators should continue to acknowledge children's questions about gender. Building on their developing understanding of gender, it is important to teach that gender (or ethnicity, etc.) does not preclude people from doing things. That is, women can be firefighters, men can cook dinner, and so on. Table 6.4 provides examples of picture books to help dispel gender stereotypes.

Child Care

Almost three in every four mothers of children under the age of 18 participate in the U.S. workforce (Children's Defense Fund, 2005). Infants, toddlers, and preschool children are in need of quality child care, and many young school-age children are in need of before or after school care while their parents work. Child care is regulated at the state level, so regulations vary across the nation. The National Child Care Information Center (http://www.nccic.org/) has a link titled State Profiles that provides information about licensing requirements by state. Additional links provide demographic information by state and requirements for credentials of early childhood care professionals.

Types of Child Care

Various types of child care are available. Although parents' selection for child care is most often governed by cost and location, some parents have other criteria. For example, some prefer the family atmosphere of home child care; others prefer a program affiliated with their religious faith, and so on.

Center Based Child Care

A child care center is a specially designed facility for large numbers of children. The maximum number of children permitted to attend at one time is usually determined by the ages of the children, the square footage of indoor and outdoor space,

Table 6.4	**Picture Books to Dispel Gender Stereotypes**

Title	Author	Annotation
The Paper Bag Princess	Robert Munsch	The princess saves the rude prince from the dragon.
Daddy Makes the Best Spaghetti	Anna Grossnickle Hines	In a typical day for this family, daddy does many tasks traditionally done by mothers.
Young Amelia Earhart: A Dream to Fly	Susan Alcott	This is a picture book biography of the female pilot Amelia Earhart.
William's Doll	Charlotte Zolotow	William is teased because he wants a doll. His grandmother helps others understand that it is okay.
White Dynamite and Curly Kidd	Bill Martin Jr. and John Archambault	Curly Kidd is a cowboy who enjoys the rodeo with his child. This book has a surprise ending.

and the number of early childhood professionals employed at the center. Some provide custodial care while others provide preschool experiences that may or may not be modeled after the programs we have discussed in this chapter.

Since the need for child care has increased so extensively over the past decades, entrepreneurs are getting into the child care business for the purpose of making a profit. For-profit centers are owned by corporations, businesses, or individuals. Many provide early childhood education programs along with custodial care.

Employer Sponsored Care

Child care sponsored by employes is a phenomenon that emerged in the 1970s in response to increasing numbers of mothers entering the workforce. Many employers decided to subsidize child care as an employee benefit. This support might be in the form of a referral list, an on-site facility, or a subcontract with a child care center. In the case of the on-site facility or the subcontracted center, the employer often provides financial support for child care.

Home Child Care

Some child care is provided in the home of a licensed caregiver. In home care settings, children are usually in mixed-age groups, but the number of children at each age level (e.g., infants, toddlers, preschool, school age) is regulated. Caregivers may have to include their own children in the adult/child ratio. These regulations vary from state to state and are based on the age of the caregiver's children and the amount of time they are in the home during child care hours.

Church or Temple Care Centers

Many child care centers and kindergarten programs are housed in churches or temples within communities; however, not all provide religious education. Some early childhood settings are established for the purpose of teaching religion along with other aspects of the curriculum. In other cases, the church or temple rents space for child care and the religious affiliation of the location has little or no influence on the program.

Nannies

Many parents choose to have care for their children provided in their own home, and this is the most expensive child care option. Most often, it is two working professional parents who employ nannies. The nanny, who may or may not live in the home, provides care only for the children living in the home, and may have additional cleaning and laundry duties. The International Nanny Association provides training for nannies.

Quality in Child Care

All children need experiences during their early years that promote healthy social, emotional, physical, and cognitive development. Quality child care supports our economy by making it possible for parents to work and by providing good learning experiences for the workforce of tomorrow. Low-income children are particularly in need of quality learning experiences as well as good nutrition and health care (Children's Defense Fund, 2005).

The quality of child care is regulated by individual states. The states develop and enforce regulations with regard to health and safety, adult/child ratio, and qualifications of personnel. However, state regulations do not always address standards for curriculum and practices in early childhood programs. The National Association for the Education of Young Children offers voluntary accreditation for child care centers, preschools, and programs for school-age children. Research indicates that accreditation correlates with improved quality of care by providing leadership and professional skills development (Eaton, 2002).

A major factor in quality of child care is the characteristics of the care providers. On the basis of research, early childhood educators are considered high-quality (Weaver, 2002) if they

▶ Voluntarily participate in health and safety program requirements.

▶ Are lifelong learners who seek opportunities to learn more about early childhood education and children's development.

▶ Have higher levels of psychological well-being.

▶ Are committed to quality care as demonstrated by planned, responsive care.

▶ Are connected to child care resources.

▶ Are financially sound. (p. 19)

Funding Quality Care

Even as we continue to learn about the importance of quality child care, the resources to support it are scarce. The cost of optimal facilities and highly trained employees cannot be absorbed totally by the consumers, many of whom are working just to meet the basic needs of the family. It is particularly difficult to find affordable care for infants, toddlers, children with disabilities, for after school care, and for parents who work weekends or odd hours (Children's Defense Fund, 2005).

Since 1990, the federal government has provided states with Child Care Development Block Grants (CCDBG) to assist with child care funding. The CCDBG program provides assistance for low-income families, for families receiving public assistance, and for those enrolled in job training or continuing education. Unfortunately, the CCDBG program has never been funded at the level needed to provide child care assistance to all eligible children. For example, in 2005, only one in seven eligible children actually received assistance (Children's Defense Fund, 2005).

Studies suggest that taxpayers get a strong return when they fund quality child care. The High/Scope Perry Preschool Longitudinal Study tracked children enrolled in high quality early childhood programs for 40 years. Findings suggested that for every $1 invested in quality early childhood programs for low-income children, taxpayers got a $17 return by increasing the likelihood that children would be literate and employed, and children were less likely to drop out of school, be on federal assistance, or engage in criminal activity. A study shorter in duration, the Abecedarian Early Intervention Project, found a return of $4 for each $1 invested (Children's Defense Fund, 2005).

Kindergarten

Recall from Part 1 of this text that kindergarten came about primarily to address the needs of children living in poverty. It was also viewed as a way to assimilate the young children of increasing numbers of immigrants into our society. During the era of WWII, many kindergartens were closed due to lack of resources, but they reopened in the prosperous post-WWII years.

Today, kindergarten is the first formal experience with schooling for young children. Although attendance is not required in nearly three-quarters of the states, a majority of children attend kindergarten. Although all states offer kindergarten, the shaded states in Figure 6.1 indicate those where children are required to attend.

Figure 6.1 States requiring kindergarten attendance.

As young children's first formal school experience, kindergarten has its unique issues. Over the past decades, there has been ongoing debate about retention, academic redshirting, transitional kindergarten and first grade, kindergarten entrance age, and full-day/half-day kindergarten.

Readiness

For the past several decades, most children in the United States have been attending kindergarten. Coupling kindergarten as the first public school experience with the emphasis during the past decades on accountability related to achievement, the issue of an individual child's readiness to begin school has become a focus. There are opposing beliefs about the requisite skills needed by children entering kindergarten and what the kindergarten experience should include. Two philosophies, maturationism and constructivism (Chapter 4), lie at the core of the readiness debate.

Maturationists subscribe to the notion that most children will eventually be ready for school if given time. If children are not ready for school, they should stay out for another year to gain maturity. Conversely, constructivists believe that schools need to be ready for the children by creating an optimal learning environment that adapts to the needs of each child. Constructivists believe that placing the responsibility on schools with financial resources and the accumulative knowledge of educators is a more palatable policy than placing the responsibility for readiness on the children.

Some children do not develop typically and have lower skill levels and abilities than their typically developing peers. Public schools are responsible for addressing the needs of these children. Educators have the resources and connections to community services to assist children with early intervention and support. The federal initiative IDEA (Chapter 3) requires programs to accommodate children with developmental delays and disabilities if appropriate. Scholars and educators agree that many children with delays and disabilities are best served in settings where they learn alongside their typically developing peers (DEC/CED, 1994).

Early childhood educators must be ready to use their knowledge to address the individual needs of each child and make needed adjustments in the learning environment, including the physical setting, the curriculum, and instructional strategies. Educators who are ready to meet the individual needs of children are those who have the following (Cassidy, Mims, Rucker, & Boone, 2003):

▶ Knowledge of children's growth and development.

▶ Knowledge of individual children.

▶ Knowledge of the social and cultural contexts in which individual children live.

▶ The ability to translate knowledge into developmentally appropriate practices.

⟩ Retention and Academic Redshirting

Academic redshirting and *retention* became common practices in kindergarten in response to increased demands for achievement and accountability that emerged in the late 20th century. "Redshirting" refers to the practice of delaying school entry for children whose birthdays occur close to the cutoff date for entry into kindergarten, and consequently who would be the youngest members of a kindergarten class. "Retention" refers to the practice of having children repeat a grade if they are not as developmentally or academically mature as their peers. These issues have been the focus of several studies and scholarly debate. Following are issues to consider regarding both practices.

Benefits Cannot Be Consistently Substantiated

There is no convincing evidence that either academic redshirting or retention provides long-term achievement gains (Graue, 2001; Graue & DiPerna, 2000; Johnson, Merrell, & Stover, 1990; Marshall, 2003). Children who are retained generally score lower on standardized measures than nonretained or redshirted children, and redshirted children score about the same as their nonredshirted peers (Graue & DiPerna, 2000). Moreover, any academic gains that appear early for redshirted or retained children disappear by third grade (Graue 2001; Graue & DiPerna; 2000; Johnson et al., 1990 Mantzicopoulos & Morrison, 1992; Marshall; 2003).

There is some indication that redshirting or retention may be differentially effective (Graue & DiPerna, 2000); however, what is unclear is a means to accurately determine who will and will not benefit. The best information we have is that it is more unlikely than likely that these practices have benefit for any individual child.

Sociocultural Issues

Academic Redshirting. Those children most commonly redshirted are Caucasian boys born in the last quarter of the year prior to the kindergarten entrance date (Graue & DiPerna, 2000). Parents may be advised by preschool teachers to hold their child out for a year, while others indicate that they want to advantage their sons in sports later. Also worthy of consideration is that little boys are not as frequently socialized in school behaviors (e.g., listening and sitting quietly) as are their female peers. This may account, at least in part, for the increased likelihood of preschool educators to recommend redshirting for boys more often than girls.

The practice of academic redshirting presents problems worth careful consideration. We have already noted one: If a child has a disability that is mistaken for immaturity, a precious year for early intervention is lost when the child is redshirted (Graue, 2001). Second, redshirting broadens the already wide range of abilities and needs within a given classroom of kindergarten children. As the skills gap among the children widens, teachers are increasingly challenged to meet the needs of all children as they plan instruction and develop curriculum.

Retention. Children most commonly retained in kindergarten and the primary grades are male children of color living in poverty (Graue, 2001; Graue & DiPerna, 2000). To complicate matters, many retainees have a poor attitude toward school (Marshall, 2003; Shepard & Smith, 1988) and are more likely to demonstrate behavior problems later in life (Graue & DiPerna, 2000). This suggests there is a cultural disconnect between the lives of some children and the expectations at school. It is a good example of the responsibility teachers must take for being prepared for the children. They must understand and acknowledge the cultural and individual natures of each child in the classroom and work to structure a learning environment that will meet their needs.

Developmental Kindergartens and Transitional First Grade

Developmental kindergartens and *transitional first grades* have become alternatives to retention and redshirting. Developmental kindergarten is designed for those children who are immature (usually the children turning 5 close to the entrance cutoff date) and might be redshirted. They do not have the knowledge and skill level of others entering kindergarten; thus, they attend a year of developmental kindergarten prior to entering regular kindergarten.

Similarly, transitional first grades are designed for children who, at the end of kindergarten, do not appear ready to succeed in the tasks of first grade. Both concepts reflect the maturationist theory that children need the gift of time.

Proponents of developmental kindergarten and transitional first grade see them as a more positive approach than redshirting or retention. Although children will spend an extra year in public school, they are promoted at the end of each year. Promotion may be from developmental kindergarten to kindergarten or from kindergarten to transitional first grade. After two years, the children in either case are in regular first grade. This practice still requires an extra year of school, and there is no conclusive evidence that the year is beneficial for children (Estok, 2005; Graue & DiPerna, 2000). Moreover, adding an additional year for some children uses resources that might be better used in other ways.

Entrance Age

Kindergarten entrance age has long been a topic of debate. Nearly one-half of the states require children to be 5 years old at or near September 1 in order to enter kindergarten. (Most states have cutoff dates between August 1 and mid-October.) Debate centers on the fact that it is often the youngest kindergarteners who demonstrate the lowest level of achievement. Given the 11 months age difference between a child who turned 6 in September of the kindergarten year and one who turned 6 in August following kindergarten, achievement differences should be expected. That is, the older child has had nearly 20% more lifetime to develop, so achievement differences are not surprising.

One means of addressing this issue has been to change the kindergarten entrance age so that children are older when they come to kindergarten; however, age seems to be a consistent factor because it is primarily the youngest children who are recommended for redshirting, retention, and transitional classrooms, regardless of entrance age policies. Changing the entrance age merely changes the age of the youngest children, so it is difficult to accept that as a solution.

An Alternative

The debate over academic redshirting and retention has polarized. It is as if children must be either delayed/retained or receive a social promotion; however, middle ground can be reached by changing their school experience without adding another year of school. Early childhood educators should identify the varied needs of children and respond accordingly. For example, if children have unusually low skill and achievement levels, consider their ages first. Perhaps they are younger than most of their peers. Then, explore appropriate interventions and adaptations in the learning environment before resorting to redshirting, retention, or transitional classrooms.

Half-Day/Full-Day Kindergarten

Today, kindergarten attendance for 5-year-olds is the norm. Most states require districts to offer kindergarten although less than one-third require children to attend. About one-fourth of the states require districts to make full-day kindergarten programs available, although all 50 states allow for extended or full-day programs.

Full-day kindergarten programs are most common in high poverty areas where federal funding for at-risk students is available to financially support the programs. They are popular in areas where children are in child care during the day anyway and may benefit from additional time in school.

Benefits and disadvantages of full-day kindergarten have been debated since their resurgence in the latter part of the 20th century. Central to the concerns of early childhood educators is the contrast between the developmental needs of 5-year-olds and the potential for full-day kindergarten to evolve into a more academic, developmentally inappropriate learning environment. On the other side of the debate is the increasing number of mothers in the workforce, which means more children are enrolled in out-of-home care. Some argue that if children are in out-of-home care, they might just as well be in school.

Research findings suggest that full-day kindergarten programs provide both academic and social benefits, at least through the primary grades (Denton, West, & Walston, 2003; Elicker & Mathur, 1997; Estok, 2005; Weiss & Offenberg, 2002). This is particularly true for children from high-poverty communities. Children who attended full-day kindergarten had:

- ▶ Higher achievement and standardized test scores.
- ▶ Better school attendance.
- ▶ Greater gains in literacy and language learning.
- ▶ Better social skills and self-confidence.

Clearly a major consideration with full-day programs is the cost. The teacher in one classroom who taught two classes in the half-day format will teach only one in a full-day format. That doubles the space and staff needed for a kindergarten program. However, the costs in terms of facilities and teachers will be partially offset by increased state aid for full-time students. Full-day kindergarten may also reduce future costs related to retention, transitional classrooms, and remedial education (Housden & Kam, 1992).

As the debate over half- or full-day programs continues, there is one central concern—what are children doing in school? Providing developmentally appropriate experiences is important in both half- and full-day programs. The *Window into the Classroom* provides a glimpse into a full-day kindergarten program.

Kindergarten Curriculum

The majority of kindergarten children have probably not yet completed the cognitive shift from preoperational to concrete operational thinking, at least at the time of school entrance. Thus, developmentally, kindergarteners are more like preschoolers than primary-grade children. Whether kindergarten programs are half-day or full-day programs, developmental appropriateness is a must. The characteristics of effective half-day or full-day programs include the following:

- ▶ Social interaction among teachers and children.
- ▶ Integrated curriculum.

Window into the Classroom

Isabel is a kindergarten teacher in a full-day program in an urban community. Until last year, she taught in a half-day kindergarten program but says she enjoys the full-day program more. "At first, I wasn't sure I'd like the full-day. But, I do like it; I don't feel like the day is so rushed anymore, and we get to do really interesting things. The children really handle the full day pretty easily, and I enjoy having half the number of children to get to know. This year, all but one would be in child care before or after school anyway; so, I think this is a good way for them to spend the day."

Around the perimeter of Isabel's classroom are five learning centers including blocks, dramatic play, art, writing, and books with a listening center. In the center are six round tables with room for four children to sit at each. Each table has shared materials (e.g., crayons, scissors, glue, and pencils) in the center, and each chair has a child's name on it.

It is 9:30 in the morning in Isabel's classroom and the children are enjoying self-selected activities at the small learning centers. Isabel is observing and interacting with the children, occasionally making notes on a clipboard. She explained, "When the children first arrive at school, we complete our weather chart and the calendar, and then have our class meeting. Because we've had some problems with sharing lately, we talked about it and role-played appropriate sharing behavior today at our class meeting. Then, we had language arts in small groups; I have two teacher's aids to help me with language arts instruction."

As the morning continued, the children had outdoor play, small group math instruction, and music. A guest from the community came in at 11:15 to read his favorite story to the class, after which they went to lunch in the school cafeteria.

After lunch, Isabel lead a shared reading activity where she read to the children from a big book (a book with print large enough that it can be easily seen as children sit in front of her on the floor) about frogs. As Isabel read, she occasionally paused to draw the children's attention to the print or photos in the book. They noted how the words flowed from left to right, that the pages were numbered in order, that the photos were things the print talked about, and that each sentence began with a capital letter.

The shared reading activity was designed to lead into their integrated unit study in the afternoon. The children had been exploring the world of pets, including kinds of pets and how to care for them. "This is my favorite time of the day," Isabel said. "I help children find books about pets or whatever we are studying. Then parent and community volunteers come in and read the books to the children in small groups. I think learning about their world through picture books helps children understand the purpose for reading and writing; and they are so interested when they select the books."

▶ Child-initiated activities.

▶ Small group and mixed-ability group configurations.

▶ Focus on social skill development.

▶ Assessment through observation and systematic data collection.

▶ Frequent parent communication.

▶ Skills instruction that builds on what children know and can do.

▶ Brief periods of skills instruction (less than 10 minutes).

 My Developing Professional View

Identify four or five things you feel should be considered when developing programs for 3- to 5-year-olds

SUMMARY

In this chapter, we have discussed the characteristics of young children age 3 to 5 years old as it relates to developmentally appropriate instruction. High-quality early childhood educators of 3- to 5-year-old children plan learning experiences that actively engage children in meaningful activities, are concrete, and build on what they already know about their world.

Over the past several decades, the number of children enrolled in preschool and kindergarten has increased, owing primarily to an increase in the number of mothers in the workforce, the needs of children living in poverty, and the need to prepare children for formal schooling in this time of accountability. In this chapter, we discussed several preschool and kindergarten programs with long, distinguished histories.

Child care is available in a variety of settings to meet the needs of families. Scholars have identified characteristics of quality child care and found that accreditation correlates with improved child care. A few political initiatives have emerged to assist families who use child care.

Children begin learning prejudiced attitudes when they are young, and it is important to foster antibias attitudes in young children. Owing to the nature of young children, such learning must stem from their daily experiences. High-quality early childhood educators capitalize on opportunities to teach tolerance in the context of daily activities.

As children's first experience with formal schooling, kindergarten has a unique set of issues that have been the center of debate over many years. These issues include retention, redshirting, readiness, entrance age, and full-day or half-day kindergarten programs. Opinions have polarized on many of these issues, raising the need for early childhood educators and scholars to seek middle ground as they work to meet the needs of all young children entering school.

⸖ Enrichment Activities

Individual Activities

1. Complete an observation in a preschool or kindergarten classroom. The observation should be long enough in duration to get a good sense of the philosophy of the program. Write a brief description of the classroom; then, discuss how you think the teacher meets the cultural and developmental needs of each child. Provide explicit examples to support your position.

2. Develop an annotated bibliography of picture books appropriate for children ages 3 to 5 years old that will support antibias teaching by presenting people with disabilities, people of color, males and females, people from all classes, and people from various religious traditions as contributing members of our society.

3. Access the website for the National Child Care Information Center (http://www.nccic.org/) to determine child care regulations in your state. How does a child care provider become licensed?

Cooperative Activity

4. Each member of your cooperative group will individually research a preschool program model (e.g., High/Scope, Head Start, Waldorf). Refer to Table 6.1 as a guide to decide how each reflects developmentally appropriate practice as set forth by NAEYC.

Advocacy Activities

5. Contact your state office of education to determine their position on kindergarten readiness. Analyze their position and determine whether the responsibility for readiness is placed primarily on the child or on the school. On the basis of your findings, write a thoughtful, reasoned letter to the state superintendent, curriculum coordinator, or another appropriate person commending the position or advocating a different one.

6. Write the federal legislators from your state and advocate for increased funding for Child Care Development Block Grants. Be sure you provide a strong rationale for your argument.

} FOR FURTHER READING

Child Care

Dombro, A. L. (2004). Child care on top of the world. *Young Children, 59*(1), 86–90.

Kontos, S., & Wilcox-Herzog, A. (2004). How do education and experience affect teachers of young children? In K. M. Paciorek & J. H. Munro (Eds.), *Annual editions: Early childhood education, 03/04.* Guilford, CT: McGraw-Hill/Dushkin.

Koralek, D. (2002). Meet Maryanne Lazarchick: An accredited family child care provider. *Young Children, 57*(1), 25–28.

Weaver, R. H. (2002). The roots of quality care: Strategies of master providers. *Young Children, 57*(1), 16–22.

Culture

Dever, M. T., & Barta, J. (1997, November/December). Giving thanks: Curricular opportunities for expanding young children's cultural awareness. *Social Studies and the Young Learner, 10*(2), 6–9.

Schmidt, P. R. (1998). *Cultural conflict and struggle: Literacy learning in a kindergarten program.* New York: Peter Lang.

Kindergarten

Cassidy, D. J., Mims, S., Rucker, L., & Boone, S. (2003). Emergent curriculum and kindergarten readiness. *Childhood Education, 79*(4), 194–199.

Ede, A. (2004). Is my child really too young for kindergarten? *Childhood Education, 80*(4), 207–208.

Estok, V. (2005). One district's study on the propriety of transition-grade classrooms. *Young Children, 60*(2), 28–31.

Harle, A. Z., & Trudeau, K. (2006). Using reflection to increase children's learning in kindergarten. *Young Children, 61*(4), 101–104.

Graue, E. (2001). Research in review: What's going on in the children's garden? Kindergarten today. *Young Children, 56*(3), 67–73.

Kato, Y., Honda, M., & Kamii, C. (2006). Kindergarteners play lining up the 5s: A card game to encourage logico-mathematical thinking. *Young Children, 61*(4), 82–88.

Marshall, H. H. (2003). Opportunity deferred or opportunity taken? An updated look at delaying kindergarten entry. *Young Children, 58*(5), 84–93.

Meier, D., & Schafran, A. (1999). Strengthening the preschool-to-kindergarten transition: A community collaborates. *Young Children, 54*(3), 40–46.

Miller, S. A. (2005). Reflections on kindergarten: Giving young children what they deserve. *Childhood Education, 81*(5), 256–260.

Preschool

Hainstock, E. G. (1986). *Essential Montessori: An introduction to the woman, the writings, the method, and the movement.* New York: New American Library.

Helm, J. H. (2003). Beyond the basics: Using the Project Approach in standards-based classrooms. *Dimensions of Early Childhood, 31*(3), 6–12.

Hendrick, J. (Ed). (2004). *Next steps toward teaching the Reggio way: Accepting the challenge to change* (2nd ed.). Upper Saddle River, NJ: Pearson Education.

Klein, A. S. (2002). Different approaches to teaching: Comparing three preschool program models. *Early Childhood News*, March/April, pp. 21–25.

Woyke, P. P. (2004). Hopping frogs and trail walks: Connecting young children to nature. *Young Children, 59*(1), 82–85.

Professional Development Resources

AMERICAN MONTESSORI SOCIETY

175 Fifth Avenue
New York, NY 10010

HEAD START BUREAU

Department of Health and Human Services
330 C Street SW
Room 2018
Washington, DC 20201
http://www.head-start.lane

HIGH/SCOPE EDUCATIONAL RESEARCH FOUNDATION

600 North River Street
Ypsilanti, MI 48198-2898
http://www.highscope.org

} SELF-ASSESSMENT

1. Describe the behaviors of an early childhood educator who uses developmentally appropriate practice in his/her early childhood setting. What does this educator do?

2. Select four characteristics of a 3- to 5-year-old that an early childhood educator should understand. Explain why awareness of these characteristics is important.

3. Select one of the models of early childhood education discussed in this chapter (e.g., Head Start, Reggio Emilia) and generally describe some of the activities you might see in that program.

4. Discuss some issues surrounding redshirting and retention in kindergarten.

5. Discuss the characteristics of an antibias learning environment for 3- to 5-year-olds. Give specific examples of antibias materials and teacher behaviors.

Scenario

You are a teacher in a full-day kindergarten program in a low SES school district. A parent comes to you and complains that she does not want her child in a full-day program. Provide a rationale for why such a kindergarten experience will not be harmful and may be beneficial to her child.

REFERENCES

Bank Street College of Education. (2003). Retrieved November 20, 2003 from http://www.bankstreet.edu/.

Barnett, W. S. (2001). Preschool education for economically disadvantaged children: Effects on reading achievement and related outcomes. In S. B. Neuman & D. K. Dickinson (Eds.) *Handbook of early literacy research*. New York: Guilford Press.

Bredekamp, S, & Copple, C. (Eds). (1997). *Developmentally appropriate practice in early childhood programs* (revised ed.). Washington, DC: National Association for Education of Young Children.

Borke, H. (1975). Piaget's mountains revisited: Changes in the egocentric landscape. *Developmental Psychology, 11*(2), 240–243.

Cassidy, D. J., Mims, S., Rucker, L., & Boone, S. (2003). Emergent curriculum and kindergarten readiness. *Childhood Education, 79*(4), 194–199.

Children's Defense Fund. (2005). *The state of America's children yearbook 2005*. Washington, DC: Children's Defense Fund.

DEC/CEC (Division of Early Childhood of the Council of Exceptional Children). (1994). Position on inclusion. *Young Children, 49*(5), 78.

Denton, K., West, J., & Walston, J. (2003). *Reading—Young children's achievement and classroom experiences: Findings from the Condition of Education 2003*. Washington, DC: U.S. Department of Education, NCES 2003-070.

Derman-Sparks, L., & A.B.C. Task Force. (1989). *Anti-bias curriculum: Tools for empowering young children*. Washington, DC: National Association for the Education of Young Children.

Eaton, D. E. (2002). Family child care accreditation and professional development. *Young Children, 57*(1), 23.

Elicker, J., & Mathur, S. (1997). What do they do all day? Comprehensive evaluation of a full-day kindergarten. *Early Childhood Research Quarterly, 12*(4), 459–483.

Estok, V. (2005). One district's study on the propriety of transition-grade classrooms. *Young Children, 60*(2), 28–31.

Graue, E. (2001). Research in review: What's going on in the children's garden? Kindergarten today. *Young Children, 56*(3), 67–73.

Graue, M. E., & DiPerna, J. (2000). Redshirting and early retention: Who gets the "gift of time" and what are its outcomes? *American Educational Research Journal, 37*(2), 509–534.

Hendrick, J. (2004). Reggio Emilia and American schools: Telling them apart and putting them together—Can we do it? In J. Hendrick (Ed.); *Next steps toward teaching the Reggio way: Accepting the challenge to change (2nd ed.)*.. Upper Saddle River, NJ: Pearson Education

Hohmann, M., Banet, B., & Weikart, D. P. (1979). *Young children in action*. Ypsilanti, MI: High/Scope Press.

Hohmann, N., & Weikart, D. P. (1995). *Educating young children: Active learning practices for preschool and child care programs*. Ypsilanti, MI: High/Scope Press.

Housden, T., & Kam, R. (1992). *Full-day kindergarten: A summary of the research*. Carmichael, CA: San Juan Unified School District. (ERIC Document ED 345 868.)

Johnson, E. R., Merrell, K. W., & Stover, L. (1990, October). The effects of early grade retention on the academic achievement of fourth-grade students. *Psychology in the Schools, 27*, 333–338.

Mantzicopoulos, P., & Morrison, D. (1992). Kindergarten retention: Academic and behavioral outcomes through the end of second grade. *American Educational Research Journal, 29*(1), 182–198.

Marshall, H. H. (2003). Opportunity deferred or opportunity taken? An updated look at delaying kindergarten entry. *Young Children, 8*(5), 84–93.

Pellegrini N. (1991) *Families are different*. New York: Holiday House Inc.

Piaget, J. (1962). *Play, dreams and imitation in childhood* (C. Gattegho & F. M. Hodgeson, Trans.). New York: Norton. (Original work published in 1945.)

Price-Williams, D. R., Gordon, W., & Ramirez, M. (1969). Skill and conservation. *Developmental Psychology, 1*, 769.

Rankin, B. (2004). Dewey, Piaget, Vygotsky: Connections with Malaguzzi and the Reggio Emilia approach. In J. Hendrick (Ed.), *Next steps toward teaching the Reggio way: Accepting the challenge to change* (2nd ed.). Upper Saddle River, NJ: Pearson Education

Shepard & Smith 1988.

Trawick-Smith, J. (1997). *Early childhood development: A multicultural perspective*. Upper Saddle River, NJ: Prentice-Hall.

Weaver, R. H. (2002). The roots of quality care: Strategies of master providers. *Young Children, 57*(1), 16–22.

Weiss, A. D. G., & Offenberg, R. M. (2002). *Enhancing urban children's early success in school: The power of full-day kindergarten*. Paper presented at the annual meeting of the American Educational Research Association, New Orleans, LA.

Early Childhood: The Primary Grades

7

Think back to your years in the primary grades. Did you have lots of opportunities to play? What kinds of literacy experiences did you have? What kinds of books did you read? Did you learn about other cultures? Did you enjoy school? Why or why not?

In this chapter, we discuss developmentally and culturally appropriate programs for young children in the primary grades. We first consider the nature of young learners age 6–8 years old and developmentally and culturally appropriate teacher behaviors in effective programs. We then address antibias learning environments and components of effective teaching in the primary grades. The typical play behaviors of 6- to 8-year-olds and various classroom and calendar configurations are examined.

After reading this chapter, you will understand:

▶ The developmental nature of children age 6–8 years.

▶ Considerations for working with children age 6–8 years.

▶ Teacher behaviors in effective programs for children age 6–8 years.

▶ Creating an antibias learning environment in the primary grades.

▶ Cultural issues related to literacy learning, the cornerstone of primary grade curriculum.

▶ Effective teaching in the primary grades.

▶ The nature of play in 6- to 8-year-olds.

▶ Classroom and calendar configurations in the primary grades.

Developmental Considerations for Primary Grade Children

Although children will vary greatly in the patterns and timing of their growth, sometime between ages 5 and 7, a significant cognitive shift happens. As presented in Chapter 2, Piaget (Piaget & Inhelder, 1969) suggests that children of this age move out of the preoperational stage of thinking and into the concrete operational stage. More recently, neuroscientists note that the brain is more efficient at this age (Bergen & Coscia, 2001). Teachers of 6- to 8-year-olds must consider what we know about this age group, along with knowledge of individual children and their cultural backgrounds. Table 7.1 provides a brief overview of the developmental nature of 6- to 8-year-olds and developmentally and culturally appropriate teacher behaviors.

Language and Literacy Development

Vocabulary acquisition for children 6–8 years of age continues to expand at an increasingly rapid rate. As children become readers, they have even more opportunities to learn vocabulary. For example, Juan encountered the word *domestic* when he was reading about pets as domestic animals. He now uses it in reference to farm animals and chores around his house. Children learn that words might have multiple meanings, like *rough surface* (coarse) and *rough day* (tough). They learn that words can be attached to other words to create a new meaning, girlfriend, for example. Most have outgrown immature language, overgeneralizations for example, and are increasingly proficient with conventional speech.

Primary grade children are learning to read, and they benefit from explicit instruction in decoding, fluency, and comprehension skills. They need many opportunities to hear stories, tell stories, read alone and with others, and explore self-selected books.

The writing skills of young children evolve on a developmental continuum. During the years from ages 6–8, typically developing primary grade children grow rapidly as writers if given opportunities to write. The developmental continuum begins with the scribbling of toddlers and evolves into circles and sticks and then strings of familiar letters (prekindergarten and kindergarten). By the beginning of first grade, most children write in invented spelling which is evidence of their letter/sound knowledge. For speakers of English, young children's invented spelling consists of only initial consonants at first. As the writer develops, ending consonants, then middle consonants, and finally vowels are added to the words.

Although children of this age will still write using invented spelling, their writing is gradually becoming more conventional. They benefit from explicit instruction on the conventions of writing, including spelling. Figure 7.1 is an example of the invented spelling of 6-year-old Elizabeth's recipe for cake. It reads: *cake, mix flour and milk and sugar together, then put in microwave, put on frosting.* It seems, for example, this child is ready to learn the *silent e* rule (cak) or that it is appropriate to move to a new line to fit all the letters of a word on the same line (togethr).

Cognitive Development

Piaget (Piaget & Inhelder, 1969) noted a cognitive shift that happens around age 7 into what he called the concrete operational stage of thinking. The shift is not, of course, abrupt nor does it happen at precisely age 7; however, around this age, increased maturity in children's cognitive abilities is evident. Moreover, children's cognitive strengths and weaknesses are more prominent because the pruning of brain synapses is taking place (Bergen & Coscia, 2001). That is, the rapid brain

Table 7.1	Appropriate Responses for Early Childhood Educators Working with Children 6–8 Years Old

What 6- to 8-Year-Old Children Do	What Early Childhood Educators Do
Language Symbolic thinking becomes more proficient and flexible. Vocabulary is rapidly increasing (~20 words per day). Are better able to express themselves.	Provide supported reading and writing activities. Gradually provide more independent reading and writing experiences. Provide many fiction and nonfiction books. Provide many and varied literacy experiences.
Cognitive Enjoy making sense of new experiences, learning is integrated and contextual. Brain synapses go through pruning so brain is more efficient to conceptualize, problem solve, reason, conserve, reverse thinking, and take perspective. Logic is deductive. Memory increases.	Integrate the curriculum, engage children in projects and inquiry. Provide many opportunities for hands-on activities, inquiry, classification, data collection, inference, and problem solving. Teach concepts like time and number. Engage children in games with rules and in team activities. Beginning from a concrete, meaningful base, extend children's understanding of more abstract concepts (e.g., long ago, far away). Provide charts, maps, and other representations for reference.
Social–Emotional More mature reasoning and perspective taking results in better understanding of right and wrong. Demonstrate the early stages of monitoring their own behavior. Focus on fairness. Strive to master skills. Have balanced judgments of others (e.g., will like someone even though the person did something child disliked). Developing a realistic sense of self, tend to compare themselves to others. Peers are increasingly important. Empathy is developing.	Engage children in conflict resolution. Communicate reasons for prohibitions. Model socially appropriate behavior. Appreciate and focus on children's strengths. Help children understand when others have greater needs. Engage them in service learning (e.g., reading to elderly). Avoid excessive competition, restricting it to primarily between or among teams. Provide cooperative activities and projects. Nurture their expressions of curiosity, helpfulness, kindness, etc.
Physical Physical growth slows. Lose baby teeth. Are more coordinated. Have increased fine motor control. Although still farsighted, binocular vision is established. Immune system is more developed.	Engage children in physical activities, avoid long periods of nonphysical activity. Provide opportunities to manipulate objects. Teach and model good health practices (e.g., washing hands often, coughing into one's elbow).

Source: Adapted from Bredekamp, S., & Copple, C. (Eds). (1997). *Developmentally appropriate practice in early childhood programs* (revised ed.). Washington, DC: National Association for the Education of Young Children.

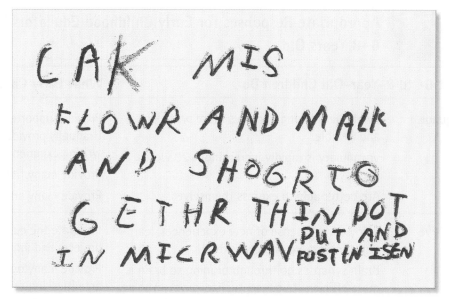

Figure 7.1. Example of Invented Spelling by a 6-year-old.

growth of the first 6 years has produced more synapses than the brain can support, so the brain prunes the synapses that are less used. This is part of normal development. Skills weaken in areas of low use and areas of high use emerge as strengths. For example, a child who has had many language experiences but few musical ones will likely have stronger literacy skills and weaker musical skills.

Although children aged 6–8 years old still do not have the ability to think abstractly in the way older children and adults do, they can think abstractly from a concrete point of reference. For example, Mia can use plastic chips to visualize the math concept of addition, and then write the operation of addition with number symbols. Even recognizing the shift in cognitive capabilities, early childhood educators still must be cautious about expecting too much.

Information Processing. The 6- to 8-year-old can now retain about five chunks of information compared to two or three for preschool children and seven for adults (Bredekamp & Copple, 1997). They can use memory strategies, such as rehearsal or mnemonics, to retain information. For example, they can remember the phone number *555-1811* with several repetitions such as *5-5-5-18-11*. The mnemonic *every good boy does fine* helps them remember the lines on the treble clef of the pi-

ano and *face* helps them remember the spaces. They have more mental structures on which to hang new understanding than do their preschool counterparts. It is now easier for them to organize information in the short-term memory so that it can be transferred and stored in the long-term memory.

Reasoning. Children in this age group can engage in deductive reasoning. For example, if A > B > C, concrete operational thinkers can deduce that A > C. Most can now conserve volume and mass, and take perspective.

Understanding Concepts. Children ages 6–8 years demonstrate an increasingly mature ability to understand concepts. For example, having experienced family life on a personal level, they can understand family life of long ago, from far away, or from a different culture, even though they have not directly experienced it in that particular context. Although sequencing events in time is still difficult, they can categorize them as past or present. Their understanding of number concepts is developing such that they know the signifier 8 does not refer only to the last item counted; rather, it refers to the entire group of 8 items. You can test that with a 5-year-old and an 8-year-old by asking each to show you 6. It is likely that the 5-year-old will point to the last object counted while the 8-year-old will indicate the entire set of 6.

Class Inclusion. Concrete operational thinkers can attend to more than one attribute at a time. For example, they know that a *girl* can be a girl and a first grader and that the classification *first graders* includes girls and boys. They understand that *cat* is a cat and an animal and that the classification *animal* includes many different species.

Physical Development

Physical development begins to slow down for children ages 6–8. Their immune systems are more developed than those of preschoolers so they experience fewer illnesses.

By this age, the brain has reached nearly adult size and works more efficiently than it has in the past. The corpus callosum, the tissue that connects the right and left portions of the brain, is more mature, which enhances mental processing (Bergen & Coscia, 2001) and is evidenced by children's improved mental abilities.

Gross and fine motor skills of children 6–8 years old have also developed beyond those of younger children. The children participate in activities that involve running, jumping, skipping, and hopping. Their muscles are developed enough to support fine motor activities including writing; however, sitting for long periods is tiring. Activities that require consistent sitting should be limited to 20 minutes or less, whereas activities where children are in and out of their seats can be longer in duration. Lively and quiet activities need to be alternated.

Although children in this age range are still a bit farsighted, their binocular vision is well established (Bredekamp & Copple, 1997). Although larger print is still necessary, they are ready for reading instruction, writing tasks, and other activities that are quite tedious for younger children.

Janine Wiedel Photolibrary/Alamy Images.

Social–Emotional Development

Primary grade children are developing a more realistic sense of self than their preschool counterparts. Whereas preschoolers are learning so rapidly that they believe they can do anything, primary grade children have a more realistic understanding of their strengths and challenges. Peers have increasing importance in their lives, and children of this age are prone to constantly compare themselves to others. In fact, they may make decisions about their competence based on their analysis of how they compare to others. For example, if a child realizes that a friend kicks the soccer ball into the goal more often than he does, he may decide that he is not good at playing soccer. Competitive individual activities will tend to amplify this tendency to compare self to others and should be limited. Team competition, where children collaborate with teammates, is more appropriate.

Primary grade children are very interested in friendships. They tend to prefer same-gender friends at school, where there are plenty of choices for same-gender playmates. In neighborhoods, where choices may be more limited, children will happily play with playmates of the opposite gender. At this age, children are quite capable of and drawn to playing games with rules. Cooperative learning (Chapter 8) and group games are very effective instructional strategies with primary grade children.

Primary grade children are developing a keen awareness of right and wrong and have a strong sense of fairness. They will participate effectively in rule making and learn conflict resolution strategies (Chapter 8).

Antibias Classrooms in the Primary Grades

Antibias classrooms value all children regardless of their cultural backgrounds. Cultural differences will have an impact on learning experiences, and early childhood educators must understand and value the cultural backgrounds each child brings to school. Family expectations influence how children develop. For example, some families place more emphasis on children becoming verbally assertive and coping with peers than on obedience. Conversely, other families value obedience over other characteristics. Understanding the family values of children in your classroom will help you understand the children's behavior and parents' expectations for their children. Your job as a teacher is not to change those family expectations unless they threaten a child's ability to feel physically and psychologically safe. For example, if a family nurtures independence to an extent that the child does not follow the rules of safe and appropriate behavior, then you should intervene.

Literacy Learning

Literacy learning refers to the activities of reading, writing, listening, and speaking and is the cornerstone of the primary grade curriculum. Obviously, it is an area on which the native language and cultural backgrounds of children have a profound effect, a topic that is discussed more fully in Chapter 10.

Cultural values vary, as does the importance families place on early literacy experiences. For example, some families may place higher value on experiences in nature than on daily book reading. Many have rich oral storytelling traditions and have fewer print literacy materials in the home. Families living in poverty have limited resources and opportunities to build a strong literacy foundation. Culture affects children's foundation for literacy as it relates to experience with literacy materials, the literacy environment, and literacy interactions (Vernon-Feagans, Hammer, Miccio, & Manlove, 2001).

Literacy Experiences. Variation in early experiences has an impact on children's ability to engage in formal reading instruction. For some children early literacy experiences are inconsistent with how literacy is defined in school, storytelling but limited book reading, for example. Children who have not had experiences with books and other print materials prior to entrance in school have not had the same opportunity to develop vocabulary and knowledge of print as have children who have had experiences with literacy artifacts (Vernon-Feagans et al., 2001). Therefore, they may lag behind other children when they enter school.

Oral language provides the foundation for literacy learning, and children come to school with a variety of language backgrounds (Braunger & Lewis, 1998). Furthermore, many books and stories reflect events and contexts that are unfamiliar to some children. As a teacher, it is your role to build on the background of experiences children bring to school as you introduce them to more public forms of literacy (Braunger & Lewis, 1998). You will want to provide many literacy experiences that depict characters from many cultures so that children can identify with story characters and plots and see themselves in literacy activities.

Literacy Environments. Not all families have the resources to provide a rich literacy foundation before their children begin formal reading instruction. This may reflect different priorities (family storytelling tradition, for example), or it may be indicative of a lack of resources (families living in poverty). The *Focus on Children* highlights issues related to children living in poverty.

Reading Interactions. Reading interactions vary among families when they read together. For example, in some families, parents and children jointly construct meaning from the text as they read and talk. As they discuss the story, they decide

Focus on Children

Challenges for Children of Poverty

Children living in poverty are at risk of poor achievement in school. The three main concerns for children living in poverty are biological and health issues, the environments in which poor children live, and discrimination.

Biological and Health Issues. Families living in poverty experience more health hazards in their living conditions and have limited access to health care due to a lack of financial resources. Other challenges for children that correlate with poverty include higher frequency of premature births, lack of immunizations, less nutritious diets, greater risk of exposure to lead, and greater likelihood of chronic ear infections and iron deficiency. Many conversations in homes are in a nonmainstream dialect that is not valued in schools, and may lack richness of vocabulary. These conditions negatively impact children's development of language and reading, and their ability to attend.

Environments. Decades of research on brain development indicates that neurological connections that support learning later in life develop in the early years. This has implications for families living in poverty because they have limited resources to provide experiences and materials needed to stimulate early development. Families that struggle to provide food and shelter do not have money to purchase magazines, newspapers, and books. Parents who are struggling to meet the basic needs of the family may have difficulty taking time away from work or coming up with money for gas so that the family can take a trip or even visit a local library.

Discrimination. Schools are part of the problem. Many poor or minority children experience a cultural clash between home and school. It is manifest in the expectations teachers hold for children who may not have the same health status and background of experiences that middle- and upper-income children have. It is also manifest in the cultural bias of literacy materials that may reflect events and contexts with which many children are unfamiliar. It is imperative that early childhood educators acknowledge these issues.

Sources: Bardige, B. (2005). *At a loss for words: How America is failing our children and what we can do about it.* Philadelphia: Temple University Press. Vernon-Feagans, L., Hammer, C. S., Miccio, A., & Manlove, E. (2001). Early language and literacy skills in low-income African-American and Hispanic children. In S. B. Neuman & D. K. Dickinson (Eds.), *Handbook of early literacy research.* New York: Guilford Press.

Laura Dwight Photography.

together what the author is saying. These children may not understand the common practice in schools where the teacher poses a question yet already knows the answer (Vernon-Feagans et al., 2001). They may not understand why the teacher would ask a question for which he already knows the answer.

The Responsibility of Schools. Literacy is not merely a decoding activity; it is a meaning-making activity that happens in particular social and cultural contexts. Whatever their native language or dialect, children must learn the language of the mainstream to function in our society. Educating parents about how to work with their children at home is part of the solution; however, it is primarily the responsibility of the schools to be certain children's needs are met. You need to do the following (Vernon-Feagans et al., 2001):

▶ Learn about the literacy practices of the children in your classroom.

▶ Remain sensitive to the impact differences might have on children's ability to function in school.

▶ Bridge incongruence between home and school by incorporating children's home styles into classroom activities.

Considering these suggestions, let's go back to the example of parents and children who co-construct meaning of text. Think about how you as a teacher might engage children in reading who have that particular family background. For example, you might use small reading groups where children are encouraged to share their understanding of the text. As each child has an opportunity to talk, you collaboratively draw meaning from the story.

⟩ Antibias Instructional Strategies

We know that children in the primary grades are increasingly able to think abstractly but still need a concrete point of reference for their learning. As with their preschool and kindergarten counterparts, antibias attitudes are best taught in the context of children's daily lives and learning experiences. The following three instructional strategies are discussed more fully in Chapter 8 but are briefly mentioned here in the context of creating an antibias learning environment.

Cooperative Learning. Group activities should be structured to include the elements of *positive interdependence, individual accountability, promotive interaction, social skills instruction,* and *group processing.* Through cooperative learning children become increasingly aware of their similarities and differences as each group member makes a positive contribution to the task. Differences become something to value rather than criticize.

Because cooperative learning highlights what children can do, it is a good way to bring together different perspectives and strengths. For example, a child with a language delay who struggles with reading may not make a significant contribution to the research aspect of an inquiry project; however, that child may be a skilled artist or have well-developed spatial sense and can organize and make significant contributions to the creation of artifacts as the group shares what they have learned.

Prejudice Reduction Activities. Specific activities are discussed in Chapter 8 that are designed to help children learn about and value differences. Such activities illuminate the shortcomings of stereotyping and the similarities among people who are different in some ways.

Conflict Resolution. Children in the primary grades are more able than younger children to take perspective. As they mediate conflict

Window into the Classroom

Neil is a first-grade teacher in a middle-income school. The class has been studying healthy lifestyles, and in the context of this unit, the children are talking about how they have developed physically over time. As part of the unit, the children brought pictures of themselves as babies.

The children are sitting in a circle and, one by one, sharing their baby pictures. Neil places them on the bulletin board as each child shares. David shared a picture of himself at age 9 months complete with details about where they lived when the picture was taken. Next, Sarah shared her picture in a long, flowing christening dress, taken when she was christened at age 2 months. This dialogue followed:

Sarah: *This is me when I was 2 months old in my beautiful christening dress. It was taken by the door of our church.*

David: *What is christening?*

Neil: *Sarah, can you answer that question?*

Sarah: *Well, ya go to church and the priest puts water on babies' heads; 'n everybody prays.*

Neil: *Some people call that christening and others call it baptism.*

David: *You can't be baptized when you are a baby; ya have to be 8 years old to be baptized!!*

Sarah: *No you don't!! I was christened when I was a baby!!*

Neil: *Families do lots of different things when it comes to religious practices. Some families believe in baptizing or christening babies and others wait until children are older. Some families don't believe in baptism or christening at all. No one is wrong; people are just different.*

Neil used this naturally occurring opportunity to teach children in his classroom about diverse religious practices. He also made the point that because something is different does not make it wrong, and that baptism and christening are not practiced by everyone. During this event, he was able to expand the children's understanding and tolerance.

and model conflict resolution strategies, teachers assist young children to take the perspective of others. They help children develop the language of conflict resolution. In the *Window into the Classroom* feature, Neil used a naturally occurring event to value difference and mediate conflict.

Integrating Content about Diversity into the Curriculum

Cooperative learning groups, conflict resolution, and prejudice reduction activities provide opportunities to overtly teach social skills and the value of differences to primary-grade children. Furthermore, integrating content about diversity into the existing curriculum will assist primary grade children to understand and appreciate differences. Primary grade children are increasingly capable of learning about events and people of long ago, far away, and different cultural backgrounds.

Integration of content about diversity into the primary-grade curriculum must be carefully done if students are to truly embrace diversity. That is, multicultural content must be integrated in such a way that concepts, skills, and ideas are taught through illustrations from a variety of cultures. Banks (1995) identifies the following four levels for integrating content about diversity into the curriculum and implores teachers to move beyond the *contributions approach* and *additive approach* levels to the *transformation* and *action* levels:

▶ *Contributions approach* includes isolated information about specific groups. For example, children study Hanukkah along with Christmas in December.

▶ *Additive approach* includes units added to existing curriculum to promote learning about others. For example, children study a unit on Native Americans that is isolated from other units of study.

▶ *Transformation* is when the curriculum is altered to integrate multiple perspectives into concepts, skills, and ideas. For example, a unit might be organized around themes like friendship or harvest celebrations where different ways of living are explored.

▶ *Action* is when the study leads students to do things that have an impact on the social–political environment (Banks, 1995). Examples might include a recycling project or reading to the elderly.

Let's look at an example. A unit on Native Americans may focus on long ago, stereotypical characterizations (e.g., feathers and war paint) and fail to depict Native Americans as members of our contemporary society (additive approach). Conversely, when Native Americans are studied in the context of integrated units on topics such as *celebrations, communities,* or *friendship*, primary grade children will learn about Native American cultures and contributions, past and present (transformation approach). They will also learn about Native Americans as members of our society today and stereotypes will be dispelled.

The study of diversity can also be integrated into science units. For example, most primary grade curricula include the study of animals. Children can learn where various animals live in the world, what cultural significance they might have for people in those areas, and what jobs, hobbies, or traditions are related to animal populations in various areas. Many Hindus for example, hold the belief of nonviolence called *ahimsa*. In practice, many Hindus do not kill animals for food; they eat a vegetarian diet.

Following are some examples of content unit themes appropriate for primary-grade children. Suggestions are included for transforming them to embrace diversity in substantial ways.

Celebrations. Most young children have participated in celebrations of some sort and find them exciting and interesting. Using their own experiences as a point of reference, primary grade children are mature enough to learn about the meaning and origin of celebrations and holidays other than their own. For example, looking across cultures, the month of December has several holidays including Christmas (Christian), Hanukkah (Jewish), Kwanzaa (African-American), and Boxing Day (British).

It is important to be cautious when young children are learning about holidays and celebrations. For example, Native American rituals such as dances and pow-wows have significance to those who participate in them, and it is inappropriate for anyone who does not appreciate or understand the significance to participate. Simply enacting a ritual should be avoided. If such a dance is demonstrated, it must be done by members of the culture, and others should be treated as guests during the activity (Derman-Sparks, 1989).

Avoid stereotyping. Help children understand that those who celebrate the same holiday may do it in different ways. This can be done by assisting them to reflect on their own family celebrations.

Never limit learning about a culture to merely the study of holidays. Children also need the opportunity to learn about the daily lives of others including diet, industry, recreation, art, and music. How have those practices come to be important in particular cultures?

Communities. Children in the primary grades are learning about their communities and will enjoy examining cultural diversity in their own and other communities. Children can learn about other characteristics of their community including roles of community members and organizations. Through interviews, classroom guests, field trips, and reading materials they can learn about what the town council does, what

Lawrence Migdale/Photo Researchers.

the school board does, or other community organizations. Some communities have health fairs, gardener's markets, patriots' days, or county fairs; children can learn about the meaning and origin of such practices. What is the impetus for a parade in your community? Is it Cinco de Mayo, the Demolition Derby, a New Year's celebration, or Mardi Gras, for example? With pen pals, they can learn about similar and different practices in other communities.

Elizabeth Crews.

The phone book is a good resource for investigating different organizations and religions in your community (Dever, Whitaker, & Byrnes, 2001). Children can learn about the history and origin of different organizations and religious traditions. Why are those organizations or religions present in your community?

By examining beliefs and traditions of community religions through classroom guests and literature, children can look for common themes across religions (e.g., honesty, kindness) that reflect universal values related to human rights (Dever et al., 2001). Of course, the study of religion must remain neutral and nondevotional; early childhood educators in public schools must be careful not to criticize or promote any religion. It is also important to communicate clearly with parents that you are not teaching a particular religion; rather, children are coming to better understand their social world by learning about several religions.

Friendship. Primary-grade children are developing social skills and friendships. In this unit, children will learn that friendships are not limited to those with the same skin color, gender, social class, religious practices, and so on (Dever et al., 2001). Friendship has more to do with how people interact. Table 7.2 is a brief bibliography of books that

Table 7.2	Examples of Books to Generate Discussions about Friendship with Primary Grade Children

Title	Author	Annotation
Jamaica's Find	Juanita Havill	This book exemplifies honesty and friendship between two young girls of different ethnicities.
The Trees of the Dancing Goats	Patricia Polacco	Friendship and compassion between Christian and Jewish families is exemplified in this book.
Amos and Boris	William Steig	Amos and Boris are two friends with different abilities. In spite of their ability differences, they each have an opportunity to help the other.
Mrs. Katz and Tush	Patricia Polacco	Based on a common bond, friendship develops between a boy and a woman, exemplifying a relationship that spans ethnicity, gender, and age.
Stellaluna	Janell Cannon	This is a story of friendship between a bat and some birds. It exemplifies that we are not wrong just because our lifestyles are different.

Focus on Diversity

Guidelines for Selecting Antibias Books and Materials

1. Examine the illustrations for stereotypes. For example, are people from nonmainstream cultures depicted in dress from long ago (Native Americans depicted in buckskin and feathers, for example) while people from the mainstream culture are depicted in modern dress?
2. Notice who the dominant characters are in plots and story lines. For example, are characters from outside the power culture (e.g., ethnic minorities, women, persons with disabilities) depicted as subservient to characters from mainstream cultures? Do this same analysis for heroes and villains in stories.
3. Select materials where characters from nonmainstream cultures are depicted as heroes, wise, strong leaders, good friends, and problem solvers.
4. Select materials where characters are depicted in nontraditional roles (e.g., women as firefighters, police officers, doctors, etc.; men as nurses, teachers, secretaries; persons with disabilities as professionals).
5. Select materials where people of various abilities are engaged in productive activity (e.g., a blind business owner, a paraplegic teacher).

exemplify friendship among those who are different in terms of ethnicity, religion, ability, gender, and age. Literature can be used to model friendships across cultures, generate discussions about friendship, and reflect on what friends do for each other.

Materials. As in preschool and kindergarten, the classroom environment should reflect diversity. Bulletin board displays, books, and other artifacts should depict people in nontraditional, nonstereotypical ways. The *Focus on Diversity* provides a checklist for selecting antibias materials that are appropriate in all early childhood settings.

Classroom Guests. Teachers should capitalize on parents and community members who might be willing to share their cultures with children. Classroom guests might share favorite recipes, stories, hobbies, or artifacts from their cultures and explain their significance. For example, Rebecca's family had a long history of raising sheep and spinning their wool into yarn. They used various plants to color the yarn, which is then sold in various markets. Rebecca shares her history with children in schools and demonstrates how she spins wool into yarn.

The Hidden Curriculum. The hidden curriculum encompasses any values that are not documented as part of the curriculum. This might include stereotypical assumptions about parents based on social class, ethnicity, religion, or sexual orientation; valuing athletic over artistic talents; or promoting gender stereotypical behaviors (e.g., girls play house and boys build with blocks). For example, there is a tendency for teachers to assume a parent does not care about a child who comes to school in clothes that are too small or unclean. In actuality, the parent may not have the funds to buy new clothes or launder them on a regular basis. Teachers must regularly reflect on their attitudes and behaviors to ensure they are tolerant of various ways of living.

Curriculum and Effective Teaching in the Primary Grades

Unlike preschool and kindergarten children, primary grade children are increasingly able to engage in formal instruction. They can sit for longer periods of time and process information more easily than younger children. The integrated approach to curriculum development (Chapter 4) is one important element of primary grade instruction. Following are some additional components of effective teaching in the primary grades.

Child-Centered Environment

A child-centered learning environment is one where the individual, cultural, and developmental needs of the children are paramount. Primary grade children learn best in an environment that involves families and provides meaningful learning experiences in a democratic atmosphere. A child-centered learning environment addresses the needs of the whole child, acknowledging that children are developing socially, emotionally, physically, and cognitively. Children enjoy a balance between structure and flexibility, independent and group activities, and required and selected activities. They share in decision making and responsibility at developmentally appropriate levels. For example, children have voice in developing expectations and rules in their classroom; they share class jobs such as taking attendance, setting out materials, and so on.

Explicit Instruction

Explicit instruction means that children are overtly taught concepts, vocabulary, and skills. The term can also apply to teaching process skills (e.g., inquiry, problem solving). Teachers explicitly teach by modeling, explaining, and presenting information in brief lessons (10–20 minutes in grades 1–3) throughout the day. Teachers focus on a particular concept, vocabulary set, or skill as they demonstrate and provide guided practice. Then, young children have the opportunity to apply the concept or use the vocabulary or skill in context.

Explicit instruction is particularly important in the primary grades when children are developing conceptual understanding, vocabulary, process skills, and skills for reading, writing, and mathematics. For example, a primary grade teacher might present a brief lesson to first graders on various end marks. The lesson would include information about when various end marks should be used, along with examples and demonstrations. Then students may have guided practice that is carefully overseen by the teacher. This is followed by opportunities to use the new learning in a meaningful context, perhaps in writing a story or nonfiction piece. The teacher draws attention to children's use of end marks during individual conferences.

Accountability pressures to increase test scores and meet *adequate yearly progress* (Chapter 2) assessments may tempt teachers to overuse explicit instruction and teach to the test. Primary grade educators must be cautious about this because overuse of explicit instruction can become tedious and lead to decontextualized learning if children do not have the opportunity to use new skills in meaningful ways. Explicit instruction is effectively used when instruction is brief and appropriately integrated with other types of activities, including more open-ended activities.

Direct Instruction

Grounded in behaviorism, direct instruction is a specific type of explicit instruction, developed by Siegfried Engelmann and others in 1964. Initial programs were developed to meet the needs of disadvantaged preschool children and were published under the title DISTAR, Direct Instruction System for Teaching Arithmetic and Reading (Adams & Engelmann, 1996). Direct instruction has led to increased reading and math achievement scores for delayed and typically developing children of all ages (Adams & Engelmann, 1996).

Balanced Literacy

Literacy learning is the cornerstone of the curriculum in the primary grades and, as discussed in Chapter 2, instructional practice has been the source of debate for decades. Balanced literacy is not a particular set of methods or a prescriptive procedure for teaching reading. Rather, it is an integration of holistic literacy activities with systematic decoding and comprehension skills instruction.

Pressley (2002) suggests that effective primary grade teachers pack their days with many literacy experiences. Effective teachers integrate features of holistic approaches and explicit instruction by immersing students in shared and independent reading of literature along with explicit decoding and comprehension skills instruction. In the most effective classrooms, teachers do the following (Pressley, 2002):

▶ Use more small-group instruction and coaching.

▶ Teach phonics with an emphasis on application during real reading.

▶ Use more higher-order questioning techniques.

▶ Involve parents.

▶ Provide extensive independent reading. (p. 189).

The balance in balanced literacy refers to balancing activities that range on a continuum from teachers performing the activity *to* children, to activities where children work independently. The *Focus on Children* describes activities on the continuum of teacher involvement. Children move toward independent activities as their abilities

Focus on Children

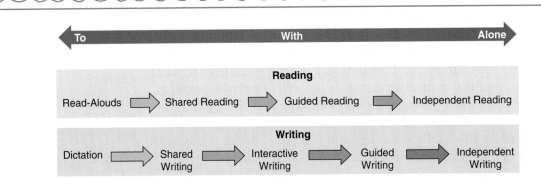

Read-alouds should be part of the curriculum for all ages as it promotes reading as a pleasurable activity. With interesting and developmentally appropriate texts, teachers model reading as a whole class activity.

Shared reading engages children in reading as they have opportunities to comment on the text, identify letters and words, and reread sections of the text while teachers model reading. Shared reading can be a small group or a whole class activity and is easily accomplished with big books.

Guided reading takes place in small, homogeneous groups of children who are functioning at approximately the same skill level. The children do the reading as educators observe, monitor, and coach as they read aloud.

Independent reading is an individual activity and is accomplished as children read self-selected books. As they read alone, they apply reading skills and strategies they have learned. Nonconventional readers might read pictures while conventional readers read the text. Primary-grade children should have access to both fiction and nonfiction text.

Dictation or *language experience* is an individual activity that involves educators, classroom volunteers, or older children writing children's stories as they dictate them. It provides a model for conventional writing and demonstrates that writing is our words written down.

Shared writing is a large group activity where educators write on chart paper in front of children. The educators think aloud as they write, making phonics and various conventions of print explicit.

Interactive writing requires educators and children to share the pen. In small groups, the educator begins writing on chart paper and invites children to write letters, words, or sentences. Their contributions are consistent with their abilities.

Guided writing is an independent writing activity but the educator is available for guidance. Educators use guided writing time to teach skills and reinforce prior learning.

Independent writing engages children in writing on their own. Nonconventional writers might write with pictures or scribbles.

Source: Gallagher-Mance, J. (1997). The reality of balanced literacy in a primary classroom. In J. L. Johns & L. Elish-Piper (Eds.), *Balanced reading instruction: Teachers visions and voices.* Dubuque, IA: Kendall/Hunt Publishing.

develop, and instructional decisions are made based on their individual, developmental, and cultural needs. In general, kindergarten and first-grade children experience more read-alouds and shared reading and writing, whereas second- and third-grade children do more guided and independent reading and writing.

Laura Dwight Photography.

National Reading Panel Report

For decades, there has been a strong focus on teaching young children to read. In 1997 under the Clinton administration, Congress charged the director of the National Institute of Child Health and Human Development (NICHHD), in consultation with the secretary of education, to appoint a panel to assess research on reading acquisition and report its findings. The panel was to discuss application of their findings, dissemination, and further needed research. The panel, known as the National Reading Panel (NRP), presented its findings to Congress in February 1999.

Owing to the large volume of studies that existed, the NRP decided to study only topics on which there were many studies (NICHHD, 1999). Furthermore, they confined their examination of research to include only experimental and quasi-experimental studies in an attempt to bring rigor to the process (NICHHD, 1999). These self-imposed limitations met with much criticism (Pressley, 2002).

In general, the NRP found support for skills-based instruction in reading; these findings have subsequently been very influential in the teaching of reading in kindergarten and the primary grades (Pressley, 2002). Following is an overview (NICHHD, 1999; Pressley, 2002):

► Instruction in phonemic awareness is effective in promoting early reading and spelling skills.

► Reading, spelling, and to a less significant extent comprehension are improved with systematic phonics instruction.

► Vocabulary instruction supports reading comprehension.

► Repeated readings of text and guided oral reading positively impact reading fluency.

► Comprehension strategies should be taught.

► Teacher in-service instruction on teaching reading can improve student reading achievement but effective in-service approaches need to be identified.

► Computer technology has the potential for improving beginning reading achievement.

Extension of Programs for 3- to 5-Year-Olds into Primary Grades

Some programs for 3- to 5-year-olds, discussed in Chapter 6, have been expanded into the primary grades and beyond. These include Waldorf, High/Scope, and Montessori, with each applying its philosophy to align with characteristics of primary grade children. Montessori schools now exist in over 100 school districts. The Montessori philosophy where teachers observe children and prepare an environment that captures their interest, stimulates their senses, and actively engages them with appealing materials has been refined to be developmentally appropriate for primary grade children. Didactic materials like map puzzles have been developed to match primary grade curriculum.

Play in the Primary Grades

Play continues to support development for 6- to 8-year-olds and should have a prominent place in the curriculum. In the latter half of the 20th century, scholars of children's play (Pellegrini, 1980; Vygotsky, 1966; Wolfgang & Sanders, 1981;

Wolfgang & Wolfgang, 1992) found support for the idea that the symbolic thinking evidenced in children's play is a developmental precursor to reading and writing. As children become conventional readers and writers, their involvement in dramatic play decreases; a cognitive shift from *player* to *worker* takes place (Wolfgang, 1974). Consistent with children's developing ability to think symbolically in more abstract ways, the play activity of children age 6–8 years old becomes increasingly more focused on games with rules (Piaget & Inhelder, 1969). These are games like hopscotch and dodgeball that are passed from adult to child. This also indicates that children are increasingly able to engage in more abstract school tasks.

Before and After School Programs

Many school-age children are in need of before and after school care while their parents work. Studies on after school programs suggest that quality programs affect children in positive ways. According to the U.S. Department of Education (Children's Defense Fund, 2005), children who participate in quality after school programs have higher academic achievement, demonstrate more socially appropriate behavior, have stronger peer relationships, and are less likely to engage in drugs and violence than their peers who are left alone after school (Children's Defense Fund, 2005).

Since 1995 and reauthorized under the No Child Left Behind legislation in 2001, 21st Century Community Learning Centers (21st CCLC) grants have provided federal funding for before and after school programs. These programs are designed to complement school programs as well as provide counseling services, drug and violence prevention, character education, and experiences with art, music, technology, and recreation. Such programs are particularly important for families living in poverty who cannot afford the estimated $3,500 per year cost of before and after school care (Children's Defense Fund, 2005). The Children's Defense Fund estimated that 1.3 million children across the nation were served by 21st CCLC programs in 2004, and that this figure falls short of the need for before and after school care.

⸾ Classroom and Calendar Configurations in Primary Grades

Since education was made available to all children late in the 19th century, schools have typically grouped children in classrooms by chronological age. As we know, each state sets a school entrance age, usually age 5 for entry into kindergarten. The idea is that children of the same age have similar needs and characteristics, so grouping children of the same age eases the task of teaching a large number of children.

Although children of the same chronological age do have common characteristics, there is also great diversity among them as they have different abilities, cultural backgrounds, and prior experiences. This along with other factors has led to the implementation of different ways of grouping children in classrooms.

Multiage Grouping

Multiage grouping dates back to the one-room school house of the 19th century. Since the 1990s, multiage grouping as been increasingly used in the primary grades, typically housing children with an age span of 3 years or more. (This must not be confused with multigrade classrooms where children from two consecutive grade levels are in one classroom. Multigrade classrooms came about as a way to address problems of overflow within grades.) The NAEYC (Bredekamp & Copple, 1997) suggests that multiage grouping, found in child care and preschool settings, is well suited for primary-grade children because it provides a family-like atmosphere.

The increased range of abilities found in multiage classrooms compared to single-age classrooms encourages teachers to acknowledge children's individual needs and interests rather than teach to the middle of the class. Multiage classrooms have the following characteristics (Hoffman, 2003):

▶ Heterogeneous groups where children bring different strengths and skills to the learning experience.

▶ Differentiated instruction designed to meet individual needs.

▶ Social interaction and flexible grouping; children are easily grouped by interest for a project, or by ability for explicit instruction.

▶ Integrated curriculum.

Many fear that multiage configurations are detrimental to the learning of older children. Although findings are inconclusive, they slightly favor multiage grouping in terms of achievement (Veenman, 1995); however, particularly in light of the accountability attached to No Child Left Behind, many teachers are concerned about adequately addressing the needs of a broad range of abilities.

The *Window into the Classroom* feature takes us into the multiage classroom of a strong, experienced teacher, Sylvia, who finds that the challenge to address individual needs varies with the particular curriculum she is teaching.

Looping

Looping is a classroom configuration where a teacher has the same students for two consecutive years as they complete two grade levels. Thus, children begin with a teacher in first grade and advance to second grade the next year in the same classroom with the same teacher. Proponents of looping believe this configuration provides continuity for educators and students in a family-like atmosphere.

The challenge of looping for teachers relates to initial preparation. During the two consecutive years, teachers teach different curricula, first grade followed by second grade, for example; however, once the 2-year cycle has been completed, the preparation demands on teachers are no different than if they taught in a traditional single-grade structure. Furthermore, many teachers and students view this configuration positively because they already know each other at the beginning of that second year. They can settle into productive work more quickly than if they had to establish rapport, set boundaries, and so on.

Homeschooling

Homeschooling emerged in the 1950s among families who were unhappy with public schools. The practice of homeschooling is now on the rise, because a significant number of homeschooled children score well on tests and are being accepted into colleges and universities (Golden, 2000). Homeschooling is now legal in all 50 states.

Families who homeschool are primarily white, middle-class, two-parent families who choose to homeschool because they feel other options do not meet the needs of their children. Often, the family's religious values are a factor. They either wish to include religious education in their children's experience or their values are inconsistent with those they feel are promoted at school. Homeschool support networks for parents have emerged.

Jim Erickson/Corbis Images.

Window into the Classroom

Sylvia teaches in a multiage classroom that houses a diverse student population, ranging in age from 6 to 8 years. She believes there are some positive aspects about multiage grouping. "You get to know the students and their parents much better [than in single-age classrooms]. Parents become your friends and allies because the relationship is sustained for longer than one school year. Of course this can happen in one year, but it takes time to build a relationship with parents and often one year isn't long enough. You're just getting to know and understand them as the year draws to a close." Sylvia continues, "Another positive aspect is that students do not have to relearn how to 'do' school for a new teacher every year. Your students from the previous year come in knowing your expectations, your general routine, etc. I think that this gives them an extra sense of security, which makes it easier to take learning risks in the classroom."

Grouped in heterogeneous dyads, Sylvia's students have been reading and discussing nonfiction books. Sylvia notes, "Students are able to support each other as they read and write together. Some dyads have same-age partners. Some have different-age partners. It is hard to tell them apart." It is fairly easy to meet students' needs in reading and writing "because I use a reading and writing workshop which meets children's individual needs and has flexible grouping" depending on what is being taught.

Mitchell and Evan make up a heterogeneous dyad. They have read several nonfiction books and are preparing to write. Following is their conversation (Read, 2000):

M: *What else did we learn? That I saw a volcano? I didn't really learn that. Evan, what did I learn?*

E: *I don't know. I'm not you. I'm not in control of your mind. I know what you learned. That you've seen a volcano.*

M: *I already knew that. I didn't learn it. I think I learned that I would be afraid of volcanoes. I never wanted to know. I should say—What should I write? Come on Evan, let's write. I never thought it would be this hard to write.*

E: *We could have written about South American temples. Asian temples.*

M: *What did I learn?*

E: *I don't know.*

M: *I learned that a man had a farm on a volcano.*

E: *And he—*

M: *Okay, I know what I'm gonna write. You don't have to tell me. (p. 94)*

Sylvia finds the challenge of multiage grouping to be the diversity of ability levels in the classroom when teaching a sequential curriculum like mathematics. To adequately address students' needs, Sylvia and her teaching partner split students by grade level. "I taught both classes of students on first-grade-level math and she taught both classes of students on second-grade level math. This works to address the needs in mathematics of both advanced and delayed students."

Some homeschooling parents purchase packaged curriculum to teach their children. Others choose to use real-life projects as the curriculum (Cloud & Morse, 2001). For example, children might take care of a farm or a garden as the basis for their learning. They learn reading, writing, and mathematics in the context of daily activities. Reflect on the child-centered curriculum and the theories of several scholars. Does this sound familiar?

Many are concerned about the development of home-schooled children. Children who are homeschooled may be socially isolated. They do not have opportunities to participate in school activities such as drama or sports. There is also concern that parents are not held accountable in the way that schools are for their children's progress.

Year-round and Traditional Schools

The United States was primarily an agricultural society when education was first made available to all children in the 19th century. To accommodate the need of families to have children available to work on the farm during the busy

summer months, schools were in session between fall and spring but not during the summer. Many districts maintain the traditional schedule but others employ a year-round schedule.

On either schedule, children in the United States attend approximately 180 days of school. On the traditional schedule, students are out of school during the summer months, for holidays, and for other times as determined by the district. The schedule for year-round schools varies among districts but is generally something like 9 weeks in school followed by 3 weeks out of school. The break following the end of one school year might be a bit longer than 3 weeks and usually happens sometime during the summer.

Year-round scheduling has come about for two different reasons. One reason is to better meet the learning needs of children and the other is to accommodate rapid growth in the size of the student body.

Learning Needs. Some believe that the summer hiatus on a traditional school calendar has a negative impact on achievement (Morse, 2002). The impact can be even more severe for children living in poverty who may not have educationally rich summer experiences like family trips, visits to the library, and summer camp. Because year-round scheduling does not include an extended break from school, a decline in achievement is less likely (Morse, 2002). Usually all children are on the same schedule for school breaks if meeting learning needs is the goal for the year-round calendar.

Accommodate Rapid Growth. Some districts employ year-round scheduling because they can accommodate approximately one-third more students with existing facilities. Students and educators are on one of three to four scheduling tracks with at least one track out of school at all times. Thus, the facilities are in continuous use while students and teachers go on and off track.

Educating Homeless Children

The numbers of children living in poverty has steadily increased since the 1970s. By the end of the 20th century, one in five children in the United States lived in poverty (Children's Defense Fund, 2000). At the dawn of the 21st century, 1.35 million children living in poverty were also homeless (Noll & Watkins, 2003/2004). Issues related to homeless children and their families are discussed in more depth in Chapter 13; here we take a brief look at the impact of homelessness on literacy learning, the chief learning goal of the primary grades.

The early experiences of most homeless children are different than those of their more affluent counterparts. Many have never been to a library or experienced a rich literacy environment with magazines, newspapers, books, and writing materials; however, many have had to take responsibility and solve problems within the family, and teachers are remiss to assume that homeless children lack critical and analytical thinking skills or that they bring nothing to the process of learning to read (Noll & Watkins, 2003/2004).

My Developing Professional View

Identify and describe some major considerations for teachers in primary grades as they plan curriculum and instruction. Think about materials, activities, and how children will be grouped.

As with all children, teachers must address the needs of homeless children developmentally and culturally, building on what they can do. Teachers must learn about the child's language and cultural background and identify things that interest the child. For example, whereas homeless children may lack school-type literacy skills, they may be adept at other kinds of literacy. They may have assisted parents who are not literate in English to complete paperwork to be admitted to a shelter or hotel. The child may have served a major role in making sense of rules, regulations, and social systems (Noll & Watkins, 2003/2004).

SUMMARY

In this chapter, we have examined the developmental nature of children in the primary grades. Children ages 6–8 usually have made the cognitive shift from preoperational thinking to concrete operational thinking. Thus, they are able to handle increasingly abstract tasks like reading, writing, and calculating. This cognitive shift can also be observed in their play. They may continue to engage in dramatic play but are interested in games with rules. There is some evidence of a relationship between children's developmental level of play and their reading and writing skills.

It is important for teachers to assess children's needs and interests as they develop curriculum and identify instructional strategies. Their individual cultural and developmental backgrounds must be considered. Children in the primary grades continue to learn about diversity, as they are increasingly able to take perspective and understand ways of living they have not directly experienced.

Literacy instruction is the cornerstone of learning in the primary grades. Early childhood scholars call for balance in terms of holistic and skills-based literacy instruction. Balance is determined by the developmental nature and needs of individual children.

Over the past several decades, other classroom configurations in addition to single-age grouping have emerged, including multiage grouping and looping. Research on the effectiveness of one over the other is not conclusive. Furthermore, schools have implemented attendance calendars where students attend school year-round and do not have an extended summer hiatus. There is some evidence to suggest that learning diminishes during summer hiatus, but it is likely that the most beneficial calendar configurations are influenced by the culture of the communities in which they reside.

ENRICHMENT ACTIVITIES

Individual Activities

1. Go to the website for your state office of education and review the curriculum guidelines for first, second, or third grade. Select a topic from the curriculum and then locate five children's books appropriate for teaching about that topic. Using the checklist on page 150, evaluate each of the books for antibias characteristics.

2. Whether highly prominent or not, most schools have a hidden curriculum, usually driven by the culture of the community. Reflect on your experiences in elementary school and decide what the hidden curriculum was. Briefly summarize the hidden values and whether or how they affected you.

3. Interview a primary grade teacher to learn about how s/he teaches reading. Determine how this teacher views the issue of balance in her/his reading instruction.

Cooperative Activity

4. Each member of your cooperative group will research the meaning, origin, and traditions of a December celebration. (You may prefer to learn about other celebrations: patriotic celebrations, festivals of light, etc.) Come together as a group and share what you have learned. Identify similarities and differences among the celebrations.

Advocacy Activities

5. Based on your knowledge of development of primary grade children, briefly describe an appropriate service learning project for this age group. Share your idea with primary grade teachers.

6. Research and develop a rationale for increasing funding for 21st CCLC programs and write a letter to the federal legislators in your state.

{ FOR FURTHER READING

Primary Grade Curriculum

Cooper, J. L., & Dever, M. T. (2001). Socio-dramatic play as a vehicle for curriculum integration in first grade. *Young Children, 56*(3), 58–66.

Dever, M. T., Whitaker, M. L., & Byrnes, D. A. (2001, September/October). The 4th R: Teaching ABOUT religion in the public schools. *The Social Studies, 92*(5), 220–229.

Edelson, R. J., & Johnson, G. (2003/04). Music makes math meaningful. *Childhood Education, 80*(2), 65–70.

Fleener, C. E., & Bucher, K. T. (2003/04). Linking reading, science, and fiction books. *Childhood Education, 80*(2), 76–83.

Johns, J. L., & Elish-Piper, L. (Eds.) (1997). *Balanced reading instruction: Teachers' visions and voices.* Dubuque, IA: Kendall/Hunt Publishing.

McDaniel, G. L., Isaac, M. Y., Brooks, H. M., & Hatch, A. (2005). Confronting K–3 teaching challenges in an era of accountability. *Young Children, 60*(2), 20–26.

Moomaw, S., & Jones, G. W. (2005/06). Native curriculum in early childhood classroom. *Childhood Education, 82*(2), 89–94.

Saab, J. F. (2001). "How do we know when we're there?" One school's journey toward developmentally appropriate practice. *Young Children, 56*(3), 88–94.

Configurations

Bellis, M. (1999). Look before you loop. *Young Children, 54*(3), 70–73.

Grant, J., & Johnson, B. (1995). *A common sense guide to multiage practices, primary level.* Columbus, OH: Teachers' Publishing Group.

Diversity

Bowman, B. (Ed.) (2002). *Essays in developing and enhancing early literacy skills of African American children.* Washington, DC: National Black Child Development Institute.

Manning, J. P., & Gaudelli, W. (2003) Perspectives: Modern myths about poverty and education. *Social Studies and the Young Learner, 16*(2), 27–29.

Swick, K. J. (2004). The dynamics of families who are homeless: Implications for early childhood educators. *Childhood Education, 80*(3), 116–120.

Professional Development Resources

CHILDREN'S DEFENSE FUND

25 E Street NW
Washington, DC 20001
http://www.childrensdefense.org/

NATIONAL BLACK CHILD DEVELOPMENT INSTITUTE

1101 15th Street NW, Suite 900
Washington, DC 20005
http://www.nbcdi.org/

NATIONAL INSTITUTE ON OUT-OF-SCHOOL TIME

Wellesley College
106 Central Street

Wellesley, MA 02481
http://www.niost.org/

NATIONAL LATINO CHILDREN'S INSTITUTE

1115 S. St. Mary's Street
San Antonio, TX 78210
http://www.nlci.org/

TEACHING ABOUT RELIGION WITH A VIEW TO DIVERSITY WEBSITE

www.teachingaboutreligion.org/

FREEDOM FORUM WEBSITE

http://www.freedomforum.org/

{ SELF-ASSESSMENT

1. Based on developmental differences, discuss some ways that teaching children age 6–8 differs from teaching younger children. Identify at least three ways the learning environment (e.g., schedule, materials, activities) might be different.

2. Provide one example of an instructional strategy that is child-centered and antibias in nature. Provide one example of an explicit instruction lesson. Provide a rationale for implementation of each example.

3. In what ways might culture influence literacy development? What are some considerations for educators regarding culture as they develop curriculum?

4. Explain *balanced literacy* in your own words.

5. Identify at least one *pro* and one *con* for each learning configuration including looping, homeschooling, and multiage grouping.

Scenario

You are a second-grade teacher in a diverse school setting. Children in your class have a range of religious (e.g., Christian, Jewish, Buddhist) and ethnic (e.g., Caucasian, Hispanic, East Indian) backgrounds. The children seem to organize in cliques based on their common backgrounds and there is occasional conflict between groups. You suspect they have prejudiced attitudes toward those who are different. Describe some strategies you might integrate into your curriculum to address their prejudiced attitudes.

REFERENCES

Adams, G. L., & Engelmann, S. (1996). *Research on Direct Instruction: 25 years beyond DISTAR*. Seattle, WA: Educational Achievement Systems.

Banks, J. A. (1995). Multicultural education: Historical development, dimensions and practice. In J. A. Banks & C. A. McGee Banks (Eds.), *Handbook of research on multicultural education* (pp. 3–24). New York: Macmillan.

Bardige, B. (2005). *At a loss for words: How America is failing our children and what we can do about it*. Philadelphia: Temple University Press.

Bergen, D., & Coscia, J. (2001). *Brain research and childhood education: Implications for educators*. Olney, MD: Association for Childhood Education International.

Braunger, J., & Lewis, J. (1998). *Building a knowledge base in reading*. Portland, OR: Nowthwest Regional Educational Laboratory; Urbana, IL: National Council of Teachers of English; Newark, DE: International Reading Association.

Bredekamp, S., & Copple, C. (Eds.). (1997). *Developmentally appropriate practice in early childhood programs* (revised ed.). Washington, DC: National Association for the Education of Young Children.

Children's Defense Fund. (2000). *The state of America's children yearbook 2000*. Washington, DC: Children's Defense Fund.

Children's Defense Fund. (2005). *The state of America's children yearbook 2005*. Washington, DC: Children's Defense Fund.

Cloud, J., & Morse, J. (2001, August 27). Home sweet school. *Time*, 47–54.

Derman-Sparks, L., & A.B.C. Task Force. (1989). *Anti-bias curriculum: Tools for empowering young children*. Washington, DC: National Association for the Education of Young Children.

Dever, M. T., Whitaker, M. L., & Byrnes, D. A. (2001, September/October). The 4th R: Teaching ABOUT religion in the public schools. *The Social Studies, 92*(5), 220–229.

Gallagher-Mance, J. (1997). The reality of balanced literacy in a primary classroom. In J. L. Johns & L. Elish-Piper (Eds.), *Balanced reading instruction: Teachers visions and voices*. Dubuque, IA: Kendall/Hunt Publishing.

Golden, D. (2000, February 11). Class of their own: home schooled pupils are making colleges sit up and take notice. *The Wall Street Journal*.

Hoffman, J. (2003) Multiage teachers' beliefs and practices. *Journal of Research in Childhood Education, 18*(1), 5–17.

Morse, J. (2002). Summertime and school isn't easy. In F. Schultz (Ed), *Annual Editions: Education, 02/03*. Dubuque, IA: McShaw-Hill/Dushkin (pp. 70–73).

NICHHD (National Institute of Child Health and Human Development). (1999). *Report of the National Reading Panel: Teaching children to read*. Washington, DC: Author.

Noll, E., & Watkins, R. (December 2003/January 2004). The impact of homelessness on children's literacy experiences. *The Reading Teacher, 57*(4), 362–371.

Pellegrini, A. D. (1980). The relationship between kindergartner's play and achievement in prereading language and writing. *Psychology in the Schools, 17*(4), 530–535.

Piaget, J., & Inhelder, B. (1969). *The psychology of the child*. New York: Basic Books.

Pressley, M. (2002). *Reading instruction that works: The case for balanced teaching* (2nd ed.). New York: Guilford Press.

Read, S. (2000). First and second graders write information text: An interpretive case study. Unpublished doctoral dissertation, Utah State University.

Veenman, S. (1995). Cognitive and non-cognitive effects of multigrade and multi-age classes: A best-evidence synthesis. *Review of Educational Research, 65*(4), 319–381.

Vernon-Feagans, L., Hammer, C. S., Miccio, A., & Manlove, E. (2001). Early language and literacy skills in low-income African-American and Hispanic children. In S. B. Neuman & D. K. Dickinson (Eds.), *Handbook of early literacy research*. New York: Guilford Press.

Vygotsky, L. S. (1966). Play and its role in the mental development of the child. *Soviet Psychology, 5*(3), 62–76.

Wolfgang, C. (1974). An exploration of the relationship between the cognitive area of reading and selected developmental aspects of children's play. *Psychology in the Schools, 11*(3), 338–342.

Wolfgang, C. H., & Sanders, T. S. (1981). Defending young children's play as the ladder to literacy. *Theory Into Practice, 20*(2), 116–120.

Wolfgang, C. H., & Wolfgang, M. E. (1992). *School for young children*. Boston: Allyn and Bacon.

Guiding Children's Behavior in Early Childhood Settings

8

Reflect on your experiences in school. What kinds of child guidance strategies did your teachers use? Do you feel like the strategies helped you learn appropriate behavior? Were your teachers more interested in controlling children or teaching them appropriate behavior? Did you feel demeaned or threatened in any way?

Guiding young children's behavior in positive ways is a multifaceted task. Early childhood educators must consider various factors: the characteristics of the learning environment, the developmental nature of the children in the environment, and the cultural values each child brings to the early childhood setting. Good teachers assess the developmental and cultural needs of individual children and structure an environment designed to teach and support prosocial behavior.

Whether from real-life experiences or the media, some children have learned violent and bullying behaviors. Early childhood educators employ strategies for addressing children's violent play and interactions with others.

After reading this chapter, you will understand:

▶ Characteristics of early childhood environments that encourage appropriate behavior.

▶ Developmentally appropriate behavior guidance strategies.

▶ Cultural considerations relative to child guidance.

▶ Strategies for encouraging nonviolent behavior.

▶ Strategies for addressing bullying.

Effective child guidance begins as early childhood educators use strategies that prevent behavior problems. Grounded in past early childhood educators like Herbart, Pestalozzi, Froebel, Montessori, and Dewey, the notion of preventative guidance is prominent today. Key to the effectiveness of prevention strategies is teachers' understanding of the nature of young children. Teachers and caregivers must understand the developmental needs and cultural values of young children, have reasonable expectations, and structure an environment that is conducive to learning and encourages prosocial behavior. Teachers who effectively manage behavior use guidance strategies that acknowledge children's individual development and cultural backgrounds, and that are designed to teach acceptable behavior.

Encouraging Environments

Early childhood environments that encourage positive, appropriate interactions align with the developmental, individual, and cultural needs of the children within. In this section, environments designed to support healthy social, emotional, cognitive, and physical development of young children of various ages are described.

Infants

Infancy is a critical developmental time for humans because, from the moment of birth, babies are developing a sense of trust. They need to know that they will be cared for and their needs will be met. A strong sense of trust acquired in infancy leads to healthy social and emotional development later in life. Infants build trust and a sense of security when caregivers respond immediately to their needs. The adult/infant ratio must be sufficient so that a caregiver is readily available to meet each infant's needs.

Sensory Learning. Infants are rapidly learning about their world as they take in information through their senses. Lack of sensory stimulation impedes growth and development. Infants need many opportunities to learn as they handle and mouth objects, focus on light and movement, and listen to voices and sounds. When they become mobile, they need objects to explore that are easily within their reach. Because infants put objects in their mouths, caregivers must be cautions about choking hazards and routine sterilization of toys and objects.

Human Interactions. As infants develop, they become interested in others. They enjoy dialogue even before they use conventional words, and need supportive interested adults to talk with them. They explore others around them, sometimes by pulling hair and grabbing, unable to understand that those behaviors may hurt another. Again, they need supportive adults who can gently and lovingly head off harmful events.

Calm Environment. Too much activity or a chaotic environment may overstimulate infants; they may startle at loud noises. Supportive adults provide a calm setting and alternate periods of activity, quiet, and sleep.

Routines. Infants are unique and have different routines for eating, sleeping, playing, and diapering. Most infants have already developed a routine at home. Communication with parents is vital so that you can use the established routine in the early childhood setting.

Toddlers

By age 18 months, toddlers are quite mobile and busy exploring, questioning, and testing their environment as they learn about their world through events, objects, and people. They are beginning to assert their independence, develop a sense of self as competent beings, and explore with no regard for their own safety.

Laura Dwight© Laura Dwight/CORBIS.

Supportive caregivers clear the environment of harmful objects (e.g., dangerous cleaning supplies, small and sharp objects), provide many carefully monitored experiences with objects and people, and encourage toddlers to take initiative.

Separation Anxiety. Most older infants and toddlers become anxious when parents leave them in a new environment. This response is known as *separation anxiety* and results in crying, sometimes for long periods of time. Separation anxiety may also occur in preschool and early school years. It is a normal reaction when parents depart. High-quality early childhood educators understand separation anxiety, respond in a comforting manner and voice, reassure the child that the parent will return, and try to engage the child in an interesting activity.

In an encouraging environment, parents are permitted to stay for a period to assist with the transition into the early childhood setting. Caregivers also caution parents to depart in an open and supportive way. Sneaking out may frighten the child and can negatively affect his developing sense of trust. Children experiencing separation anxiety may be comforted by a *transition object* (a favorite object from home) and should be permitted to have one.

Freedom within Limits. Toddlers need the security that routine and structure provide, yet they need some freedom with the routine and structure. Supportive teachers provide reasonable choices within a safe environment. For example, a toddler can safely decide whether to color with markers or crayons but cannot decide to play outside when there is no one to accompany her. The adult/child ratio must be sufficient so that all children can be carefully monitored.

Laura Dwight Photography.

Routines. Like infants, toddlers thrive on routine. It helps them know what to expect which, in turn, helps them feel physically and psychologically safe in their environment. Early childhood educators must also be consistent with their expectations to support children's psychological safety. For example, it is inconsistent to forbid running inside one day, and ignore it the next.

Human Interaction. Most toddlers have a desire to interact with other children. Yet, although they enjoy the company of other children, they are quite egocentric and have limited ability to delay gratification. From their egocentric point of view, sharing is difficult. The encouraging environment acknowledges this and contains multiples of various toys in case of conflicts.

Toddlers lack appropriate language and moral development to react to situations in socially appropriate ways. Thus, it is not unusual for them to have tantrums or become defiant when they do not get what they want. In a supportive environment, early childhood educators understand this and respond in firm yet warm and understanding ways. For example, if a child is fussing because it is not yet his turn, the caregiver might say, "I know it is difficult to wait. You can sit on my lap if that helps." In this case, the early childhood educator acknowledged the feeling for the child and provided understanding and comfort.

Preschoolers and Kindergarteners

Children 3 to 5 years old continue on the developmental path on which they embarked as infants, demonstrating new skills and understandings almost daily. They may do something today that they could not do yesterday. In a supportive environment where early childhood educators are accepting and warm, yet firm, preschoolers and kindergarteners will develop a positive sense of self and their interactions with others will become increasingly more socially appropriate. They are interested in friendships and cooperative play. Warm support from adults assists them to learn to share, delay gratification, and take others' perspectives. For example, if children are having difficulty sharing, you might suggest *trading*, where one child offers to trade a toy for the desired one.

Sense of Self. The self-concept of preschoolers and kindergarteners is quite fragile but will flourish if interactions with adults are warm and positive. To this end, they need activities designed to develop their sense of competence and positive self-worth including many opportunities to take initiative, learn from mistakes, and interact with objects and people in positive ways. Teachers must clearly understand how a positive sense of self develops. Merely telling children they are special and teaching them songs and poems about being special is not enough. Children learn to feel special through positive interactions and daily support. Supportive teachers acknowledge that we all make mistakes and assist children to be accepting of their mistakes and learn from them.

The Influence of Culture on Self-Confidence. Children's perceptions of self are derived from the cultures in which they live (Marshall, 2001). Early childhood educators who understand various cultural norms as well as individual differences are well positioned to support children's developing self-confidence. Many families that have lived in the United States for several generations adhere to the traditional values of their ancestors.

In Western cultures, independence, individuality, and willingness to explore new situations are viewed as characteristics of confident children. Conversely, in cultures influenced by Confucian and Taoist philosophies, self-restraint and control of emotional expressions are signs of social maturity and self-confidence (Marshall, 2001). Assertiveness, in these families, may be viewed as immaturity. Many (not all) families with African-American, Latin American, and southern European ancestry view cooperativeness and interdependence, rather than individuality, as indicative of healthy self-confidence (Marshall, 2001).

Teachers who embrace the Western ideals of the cultural mainstream must expand their concept of healthy self-confidence to include the ideals of others. Many families nurture cooperation, sensitivity, and modesty in their children over assertiveness and autonomy (Marshall, 2001). Frequent and ongoing communication with parents, including home visits, is a way for you to learn about the values of individual families.

Culturally Relevant Environments. Children of all ages function best in an environment where they feel accepted and valued. Thus, learning environments that reflect the multicultural nature of our society are an important component of an encouraging learning environment. Children need to see pictures of people who look like them and need to engage with objects that are culturally relevant for them. Cultural diversity should be thoughtfully reflected in dramatic play, books, bulletin board displays, visitors, and so on. For example, include food boxes and packages from a variety of cultures in housekeeping play. Invite adults from various cultures to share a favorite story.

Routine. Routine and structure are important for the physical and psychological well-being of preschoolers and kindergarteners. Like toddlers, they need some freedom within the structure of the environment, and they can handle a broader array of choices than toddlers. For example, 3- to 5-year-olds can choose an activity among block play, painting, listening to a story, or molding with clay. Making choices and engaging productively with others supports their developing self-concept in positive ways.

Transitions. Along with routines, children need support as they transition from one activity to another. Figure 8.1 provides a simple guide for smooth transitions that can easily be remembered with the acronym EAT. The *E* stands for *expectations*. Be certain that your expectations in terms of noise level and the children's capabilities are reasonable and developmentally appropriate. For example, expect that they will talk with each other and make some noise as they put toys away.

The *A* stands for *alerting* children that the transition time is approaching. For example, you might say, "It will soon be time to pick up our toys so we can go outside." A routine song or saying is a good way to accomplish this.

The *T* stands for *transition alternatives*. Children need to know what alternative activities are appropriate in case they are ready for the next activity before the others. That means there is a designated activity, looking at books for example, in which children engage when waiting for others to get ready to move on. If you do this regularly, children will automatically select a book to look at while waiting for others.

Expectations. Children ages 3 to 5 years old are increasingly able to understand rules for behavior. When teachers are clear and consistent with their expectations, children learn appropriate behavior.

Play. Opportunities for constructive, dramatic, and sociodramatic play are essential in preschool and kindergarten. Dramatic and sociodramatic play not only support the many aspects of learning discussed in Chapter 4, they also provide a release for children's stress or anxiety. For example, it is comforting for the child adjusting to a new sibling to play mommy or daddy with a doll. The child who is fearful of dogs might pretend to have an imaginary dog during play. Opportunities to play out stressful events and feelings help children move past them.

Taking Responsibility. Preschool and kindergarten children can take responsibility for many things in their classrooms. They can clean up toys and put them away in their proper places, pass out snacks or instructional materials, and so on. Taking responsibility builds a sense of competence and self-confidence.

Cooperation vs. Competition. When competitive activities are promoted in preschool and kindergarten, children's tendencies to compare themselves to one another are amplified. They are quick to identify themselves as successful or a failure based on the results of the competitive activity. Over time, a compilation of competitive activities where children experience failure can have devastating and lasting negative effects.

Preschool and kindergarten children can begin learning to work cooperatively. They work well in pairs on well-defined tasks with clear limits for behavior. The *Window into the Classroom* describes how Ms. Renée's kindergarten children worked cooperatively to learn about owl pellets.

Room Arrangement. The physical arrangement of the learning environment impacts children's behavior. This topic is discussed more fully in Chapter 12, but following are some general considerations for arranging a learning environment that will promote prosocial behavior.

▶ Be certain the group activity area is large enough that children can sit together without crowding.

Ellen B. Senisi/The Image Works.

Myrleen Ferguson Cate/PhotoEdit.

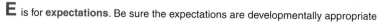

E is for **expectations**. Be sure the expectations are developmentally appropriate

A is for **alerting** children that the transition is coming.

T is for **transition alternatives** to productively occupy them as they wait for others.

Figure 8.1 **Supporting smooth transitions from one activity to another.**

Bob Daemmrich/The Image Works.

▶ To avoid conflicts, separate quiet and noisy small group activity centers. For example, blocks and dramatic play might be in one section with books and listening in another.

▶ Have clear and open pathways so children can easily move around the room without getting in each other's way or tripping.

▶ Store some materials within children's reach so they are not dependent on adult assistance to retrieve them. Teach them appropriate care of the materials.

▶ Be certain there is ample space for each small group activity. For example, the block area needs enough space for elaborate constructions and the book area needs space for several children to read books at one time.

Primary Grade Children

During the primary grade years (ages 6–8), children undergo a cognitive shift (Piaget & Inhelder, 1969) that enables them to learn social skills that set a path for later social development. By this time, young children have fairly well-developed perspective-taking abilities. While the 3- to 5-year-olds may believe they can learn to do anything, primary grade children have a more realistic sense of self. Peers are becoming increasingly important and friendship means more than just having someone to do things with. It is now a reciprocal relationship where friends do things for each other.

Just as in preschool and kindergarten settings, culturally relevant environments, smooth transitions, and appropriate room arrangements must be considered in primary grade classrooms. Because primary grade children are further along on the developmental continuum, they are able to take more responsibility and engage in more cooperative activities than are younger children.

Taking Responsibility. Primary grade children have the skills to take much responsibility for the daily running of their classroom. If expectations for behavior are taught, they can change wall and bulletin board displays, take lunch count, set out

Window into the Classroom

Ms. Renée's kindergarteners have been learning about birds. They have been examining several stuffed bird specimens and learning descriptive words as they read and write about birds. They have also gone on a nature walk where they spied several different kinds of birds in their natural habitats.

Ms. Renée had some stuffed owl specimens and owls became a focus of the bird study. From books, the children learned many things about owls, including the fact that they feed mostly on mammals and, if the prey is small enough, the owl will swallow it whole. Later, the owl regurgitates pellets of bones, fur, feathers, and anything else it cannot digest. (Sterilized pellets are available commercially; they should never be gathered from the natural habitat due to risk of disease.)

Today, the children are working in cooperative pairs to examine owl pellets that Ms. Renée ordered from a local source. One child in each pair has tweezers for taking apart the owl pellet. The other has a picture chart to record the items found in the pellet. (The chart has pictures of mouse bones and fur because the local owls feed primarily on mice.) As one child finds a piece of bone or fur, the children talk, compare the piece to the pictures, and identify it. The other child then makes a tally mark in the appropriate place on the chart. The children are free to trade jobs if they wish. At the end of the activity, children review their data and share their findings.

(The pictures on the chart are accompanied by the name of the item, jaw bone for example, to provide a print activity for the kindergarteners. More detailed text can be added if the activity is done with primary grade children.)

and clean up materials for routine activities, record attendance, care for class pets, and so on. *The Focus on Children* takes you into Mindy's classroom, where second graders take responsibility for jobs in their classroom.

Cooperation vs. Competition. As with preschool and kindergarten, competitive activities should be limited in the primary grades, because, similar to their younger counterparts, primary grade children may quickly label themselves as failures. Primary grade children will, however, enjoy a limited amount of team competition that requires cooperation within the teams.

In addition to considering the developmental stages of primary grade children, their cultural backgrounds must be considered as well. Attitudes about cooperation and competition are formed in the family, and children's family backgrounds vary with regard to this issue. The continuum of individualism to collectivism refers to the degree to which the family culture values individual accomplishment (individualism) or the well-being and accomplishments of the group (collectivism) (Trumbull, Rothstein-Fisch, Greenfield, & Quiroz, 2001). While individual family values fall somewhere on the continuum, about 70% of the world's cultures fall closer to the collectivist end (Trumbull et al., 2001). On the other hand, the dominant culture in the United States is situated on the individualistic end of the continuum. Thus, many children in our nation's public schools may have different cultural values with regard to this issue.

Conversely, well-structured cooperative activities generally support children's growth and development. They help children:

▶ Build a sense of community.

▶ Illuminate the individual strengths each brings to the activity.

▶ Learn to value contributions of others.

▶ See themselves as a valuable contributor to the group's shared goals.

David Young-Wolff/PhotoEdit.

Focus on Children

As the day begins, Mindy greets her second-graders as they enter the room one by one. Mindy casually opens her desk, takes out a tube of hand lotion and begins applying it to her hands, while still greeting new arrivals. As children enter the room, they hang up their jackets and store their backpacks as they chat to each other. Some are placing homework papers on her desk while others are adding interesting bits to the morning news. All children mark on a piece of chart paper under either *school lunch* or *brought lunch*.

Beginning the day's activities, most of the children are in their seats silently reading a book of choice found in their desks or the class library. However, some children are busy with other tasks. One child changes the calendar to reflect the correct date and marks the weather sign that appropriately characterizes the day's weather. Another marks the attendance and calculates the lunch count. She subsequently approaches Mindy to indicate that she is now on her way to the office to turn in the attendance. Two boys are setting out the materials to be used for Writer's Workshop (paper, stapler, etc.), which will begin at 9:30. Finally, one child is feeding the class pets while another waters the class plants. (Not all of the plants are watered each day, and they need weekly doses of plant food. This information is recorded daily on a wall chart so the plant caregiver knows what to do.)

Mindy believes that children learn and build a sense of competence and self-worth when they carry out responsibilities that are within their developmental capabilities. She said, "I used to do everything for children until I realized that they could do it for themselves." About bulletin boards she said, "I even used to make the most spectacular bulletin boards until I realized that I was the only one who ever looked at them! Now, the children do the bulletin boards in my room. It allows me to spend my time more productively and they learn from doing it and have ownership of the bulletin boards." She went on to comment that children even take responsibility for teaching each other how to do the class jobs. "I do the job the first time and teach one child how to do it. Then, as the class jobs rotate, each child teaches the next child until all of the children know how to do each job. They learn responsibility and it gives me more time for study, organization, and planning."

Cooperative Learning

Positive Interdependence

Individuals are linked so that one cannot succeed without the others.

Individual Accountability

Each collaborator is individually accountable for a portion of the task.

Promotive Interaction

There are opportunities to promote the success of others.
(e.g., assisting, encouraging.)

Interpersonal and Small Group Skills

Interpersonal and small group skills are taught.

Group Processing

Collaborators discuss how well they are achieving their goals and developing working relationships.

Figure 8.2 Elements of cooperative learning.
Source: Johnson, D.W., & Johnson, R. T. (1999). The three Cs of school and classroom management. In H. J. Freiberg (Ed.), *Beyond behaviorism: Changing the classroom management paradigm.* Boston: Allyn and Bacon.

Cooperative learning helps children build a sense of competence as they perceive that they are a valued, contributing group member. Figure 8.2 outlines the elements of well-structured cooperative learning activities. The scenario of Ms. Renée's kindergarten class is an example of a cooperative activity where kindergarten children are grouped in pairs, each with a job that is necessary to complete the task at hand.

Managing Environments and Guiding Behavior

Effective management of early childhood environments results in a social and physical atmosphere that supports development and learning. Continue to reflect on your own experiences in school. Do you remember any teachers who you felt were overly controlling? Do you remember guidance strategies that helped you learn?

For decades, management has been a primary concern to early childhood educators, experienced and novice alike. Guiding behavior is a major component of managing the environment and early childhood educators who successfully guide behavior find management in general to be easier. The importance of planning and preparation; providing engaging, interesting, learning activities; and capitalizing on children's strengths, as discussed in Part 2 of this text, cannot be ignored when considering management issues.

High-quality early childhood learning environments embrace two ideas from the past. First, as suggested by Froebel and others, children are inherently good. Second, as promoted by Dreikurs and others, a democratic learning environment is optimal.

Children Are Inherently Good. Children are not born knowing the ways of their culture or how to function happily and productively within it. Parents, teachers, and caregivers have the responsibility to teach them about their social world. Children should be viewed as good human beings who have not yet learned all there is to know about appropriate behavior.

Democratic Environments. We live in a democratic society in the United States, and early childhood settings should reflect life in the broader culture. That is, we live in a free society yet limits are imposed on our behavior to ensure physical and psychological safety for everyone. For example, we enjoy freedom of speech but it is unlawful to maliciously slander another. We have laws designed to balance our freedom with safety. Such should be the case for young children as well.

Research on behavior guidance suggests that environments where teaching children self-discipline is emphasized over externally imposed control show greater promise of improvement in learning and achievement (Freiberg, 1999). If the goal is to teach self-control and self-governance, then using methods with the intent to control seems counterproductive.

General Considerations for Guiding Behavior

Early childhood educators in well-managed early childhood environments have some common goals. They want children to learn to (a) be self-governing, (b) work together productively, and (c) learn appropriate behavior toward others. This section provides some general considerations for early childhood educators as they address these goals using strategies designed to teach appropriate behavior. General considerations include (a) providing choices, (b) using praise effectively, and (c) understanding the limitations of punishment.

Choices

Adults make choices about their lives everyday, but children live in a world where they have limited power to make decisions about their lives. That is as it should be. Children are, of course, not mature or socialized enough to take complete charge of their lives. However, as a component of a democratic encouraging environment, they can take charge of some things, and opportunities to make choices support children's positive sense of power and competence. Toddlers can handle two alternatives while older children can handle more.

Giving children the choice to *do as I say or suffer the consequences* is not an effective way to empower children. To empower children and build their confidence as independent beings, you must be certain that all alternatives are positive ones. For example, toddlers can choose whether to wear the blue bib or the yellow bib during lunch, but the choice of whether or not to wear a bib is not given. A first grader should be able to choose the topic for her writing project, but the choice of whether or not to write is not given.

Praise

Effective praise is specific, immediate, and provides children with some helpful information about themselves. Nonspecific comments such as "good job," give a child very little information about her/himself. It is more helpful and effective to provide specific information. For example, after watching Tad put away the materials from the word working center, Ms. Thompson said, "I noticed you got all of the tools put away on the workbench today and you hung each right next to its picture. I can see that you want to take good care of them so they will be there for you to play with

tomorrow." Mr. Fukui was specific when he gave Mia, a first grader, feedback on the story she was writing when he said, "I really feel like I know the characters in your story because you have used adjectives to describe them so well. Here you tell me that the dog is big and brown and likes to lick people. I can picture that dog in my mind!" This type of praise gives children useful information that can be applied to future experiences.

Misuse of Praise. Teachers must be careful not to use praise and rewards to manipulate behavior. An example of a manipulative comment is, "I like the way Jack is ready for circle time." A statement like this is often used to get others to do exactly as Jack is doing. The focus is on pleasing the teacher, rather than on the value of the next activity. If learning experiences are engaging and the guidelines for smooth transitions are followed, children will probably get ready for the activity if you say, "We can get started with our next activity as soon as everyone is ready."

Punishment

Punishment is any punitive response to behavior that is intended to eliminate the behavior. Educational scholars warn against punishment because, in the long run, it can be harmful to children, particularly if it is used excessively. Moderate forms of punishment (e.g., arbitrarily taking away privileges, gentle swats) do not eliminate undesirable behaviors; they only temporarily suppress them (Freiberg, 1999). Other limitations include the following (Freiberg, 1999):

▶ Punished behaviors often reoccur when the punisher is not present.

▶ Public reprimands may be desirable for children who seek any type of attention. For some, negative attention is better than no attention at all.

▶ Punishment models behavior we do not want to teach children (hitting, for example).

▶ There may be emotional side effects (e.g., promotes negative self-image; child hates coming to school or child care center).

▶ Punishment that is most likely to extinguish undesirable behavior is severe and beyond legal and ethical limits. (p. 9).

The use of corporal punishment is almost nonexistent in care and education settings today. Moreover, states inflict severe penalties on educators who use any kind of severe punishment on children. Early childhood educators must be certain that no response to children's behavior is dangerous, degrading, disrespectful, or in any way physically or psychologically harmful. Children must feel safe at all times.

⟨ Developmentally Appropriate Guidance Strategies

Appropriate behavior guidance varies based on the developmental stages of the children. Expectations and responses to their behavior must acknowledge what children are reasonably able to do.

Infants

Infants are not developed enough to take responsibility for their behavior; they do as they wish with the goal of having their needs met. Managing the behavior of infants is very individual. Schedules for diapering, eating, playing, and sleeping vary, and caregivers must respect and adhere to infants' individual schedules. Trying to get all infants on a particular schedule to ease the work for caregivers does not support infants' healthy development.

Respond to Crying. Caregivers must respond to the cries and movements of infants. A cry indicates some type of distress and good caregivers carefully analyze what it might be. For example, if it is almost feeding time, the infant is probably hungry. If the infant ate an hour ago, however, it is probably some other type of discomfort (a gas bubble, for example). High-quality caregivers learn to read the signals of individual infants.

Bill Aron/PhotoEdit.

It is sometimes difficult to decide what the infants' distress might be, but whatever the reason for crying, it is important to respond in a calm and tender way. Gentle holding and a calm, warm voice are appropriate. Speaking to them in a harsh voice, shaking, and slapping are inappropriate ways to respond.

Curiosity. As infants become mobile, they will demonstrate a natural curiosity about each other, and this may result in hair pulling, poking at eyes, grabbing ears, or even biting. This is one of those times when caregivers assert control so that the psychological and physical safety of other infants is safeguarded. Gently pick up the curious infant and move her out of reach of the others. Then, talk with her in a warm and gentle voice about the feature she was exploring. "Yes, those are Ivan's eyes. You have eyes too, and so do I," pointing as you speak.

Toddlers

Toddlers are learning appropriate and safe behavior and have reached an age when they can begin to take some responsibility for their behavior. They are in the *extrinsic consequences* stage of moral development, which means they are aware that they must submit to adult authority and behave in certain ways because adults impose consequences if they do not (Kohlberg, 1984). That is, *good* behavior is followed by desirable consequences and *bad* behavior is followed by undesirable consequences.

It is doubtful that responding in punitive ways will teach toddlers appropriate and safe behavior. Furthermore, their point of view is very egocentric, which makes reasoning with them difficult and futile. They often lack the experience to understand what they want to communicate and the language with which to communicate it.

Toddlers learn when caregivers respond in ways designed to teach them what appropriate and safe behavior is. For example, a supportive caregiver might say, "I can't let you hit Jamaica with the stick because it might hurt her. But, you can hit this drum with it." In this case, the caregiver firmly, yet warmly stated the prohibition while emphasizing what is allowable.

Redirecting Behavior. Toddlers are curious about their world and enjoy exploring it. Even in an environment that has been cleared of harmful objects, they will find a prohibition (climbing and standing on a chair, for example). This is best addressed by redirecting the child to a safer behavior while providing an explanation. For example, with the toddler who is standing on the chair, a caregiver might say, "I can't let you stand on the chair because you might fall. But, I can let you stand on this balance beam if you like." Or, "It isn't safe to stand on the chair but you may sit on it." Again, the caregiver goes beyond stating the prohibition and suggests acceptable behavior.

Toddlers will frequently get into conflict with each other, primarily over things (as opposed to relationships). This may result in grabbing, hitting, biting, and most certainly crying. Redirecting children is useful here because it honors their developmental stage. That is, due to their egocentric nature, sharing is difficult for them; however, they may find another toy or activity pleasing if gently redirected.

Redirecting is particularly easy if you have multiples of the most popular toys. Again, it is important to put language with your behavior. For example, a caregiver

Stuart Cohen/The Image Works.

might redirect a toddler by saying, "I can't let you take the red car from Molly because she is using it and that would make her sad. But, I have another red car right here for you to play with." If there are not two red cars, the child might be easily directed to another favorite toy. What the child is learning is that his needs can be met without disrupting or hurting another.

Sharing. Although sharing is difficult for toddlers, they are beginning to learn about it. As toddlers get older and gain experience interacting with peers, caregivers can help them understand sharing. This might begin by helping them to trade one toy for another. For example, if Julie wants the red truck, you can help her find another truck to trade for it. This is best tried when at least one of the children is not overly passionate about having the toy. If both are determined to have the toy, redirection will be best.

Logical and Natural Consequences. Use of logical and natural consequences dates back centuries to Native American cultures. The age-old practice has important applications in today's society. As discussed in Chapter 2, it is particularly prominent in the more recent work of Dreikurs (Dreikurs, Grunwald, & Pepper, 1982).

Natural consequences flow naturally from the behavior. For example, if a toddler touches the hot stove, he will get burned. If he goes outside without his mittens, his hands will get cold. *Logical consequences*, however, are determined by adults and are a logical result of the problematic behavior. For example, if a toddler runs into the street, a logical consequence is that she must play inside, away from the street.

Teachers deliver logical consequences in a firm yet nurturing way rather than in a punitive manner (Dreikurs, et al., 1982). For example, if the toddler begins playing in his food, mealtime ends. You might say, "Oh, you are playing in your food; you must be done eating. Let's wash up and get down." It is important to be consistent and follow through with logical consequences immediately.

Time Away. Time away, or time-out, can be used effectively as a logical consequence for problematic behavior, but teachers must be cautious that it is not used as a punishment. This is a line that is easy to cross. For example, as a logical consequence, you might require a child to take some *time away* from a particular prohibition to calm down. Using a firm yet friendly voice, you might say, "I can see that you are angry, but I can't let you hit Lindsey; that hurts her. Please go to the rug

Focus on Diversity

Historically, many Native Americans guided their children's social learning through stories, modeling, and logical consequences. Many Native American families continue that tradition today. Elders tell stories promoting values like *sharing* and *honesty.* They teach by modeling appropriate behavior and expecting children to follow their lead.

Continuing to abide by ancient beliefs, corporal punishment is not practiced in many Native American families today. A value passed down through many centuries of Native Americans is that hitting a child will "hurt the spirit." When children misbehave, they experience logical consequences and adults talk with them about what they did and what they learned from the experience. For example, if a child touched a knife and got a cut, a parent might ask the child what she had learned from that experience. The parents also share their expectation that the child will not commit the prohibition again.

Source: Ed Galindo, personal communication, September 2003.

until you can calm down and we can talk about it." Although you will likely encounter some protest, removing the child from the prohibition is a logical consequence for the problematic behavior. Teachers use time away as an opportunity to teach by talking about what is wrong and about appropriate alternative behaviors. If the child is handled in a gentle, warm, yet firm way, she will eventually learn that hitting is inappropriate.

Conversely, if you use punitive language, time-out or time away becomes a punishment. Note the difference in the following example. "You stop hitting Jamaica right now! Now go over and sit in that time-out chair until I tell you to get up!" A directive such as that is usually followed by much protest and you will probably have a struggle getting the child to the time-out chair. Now, the consequence has become a punishment.

Some things to remember about time-out or time away are as follows:

▶ It must meet the objective of helping a child develop self-control.

▶ A child should never be placed in isolation.

▶ Its use must flow logically from the problematic behavior (e.g., a child who is hitting is removed from the group for the safety of everyone).

▶ It should never be humiliating (e.g., don't put the child on public display in a time-out chair).

It is important to look for alternatives to time-out (Preuesse, 2005/06). For example, can the environment be rearranged to prevent problematic behavior such as running in the classroom? Can you redirect the behavior or take time to teach an alternative behavior?

The Out of Control Toddler. Reflective of their egocentric nature, toddlers can become so distraught over a prohibition that they get out of control. They might throw a tantrum or become aggressive with you or with another child. In this case, it may be necessary to physically restrain the toddler by holding tightly so that she will not hurt herself or others. When doing this, you must be certain to hold the child only tight enough to ensure everyone's safety (including the acting out child) and to talk in a calming voice. It is futile to try and reason with any toddler, particularly one who is out of control, and doing so may even escalate the behavior.

If toddlers are continuously out of control, it may be a sign of more serious behavior problems. If excessive tantrums and acting out continue, you should recommend an evaluation.

Preschoolers and Kindergarteners

Children ages 3–5 are becoming less egocentric and are increasingly able to reason. They are still in the extrinsic consequences stage of moral development. Although strategies used with toddlers might be successfully used with preschoolers (e.g., redirecting attention, time away), there are other effective strategies to use with the more mature preschoolers and kindergarteners that will help them learn appropriate behavior and problem solving skills.

Active Listening. When a problem arises, one of the first things early childhood educators need to assess is who owns the problem. If physical or psychological safety in the learning environment is threatened, then the adult owns the problem. If the child is disillusioned because she

Figure 8.3 **Characteristics of active listening.**

Bob Krist© Bob Krist/CORBIS.

is not getting her way or something is not working to her satisfaction, then the child owns the problem. Supportive early childhood educators use *active listening* to encourage children to solve problems they own rather than act inappropriately.

By engaging in active listening, you do not solve the child's problem; rather, you assist the child to verbalize the problem, understand it, and confront it. Some preschoolers, particularly 3-year-olds, may not participate fully in active listening. Most children, however, will learn to participate. Figure 8.3 outlines the steps of active listening and the *Focus on Children* is an example of how active listening is implemented.

Conflict Resolution. By engaging in conflict resolution, early childhood educators are teaching children how to solve problems in socially appropriate ways. Although many 3-year-olds are not mature enough to participate, conflict resolution is a strategy that will be useful with most preschoolers and kindergarteners. During conflict resolution, the teacher mediates the conflict, assisting each child to express his or her needs, describe feelings, discuss solutions, and agree on a solution. With children this age, the adult usually has to assist by suggesting appropriate solutions. Figure 8.4 outlines the steps of conflict resolution, and the *Window into the Classroom* on p. 176 provides an example of its implementation.

Focus on Children

Kara is a caregiver who works with 3- to 5-year-old children. The children in her care enjoy outside play twice a day. Today, however, Kara notices that 5-year-old Maggie is dawdling at the art center and is not preparing to go outside as she usually does.

Kara: *Maggie, aren't you going to get your jacket and go outside?*

Maggie: *Ya, I will but I'm not ready yet. [She continues to dawdle.]*

Kara: *Maggie, do you have a problem with going outside today?*

Maggie: *Well, before, when we were outside, a dog was barking on the other side of the fence.*

Kara: *Oh, I see. It sounds like that frightened you. [The play yard was completely fenced so there was no danger of the dog harming the children.]*

Maggie: *Ya. He barked loud and mean and I saw his teeth.*

Kara: *Oh, and that scared you didn't it?*

Maggie: *Ya. But it's a good thing dogs can't get into our play yard. [With that comment, Maggie went outside.]*

Conflict Resolution

In early childhood settings, early childhood educators mediate conflict by guiding the conflicted children through the following steps. Early childhood educators assist children who have difficulty verbalizing. Preschoolers particularly need assistance in generating and evaluating solutions.

Step 1: Identify the problem.

Step 2: Generate solutions.

Step 3: Evaluate solutions.

Step 4: Select a solution.

Step 5: Try it out.

Step 6: Talk again to evaluate the results.

Figure 8.4 Elements of conflict resolution.

I Messages. Recall our earlier discussion about child-owned and adult-owned problems. Early childhood educators use *I messages* to communicate an adult-owned problem to young children. An I message communicates what the problem is, why it is a problem, and how you feel about it. Examples are as follows:

> When you are talking to your neighbors while I'm talking to the class, you can't pay attention to what I'm saying, and I feel like you don't care about what I'm saying.
>
> When you run inside, you are ignoring our classroom rules and I feel like you don't care about anyone's safety.

After you state your *I message*, talk about solutions to the problem. Help young children determine what is an appropriate behavior.

Natural and Logical Consequences. Just as with toddlers, applying natural and logical consequences with preschoolers and kindergarteners will help them learn appropriate behavior. For example, if a child is marking on another's paper, the logical consequence might be that she will be directed to another activity or be required to put the crayons away. In cases like this, children must always understand that they will have the opportunity to try the activity again.

Primary Grade Children

Sometime around age 7 (first grade), a shift in young children's moral development is observed. They move from the extrinsic consequences stage of moral development to the *natural consequences* stage (Kohlberg, 1984). At this stage of development, egocentrism has diminished and children are able to empathize with others (take another's point of view). They increasingly understand their social world and that chaos will result if everyone tries to talk at once, for example. Children of this age are increasingly able to reason and problem solve.

Children in the primary grades continue to benefit from strategies already discussed, including active listening, conflict resolution, and natural and logical consequences. Because of their maturing ability to reason and articulate, they will participate more fully in active listening and conflict resolution by suggesting reasonable alternatives.

Determining logical consequences for primary grade children is sometimes quite simple. For example, if a child misuses a piece of playground equipment, she is not permitted to use that equipment until she is ready to demonstrate proper use. However, some problematic behaviors of children this age are more complex. For example,

Scholastic Studio/© Index Stock Imagery.

primary grade children are increasingly aware of right and wrong, truth and untruth. They know that lying is wrong. Because lying affects the ability of others to trust, the logical consequence for lying is that trust must be re-earned. For example, you give the child opportunities to earn trust in small ways first (e.g., showing responsibility for care of materials). The child gradually earns the right to be trusted in larger ways (e.g., serving as office messenger).

As children get older, their ability to delay gratification and to reason mature, enabling them to better take ownership of their problems and find solutions. This opens new doors for introducing new behavior guidance strategies.

Class Meetings. Whole group *class meetings* can be used for social problem solving or to address educational or diagnostic needs, or they may be open-ended (Glasser, 1969). Class meetings are carried out in a democratic manner and provide a safe environment for all voices to be heard.

Social problem solving class meetings are useful for addressing problems that affect the entire class. For example, run-and-chase games on the playground may be getting too rambunctious or there may be excessive arguing over a limited number of tether

Window into the Classroom

Matt, a kindergarten teacher, is moving from one interest center to another where the students in his classroom are engaged in activities of their choice. He is talking with Julia who is telling him about her drawing when he hears shouting from the block center and he notices Brad and Lisa both tugging on a dump truck.

Brad: *I had it first!!*

Lisa: *But I need it and you weren't touching it!!*

Brad: *Ya 'cause it's parked for now, but I'm gonna drive it on my road later!!*

Matt: *Oh, I can see that you are having a problem. Let's see how we can work this out. Brad what do you want?*

Brad: *I want the truck 'cause I had it to drive my loads but it's parked for now 'cause I was building my road.*

Matt: *I see; and Lisa, what do you want?*

Lisa: *I just wanted to put it in my truck station that I made with my blocks.*

Matt: *I see. You both want the truck at the same time. How can we solve that problem?*

Brad: *I had it first and I need it!!*

Matt: *Okay, one thing we could do is let Brad finish his turn. Then, in 5 minutes, you can let Lisa have a turn for 5 minutes. Think about doing that. Or, another solution is to get one of the smaller trucks from the shelf for one of you. Do you have any other ideas?*

Brad: *I want to keep it for 5 minutes 'cause I don't like the red truck.*

Lisa: *Ya, I want it for 5 minutes too.*

Matt: *So, Brad, I'll set the timer for 5 minutes and then you'll share with Lisa?*

Brad: *Ya.*

[The children continue playing. When the timer rings, Lisa gets the truck and takes it to her truck station. Brad does not protest but asks Matt to again set the timer for 5 minutes. At the end of the choice period, Matt talks with Lisa and Brad.]

Matt: *How did it work for you to use the timer and share the truck?*

Brad: *It was okay.*

Lisa: *Ya, but, maybe we can get another truck that has a dumper on it.*

Matt: *That would be nice, wouldn't it? But, I think you found a great way to share the one we have.*

balls. These are all problems that children can discuss and resolve in a class meeting.

At the beginning of the school year, the social problem solving strategy can be used to establish classroom rules. Participating in a democratic process to establish class rules gives children a sense of ownership of those rules, which means they may be more likely to follow them.

During the class meeting, children come together under the careful guidance of the teacher to identify the problem and discuss solutions. Figure 8.5 outlines general characteristics of class meetings.

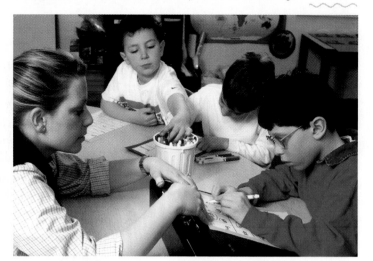

Laura Dwight Photography.

Prejudice Reduction Activities. Prejudice, discrimination, and stereotyping sometimes lie at the core of inappropriate behavior. Children in the primary grades may make fun of, isolate, or mistreat children who look or act differently. Primary grade children are acquiring the ability to take perspective and will benefit from activities designed to reduce prejudice. However, early childhood educators must cautiously evaluate such activities for developmental appropriateness. For example, contrived activities where children are excluded purportedly to learn what discrimination feels like should be avoided with young children.

Figure 8.6 outlines some general guidelines for reducing prejudice in early childhood environments. The *Focus on Diversity* on page 179 provides an example of two activities that are appropriate for primary grade children.

Children with Special Needs

Early childhood educators must be able to read the behavioral cues of children with disabilities and respond in ways that teach and support appropriate behavior. For example, if a child who has tactile defensiveness (extreme sensitivity to touch) frequently has episodes of crying, carefully analyze the context of those episodes to identify the antecedent to crying (Cook, Klein, Tessier, & Daley, 2004). When the

General Characteristics of Class Meetings

Sit in a Tight Circle. A circular seating arrangement ensures that no child is left out of the conversation because s/he cannot see or hear.

The Teacher Does Not Have a Particular Seat in the Circle. The teacher facilitates the meeting, but is not the center of it. In addition, the teacher can sit by children likely to act out to restrain them or by noncommunicative children to encourage them.

Meetings in Primary Grades Should Last Only 10–15 Minutes. It is difficult for young children to maintain attention for longer periods.

Meetings Should Be Held Regularly. Meetings might be daily but no less than once per week.

Meeting Topics Can Come from the Teacher or Students. Everyone's concerns should be addressed.

No Put Downs. Everyone's perspective is valued.

Figure 8.5 Elements of a Class Meeting.
Source: Glasser, W. (1969). *Schools without failure.* New York: Harper & Row.

Guidelines for Reducing Prejudice

1. Use teaching materials that include positive and realistic images of social, ethnic, racial, and other cultural groups in a consistent, natural, and integrated way.

2. Permeate the curriculum with different faces of members of other social, age, racial, and ethnic groups, and help the students differentiate between the individual faces.

3. Use films, videos, books, recordings, photographs, etc., to expose children to members of different racial and ethnic groups.

4. Involve children in structured interracial contact situations that have the following attributes:
   ✔ Cooperation is emphasized rather than competition.
   ✔ Individuals have equal status.
   ✔ Individuals have shared goals.
   ✔ The contact is approved by authorities such as parents, principals, and teachers.

5. Involve children from different racial, ethnic, and social groups in cooperative learning activities (Banks, 1994).

6. Address a child's negative response to a cultural difference as soon as it occurs, and help the child understand why he/she is uncomfortable.

7. Explain why some reactions can hurt feelings, and suggest alternatives.

8. Be uncompromising about a rule that no aspect of individuality, be it gender, race, ethnicity, disability, religion, social class, or any other, is ever an acceptable reason for excluding or teasing another child.

9. Intervene immediately when a child is excluded and comfort the target of the action. Do not ignore, excuse, or do nothing due to fear.

10. Learn to use conflict resolution strategies *(Derman-Sparks, 1989).*

Figure 8.6 Prejudice reduction guidelines.
Sources: Banks, J. A. (1994). *An introduction to multicultural education.* Needham Heights, MA: Allyn and Bacon. Derman-Sparks, L., & the A.B.C. Task Force. (1989). *Anti-bias curriculum: Tools for empowering young children.* Washington, DC: National Association for the Education of Young Children.

teacher knows what prompts the episodes, the environment can be changed to avoid that circumstance in the future. In this case, let's say you notice the episodes happen during circle time. The child might be feeling crowded by other children, a problem that can easily be remedied by moving him to the edge of the group.

Children with disabilities deserve the same considerations as typically functioning children. One such consideration is that children with disabilities respond to logical consequences and do not necessarily need contrived ones. For example, when teaching a deaf child to sign, correct responses are reinforced by your response rather than a piece of candy. Considerations for working with children with special needs are examined more fully in Chapter 11.

Cultural Considerations

Mutual respect and understanding are critical to working with children and families. Embracing narrow expectations for children's behavior and believing there is only one right way to guide children's behavior ignores cultural differences

Focus on Diversity

Children often isolate, mistreat, or make fun of those who are different. Following are two activities appropriate for children in the primary grades designed to reduce prejudice.

Activity 1. Have the children in your class collect pictures of people from many different ethnic and racial backgrounds who are smiling. Display them on a bulletin board and discuss with the children that people from all backgrounds smile when they are happy. Smiling is an international sign of goodwill. Talk about other things that may be common across cultures (e.g., sense of accomplishment, friendship).

Activity 2. Display the following sentences on a bulletin board along with book covers, videotapes, and wrapped packages.

   Don't Judge a Book by Its Cover

   Don't Judge a Video by Its Cover

   Don't Judge a Gift by Its Wrapping

   Don't Judge People by Their Appearance

Discuss children's experiences with books, videotapes, and presents. Were you surprised at what was inside? Did you form an accurate opinion from the cover? Discuss how we sometimes judge people by their appearance before we know what is inside.

Source: Byrnes, D. A. (1995). *"Teacher, they called me a _____!":* Confronting prejudice and discrimination in the classroom: Anti-Defamation League and Utah State Office of Education.

children may bring to school. Early childhood educators must understand the values of the home culture and work with parents to structure an encouraging learning environment and to determine effective behavior guidance strategies.

Schools and early childhood centers typically view the mainstream values of hard work, individual accomplishment, and productivity as most important. Yet, in many homes, the values of creativity, artistic expression, and collective efforts are deemed most important. Institutional bias toward mainstream values develops and often results in children from culturally different populations receiving more negative interactions from early childhood educators.

Cultural differences in relation to child raising must be understood and addressed as early childhood educators develop expectations and implement guidance strategies. Perhaps the most fundamental difference lies in family value differences on the individualism–collectivism continuum (Trumbull et al., 2001), introduced earlier. Another cultural difference relates to incongruence between early childhood educators and parents' attitudes about their roles in the child's life.

Individualism vs. Collectivism

As noted earlier, family values vary with regard to emphasis on the individual or the group (individualism or collectivism). Many early childhood educators align with the dominant culture of the United States where individualism is valued. Yet, they work with children from Native American and Latino families that might be oriented toward collectivism, or African American families whose values often lie somewhere in the middle (Trumbull et al., 2001). Neither way of being is right or wrong; they are merely different. (A note of caution is appropriate here. It is important for you to understand cultural norms yet consciously refrain from stereotyping. That is, there is much diversity among families that share any culture. Using the term *some or many families* helps avoid stereotyping.)

We discussed earlier the implications of the individualism–collectivism continuum for cooperative versus competitive activities. We also noted that cooperative activities are more congruent with the developmental nature of young children who have fragile, developing self-concepts. Following are additional implications of the individualism–collectivism continuum for how children express themselves, how materials are used, and how they self-identify.

Expression of Opinions. Although children in collectivist families are often taught to take responsibility and demonstrate leadership, many are taught that it is inappropriate to express an opinion to older people. For example, in some Native American families, children take responsibility for the care of younger siblings or certain household chores, but they respectfully defer some knowledge to elders. Although children are free to consult the authority of a text or an elder, they often keep their opinions to themselves (Trumbull et al., 2001). Teachers must find culturally acceptable ways for children to express themselves. This might be as part of a cooperative group, for example.

Use of Materials. In collectivist families, the boundaries of property ownership are more permeable than in individualistic cultures (Trumbull et al., 2001). Children will readily share their materials with less regard than their individualistic peers or teachers for the return of the materials. It is not that they are careless; rather, the notion of personal property is not an important one (Trumbull et al., 2001).

Scholastic Studio 10/© Index Stock Imagery.

This has implications for teachers. One way of acknowledging collectivist values is by arranging materials in such a way that they are shared. For example, children may use paper, markers, and crayons from a common source rather than a personal one if they choose. As a group, children are responsible for cleaning up and taking care of all materials. Children may be given a choice of using shared materials or their own.

Independence and Helpfulness. Families place different emphasis on children developing independence and helpfulness. Individualistic families value children's ability to complete a task independently and excel on their own. Collectivist families place higher value on helpfulness (Trumbull et al., 2001). Common among Latino families is teaching children to help each other with academic and housekeeping tasks. For example, if Jamie is having trouble getting all of the blocks put away, Carlos might lend her a hand before he finishes his own task. Understanding these different perspectives assists teachers to accept various behaviors.

Understanding Roles

As an early childhood educator, you will benefit from getting to know parents and from learning as much as possible about what the family values. This can be accomplished through home visits and regular communication, using interpreters if necessary. Following are some issues on which family values differ.

Helping with School Work. Early childhood educators from the mainstream culture often expect parents to assist their children with homework or with preparation for a school task (e.g., gathering materials for a project). If parents do not readily participate, they are sometimes labeled as *disinterested* or *parents who don't care*. However, it is a rare parent who is not interested or does not care about his or her child. Caring is evidenced in many homes by the meticulous care given to their children's meals and clothing, by involving them in regular family activities, and so on.

Early childhood educators must consider, first, the parents' level of education. Many immigrant parents, for example, do not have much formal education; that, coupled with the fact that they have a native language other than English, makes the challenges of helping children complete school tasks daunting. Moreover, some parents did not have positive experiences in their own schooling, and that influences their expectations for their children's experience. It may be difficult for those parents to invest time and energy in something they feel is negative.

For other parents, it is beyond the scope of their parenting role as they see it to help with school tasks (Trumbull et al., 2001). Many feel it is their job to care for the children by providing for their needs and socializing them at home, and it is the teacher's job to educate children. These parents view teachers as qualified to do their jobs and feel it is insulting to challenge a teacher or to presume to teach their children at home.

Parenting Advice. Similarly, parents who feel your role is only to educate their children may not appreciate receiving parenting advice (Trumbull et al., 2001). They believe teachers are responsible for socializing children in the early childhood setting but not at home. Careful communication with parents will let you get to know one another and understand what each of you values.

Using Praise. Children coming from a collectivist orientation at home may not appreciate having praise lavished on them, particularly in public. They have learned from their parents that praise singles one out whereas criticism has a normative effect and aligns children with others (Trumbull et al., 2001). Although you may think children are building a positive self-concept as a result of public praise, it may actually be making some children uncomfortable. During conferences, many parents may prefer to hear more about where the child needs to improve rather than what he does well.

Supporting Nonviolent Behavior

Young children are in the process of learning social interaction habits; unfortunately, some have viewed real-life violence. They may have seen someone assaulted, may have laid on the floor to avoid flying bullets, been beaten themselves, and so on. These experiences may lead to aggressive or violent behavior, poor achievement, and emotional distress (Slaby, Roedell, Arezzo, & Hendrix, 1995). Other children have learned aggressive and violent behaviors from the media or may see it as a way to cope with their lives.

There are three different roles children might take in a violent situation: *aggressor, victim,* or *bystander* (Slaby et al., 1995). Without help, the aggressor's behavior may turn into criminal behavior in later life, the victim may remain a victim, and the bystander may continue to support violence by passively accepting it (Slaby et al. 1995).

Violent behavior is learned and it can be unlearned. It is easier for young children to unlearn inappropriate behavior than for older children for whom the behaviors may be more deeply ingrained (Slaby et al., 1995). Early childhood is a critical time for addressing persistent inappropriate behavior. Following are some general guidelines for teachers and caregivers to help children unlearn aggressor, victim, and bystander behaviors.

Be a Good Role Model. First and foremost, early childhood educators must be good role models for young children in their classrooms. This means that they do not yell, shout, or harshly scold children; rather, they talk with children in a firm, friendly voice. They get on the child's level to talk about problems and use logical consequences for inappropriate behavior. They do not tolerate violent behavior by ignoring it. They ensure the early childhood environment has predictable routines and feels safe for all children.

Conflict Resolution. Often children learn violent behavior as the best way to feel physically and psychologically safe. These are usually children who do not have good role models for resolving conflict. Early childhood educators must teach young children appropriate ways to solve problems by using

Chris Minerva/© Index Stock Imagery.

the conflict resolution strategies we discussed earlier. Through experience with conflict resolution, young children practice perspective taking and problem solving and learn the language of compromise.

Be Alert. Aggressive and violent situations always have an aggressor, a victim, and usually bystanders. They will most likely take place during activities of high social interaction (Slaby et al., 1995), such as dramatic play, block play, and outdoor play. Early childhood educators need to be especially alert to inappropriate behavior and be ready to intervene during these activity times. Problems may also occur when children are sitting or standing in close quarters, something you might wish to avoid.

Encourage Discussion. Children have many issues in their lives that may lead to aggressor, victim, or bystander behavior. Issues vary from children experiencing violence in real life, to those who struggle to make friends. Children need opportunities to talk about things that create stress in their lives. Through a strategy called *bibliotherapy*, early childhood educators use children's books as a means of inviting children to open up and talk about difficult issues. Bibliotherapy supports discussion because children can focus on the characters in the book rather than on themselves. Table 8.1 provides a few examples of high-quality children's books for generating discussion.

Cooperative Learning. Meaningful, engaging cooperative learning experiences are important. This gives children the opportunity to address common goals, capitalize on individual strengths, and share leadership. By capitalizing on individual strengths, children learn to accept and appreciate each other.

Redirect Violent Play. Play is very important to all aspects of children's development and learning. They use it to master experiences, try out new skills, play out anxiety, and feel powerful (Levin, 2003). Banning violent play completely (as long

Table 8.1   Examples of Children's Books to Engender Discussion

Title	Description	Theme
Bourgeois, P. (1993). *Franklin Is Bossy*. Scholastic.	Franklin encounters problems with his friends because of his tendency to be bossy.	Friendship and perspective taking
De Paola, T. (1973). *Nana Upstairs and Nana Downstairs*. Putnam.	Grandparents age and eventually die.	Grief
De Paola, T. (1990). *The Knight and the Dragon*. Putnam.	The knight and dragon are supposed to be enemies but learn to be friends instead.	Friendship
Hoban, R. (1960). *Bedtime for Francis*. Harper & Row.	Francis is afraid of the dark.	Fear
Vorist, J. (1987). *Alexander and the Terrible, Horrible, No Good, Very Bad Day*. Aladdin Paperbacks.	Unfortunate things keep happening to Alexander.	Anger
Cohen, M. (1967). *Will I Have a Friend?* New York: Aladdin Paperbacks.	On the first day of school, Jim worries that he will find a friend.	Feeling connected
Abercrombie, B. (1990). *Charlie Anderson*. Aladdin Paperbacks.	Sarah and Elizabeth learn that their cat has two homes, just like they do.	Divorce

as no one is getting hurt) denies children the opportunity to understand or come to bear violence they may have experienced in real life or through the media.

The needs of children who experience media violence are more easily addressed than the needs of those who have experienced real-life violence. Media sensationalizes violence by failing to show the devastating consequences of assaults and shootings. In addition, the market is flooded with superhero figures for children's play. Because playing superhero makes children feel powerful, it is very attractive to them. The first step in addressing violent play learned from the media is to talk to parents about the effects of viewing too much violent media and suggest alternatives to media viewing.

The next step is to redirect children's violent play. The role of teachers is to be sensitive to the needs of individual children and recognize their need for violent play (again, as long as no one is getting hurt). At the appropriate point (probably after a few minutes), such play can and should be redirected.

©Ellen B. Senisi.

To redirect violent play, early childhood educators must first recognize that toy guns and knives have no place in an early childhood setting. They are realistic and it is unlikely that children will use them for anything other than their intended purpose. However, children will use other objects, a stick for example, as a gun or knife. Just as the child labeled the stick as a gun, you can suggest that it become something else. You might say, "Now let's pretend that your stick is a magic wand and you wave it to make the mean people nice." Directives like this help children create new themes for their play. If you can do it without being obtrusive, join the play to assist children with creating new themes.

Bullying

Bullying is any negative behavior intended to hurt another (Brinson, 2005) Historically, research (Gropper & Froschl, 1998) suggested that boys are three times more likely to engage in bullying than girls, and that boys and girls are equal recipients of bullying. More recently, scholars and educators are acknowledging that bullying is just as prevalent among girls (Brinson, 2005).

Although bullying is more prominent in upper and middle grades, it happens in the early years too. The following strategies are useful for preventing bullying in early childhood settings:

- ▶ Talk about teasing and bullying. Use bibliotherapy to support discussions.

- ▶ Engage children in rule making for the classroom. Write the rules in the children's own words. They may also enjoy working in pairs to illustrate the rules.

- ▶ Use noncompetitive games as a means of fostering cooperation.

- ▶ Provide activities to help children relieve stress along with a cool down area.

- ▶ Communicate with parents about what is going on at school and share strategies for addressing bullying.

- ▶ Foster friendships and empathy.

- ▶ Talk about differences in positive ways (Froschl & Sprung, 1999).

- ▶ Discuss the issue of girls who are bullies so that children understand that girl bullies are not excused, that boys do not have to tolerate bullying from a girl, and that bullying from anyone is not acceptable (Brinson, 2005).

David Young-Wolff/PhotoEdit.

SUMMARY

Effective classroom management and behavior guidance begin with an encouraging environment where children's developmental and cultural needs are addressed. Successful behavior guidance strategies are determined by children's developmental levels and cultural backgrounds. Toddlers may benefit from having their behavior redirected or from time away from the prohibition, whereas older children have the reasoning ability to engage in strategies like active listening and conflict resolution. Logical and natural consequences are designed to teach appropriate behavior, but punishment is not.

A critical element of behavior guidance is to understand the family values of children in the early childhood setting. Family values highly influence how children behave and may or may not be congruent with expectations at school. Early childhood educators must communicate regularly with families to understand children's individual cultural backgrounds and adjust the early childhood environment to meet the needs of all children.

Children engage in violent behavior and bullying for a variety of reasons. Early childhood educators must understand those reasons and then employ strategies such as bibliotherapy and cooperative activities that help children learn nonviolent behaviors.

My Developing Professional View

Begin to articulate how you will guide children's behavior. Be sure to consider how you will structure the environment and address problematic behavior.

‹ ENRICHMENT ACTIVITIES

Individual Activities

1. Observe an early childhood educator to identify two or three guidance strategies s/he uses. Describe the strategies. Are they effective? Do they all work with all children? Elaborate.

2. Interview two early childhood educators to learn how they adjust the classroom environment and behavior guidance strategies to meet the individual needs of children in the classroom. What are the common elements of the two early childhood settings? What are their differences? Do the early childhood educators consider developmental, ability, and cultural differences when it comes to child guidance? What are those considerations?

Cooperative Activities

3. In cooperative groups, research children's books that might be used for bibliotherapy. Divide the task by identifying a focus for each group member (bullying and friendship, ethnic differences, ability differences, children's fears, etc.). Each group five member must identify at least five books. Combine your efforts to develop an annotated bibliography.

4. Puppets are another way to help children talk about important issues. As with books, children focus on the characters portrayed by the puppets rather than on themselves. In your cooperative group, create a brief dialogue between two puppets, where one is put down by the other, that could be used as a discussion starter. Be sure your dialogue is relevant for young children (Byrnes, 1995).

5. There is evidence to suggest that excessive media viewing contributes to desensitizing young children to violence. Divide various media sources among members of your cooperative group (e.g., cable TV, PBS, regular programming, DVD games for young children). Spend 5 hours viewing your

media source at different times of the day and on different days of the week. How much violence is depicted (in approximate minutes)? What are the consequences of violent acts? Compare your findings in your cooperative group. What media source is the least violent? Which is the most violent?

Advocacy Activity

6. Identify a manufacturer of violent toys for children (e.g., toy guns, violent video games). Write a letter presenting a reasoned argument against the production of violent toys. Suggest an alternative.

⸱ FOR FURTHER READING

Encouraging Classrooms

DeVries, R., & Zan, B. (2005/06). When children make rules: In constructivist classrooms, young children's participation in rule making promotes their moral development. In K. M. Paciorek & J. H. Munro (Eds.), *Annual Editions: Early Childhood Education, 05/06*, 134–136.

Stone, J. G. (2001). *Building classroom community: The early childhood teacher's role.* Washington, DC: National Association for the Education of Young Children.

Vance, E., & Weaver, P. J. (2002). *Class meetings: Young children solving problems together.* Washington, DC: National Association for the Education of Young Children.

Prejudice Reduction

Byrnes, D. A. (1995). *"Teacher, they called me a _____!": Confronting prejudice and discrimination in the classroom.* USA: Anti-Defamation League and Utah State Office of Education.

Paley, V. G. (1992). *You can't say you can't play.* Cambridge, MA: Harvard University Press.

Behavior Guidance

Bakley, S. (2001). Through the lens of sensory integration: A different way of analyzing challenging behavior. *Young Children, 56*(6), 70–76.

Flicker, E. S., & Hoffman, J. A. (2002). Developmental discipline in the early childhood classroom. *Young Children, 57*(5), 82–89.

Gartrell, D. (2004). *The power of guidance: Teaching social–emotional skills in early childhood classrooms.* Clifton Park, NY: Delmar Learning.

Gartrell, D. (2006). Guidance matters: A spoonful of laughter. *Young Children, 61*(4), 108–109.

Kohn, A. (1996). *Beyond discipline: From compliance to community.* Alexandria, VA: Association for Supervision and Curriculum Development.

Kohn, A. (1993). *Punishment by rewards: The trouble with gold stars, incentive plans, A's, praise, and other bribes.* New York: Houghton Mifflin.

Marshall, H. H. (2001). Cultural influences on the development of self-concept: Updating our thinking. *Young Children, 56*(6), 19–22.

Preuesse, K. (2005/06). Guidance and discipline strategies for young children: Time out is out. In K. M. Paciorek & J. H. Munro (Eds.), *Annual Editions: Early Childhood Education, 05/06*, 137–139.

Violent Behavior

Froschl, M., & Sprung, B. (1999). On purpose: Addressing teasing and bullying in early childhood. *Young Children, 53*(2), 70–72.

Levin, D. (2005/06). Beyond banning war and superhero play: Meeting children's needs in violent times. In K. M. Paciorek & J. H. Munro (Eds.), *Annual Editions: Early Childhood Education, 05/06*, 140–143.

Levin, D. E. (2003). *Teaching young children in violent times: Building a peaceable classroom (2nd ed.).* Washington, DC: National Association for the Education of Young Children.

⸱ SELF-ASSESSMENT

1. Identify some characteristics of an encouraging environment for different ages of children, including infants, toddlers, preschool and kindergarten children, and primary grade children.

2. Explain why it is important to understand the individual cultures of children in your early childhood setting. Provide a specific example.

3. Explain the EAT acronym as it relates to transitions. Provide an example of how you would effectively facilitate transitions in a particular setting (e.g., toddlers, kindergarteners).

4. Provide an example of an effective behavior guidance strategy for different stages of development, including infants, toddlers, preschool and kindergarten, primary grades.

5. Characterize a class meeting.

6. Explain the concepts of *individualism* and *collectivism* as they relate to a family's ways of being.

7. Describe some considerations for addressing bullying in an early childhood setting.

Scenarios

1. You are a teacher of toddlers. Jamie and Kim both really enjoy playing with a particular red truck and frequently argue over who gets to have it. There are other trucks in that play area but they both like the red truck. How might this situation be handled?

2. You are a second-grade teacher. You keep several pencils in the writing center for the children to use if necessary. One day, you notice that there is only one pencil at the writing center so you remind the children to return any of your pencils they may have. Three days later there is still only one pencil in the writing center. You are puzzled but forget about it until you notice about 15 pencils in Marcia's desk. When you query her, she denies that she took the pencils from the writing center. How should this situation be handled?

REFERENCES

Banks, J. A. (1994). *An introduction to multicultural education.* Needham Heights, MA: Allyn and Bacon.

Bredekamp, S., & Copple, C. (Eds.) (1997). *Developmentally appropriate practice in early childhood programs* (revised ed.). Washington, DC: National Association for the Education of Young Children.

Brinson, S. A. (2005). Boys don't tell on sugar-and-spice-but-not-so-nice girl bullies. *Reclaiming Children and Youth, 14*(3), 169–74.

Byrnes, D. A. (1995). *"Teacher, they called me a _____!": Confronting prejudice and discrimination in the classroom.* USA: Anti-Defamation League and Utah State Office of Education.

Cook R. E., Klein, M. D., & Tessier, A., in collaboration with Daley, S. E. (2004). *Adapting early childhood curricula for children in inclusive settings.* Upper Saddle River, NJ: Pearson, Merrill, Prentice-Hall.

Derman-Sparks, L., and the A.B.C. Task Force. (1989) *Anti-bias curriculum: Tools for empowering young children.* Washington, DC: National Association for the Education of Young Children.

Dreikurs, R., Grunwald, B. B., & Pepper, F. C. (1982). *Maintaining sanity in the classroom: Classroom management techniques* (2nd ed.). New York: Harper & Row.

Freiberg, H. J. (1999). Beyond behaviorism. In H. J. Freiberg (Ed.), *Beyond behaviorism: Changing the classroom management paradigm.* Boston: Allyn and Bacon.

Froschl, M., & Sprung, B. (1999). On purpose: Addressing teasing and bullying in early childhood. *Young Children, 54*(2), 70–72.

Glasser, W. (1969). *Schools without failure.* New York: Harper & Row.

Gropper, N., & Froschl, M. (1998). The role of gender in young children's teasing and bullying behavior. Paper presented at the American Educational Research Association Annual Meeting, April 19–23, 1999, Montreal, Quebec, Canada.

Johnson, D. W., & Johnson, R. T. (1999). The three Cs of school and classroom management. In H. J. Freiberg (Ed.), *Beyond behaviorism: Changing the classroom management paradigm.* Boston: Allyn and Bacon.

Kohlberg, A. (1984). *The psychology of moral development.* San Francisco: Harper & Row.

Kohn, A. (1993). *Punishment by rewards: The trouble with gold stars, incentive plans, A's, praise, and other bribes.* New York: Houghton Mifflin.

Levin, D. E. (2003). *Teaching young children in violent times: Building a peaceable classroom (2nd ed.).* Washington, DC: National Association for the Education of Young Children.

Marshall, H. H. (2001). Cultural influences on the development of self-concept: Updating our thinking. *Young Children, 56*(6), 19–22.

Piaget, J., & Inhelder, B. (1969). *The psychology of the child.* New York: Basic Books.

Preuesse, K. (2005/06). Guidance and discipline strategies for young children: Time out is out. In K. M. Paciorek & J. H. Munro (Eds.), *Annual Editions: Early Childhood Education, 05/06,* 137–139.

Slaby, R. G., Roedell, W. C., Arezzo, D., & Hendrix, K. (1995). *Early violence prevention: Tools for teachers of young children.* Washington, DC: National Association for the Education of Young Children.

Trumbull, E., Rothstein-Fisch, C., Greenfield, P. M., & Quiroz, B. (2001). *Bridging cultures between home and school: A guide for teachers.* Mahwah, NJ: Lawrence Erlbaum Associates.

Assessing the Child in Early Childhood Settings

Reflecting on your own experiences as a young child in school, what do you remember about assessment of your learning? Did you take tests? Did you have other kinds of assessments? Do you think sometimes your learning was being assessed and you did not know it? How did you feel about being assessed? How was your progress communicated to your parent(s) or guardian(s)? How would you like your learning to be assessed in this class? In this chapter, we address the many aspects of assessment in early childhood settings.

Assessment is the process of gathering data about an individual student, a group of students, or a program. *Evaluation* is the process of interpreting those data to make decisions about the progress of individuals or groups of students, or the impact of a program. The type of assessment data to be gathered depends on the purpose of the evaluation, which might include informing curriculum development, appraising children's progress, or identifying the strengths and weaknesses of programs. No single assessment provides a complete evaluation. Rather, data gathered from multiple measures over time provide the only valid and reliable evaluation.

On the basis of assessment data from multiple sources and knowledge of the context, early childhood educators evaluate individuals, groups, and/or programs. From the evaluation, they make informed decisions and change practice to better meet children's needs and program goals. Figure 9.1 depicts the cycle of assessment, evaluation, decisions, and change.

After reading this chapter, you will understand:

▶ Types of assessments used in early childhood settings.

▶ Developmentally appropriate assessment practices for young children.

▶ Issues related to standardized testing of young children.

▶ The connection between assessment and curriculum.

▶ Cultural considerations related to assessment of young children.

▶ The influence of social and political factors on assessment for young children.

▶ The difference between assessing individuals and programs.

Types of Assessment in Early Childhood Settings

Effective learning environments build on what children know and can do; thus, the primary purpose of assessment is to inform instruction and curriculum development. Developmentally appropriate assessment encompasses multiple measures over time, is ongoing, and is authentic. *Authentic assessment* involves collecting data from various sources stemming primarily from children's daily learning activities. Assessment may be *formative*, that is, an informal check to determine children's progress and learning needs. Formative assessment takes place daily as early childhood educators observe and interact with children. It informs daily planning in the learning environment. Assessment may be *summative*, which is a more formal, comprehensive assessment. Summative assessments document achievement or ability.

Observation

The practice of observation is rooted in the *child study movement* when social reform led to an interest in child development. It continues today to be a primary means of assessing childrens social, emotional, cognitive, language, and physical development in early childhood settings. Observation is a systematic means of collecting data on individual children and groups of children as they initiate and engage in daily activities in preschool, public school, and child care settings. It is systematic because it takes place regularly, and each observation is considered in light of previous

Figure 9.1. **Cycle of assessment and change.**

Jamal—10:00 am —7-11-03

He was lying on the play pad looking at the star/moon mobile. After a few minutes, he rolled over, pushed himself up, and then rolled back into a sitting position. I've never seen him do that before!

Figure 9.2. Sample of an anecdotal record.

observations. Before observing, it is critical that early childhood educators determine the purpose of their observation and identify a particular focus.

Early childhood educators keep both formal and informal records of their observations. Following are some ways to document children's behaviors in early childhood settings.

Anecdotal Records and Field Notes

Anecdotal and field notes are narratives that describe children's behavior in light of the purpose of the observation. They are relatively easy to complete and require only paper and pencil. Anecdotal records and field notes are useful for recording any type of information and can be kept in chronological order in a folder for reference. Teachers review the notes when planning activities to build on what children can already do.

Anecdotal Notes. Anecdotal notes are fairly short. Depending on the focus of the assessment, early childhood educators briefly record what they have observed. Figure 9.2 provides an example of an anecdote about the physical development of 6-month-old Jamal who just sat up for the first time. Anecdotes should always be dated so that growth over time can be noted.

Field Notes. Field notes also take the narrative form but are somewhat longer than anecdotal notes. One approach to writing field notes is to divide a piece of paper by drawing a vertical line about two-thirds of the way across the paper. In the wider column, teachers objectively record what they observe, being careful not to interject subjective comments. This serves as an objective record of what happened. The narrower column is for recording subjective thoughts about the observation later as the teacher reflects on the observation. Figure 9.3 is a field note sample of 5-year-old Maria during dramatic play. Her teacher notes her use of background knowledge about food, prescriptions, and baby care as well as her appropriate use of literacy artifacts. Teachers often develop unique forms of shorthand in order to quickly record their observations.

Time Samples. Another useful observation tool, time samples can be used to observe whether a particular behavior occurs and how frequently it occurs during a particular period. It is also a useful strategy for identifying cues or antecedents to the behavior. For example, 4-year-old Max has difficulty focusing on any particular activity during free choice time. As his teacher, you may wish to observe him during several 10-minute periods to determine how frequently he moves from one center to another and whether there seems to be impetus for his moving on. A note of caution, however: be mindful that a few time sample recordings may or may not accurately reflect the entire school experience (Pucket & Black, 1994), so you will want to consider other data in your evaluation.

Event Samples. Event samples entail observation of events or categories of events as they occur (Pucket & Black, 1994). For example, a teacher may want to observe

9-5-03 — Maria

Playing alone in the housekeeping center— in the kitchen-- she picked up a plastic ham and called it yogurt.

family is vegetarian

She went to doll bed and picked up the doll— diapers doll w/ a cloth and holds doll to her chest "Go to sleep now baby" -- "Oh dear baby Isabelle has a fever."

Maria has a new baby sister.

Picks up phone book-- opens then dials phone. "My baby has a fever." "Um - yes" "ok" wraps baby in blanket as Jamie and Sophie enter.

She knows something about the purpose of the phonebook.

Maria picks up a piece of paper. "This is my baby's 'cription", she begins scribble on the paper.

She has a concept of a prescription as a written artifact.

Figure 9.3. Sample of field notes.

what type of literacy events will engage Jill, who is a kindergartener with a language delay. The findings might be recorded on a teacher constructed chart such as the one in Figure 9.4.

As Jill's teacher, you will note that she does not show interest in books or writing but does engage with literacy artifacts during dramatic play. You conclude that dramatic play might serve as a vehicle for engaging Jill with literacy in ways that may lead to more interest in books and writing later.

Audio/Video and Photographic Recordings

Audio/video recordings and photographs are a precise means of preserving children's behavior. They provide useful data for capturing cognitive, language, and social development, as well as thinking skills. Short excerpts from the recordings can be compiled on a CD-ROM as part of a show portfolio (discussed in the next section) to document achievement at various times during the year.

Audio Recordings. Children's language development, storytelling, and reading behaviors can be audio recorded so that their progress over time can be evaluated. Although the presence of technology might affect a child's performance, most perform normally once they get used to being recorded.

Video Recordings. Video recording is a way to capture precisely what children say and do. Analysis of video recorded episodes allows teachers to note cognitive,

Michael Newman /PhotoEdit.

Child's name: Jill M.

Date of Observation	Literacy Artifacts in Dramatic Play	Book Center	Listening Center	Writing Center
1/15/04	//			
1/16/04	//			
1/20/04	/		/	
1/21/04			/	

Comments:

Figure 9.4. Example of event sampling chart.
Source: Adapted from Puckett, M. B., & Black, J. K. (1994). *Authentic assessment of the young child: Celebrating development and learning.* New York: Macmillan College Publishing.

language, and social development as children engage in dramatic play, perform group inquiry projects, or interact at learning centers. Again, the technology will cease to be a distraction as children become accustomed to its presence.

Photographs. Although only a quick snapshot in time, photographs are useful for capturing finished products. Children's constructions (e.g., blocks, clay) can be photographed and compared over time to note the development of their creative thinking, collaborative interactions, or other developing skills. Photographs also provide a way to preserve constructions long after they have been taken apart.

Checklists

Whether it is the first observation of an infant rolling, a kindergartener identifying letters of the alphabet, or a second grader's use of adjectives in her writing, checklists provide a means of documenting children's mastery of skills. They can be used to record data about social, emotional, cognitive, language, or physical development.

Checklists provide information at a glance and are not only informative for the teachers but are easily shared with parents. You can make a quick check of individual children's progress as well as the progress of the entire group of children. You can develop checklists that reflect developmental benchmarks, state or local curriculum standards, or other expectations for children. They may be purchased commercially or developed by individual teachers. Figure 9.5 is an example of a teacher-made checklist from a kindergarten classroom that focuses on individual literacy learning.

Portfolios

A portfolio is a collection of artifacts that documents what children can do and what interests them. Artifacts must reflect learning goals established for the child. Collected over time and stored in a binder, in a box, or on a CD-ROM, artifacts might include drawings, written pieces, photographs, and tape recordings of a child telling or reading a story. Teachers and children decide together what artifacts will be included in the portfolio.

| child's name _____ | | | | | | | | | | | | | | | | | | | | |
| date _____ | | | | | | | | | | | | | | | | | | | | |

skill							date											comments
listens attentively																		
responds appropriately to 2-step directions																		
responds appropriately to 3-step directions																		
phonemic awareness																		
print awareness																		
identifies front/back, left/right, top/bottom of book or text																		
recognizes letters in name																		
writes name																		
recognizes most letters																		
recognizes all letters																		
recognizes most consonant sounds																		
recognizes all consonant sounds																		
recognizes vowel sounds																		
reads words																		
creates print with scribbles or marks																		
writes letters																		
writes with immature invented spelling																		
writes with mature invented spelling or conventional print																		

Figure 9.5. Sample checklist for literacy in kindergarten.

Cindy Charles/PhotoEdit.

Reflection

Reflection is central to the usefulness of a portfolio (Smith, 2000). As children talk about what to include in their portfolios, they reflect on their activities, what they did and what they are learning. For example, 4-year-old Zoe thought about how difficult it was to mix the paint to just the right shade of green for her dinosaur picture. She started with too much blue and had to keep adding yellow until she decided it was just right. Reviewing the story he wrote about playing with his brothers, 7-year-old Alex recalled when he first learned how to write words in plural form. He noticed three plural words in this story.

Teachers purposefully engage children in reflection as they help them compile their portfolios. They guide discussion by asking children to tell them about a particular piece or note a new skill, correctly reading *silent e* words, for example. They assist children to self-assess their learning and then select artifacts that document it.

Purposes

Portfolios can serve two general purposes, and artifacts included in the portfolio will vary depending on the purpose. *Working portfolios* document growth and engage teachers in formative assessment and children in self-assessment. On the other hand, *show portfolios* document achievement and provide information for summative assessment. *Show portfolios* can be sent to the next level with the child and both types can be shared with parents.

Working Portfolio. A working portfolio documents growth and is a collection of artifacts selected to demonstrate change over time. For example, Juan is a first grader who selected his latest written story for inclusion in his portfolio because he had correctly used three exclamation marks and one question mark. The class had a minilesson that day on end marks, and Juan looked for opportunities to use the end marks appropriately when he wrote his story. Looking back at the other writing artifacts in his portfolio, he noticed that he had never used anything other than a period to end a sentence. Having these dated artifacts provided a means for seeing his progress with using end marks in his writing.

Show Portfolio. A show portfolio documents achievement and will be somewhat different than a working portfolio. It will include artifacts that show children's accomplishments based on a set of achievement standards. The standards might be those mandated by the state or the district, in the case of school-age children, or developmental benchmarks, in the case of infants, toddlers, and preschool children. Rather than including artifacts that can be compared over time, a show portfolio will include pieces that best document children's highest achievements relative to the standards. A single show portfolio can follow each child from grade to grade by documenting information on a CD-ROM.

Using Portfolios to Conference with Parents. Prior to conferencing with parents, they should have information about your philosophy of teaching, learning goals for their child, instructional strategies, and curricular topics. During conferencing, portfolios are helpful because, as you talk about learning goals and the particular child's progress, the artifacts serve to exemplify and explain. For example, going back to Zoe, as you discuss her behavior trying to create the right shade of green, you can share the finished product. As you talk about Alex and his ability to write in plural form, you can share the artifacts that demonstrate change over time. Before ending the conference, solicit information on what the child does at home and how it may be consistent or inconsistent with what the portfolio documents.

Age Appropriate Portfolios

Although there is variation based on children's developmental level, portfolios can be used as an assessment tool with young children of various ages. Kindergarten and primary grade children can discuss why they feel a specific artifact should be included in the portfolio. Through collaborative reflection with the teacher, they can discuss how an artifact demonstrates a specific accomplishment or interest. They can point out how the artifact provides evidence of what they have learned.

The reflective thinking of preschool children will be less mature than that of school-age children, but their ability to participate in creating a portfolio should not be underestimated (Smith, 2000). Initially, preschool children might simply say, "I like it" as a reason to include the artifact. With practice over time and with the teacher's guidance, they will elaborate their comments about their artifacts noting details and specific reasons for the artifact being worthy of inclusion (Smith, 2000).

Home Visits

Home visits, discussed in more detail in Chapter 13, can assist early childhood educators with assessment. Home visits done early in the year provide an opportunity for early childhood educators to learn about children's needs and interests by talking with their parents and by observing them in their home setting. This information will assist early childhood educators to plan appropriate activities and involve the parents in ways that are meaningful for them and culturally relevant for their children. Although a visit to the home will provide the richest source of information, a call will provide an opportunity to acquaint yourself with the parents if there is insufficient time for you to visit each home.

The Work Sampling System

For many years, early childhood educators have been using the *work sampling system*, developed by Samuel Meisels. The work sampling system is a comprehensive, developmentally appropriate assessment system that combines some of the strategies we have discussed. It is designed to document children's growth and development over time in seven domains including the following (Meisels, 1993):

▶ Personal and social

▶ Language and literacy

▶ Mathematical thinking

▶ Scientific thinking

▶ Social studies

▶ Art and music

▶ Physical development (p. 37)

Meisels has published performance indicators for each domain.

The work sampling system is an ongoing assessment system that has three components: (a) checklists, (b) portfolios, and (c) summary reports (Meisels, 1993). Each addresses the seven domains and is completed for each child in the fall, winter, and spring.

Developmental Checklists. Developmental checklists address common expectations for achievement of young children across ages. Over time, teachers observe and record information about children's skills, knowledge, and achievements. These checklists are available commercially and are accompanied with observation guidelines so that you can be consistent as you observe all children in the group. The checklists provide a profile of children's progress at a glance so that you can look at the growth of individual children or make comparisons among children (Meisels, 1993).

Portfolios. In the work sampling system, portfolios address the seven domains and contain two types of items, *core items* and *other items*. The core items are samples collected from each child of repeated work. For example, a writing sample from a particular activity is collected from each child in the fall, again in the winter, and finally in the spring (Meisels, 1993).

Summary reports are completed for each child three times per year. On the basis of your observations and accumulated records, you write a brief summary of children's performance based on specific criteria (Meisels, 1993).

Standardized Tests

If a test is standardized, it means that it is administered in the same way in all contexts so scores can be reliably compared. Usually, test developers determine a level of validity and reliability for their standardized instruments so users can be confident that they are consistently measuring what the test intends to measure. It is difficult to acquire strong validity and reliability on standardized instruments for young children and this is discussed later.

There are many different types of standardized tests that have been developed for different purposes, including (1) diagnosing delays or disabilities, (2) measuring achievement, and (3) measuring readiness for entrance to a particular grade. Table 9.1 is a small sampling of different standardized tests for young children to provide an idea of types of test on the market. College and university libraries maintain detailed information on all standardized tests.

Linking Assessment and Curriculum

Although assessment is used to evaluate programs and meet accountability needs, it is important to remember that the primary purpose of assessment is to inform curriculum development and identification of appropriate instructional strategies. Information from multiple data sources is used to identify children's skill levels, background knowledge, and interests. Teachers use this information to decide what content and skills need to be taught and how to teach them.

Table 9.1	Examples of Standardized Tests for Young Children
Test Name	**Function**
Bayley Scales of Infant Development, 1–42 months	Assesses intellectual and psychomotor functioning
Diagnostic Inventory for Screening Children, birth to age 5	Identifies developmental delays in motor, language, memory, social, self-help skills, and auditory and visual attention
Preschool Development Inventory, ages 3–6	Parental report of language, motor, self-help, social skills, and descriptions of behavior patterns
Preschool and Kindergarten Behavior Scales, ages 3–6	Evaluates social skills and problem behaviors
Metropolitan Achievement Test, preschool through grade 12	Measures achievement in reading, math, and language
BRIGANCE Diagnostic Inventory of Basic Skills, kindergarten to grade 6	Measures academic and readiness skills
Stanford Early Achievement Test, kindergarten through grade 3	Measures achievement in reading, math, language, and environment
DIBELS, prekindergarten through grade 5	Used for readiness and achievement; prekindergarten measures oral language, phonemic awareness, letter knowledge, graphophonemic awareness, story retelling, and oral reading
Battelle Developmental Inventory, birth to age 8	Identifies children's developmental strengths and weaknesses
Callier-Azusa Scale, birth to age 9	Individually administered to children with severe disabilities to identify developmental levels

Focus on History

Increased Standardized Testing

By the 1970's, increasing availability of federal and state resources for schools heralded a strong accountability movement nationwide. The federal government became more involved in educational funding, and this resulted in legislation that affected preschool and school-age children, particularly those with disabilities.

In Part 1 of this text, we discussed federal legislation relative to early childhood education. For example, the Maternal Child Health and Mental Retardation Act and the Economic Opportunity Act of 1964 required the provision of educational and social opportunities for all children. PL 94-142, in 1975, mandated a free and appropriate education for all children age 3 and older (Kelly & Surbeck, 2000). Subsequent iterations of this legislation including PL 99-457 in 1986 and the Individuals with Disabilities Act (IDEA) in 1990 endorsed special education and related services for preschoolers (Kelly & Surbeck, 2000). Although these initiatives did not limit assessment to standardized tests, and required multiple assessment measures for evaluation, they continued to promote testing as a means to determine what services, if any, individual children needed. The increased focus on test scores quickly became a way to hold school districts accountable for students' achievement.

As teachers prepare lesson plans, they refer frequently to assessment documents. These documents help them determine when all students need instruction on a particular topic or skill and when only some students need it. For example, Max noticed that five of his second graders were using *s* to make words plural. So, he grouped those five children for a brief lesson on making words plural and making words possessive. Particular group configurations last only as long as needed to teach a particular skill.

Field notes and anecdotal notes contain valuable information about children's interests. For example, Marie noticed a group of her 3-year-olds playing *pets* in the dramatic play area. She later groups them to listen to a story about pets.

Assessment Issues

In recent decades, assessment of young children has become controversial. There is some tension between early childhood educators or scholars and other groups (e.g., policy makers, administrators) about how young children should be assessed, particularly as it relates to standardized testing. There are several considerations for designing assessment procedures for young children.

Align Assessment with the Nature of the Child

Young children are not miniature adults; rather, they are on a developmental path toward adulthood. During their early years, children think differently than adults or older children. They do not think in the abstract and they base their understanding of the world on their unique prior experiences. Because of these characteristics, young children learn best as they interact with people and objects in their environments.

Although general patterns in children's development have been identified, their learning patterns are varied and often inconsistent; in other words, no two children develop in exactly the same way. The National Association for the Education of Young Children (NAEYC) and the National Association of Early Childhood Specialists in State Departments of Education (NAECS/SDE) call for assessment that is aligned with the nature of young children (Bredekamp & Copple, 1997; NAEYC & NAECS/SDE, 2004). They assert that assessment must be developmentally, culturally, and linguistically responsive, connected to children's daily activities, and inclusive of families. They further assert that early childhood educators must receive appropriate professional development to help them understand assessment techniques and purposes, including (1) making sound decisions about teaching and learning, (2) identifying significant concerns that may require focused intervention for individual children, and (3) helping programs improve their educational and developmental interventions (NAEYC & NAECS/SDE, 2004, p. 52). This means that if assessment is to consistently provide dependable information, it must include multiple and varied data sources, and data gathered over time, so that patterns and idiosyncrasies in individual children's growth and development can be identified.

Infants and Toddlers

In child care settings for infants and toddlers, caregivers use authentic assessment. Authentic assessment is integrated with learning experiences, is ongoing, and takes place in the context of daily activities. As infants and toddlers engage in daily activities, caregivers observe and record descriptions of their social, emotional, physical, cognitive, and language development. They keep careful records of children's eating, sleeping, toileting, language, social, and physical behaviors. Caregivers acknowledge that whereas there are some general expectations for children's development, children also demonstrate individual patterns of development.

Ellen Senisi/The Image Works.

Infant and toddler caregivers systematically compile descriptive anecdotes and behavior schedules over time. They couple this information with what they learn from parents to develop a comprehensive picture of the child. This not only provides information on children's developmental progress but also informs curriculum development. Assessment leads to evaluation of children's needs, which leads to decisions about changing the curriculum (Figure 9.1).

Preschool, Kindergarten, and Primary Grade Children

Teachers in programs serving children ages 3–8 also use authentic assessment. Because children function best when activities are meaningful, activities contrived solely for the purpose of assessment are used minimally. Teachers assess children using a variety of data sources: children's artwork and written artifacts; anecdotal records and checklists; summary reports; and tape recordings of conversations, storytelling, or reading. Systematic records of children's growth and development are kept.

Standardized Testing in Early Childhood Settings

Standardized tests provide useful information when considered in conjunction with multiple sources of assessment information and over time. However, they must be used cautiously. No single assessment measure supplies all information about a child or group of children. Following are some issues to consider regarding the use of standardized tests with young children.

Developmental Considerations

It is difficult to obtain valid and reliable results when testing young children because they have limited ability to think beyond the scope of their personal experiences.

Because of this, they respond to test questions based on their direct experience, which may or may not match the "correct" answer to the test question.

Another consideration is the testing circumstance, which requires young children to engage in multiple cognitive tasks: following directions, understanding the question, discerning an appropriate response, and marking it. Moreover, they must do all of that on their own. The teacher, who is usually quite supportive and helpful, cannot provide assistance. Scholars (Dever & Barta, 2001; Fleege, Charlesworth, Burts, & Hart, 1992; Wodtke, Harper, Schommer, & Brunelli, 1989) have found that young children demonstrate stress when they take standardized tests.

Inappropriate Labels

When decisions are based solely on test results, children may be inappropriately labeled as delayed or deficient. Teachers must be cautious not to label a child based on a single test score. Additional assessment measures, including observation and interviews with parents and other caregivers, are used to inform decisions, including decisions to place children in special programs.

High-Stakes Testing

The term high-stakes in the context of testing means that test results have life-altering implications. For individual children, these implications include retention

Window into the Classroom

Ms. Cook is a kindergarten teacher who uses many forms of assessment to identify the needs, accomplishments, and interests of her students. Here is her story.

Observation

As I watch my students interact, listen to their chatter and feel them struggle, I have the single most effective form of assessment. I do not have to wait for results; I have immediate insights into a child's learning.

Observation enables me to see the critical thinking skills of my kindergarten children. One day, I wrote four word cards and placed them in an envelope with a question. I asked the children to tell me which word they thought was the best answer. The children would sound out each word and then use their thinking skills to determine their answer. One of the questions was, "Which is the brightest among the sun, moon, stars, and lamp?" Peyton thought for a moment and replied, "The moon." I said, "Tell me about the moon being the brightest." He replied, "The moon is so bright it can shine in the dark. One night it shined through my window and I could see my room even though it was dark!"

The next day, I got another window into Peyton's critical thinking skills. As our class created a map of our town on a plastic play rug, Peyton noticed that the children had drawn the parking spaces in the Wal-Mart parking lot much too small for him to park the toy cars. He proceeded to get a toy car and use it to measure the spaces he created in his parking lot beside the zoo. He could drive his car and park in every space!

Work Samples

I appreciate collecting student work samples as part of their portfolios. Developmental rubrics help to identify indicators of a child's current skill level and to determine what concepts to target at that skill level. It is not enough to know what a child's skill level is. Early childhood teachers need to understand the developmental continuum and we need to be able to articulate to parents how they can best help their child. Work samples help me articulate to parents what their child can do and how they can support their child's learning.

Standardized Assessment

I use the DIBELS (Dynamic Indicators of Early Literacy Skills). It is short and provides immediate results. It is structured so that I can test interventions frequently and evaluate the success of the instruction. It also provides benchmarks, which helps me communicate with parents what it means to "be on grade level." I can print out class reports too. The scores are for teacher use and are not reported.

My colleagues and I are often frustrated when asked to spend valuable instructional time on standardized tests that are lengthy or that do not inform our classroom instruction.

and special placement. For a school or district, the availability of some funding rests on high-stakes test results.

High-stakes testing is often promoted by politicians and supported by the taxpayers who elect them as a means of holding schools accountable for students' learning. Test scores are preferred because they are tangible and easily obtained; however, they provide a narrow view of accomplishments.

Policy makers often aspire to ideals like *all children will read on grade level*. Although teachers should rightly be concerned if children continuously demonstrate developmental delays, they must remember that children vary in the timing of their growth and development. Their progress *over time* should be considered as important as their development at a particular *point in time* (e.g., at the point of testing).

Results Are Not Precise. Grade level is a construct determined through the process of norming and it cannot be precisely defined. To develop a norm-referenced test, it is administered to groups of children and then scores are extrapolated. For example, the test may be given to groups of first graders and second graders in the first month of school. Then the difference between the average first-grade score and average second-grade score is divided into nine equal intervals to represent the nine months of school between the first month of first grade and the first month of second grade. Then, students are given grade equivalency scores such that 1.4 represents

Table Mesa Production/© Index Stock Imagery.

first grade, fourth month; 2.1 represents second grade, first month, and so on. The process inappropriately assumes consistent, systematic development within and between children.

Another consideration related to norm-referenced tests is the population used in the norming process. Was the test normed using a diverse population of children or a homogeneous population? The test is reliable and valid only for groups that match the norming population.

Test-Driven Curriculum. High-stakes testing may lead to a narrow, test-driven curriculum (James & Tanner, 1993; HEL, 2003) if educators fear consequences for poor test scores (e.g., scores printed in the newspaper or on the Web, loss of job). Teachers have indicated three concerns related to the test-driven curriculum that affect young children: (1) Pressure to achieve high test scores means that teachers focus most of their teaching on content that will appear on the test (HEL 2003). (2) They feel they lose valuable instructional time that is spent teaching test-taking skills (Chapter 7). (3) They may feel compelled to retain children if a high-stakes test is scheduled for the next grade level.

Addressing Low Scores. Standardized test scores for individual children must be considered in conjunction with observational data. It is not unusual for observations to indicate that a child is achieving at an appropriate level yet s/he receives a low standardized test score. This could be because the child was tired or ill when the test was administered. For many young children, testing is culturally foreign and irrelevant. Others become anxious about tests and many have not yet developed test-taking skills.

Cultural Issues in Assessment

The need to appropriately assess young children who are not members of the cultural mainstream is the result of two social movements. The first is the movement toward more federal legislation that began in the 1960's and continues.

Advocating for the Child

No Child Left Behind Act

Historically, continuation of funding for compensatory preschool programs, special education programs, and other related programs depended on evaluation that indicated children were showing achievement gains. Because policy makers perceived tests as an easy and inexpensive way to measure progress, test scores became the yardstick for measuring whether or not schools were meeting standards and whether or not educational innovations were funded.

The *No Child Left Behind Act of 2001* (NCLB) exemplifies the continuing national focus on test scores and embodies the high-stakes (life-altering implications) status of tests. A reauthorization of the Elementary and Secondary Education Act implemented by the G. W. Bush administration under Secretary of Education Rod Paige, the Act, still in place today, focuses on accountability of school districts for making *adequate yearly progress*, measured by standardized test scores. Under the NCLB, schools may be deemed *failing* due to inadequate student progress as measured by standardized measures and graduation rates. Furthermore, any school deemed *failing* will be *failing* in all grades.

Although the NCLB does not require testing prior to third grade, most states have state-mandated testing in the primary grades. Thus, kindergarten and the primary grade teachers are expected to prepare children well for the next level, and this may result in tension among teachers.

What is the source of the tension?

1. The consequence for failing schools is loss of some federal resources. Schools most likely to be deemed failing are those where there is the most poverty and cultural diversity, owing to the culturally biased nature of tests.
2. Teachers can be reprimanded and fired when adequate yearly progress, defined by test scores, is not achieved.
3. It is unlikely that successful schools can accommodate all students eligible to transfer from failing schools; furthermore, in rural areas, there may not be another school nearby to accommodate transfers.

As advocates for young children, it falls to professionals in early care and education to employ developmentally appropriate practices, outlined in chapter 4, while collecting multiple forms of assessment data to both inform practice and document children's achievement.

The second is the changing demographics in the United States. According to the Federal Interagency Forum on Child and Family Statistics (1997), the number of non-whites and Hispanics is estimated to reach 45% of the total population by 2020 and the number of minority group young children will increase accordingly.

Culturally and Linguistically Diverse Children

Children are considered culturally diverse on several characteristics including class, ethnicity, language, ability, and religion. For preschool, kindergarten, and primary grade children the main socializing influence has been the family. Thus, children from non-mainstream families most likely bring different experiences, values, attitudes, and behaviors to their school experiences. Consequently, the knowledge base and frames of reference they use are different than those used in the dominant educational culture. If assessment is to be valid, reliable, and fair, these factors must be taken into consideration when assessing children from non-mainstream groups.

Barriers to Accurate Assessment

No assessment instrument or mode is free of bias, including observation. The following factors must be considered with regard to assessment of children in our nation's schools.

Cultural Experiences. Cultural differences affect not only the way learning takes place, but also what is learned because it is the things relevant to the culture of each individual that are recalled and understood. This is particularly true for young children because they base their understanding of the world solely on personal experience. Children living in poverty or in homes from non-mainstream cultures may not be able to respond accurately to assessment materials that draw on experiences they have not had. Even when assessing via observation, teachers must understand the cultures of the children in their early childhood settings.

Cultural Values. Culture influences values that individuals bring to school. This can be as basic as a variation in the understanding of what it means to be *gifted*, for example. Most mainstream Americans define a gifted child as one who shows high achievement or potential in general academic, creative, psychomotor, or intellectual aptitude. In contrast, when many Mexican Americans identify a child as *gifted*, they consider traits such as obedience, common sense, and self-reliance to be just as important as the trait of intelligence. Thus, conventional assessments to identify *giftedness* may be culturally foreign to many children.

Language. Language barriers impede the accuracy of assessment. Many children are not speakers of English or they speak a nonstandard dialect of English. In both situations, the young child's ability to communicate and understand meaning from the cultural mainstream is limited. Teachers must understand the communication style of children in their settings. Furthermore, assessment is impeded if the child and the evaluator do not speak the same language with fluency. The validity of assessment relies on children being assessed in their native language or dialect by someone who speaks that language or dialect fluently.

Following are some important considerations related to administering standardized tests to nonnative English speakers (Stefanakis, 1998):

▶ Bilingual students take more time to complete a test, which may invalidate timed tests.

▶ A systematic, sequential testing approach may be unfamiliar and of questionable validity for bilingual students.

▶ Careful evaluation of native language proficiency must precede any assessment of learning potential.

▶ Decision making on behalf of bilingual students must encompass multiple assessment measures (p. 11).

The *Focus on Diversity* on the next page exemplifies these issues.

Culturally Appropriate Assessment

Portfolio assessment as an alternative to testing has the potential to improve educational opportunities for children from diverse backgrounds. Portfolios offer early childhood educators excellent opportunities to measure children's achievement against themselves, recognize individual children's strengths, and to reflect on the knowledge and background they bring to school (Au, 1997). Portfolios should weigh heavily in instructional decision making.

Instruction must build on what children bring to the learning situation (Au, 1997). This is particularly important for young children because they do not think beyond their own experiences. Teachers must implement learning experiences that reflect and build on the knowledge and experiences children bring to their learning tasks. For example, imagine a teacher who is teaching comprehension skills using a story about a trip to the circus as his instructional vehicle. Children who have actually been to a circus are advantaged

 My Developing Professional View

Identify different purposes for assessment and suggest appropriate assessment tools for each.

Focus on Diversity

Antibias Assessment

Our nation's schools have not identified effective testing approaches for all children in a system that increasingly relies on test-based accountability to promote educational change (Solano-Flores & Trumbull, 2003). English language learners, children living in poverty, and children from nonmainstream cultures often lack background experiences to succeed on standardized tests.

Two primary issues surface. First, tests are cultural products created from a particular paradigm. No matter what efforts are made to span cultures, it is virtually impossible to test the same construct across populations of children. Second, the testing experience interacts with the linguistic and cultural background of the test taker (Solano-Flores & Trumbull, 2003). Following is an example.

A portion of a standardized test is designed to measure comprehension skills of kindergarteners. On this individually administered standardized test, the teacher first reads a story called "Cat's Birthday Party." In this story, Cat anxiously anticipates her party, which will be complete with balloons, a cake with candles, and presents. Then, the teacher poses comprehension questions about the story to which the child responds.

Many groups of children are challenged to succeed in this test example. English language learners are limited by the extent of their developing expressive and receptive use of English. In addition, celebrations, including birthdays, are culturally defined and practices vary. For example, not all cultures incorporate a cake, candles, and balloons into a birthday celebration. Many children living in poverty or those whose religious beliefs do not permit participation in birthday parties may have never experienced a birthday party at all. Children who have experienced a birthday party such as the one in the story bring a background of experience to the testing situation that better enables them to succeed on the test.

Recommendations

Santos (2004) provides some guidelines for assessing culturally and linguistically diverse groups of children that are helpful for testing situations.

1. Honor families' preferred language or mode of communication by having persons fluent in the preferred language conduct the assessment. In addition, review the assessment tool to determine whether it is sensitive to cultural norms and language usage.
2. Choose materials that are nonstereotypical and that acknowledge diversity related to gender, class, religion, ethnicity, family structures, and so on.
3. Seek assistance from a cultural guide (e.g., family or community member from the particular culture) to confirm interpretations of the assessment.
4. Use a cultural guide to assist with the oral or written report of the results. Check on the possibility that perceived developmental delays are related to particular cultural practices, difficulties in translation, etc. (p. 49)

because they have a context for understanding the story. Those who have had multiple opportunities to hear stories and see pictures about the circus are also advantaged. Those who have never experienced a circus either directly or through stories are clearly disadvantaged.

Children must be given alternative ways to create portfolio artifacts to demonstrate what they know. For example, a child might have a clear understanding of the story about the circus (receptive language) but, due to a language delay, have difficulty expressing what she knows (expressive language). Given the opportunity to express herself in a drawing enables her to demonstrate what she knows.

Assessing Children and Programs

Assessment of programs, or program evaluation, indicates how well programs are meeting their goals. Program evaluation should not be used to evaluate individual children; rather, general accomplishments of the group are considered. The program goals provide a framework for the evaluation. Multiple data sources, including demographic information on students and general indicators of student achievement, are considered in a comprehensive program evaluation.

Standardized tests provide a useful component of a program evaluation. If the goal is to evaluate the program, evaluators must be careful to focus on the program rather than on individual children. There are ways to administer standardized tests to ensure the focus is on the program goals rather than on individual children.

Not all children are tested. Administer the test to a random sample of children, rather than all children. Accurate data will be obtained because the random sample will be representative of the total population. Nevertheless, if scores for every child do not exist, it is unlikely that individual children's scores will become the focus.

Children do not take the entire test. The total population of children can be randomly divided in half; then, one half of the test is administered to one group and the other half to the other group. Using this strategy, all children are tested, each sample is representative of the total population, and no child takes the entire test. With different data on each child, it is again unlikely that individual test scores will become the focus.

Names are omitted. Perhaps the easiest way to avoid misuse of standardized tests designed to evaluate programs is to omit children's names from the test altogether. Include important demographic data but no names. In that way, a particular score cannot be traced back to an individual child. The focus remains on the program.

With program goals as the guide, additional program evaluation data include random samples of students' artifacts, checklists, and other assessment documents. Interviews with teachers, students, and parents may also be conducted.

SUMMARY

Assessment data provide information about individuals and groups of children that are used to plan instruction and develop curriculum. Assessment data also indicate the degree to which programs are meeting their goals. If assessment is to inform decision making, the assessment must encompass multiple data sources gathered over time.

There are several considerations regarding assessment in early childhood settings. First, assessment must be aligned with the developmental nature of young children. Second, although standardized test results may have some value, high-stakes testing must be avoided. Third, no assessment is free of bias. Culture or the experiences children bring to the testing situation highly impacts the results.

Program evaluation is framed by the goals of the program and focuses on the program rather than on individual children. Strategies exist to ensure that data collected for program evaluation are used to that end and not to evaluate individual children.

⸭ ENRICHMENT ACTIVITIES

Individual Activities

1. For a period of 2 weeks, pay particular attention to articles about education in your local newspaper. How prominent is the theme of testing? In general, what do the articles say about testing and what are the implications for young children?

2. Complete an observation of a child in an early childhood setting. Record your information using the field note format described in this text. First, decide what the focus of your observation will be (e.g., language, social interactions). Then, write your objective field notes and finally, review them and add subjective inferences. What have you learned about this child?

3. Visit your institution's library to find information on standardized tests for young children. Identify a focus (diagnosis of language development, for example) and identify three tests for that purpose. Briefly describe each test's contents and procedures.

Cooperative Activity

4. In cooperative groups, conduct interviews with early childhood educators about their beliefs and methods of assessment and evaluation. Be sure your interviewees span several levels so that a variety of early childhood educators, from infant, toddler, pre-K, kindergarten, and primary grade settings, are included. As a group, share what you learned. What are some common themes? What is unique to a particular setting? What do these early childhood educators believe about assessment and evaluation? What do you think influences their beliefs?

Advocacy Activity

5. Go to the website for your state office of education. Research standardized testing practices for young children in your state and decide whether the practices are developmentally appropriate or inappropriate. Write a letter to a state official (e.g., legislator, state office official) commending appropriate use or advocating against inappropriate use of standardized testing for young children. Support your position.

} FOR FURTHER READING

Billman, J., & Sherman, J. (2003). *Observation and participation in early childhood settings (2nd ed.).* New York: Allyn and Bacon.

Dever, M. T., Falconer, R., & Kessnick, C. (2003). Implementing developmentally appropriate practices in a developmentally inappropriate climate: Assessment practices in kindergarten. *Dimensions of Early Childhood, 31*(3), S. Kontos & L. Dunn, Guest Ed., 27–33.

Dodge, D. T., Heroman, C., Charles, J., & Maiorca, J. (2004). Beyond outcomes: How ongoing assessment supports children's learning and leads to meaningful curriculum. *Young Children, 59*(1), 20–28.

Kohn, A. (2000). *The case against standardized testing: Raising the scores, ruining the schools.* Portsmouth, NH: Heinemann.

McAfee, O., Leong, D. J., & Bodrova, E. (2004). *Basics of assessment: A primer for early childhood educators.* Washington, DC: National Association for the Education of Young Children.

Santos, R. M. (2004). Ensuring culturally and linguistically appropriate assessment of young children. *Young Children, 59*(1), 48–50.

Smith, A. F. (2000). Reflective portfolios: Preschool possibilities. *Childhood Education, 76*(4), 204–208.

Stefanakis, E. H. (1998). *Whose judgment counts? Assessing bilingual children, K–3.* Portsmouth, NH: Heinemann.

} SELF-ASSESSMENT

1. Explain the difference between formative and summative assessment. Give an example of each type of assessment.
2. Select four types of assessment discussed in this chapter and explain what you might learn from each.
3. Discuss ways early childhood educators can make connections between the curriculum and assessments. Provide specific examples.
4. Discuss important cultural considerations related to assessment.
5. Explain the term *high-stakes test.*
6. Explain the difference between a *show portfolio* and a *working portfolio.*

Scenarios

1. You are interviewing for a position as head teacher for toddlers in a child care center. Respond to the center director's question about how you plan to assess the growth and development of the children in your care.
2. You are a first grade teacher. A parent comes to you very upset because her child's reading, math, and language scores on the Metropolitan Achievement Test are in the 60th percentile, yet she earns A and B grades. Describe other evidence you might have to support the A and B grades.

} REFERENCES

Au, K. H. (1997). Commentary. In B. P. Farr & E. Trumbull, *Assessment alternatives for diverse classrooms* (pp. 309–312). Norwood, MA: Christopher-Gordon Publishers.

Billman, J., & Sherman, J. (2003). *Observation and participation in early childhood settings (2nd ed.).* New York: Allyn and Bacon.

Bredekamp, S., & Copple, C. (Eds.). (1997). *Developmentally appropriate practice in early childhood programs* (revised ed.). Washington, DC: National Association for the Education of Young Children.

Dever, M. T., & Barta, J. J. (2001). Standardized entrance assessment in kindergarten: A qualitative analysis of the experiences of teachers,

administrators, and parents. *Journal of Research in Childhood Education, 15*(2), 218–231.

Federal Interagency Forum on Child and Family Statistics. (1997). *America's children: Key national indicators of well-being.* Washington, DC: U.S. Government Printing Office.

Fleege, P. O., Charlesworth, R., Burts, D. C., & Hart, C. (1992). Stress begins in kindergarten: A look at behavior during standardized testing. *Journal of Research in Childhood Education, 7*(1), 20–25.

HEL. (2003). Teaching and learning in a high-stakes environment. *Harvard Educational Letter, 19*(4), 1–2.

James, J. C., & Tanner, C. K. (1993). Standardized testing of young children. *Journal of Research and Development in Education, 26*(3), 143–152.

Kelly, M. F., & Surbeck, E. (2000). History of preschool assessment. In B. A. Bracken, Ed. *The psychoeducational assessment of preschool children* (3rd ed., 1–18). Boston: Allyn and Bacon.

Meisels, S. J. (1993). Remaking classroom assessment with the work sampling system. *Young Children, 48*(5), 34–40.

NAEYC & NAECS/SDE. (National Association for the Education of Young Children & National Association of Early Childhood Specialists in State Departments of Education.) (2004). Where we stand on curriculum, assessment, and program evaluation. *Young Children, 59*(1), 51–53.

Puckett, M. B., & Black, J. K. (1994). *Authentic assessment of the young child: Celebrating development and learning.* New York: Macmillan College Publishing.

Santos, R. M. (2004). Ensuring culturally and linguistically appropriate assessment of young children. *Young Children, 59*(1), 48–50.

Smith, A. F. (2000) Reflective portfolios: Preschool possibilities. *Childhood Education, 76*(4), 204–208.

Solano-Flores, G., & Trumbull, E. (2003). Examining language in context: The need for new research and practice paradigms in the testing of English-language learners. *Educational Researcher, 32*(2), 3–13.

Stefanakis, E. H. (1998). *Whose judgment counts? Assessing bilingual children, K–3.* Portsmouth, NH: Heinemann.

Wodtke, K. H., Harper, F., Schommer, M., & Brunelli, P. (1989). How standardized is school testing? An exploratory observational study of standardized group testing in kindergarten. *Educational Evaluation and Policy Analysis, 11*(3), 223–235.

Children Who Are Linguistically Diverse

Are you monolingual? Are you bilingual? Do you speak several languages?
Do you speak a nonmainstream dialect of English? Most early childhood
educators in the United States are monolingual; they speak only one
language, American English. This means that finding themselves working
with a child for whom English is not the first language, and whose English
language skills may be very limited, can be daunting. It is important for all
early childhood educators to realize that they can have a positive effect in
motivating those children to learn English, and they are also a key factor in
promoting acceptance of linguistic diversity among all the children and
their teachers and caregivers.

The language a child uses at home is closely tied to her/his identity, values,
beliefs, and behavior; in effect the child's language is the child's culture.
Therefore, it is vitally important that the language used by a child is
respected and acknowledged. In order to do this, early childhood educators
must have some understanding of linguistic diversity.

After reading this chapter you will understand:

▶ The issues involved in language differences in the United States.

▶ The variety of linguistic differences you may encounter in young children.

▶ Theories about second language acquisition.

▶ The stages of acquiring a second language.

▶ Factors affecting second language acquisition.

▶ The role of the early childhood educator in promoting second language
  acquisition.

⧘ The Challenge

Prior to the industrial era, each community and its educational institutions shared a common language and culture. Today, most communities include individuals and families who come from diverse cultural backgrounds and who have linguistic traditions that differ from the American mainstream group, the Euro-American middle class, who speak Standard American English (SAE). These linguistic traditions may be those of a different language (such as Spanish), a different accent, and/or a different dialect. The accent a speaker uses refers to how the uttered words are pronounced, and an accent differs from SAE only in pronunciation. A dialect, on the other hand, is usually spoken with an accent different than SAE but has additional differences in grammar and often in vocabulary as well.

Standard American English is not a uniform linguistic style; there are several versions of SAE and no one "dialect" has been identified as such (Wolfram & Christian, 1989). However, in each community the speech of a particular group, usually those from the middle class who form the influential core of the community, tends to be identified as the standard for use in business, education, the media, and other formal situations in which clear communication is needed. For example, the SAE acceptable in the southern states differs in both accent and dialect from that accepted in the West or other regions of the United States.

Within each early childhood setting there may be found a variety of linguistic traditions among the young children and the educators. In any given setting, the teacher may speak using one form of American English (AE) and the young children may all use a different form of AE; or the educator and some of the young children may share a language tradition while other young children share another. In other settings there may be several young children whose first language is one other than AE, and these young children may or may not share the same first language.

One fact is certain: in the future all early childhood educators must expect to encounter language diversity in their settings. In 2000, over 27 million people in the United States spoke a language other than English at home (U.S. Census, 2000). The population of those who speak with an accent or dialect is myriad. It is mistakenly assumed that the children who are linguistically diverse are immigrants; however, the fact is that many of these children are American born.

Those who do not speak SAE in our society are at a disadvantage. They are often stereotyped as less intelligent and therefore less useful socially, financially, and politically. Teachers have lower expectations of both second language learners and those with pronounced dialects. The difficulties involved with assessing the academic achievement of non-SAE speaking children have often resulted in the inappropriate placement of these children in special education classes for children with disabilities (Chapter 11).

The Controversy

Ever since a constitutional amendment to make English the official language of the United States of America was introduced in 1981 by U.S. Senator S. I. Hayakawa, the use of other languages in education and the political arena has been highly

Something to think about!

How many of you reading this speak a language other than American English at home?

How many of you use the accepted SAE for your region?

Do any of you acknowledge that you speak with a pronounced dialect or accent that differs from the accepted regional SAE?

controversial. This movement was not successful, but the controversy about bilingual education and efforts to accommodate linguistic minorities continues (Ovando, Combs, & Collier, 2006).

The case against accommodating linguistic diversity in our educational and governmental institutions is brought by those who mistakenly believe that the use of other languages is divisive and has the potential to be subversive. They also believe that unless children are forced to switch completely from their home language or dialect to SAE, they will never become productive members of society and will become a financial drain on the nation. English as a common language is seen as a means of resolving conflict in this nation of ethnic, religious, and linguistic diversity, and also as the prime means of attaining social and financial advancement (Crawford, 1992).

Advocates for accommodating linguistic diversity, who oppose the English only movement, see things from a different perspective. They agree that it is essential for all children in the United States to master the English language, but they emphasize the advantages of bilingualism (and even bidialectism). They also acknowledge the dangers of ignoring the importance of a child's first language or dialect. In the past, many non-English speaking immigrants succeeded in learning the language; however, many did not and ended up failing to find a niche in society. With the larger numbers of linguistically diverse students in our schools today, we cannot afford the social and financial cost of such failures (Gollnick & Chinn, 2006).

© Bettmann/CORBIS.

Public schools in the United States are bound by the Lau decision (1974), when the U.S. Supreme Court ruled in *Lau v. Nichols* that the San Francisco School District violated the 1964 Civil Rights Act. This case established the right of children in public schools to receive instruction that they are able to understand. Because of this case, laws were enacted to guide school districts in providing programs for those children who did not speak English fluently enough to learn in a monolingual English language classroom.

There are three aspects of language that teachers must consider:

1. Language is used to communicate emotions, thoughts, opinions. It is the common bond of each group that shares everyday values, beliefs, and behaviors (Gollnick & Chinn, 2006), and without it societies would not survive.

2. Language has an effect on the individual and cultural identity of each person (Gollnick & Chinn, 2006). It is used to socialize the young into their cultural group, and it distinguishes one group from another. Through language and its patterns, children learn with whom they can identify and how to interact with them.

3. Language is the means of connecting with other people. By adjusting language patterns and vocabulary to those of another group, an individual can connect with those other groups or cultures, and be accepted and considered to be trustworthy (Dicker, 1996).

Linguistic Differences

Language diversity among citizens in our nation includes differences in dialect, accent, spoken or not spoken, and languages other than English. Language differences and the role of early childhood educators who encounter language diversity are discussed below.

Dialects

Everyone speaks a dialect, which is a regional or social variation of a given language. It is set apart from other varieties by differences in grammar, pronunciation, and vocabulary. As we noted earlier, no one "dialect" has been identified as the SAE dialect (Wolfram, Adger, & Christian, 1999; Wolfram & Christian, 1989), nor is any dialect good or bad in itself. However, some dialects are considered more acceptable than others for use in particular social or business contexts. If you have never seen it, ask someone (probably older than you are) about the classic TV comedy *The Beverly Hillbillies*. The humor was based on a clash of cultures, and a large part of this was in the dialectical differences and the misunderstandings that arose from them.

Teachers often take one of the following approaches when working with non-SAE speakers: (a) they constantly correct the "errors" of Standard English learners (SELs) in an attempt to replace the students' dialect with SAE; (b) they believe that learning SAE is unnecessary, or (c) they encourage the use of both dialect and SAE in appropriate situations (Diaz-Rico & Weed, 2002). Most often, teachers feel that they must not accept or endorse any dialect other than the local SAE dialect in the classroom, and they insist on the use of the latter (Roberts, 1985). Although it is true that it is important for academic, financial, and social purposes that children master SAE, it is nevertheless true that the best means of communicating with a child is through the child's own first language, even if it is a dialectical variation of SAE.

In order to understand the child, the teacher must understand the child's language and culture (Labov, 1969; Grant & Wong, 1994). As a teacher, you become the bridge for children between their own languages and SAE. Teachers must directly help children with translations (as they would with a foreign language speaker) while at the same time respecting the child's dialect. The goal is to help the child become "bidialectic," that is, able to understand and use both her/his own home dialect and SAE.

Bill Bachmann/Alamy Images.

Dialect Errors: Points to Consider

Don'T Interrupt a Child to Correct Her/His Speech:

▶ If the teacher interrupts the child to correct her speech, the child may not even hear the correction; the child only notices that she has been interrupted.

▶ If the teacher constantly interrupts the child to correct him, this may discourage the child from speaking at all.

▶ If the child gets the impression that the teacher thinks the way she speaks is unacceptable, and therefore "bad," this will affect her self-confidence and hinder her success at school more than using a dialect does.

Always Use Standard American English Speech to the Children:

▶ The most effective way to teach SAE is to use it, thereby "modeling" SAE speech for the children.

▶ The child will correct himself if he is motivated to use SAE.

Black English

The dialect used in many working-class African-American communities (Owens, 1992; Wolfram, Adger, & Christian, 1999) is often referred to as Black English, vernacular Black English, African-American vernacular English (AAVE), or Ebonics. Approximately 80% of African-Americans use Black English most of the time, 19% use SAE, and 1% use other dialects (Woffard, 1979). Black English is viewed as a legitimate language system with its own regular rules of syntax and vocabulary; however, it has many features in common with SAE. Southern English, southern white nonstandard English, and Black English have many common characteristics (Wolfram, Adger, & Christian, 1999). The main differences lie in tone, speaking rate, and unique lexicons (Owens, 1992).

Role of the Early Childhood Educator

▶ When children arrive at school or preschool they have been communicating effectively with their home dialect for 3 to 5 years. Remember that children bring an already formed dialectic linguistic history with them to school or preschool (NAEYC, 1995; Hollie, 2001).

▶ Focus on the ending sounds of words (ask, helping, with).

▶ Show children how contracted forms relate to full forms of words (ain't = are not).

▶ Avoid using phonics instruction as pronunciation instruction (Labov, 1972).

Table 10.1 and the *Focus on Diversity* highlight some important information for teachers who work with speakers of Black English and other dialects.

Table 10.1   Black English/African–American Vernacular English (AAVE)

Typical Characteristics of Black English/AAVE	AAVE	SAE
The "th" at the end or middle of word not sounded, or replaced by "f" or "v"	aufor wif smoov	author with smooth
Consonant digraphs not spoken as two distinct sounds, but as one sound	ax	ask
Omission of plural marker "s" *(not required if with adjective indicating quantity)*	There are three girl.	There are three girls.
Omission of possessive marker "s" *(not required if possession is indicated by word position)*	The man car. . .	The man's car. . .
Omission of "ed" on past tense verbs	Yesterday Bobby play at my house.	Yesterday Bobby played at my house.
Use of habitual "be"	She be at school.	She is at school
Verb agreement	The boy run to the store.	The boy runs to the store.
Use of double negative	I ain't got nothing.	I don't have anything.
Wide range between highest and lowest voice tone.	Greater range	Smaller range

Sources: Wolfram, W., Adger, C., & Christian, D. (1999). *Dialects in schools and communities.* Mahwah, NJ: Lawrence Erlbaum Associates; Hollie, S. (2001). Acknowledging the language of African American students: Instructional strategies. *English Journal, 90*(4), 54–59; Owens, R. E., Jr. (1992). *Language development.* New York: Macmillan Publishing.

Focus on Diversity

African-American Standard English learners may have difficulties because of the following:

- The relationship between the spoken language and the written or spelling form is unclear due to linguistic differences.
- Final sounds in words are linguistically unfamiliar to them.
- AAVE contains historically and linguistically based sound changes that create many homophones.
- There is a tendency to rely on the form and meaning of words in their context and to mistrust the alphabet.

Source: Cited in Hollie, S. (2001). Acknowledging the language of African American Students: Instructional strategies. *English Journal, 90*(4), 54–59.

⟩ Accents

When we hear people pronounce words differently, we describe them as having an accent. Southerners visiting New York will exclaim that they cannot understand the strange accent of the New Yorkers. Conversely, those in New York may be fascinated by the Southern slow speech, long vowels, and use of "y'all" (which incidentally is derived from the old English plural form of "you"). No linguistic group is considered to have an accent until they leave their home territory.

Our accent depends on the speech form and pronunciation with which we are surrounded as we develop our native language skills. For example, Falconer's sons were born in Canada and have North American/Canadian accents, even though both their parents speak with a British accent. Japanese and Chinese native speakers are unable to pronounce the sound of "l" because it is nonexistent in the language they grew up speaking. They tend to begin English words having an initial "l" sound with an "r" sound (e.g., they say "right" for "light"). Growing up in Hong Kong, Falconer became accustomed to two forms of her first name. Her English friends called her "Renée" and her Chinese friends called her "Lenée." It is difficult for anyone who learns another language after the age of 12 years to speak it without a discernible accent.

According to research done at the University of Pennsylvania, as reported by the ABC News show *20/20* on September 3, 1999, regional accents in the United States are growing more distinct rather than more similar. Listen carefully to your peers. Does anyone have an accent that is noticeably different than that of everyone else in the group? Find out where they have lived, for how long, and at what age. Do you judge people on the basis of their accents? If so, in what way?

⟩ Sign Language

All languages are communication systems made up of vocal or nonverbal messages (Gollnick & Chinn, 2006). Hearing impaired individuals worldwide have developed communication systems based on signs. American Sign Language (ASL) is the system used most extensively among deaf individuals in the United States and Canada, and Signed English (SE) is the most common system used to communicate with the hearing. Children who are hearing impaired learn the rhythms and syntax of signing as easily as hearing children learn spoken language. Those who have hearing parents do not usually learn ASL until they attend a school for the deaf. Many deaf individuals are bilingual in ASL and spoken English.

ASL is recognized as a language complete with a complex and well-regulated syntax and vocabulary; however, it does not match completely with written or spoken English (Smith, 2001). Therefore, when communicating with the hearing population, deaf individuals tend to use SE, which parallels spoken English. Interpreters on television or at a meeting usually use SE (Swank, 1997).

Focus on Children

Following are websites that have information on how young children learn sign language.

Search the American Sign Language Dictionary. Enter your query below: Tips for searching. ... Hand signs from the American Sign Language ... http://www.masterstech-home.com/ASLDict.html

The Alphabet. American Sign Language. A. B. C. D. E. F. G. H. I. J. K. L. M. N. O. P. Q. R. S. T. U. V. W. X. Y. Z. Want to see fingerspelling in action? Think you've got it down? ... http://where.com/scott.net/asl/abc.html

Learn American Sign Language (ASL) and Signed English (SE). ... American Sign Language (ASL) for the Deaf: Series 1. American Sign Language (ASL) vs. ... http://www.lessontutor.com/ASLgenhome.html

American Sign Language. Major Sites. Dictionaries and ASL Lessons, ASL History. Deafness. ... http://www.fcps.k12.va.us/DIS/OHSICS/forlang/amslan.htm

Sherman Wilcox. Department of Linguistics. ... American Sign Language as a Foreign Language. ... ASL as a Foreign Language Fact Sheet. ... http://www.unm.edu/%7ewilcox/as/fl.html

Signing Time is a sign language video series for hearing infants and children that teaches them basic American Sign Language (ASL). ... http://www.signingtime.com

Welcome to Bright Tykes! ... The first in our series of videos is *Read the Signs, Sign Language for Preschool Literacy.* An innovative video that combines early literacy topics with Sign Language and Spanish! ... http://www.bright-tykes.com

An interesting extension of sign language is its use with very young hearing children who are able to learn a sign language system to communicate with adults before they are able to speak. If you want to know more about this and the ASL and SE sign languages, explore the websites listed in the *Focus on Children*.

Speakers of Languages Other than English

Bilingualism, the ability to use two languages, is not valued as highly in the United States as it is in most other nations. Moreover, some people consider that an individual must be fluent in both languages to be considered bilingual, whereas others believe that only a certain level of competency is required to be considered bilingual (Baca & Cervantes, 1998).

Bilingual Education

The main goal of bilingual education is to teach children the knowledge, concepts, and skills they need to succeed. The best way to do this is through children's first language until they have mastered sufficient English to successfully learn in English. This is vitally important because English language learners (ELLs) who are not able to keep up with schoolwork will eventually drop out before completing high school. Imagine if this class you are in now were taught in a language you were learning and did not know well! How successful do you think you would be? This is a major factor in the fact that children from underrepresented populations have higher dropout rates than those of the dominant culture.

There are two forms of bilingual education used in schools. *Transitional* bilingual programs focus on moving from the home language and culture as a means of instruction to the use of American English and mainstream culture as soon as is feasible. The home language is used only to make the transition to learning in American English, and it is phased out gradually. The goal of *maintenance* bilingual programs is to help young children function and learn effectively in both the home language and American English, and to become bilingual and bicultural. The *Focus on Diversity* takes you into a maintenance bilingual program.

English as a Second Language

Transitional and maintenance programs must not be confused with English as a Second Language (ESL) programs. In ESL programs, instruction is given exclusively in English, and students are immersed in an English language learning environment. ESL teachers employ strategies to assist English language learners. The goal is to assimilate the ELL student into the linguistic mainstream as quickly as possible. Early childhood educators must be cautious not to disregard young children's home language and culture. With very young children in particular this can lead to loss of the home language (L1).

It is extremely important for early childhood educators to learn about the home language and culture of children in the setting and to be aware of the problems associ-

Focus on Diversity

Kayley is a kindergarten teacher in an urban school serving a population that is approximately 70% Hispanic and 30% Caucasian. Other ethnic groups make up less than 1% of the population. Kayley is bilingual, knowing English and Spanish. With two half-day sessions of approximately 18 kindergarteners in each, Kayley's program is a dual immersion language program. In this case, the curriculum is presented in both Spanish and English. This is different than an English as a Second Language (ESL) program where, although the teacher may be bilingual and talk with children in their native language, the curriculum is delivered in English only. Both Spanish- and English-speaking children were placed in this dual immersion kindergarten by parent choice.

When the children first came to school in August, Kayley did initial assessments to inform her curriculum development. She assessed individual children in their own language to determine their developmental levels.

In Kayley's kindergarten classroom, the curriculum is delivered in Spanish on Monday and Tuesday and in English on Wednesday and Thursday. On Friday, the curriculum is delivered in both languages. Following is an excerpt of a whole group interactive writing experience on a Friday. The class is talking and writing about things that are red.

Kayley: [To the class.] Let's write some things that are red? What can you think of that is red?
Juan: Una manzana.
Kayley: [Writing on the chart.] Una manzana es—Juan, puedes escribir roja?
Juan: [Comes to the chart and writes.] roja
Kayley: Que mas?
Missy: Stop sign.
Kayley: [Writing on the chart.] A stop sign is—Missy, can you write red?
Missy: [Comes to the chart and writes.] red
Kayley: What else?
Maria: Pizza.
Kayley: [Writing on the chart.] Pizza is—Maria, can you write red?
Maria: [Comes to the chart and writes.] red
Kayley: What else is red?
Xochilt: Un boli.
Kayley: [Writing on the chart.] Un boli es—Xochilt, puedes escribir rojo?
Xochilt: [Comes to the chart and writes.] rojo
Kayley: Que mas?
Alex: Fire is red.
Kayley: [Writing on the chart.] Fire is red.

On this day when the curriculum is delivered in both languages, Kayley is following the lead of the children. If they respond in Spanish, she writes and speaks in Spanish. If they respond in English, so does she. In this dual immersion program, not only do native Spanish speakers learn English, but native English speakers learn Spanish.

Kayley assesses children in her kindergarten classroom primarily by observation. She sets goals for the children and then observes their progress. At the end of the year she assess children's learning in their native language first and then in the other language. Children are required to take a standardized *End of Level* test in English.

In a program such as this one, all children receive the "gift" of being bilingual—learning in their native language and in another language. Kayley notes that the children do not focus on their ethnic differences; rather, they make friends across cultures. Assistance is reciprocal as they work in both languages.

ated with children losing their first language. This can be attributed to negative feelings toward the first language engendered by the attitudes of others. The loss of a child's first language can result in difficulties with family interactions, low self-esteem and community pride, and a lowered ability to learn English successfully (NAEYC, 1995).

Nonverbal Communication

Within the whole process of communication, nonverbal communication can be very important. It expresses meaning through attitudes, actions, personality, dress, or mannerisms, and can either augment or replace verbal communication. For example, a thumbs-up sign reinforces an encouraging remark: a frown contradicts that same encouraging comment. A shake of the head communicates "no" to the observer.

Nonverbal communication is more closely linked to culture than is the spoken word. For example, a pat on the head is a positive action to some groups but offensive to others. European American teachers exhort children to "look me in the eyes" as a sign of compliance or honesty. However, this is considered a disrespectful and defiant action by some, African-Americans and Hispanic Americans in particular. The acceptable distance maintained between people varies. Most Americans maintain a distance of about 20 inches, whereas some groups are used to standing much closer to each other when talking, and others stand much further apart.

It must be realized that discussion about cultural nonverbal behavior refers to generalizations about cultural dispositions. Individual members of each group may behave differently from each other depending on their experiences. Nonverbal communication must be seen as the context in which verbal communication takes place, and context is always important to meaning and interpretation.

▧⟩ Acquiring a Second Language

Acquiring a second language (L2), or even a third, fourth, or fifth, means learning how to use that language to communicate effectively with those for whom it is a native language (L1), not just learning the grammatical rules and vocabulary. English is the main vehicle of expression in our schools and children need to acquire proficiency in English in order to succeed. To meet the needs of the many students who enter our schools speaking languages other than English or even SAE, teachers must teach basic speaking and listening skills as well as literacy. People are able to form societies because they can communicate, using some form of language. Schools are the means of socializing the young for success in our society by teaching them the requisite knowledge and skills to maintain social interaction and achieve positions and individuality (Diaz-Rico & Weed, 2002). Teachers that are informed about language acquisition and use are better able to build the bridges between a child's home culture and the school culture and to make schools dynamic and creative learning environments. If you are interested in knowing more about second language acquisition, *Bilingual & ESL Classroom: Searching in Multicultural Contexts* by Ovando, Combs, & Cottier, 2006, is an excellent reference.

Theories of Second Language Acquisition

The characteristics of language and how it evolves have fascinated people since the time of the Greek and Roman empires. In Medieval times, Latin was the model on which grammar was based. The early grammarians believed that there were certain "correct" ways to use language, and these were "prescribed" as the only forms acceptable. This evolved into the traditional method of teaching foreign languages, by memorizing vocabulary, learning verb forms, and translating texts. If you have ever learned a foreign language, this was probably the way you were expected to learn it. Greater value was placed on knowing the grammatical rules and structure of a language than on being able to speak it. Later the behaviorist approach to language acquisition added oral drills and repetition to this, based more on the correct form of the language rather than on meaning (Diaz-Rico & Weed, 2002).

New theories about language acquisition and development emerged in the last century. Recall from Chapter 5, two conflicting theories were put forward by B. F. Skinner and Noam Chomsky. Skinner's theory that language was learned by reinforcing what young children memorized and said (behaviorist) was challenged by Chomsky who argued that if this were so, then young children would not be able to understand any sentences they had never heard before. Chomsky (1959) asserted that this is clearly not the case, and he proposed a theory that the mind actively processes language through a language acquisition device (LAD) that constructs rules by unconsciously internalizing grammar (innatist).

There are three major groups of theories about second language acquisition (SLA), behaviorist, innatist, and interactionist. From the behaviorists' point of view, influenced by Skinner, L2 learners need to have opportunities and patterned practices to imitate language patterns and need much repetition focusing on grammar, and their errors should be corrected as soon as possible (Peregoy & Boyle, 2000). The innatist perspective, influenced by Chomsky (1959) and developed by Krashen (1982), states that L2 learners acquire a second language in the way that people acquire their first language. Innatist theorists believe that L2 learners will naturally acquire their L2 unconsciously from teachers, books, and friends, and that L2 learners will naturally correct their errors themselves and that in this way they acquire their L2 effectively with more motivation and lower anxiety. The interactionist theorists consider that L2 learners acquire their L2 through interaction with people. They emphasize second language acquisition through communication with others, accompanied by input L2 learners can understand. This can be achieved when native speakers of the second language speak more slowly and distinctly, use simple vocabulary, and use gestures.

The *Focus on Children* describes five contemporary theories about second language acquisition and the appropriate learning environment for young children with regard to each. Can you identify which SLA perspective, behaviorist, innatist, or interactionist, has the most influence on each theory?

Language Acquisition Stages

It takes a long time for L2 learners to achieve fluency in a language. During the process of learning and acquisition, the L2 learner makes many mistakes in both the receptive (listening, reading, and understanding) and expressive (speaking and writing) areas of the language. Furthermore, not every L2 learner acquires the proficiency of a native speaker. A person may be able to comprehend the written and spoken forms of a language well, but not be able to speak or write it with fluency. Recall from Chapter 5 that, as young children acquire their native language, the ability to receive or understand a language (receptive) comes before the ability to produce the language in written or spoken form (expressive). Receptive skills develop before expressive. The process of learning a second language happens in the following stages as proposed by Krashen (1982).

Comprehension or preproduction stage. The ability to understand the language (receptive skill) is developing, but expressive skill is limited. Often, L2 learners go through a period of silence at this time, lasting from 1 or 2 weeks to several months. In order to associate sounds with meaning, listening is important at this stage.

Focus on Children

Theory

The Monitor Model Theory

Chomsky's work influenced the monitor model of second language acquisition developed by Krashen (1982), and this in turn became the theoretical base for the natural approach to learning and teaching another language. In his monitor model, Krashen proposed that the acquisition of a second language occurs in a predictable order, but only if understandable input is received and emotions do not block understanding. He also proposed that the use of the language is edited by an internal "monitor." To summarize, Krashen postulates the following five premises:

1. The *acquisition* of a language leads to fluency, while *learning* a language involves knowing the rules of the language (acquisition–learning hypothesis).
2. People master the rules of a language in a predictable order (natural order hypothesis).
3. Second language learners or acquirers edit language for accuracy as they use it (monitor hypothesis).
4. Languages are acquired only by understanding messages (input hypothesis).
5. Certain mental and emotional blocks can inhibit complete understanding of messages (affective filter hypothesis).

Communicative Competence Theory

The idea behind the theory of communicative competence (Hymes, 1962) is that knowing when, where, and how to use a language suitably and effectively is more important to meaning than mere correct grammatical usage. Four dimensions of communicative competence have been outlined by Canale (1983):

1. *Grammatical competence* focuses on the ability to speak and write using correct vocabulary, grammar, pronunciation, and spelling.
2. *Sociolinguistic competence* refers to knowing how to use the language in particular situations, taking into account the purposes of the communication, the participants' relationship, and the social norms.
3. *Discourse competence* refers to being able to put together written and spoken words and sentences into meaningful communication. Even grammatically correct sentences can lack meaning.
4. *Strategic competence* refers to using language, both verbal and nonverbal (as in gestures and body language), to ensure understanding. An example is raising the voice to underline a point or using a gesture to add emphasis to what you say.

Appropriate Learning Environment

The Monitor Model Theory

What does this mean for early childhood educators? Children will produce some language involuntarily but will need certain guidance and rules. As children go about their daily activities they will learn and use language, and an alert educator can catch "teachable moments" or address language errors overheard during discussions in a later lesson. Furthermore, young children must feel that their native language is valued and that they will successfully become bilingual.

An educator cannot expect mastery of a grammatical rule even after direct teaching and/or practice because language learners search for patterns and order in what they hear or see. They will only master these rules gradually in the natural order, similar to that found in first language development. For example, the correct use of the negative form is mastered after (a) first using it outside the sentence ("Not like it now"), (b) using it between the subject and the verb ("I no like this one"); and (c) using it in the correct place ("I don't like this one") (Dulay, Burt, & Krashen, 1982). Teaching the rules does not result in language acquisition, but a language-rich learning environment helps acquisition. Early childhood educators must use various ways, including visual and kinesthetic strategies, to make sure young children understand what is said. Finally, language acquisition is enhanced by a nonthreatening, accepting, and supportive environment.

Communicative Competence Theory

Educators must include active and interactive experiences in the learning environment to promote all the dimensions of communicative competence. In the early years, small groups interacting at centers are ideal, and the adults in a classroom setting must promote communication among children and between children and adults.

Sociolinguistic competence skills are important for L2 learners, and are taught in kindergarten and first grade even to English speaking students; however, they re often neglected in higher grades.

Focus on Children (continued)

Theory	Appropriate Learning Environment

Discourse Theory

The basic idea behind discourse theory is that the more L2 learners talk, the more language is acquired, and this is the key to second language acquisition. Interacting verbally with others allows L2 learners to internalize language patterns and structures and master expressions (Brown & Yule, 1983; Fox, 1987; Hatch, 1992). According to Selinker (1991), in conversing with others, L2 learners generate an "interlanguage" based on (a) their capability with their first language, (b) what they know about the second language, (c) their capacity to use language, and (d) their general knowledge and experience.

Discourse Theory

Early childhood educators must provide frequent and various occasions for L2 learners to talk with those for whom English is their first language.

The Social Context Theory

The development of language is enhanced by interaction with others in social contexts. Although this is an important aspect of the monitor model, communicative competence theory, and discourse theory, when examined from the perspective of social and cultural interaction as well as pure communication (Vygotsky, 1978), thought development is added to language development and acquisition. By interacting with others who have more advanced English language skills than their own, second language acquisition is enhanced and the L2 learners can acquire a wider vocabulary and develop more complex language structures. In addition, they learn about the cultural and social aspects of language use.

The Social Context Theory

Understanding this theory should encourage early childhood educators to provide a learning environment in which young children are encouraged to talk in pairs or small groups while completing learning activities.

Brain Research Theory

The foremost function of the brain is to learn (Caine & Caine, 1994; Hart, 1983; Nummela & Rosengren, 1986). Learning methods that use knowledge of how the brain functions have been developed by a number of present-day educators. Language acquisition can be aided by the principles of brain-based learning:

1. The brain can carry out numerous processes at the same time.
2. The whole body and mind is involved in learning.
3. The hunt for meaning is instinctive.
4. The brain seeks out and generates patterns.
5. Emotions have a direct impact on memory.
6. The brain deals with parts and wholes at the same time.
7. Focused attention and peripheral awareness are both involved in learning.
8. Both conscious and unconscious processes are involved in learning.
9. Memory includes both spatial and rote learning.
10. Optimal learning takes place when facts and skills are set in natural, spatial memory.
11. Learning is improved by challenge, suppressed by threat.
12. Each brain is unique.

Brain Research Theory

Use a variety of modes and strategies for learning experiences. Include conversational opportunities at all times.
All aspects of physical, emotional, and social well-being should be considered at all times. Language learning should be the product of meaningful and authentic activities.
Language learning environments and teaching methods should stimulate the brain to actively find patterns and generate meaning. Language learning should take place in an atmosphere of respect, acceptance, and support. Vocabulary and grammar (parts) can be learned through discussions, problem solving, reading, singing, etc. (wholes), in authentic situations.
A rich environment with music, art etc., stimulates language learning. Students need to reflect on and reexamine what they learn to enhance understanding. Memorization (rote) and authentic new experiences (spatial) are both important.
Real and purposeful language activities consolidate learning of disconnected language skills.
An accepting, supportive, and stimulating learning environment promotes language acquisition.
Teachers should use a wide variety of strategies and learning modes to meet the needs of L2 learners.

Sources: Diaz-Rico, L. T., & Weed, K. Z. (2002). *The cross-cultural language and academic development handbook: A complete K–12 reference guide* (2nd ed.). Boston: Allyn and Bacon.
Caine, R., & Caine, G. (1994). *Making connections: Teaching and the human brain.* Menlo Park, CA: Addison Wesley.

Early production. The L2 learner may attempt a few single- or double-word utterances, and mispronunciation is common. Understanding is improving. As with toddlers, *telegraphic speech* or short phrases with the article are typical (e.g., "I go school") (Lopez & Gopaul-McNichol, 1997).

Speech emergence. More complex and lengthier sentences are used in this stage. The L2 learners generate their own sentences but make many grammatical mistakes. The mistakes usually reflect transference of rules from the first language (Lopez & Gopaul-McNichol, 1997).

Intermediate fluency. Engaging in conversations and producing narratives with connected thought occur in this stage; however, thinking in the second language is still slower than in the first language. Receptive skills are now sufficient for good understanding; however, translating information still occurs to help understanding.

Advanced fluency. Receptive and expressive skills are well developed; however, information is still processed more slowly in L2 for such tasks as retrieval, memorization, and encoding (Lopez & Gopaul-McNichol, 1997). Information encoded in the L1 probably will be more easily retrieved in the L1, so at first the learner will have to translate information. For example, when writing out a recipe from the learner's native country in the second language, that recipe may have to be recalled in the first language and then written in the second (Thomas & Damino, 1985).

Second language learners may still process information more slowly than other children even though they may have expressive and receptive language skills that appear to be adequate. Because this is normal progression in language acquisition and learning, teachers must be careful not to unnecessarily refer L2 learners for special education classes (Chapter 11).

Cummins (1984) studied the language of L2 learners and found that after 2 years of ESL instruction the students were able to use adequate English to function in social situations, a level of language acquisition that Cummins called *basic interpersonal*

Bonnie Kamin/PhotoEdit.

communicative skills (BICS). Nevertheless, these language skills were insufficient for the students to function adequately in academic situations, where the language skills needed were very different. His research found that attaining *cognitive academic language proficiency* (CALP) took up to 7 years of language learning. The reason is that academic language is highly content driven and is laden with specialized vocabulary and concepts that are not encountered frequently and that have more complex syntax (Cummins, 2000), very unlike social conversational language. If an early childhood educator fails to acknowledge or recognize these differences, the cost for young children can be high.

Role of the Early Childhood Educator. Developmentally appropriate language activities can promote the development of CALP, or the *academic register* as it is sometimes called. Children should be encouraged to look at how they use their own language, be it a dialect or another language, for different purposes and in different settings (Wong-Fillmore, 1999). Being aware of this should help children understand the different forms of English used in social and academic situations. Language should always accompany learning experiences, first through hands-on activities, then more often through the use of written materials using decontextualized language. The emphasis should be on both meaning and use. The *Focus on Children* and the *Focus on Diversity* highlight some important considerations for early childhood educators.

Factors Affecting Second Language Acquisition: Social, Emotional, and Cognitive

Mere exposure to a language is not sufficient to achieve a level of advanced fluency. How close each English language learner comes to achieving advanced fluency, and how quickly this level is attained, depends on various influences emanating both

Focus on Children

English language learners encounter many challenges as they develop as speakers of English. Following are some examples.

Can You Read This?

Acdorcing to rsareech at an Elingsh uinervtisy, it deosn't mttaer in waht oredr the ltteers in a wrod are, the olny iprmoetnt tihng is taht the frist and lsat ltteer is at the rghit pclae.
The rset can be a toatl mses and you can sitll raed it wouthit a porbelm.
Tihs is bcuseae we do not raed ervey lteter by itslef but the wrod as a wohle.

The Difficulties of the English Language

Imagine having to sort out the meanings of these sentences if you were an English language learner!

- The bandage was wound around the wound.
- The insurance was invalid for the invalid.
- The town dump was so full it had to refuse more refuse.
- The farm was used to produce produce.
- The soldier decided to desert his dessert in the desert.
- After a number of injections my jaw got number.
- When I saw the tear in my dress, I shed a tear.
- A bass was painted on the bass drum.
- The farmer taught his sow to sow seeds.

from the social context in which the learner lives and from the characteristics of the learner as an individual. Each person is influenced by both sociocultural and psychological factors.

Learning a language happens in a social and cultural context. Interacting and conversing with others is the only way to learn either a first or second language. These social interactions are important in second language acquisition, because through them ELLs learn how to use the language appropriately and understand cultural expectations and behavior. In addition, the learners come to the learning environment as products of a cultural group, which means that they have learned certain ways of behaving and interacting typical of that culture (Diaz-Rico & Weed, 2002).

Emotional and cognitive (psychological) factors also influence second language acquisition and learning. This in turn enables or hinders the ease with which young children acclimate to the culture of the second language and are able to process what they hear and to respond with meaning (Diaz-Rico & Weed, 2002). Factors such as acculturation variables, the social status of the learner's first language, and the learner's proficiency in the first language, learning style, motivation, self-esteem, and attitudes all affect the process of acquiring a second language (Diaz-Rico & Weed, 2002; Gopaul-McNichol & Thomas-Presswood, 1998). The following influences match well with the theories about language acquisition described earlier in the chapter.

Focus on Diversity

Language is a key element of culture because it enables us to communicate within our families and communities. Moreover, it is through social interaction within families and among other members of our culture that we learn language. Learning a language other than one's native language is a feat far greater than just learning words; it involves learning the cultural aspects of the language as well.

Idioms are phrases that have meaning within a particular culture. The sense of these phrases has been socially constructed within that culture; however, they pose a challenge to those learning our language because their connotations are different than the meanings of the conjoined words within them. Thus, they cannot be understood by merely translating them.

Following are some idioms common to American speakers of English. As you read them, think about times you have used these idioms; then, imagine how English language learners might understand them.

- Time flies.
- A bird in the hand is worth two in the bush.
- What's good for the goose is good for the gander.
- When the cat's away, the mice will play.
- I'm going ape.
- It's the greatest thing since sliced bread.
- I have a frog in my throat.
- You're jumping from pillar to post.
- I'm all puffed up.
- When you have a bigger mouse, you build a bigger mouse trap.

This raises two (of many) considerations when working with English language learners. First, conversations must be clear and comprehensible for young children, particularly English language learners. Avoid use of idioms and slang. Second, it is important to learn a few basic phrases in the native language of children within your early childhood setting so you can communicate in their language. The local school district office as well as some parents are good resources for learning another language.

Exposure to target language. Exposure to a second language must be frequent and lengthy, but, even more valuable, the input of that language must be comprehensible (Cummins, 1994; Krashen, 1995). The L2 should be used at a level just above the ELL's current level. The interaction of this with the learner's individual characteristics will have an impact on the acquisition of the L2.

Language learning environment. The environment in which the ELL learns the L2 is an important element in the acquisition of the target language. Language acquisition is facilitated if the environment allows for the young child's active participation in rich experiences and exposure to concrete images to help language concepts develop. It is also facilitated through interaction with speakers of the target language who use comprehensible speech and who are linguistically aware. The need for comprehensible input in the learning environment links with the previously mentioned factors related to target language exposure. In addition, an optimal learning environment will enhance acquisition if the learner possesses the best possible characteristics for learning.

Characteristics of the learner. The characteristics of each young child have an impact on the outcome of exposure to the target language and the nature of the language environment (Gopaul-McNichol & Thomas-Presswood, 1998). These characteristics are age, cognitive abilities, motivation, personality, self-confidence, and level of oral and literacy competence in the L1 (Cummins, 1994; Tabors, 1997).

Loss of the First Language

If children learn English at an age when their first language is not yet well developed, they can lose the use of that home language (Wong-Fillmore, 1991). This happens most often in cases where children feel that their first language is considered inferior to English, and they are pressured not to use it by peers or by well-intentioned educators. This loss of the home language can result in a serious disintegration of family relationships when the child can no longer communicate effectively with his/her parents or grandparents. Teachers should encourage the family to persist in using the child's first language at home.

Focus on Children

Barriers to academic success for linguistically diverse children include differences in culture as well as language. Here are some practical instructional suggestions to eliminate the limitations imposed on learning by cultural differences (Cadzen, 1986). Some of these culturally responsive strategies are examples of the best practices as used by many creative and child-centered teachers in both monocultural and multicultural classrooms.

1. Use the children's own words to create beginning reading texts. These books could be illustrated "key words" such as house, dog, etc., or they could be simple illustrated stories about personal events dictated by the children.
2. Group L2 learning children with native English speakers, giving all the children the opportunity to be leaders and participants.
3. Allow children to practice following and giving directions in learning centers or large group activities, for example, turning pages during reading, using pictures to tell a story, noting the names of the main characters.
4. Refrain from forcing children to participate; wait for them to volunteer.
5. Learn some key words in the L2 learning child's first language (e.g., good, yes, hello, the numbers 1 through 10, bathroom).

Children learn languages more easily than do adults. Before the age of 5 years, acquiring additional languages is similar to the process and competence of first language acquisition. Developmentally appropriate, language-rich, early childhood learning environments are optimal for supporting young children's language acquisition and development in L1 and L2. How language input is processed is influenced by the learner's cognitive abilities, and the level to which the learner participates in verbal interactions and language experiences depends on personality, self-confidence, and motivation.

The young child's home language is the foundation on which skills in additional languages are built. Receptive language will develop first, as in L1, followed by expressive language. As with first language acquisition, early childhood educators should expect a silent period while receptive language develops (Tabors, 1997). Falconer noticed this with most of the ELL first-grade children she taught in international schools. Literacy in the home language, L1, will transfer to the L2 (Krashen, 1994). An ELL who has developed both oral fluency and literacy skills in the L1 will more quickly acquire oral fluency and literacy skills in the L2.

Figure 10.1 summarizes and depicts the reciprocal interactions of factors affecting second language acquisition.

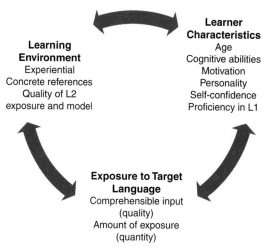

Figure 10.1. Factors affecting second language acquisition.

Summary

Early childhood educators are challenged to work effectively with children who are not native speakers of Standard English. Linguistic differences among young children take several forms including differences in dialect, accent, and native language. Furthermore, children with hearing disabilities communicate with sign language (American Sign Language or Signed English).

Second language acquisition is a complex task, although it is most easily completed in the early years. Theories of second language acquisition posit that it is a process that evolves in stages. Second language acquisition is affected by the quality and quantity of exposure to the target language. Young children need comprehensible input to support their learning. The early childhood environment must have concrete references and social interaction. The amount of exposure to the target language and the nature of the learning environment are influenced by the nature of the learner. The learner's age, motivation, self-confidence, and cognitive abilities all influence language acquisition.

Early childhood educators must respect the home language of all young children in their setting whether the variation is dialectical, another language, an accent, or sign language. Furthermore, the environment of a high-quality early childhood setting where young children are actively and interactively engaged with objects and people is also optimal for second language acquisition.

My Developing Professional View

Articulate your developing view of how you will address the needs of non-native English speakers in your early childhood setting.

◦ ENRICHMENT ACTIVITIES

Individual Activities

1. Read *From Far Away* by Bob Munsch and *From Anna* by Jean Little; both are available in a children's library or on Amazon.com. Each is a story about North American immigrants. Write a brief response to these books.

2. Explore the local library and/or bookstores to find children's books written in languages other than English. Develop an annotated bibliography.

3. Watch a foreign language TV channel and make note of nonverbal communication (gestures, facial expressions, distance between conversing people, etc.).

4. Visit a school or child care setting and observe any young children who are English language learners or dialect speakers. From field notes, write a brief overview of your observations.

5. Interview a teacher who has non-English speakers or dialect speakers in the classroom. Ask her about strategies she uses to help them acquire Standard American English.

Cooperative Activity

6. Using your state office of education as a resource, identify languages other than English that are spoken in schools in your state. Have each member of the group select one to learn. (If you are bilingual or multilingual, select a language you do not already know.) Using resources on your college or university campus, learn at least six conversational phrases in the language you selected (I'm glad to see you today. It's your turn. This is the bathroom. Etc.) Then, each group member teaches what s/he has learned to others in the group; the result is each of you will know a few conversational phrases in four different languages.

Advocacy Activity

7. Develop a campaign brochure (hypothetical) imploring citizens to vote against an English-only law. Your brochure must justify your position.

◦ FOR FURTHER READING

Espinosa, L. M. (2005). Curriculum and assessment considerations for young children from culturally, linguistically, and economically diverse backgrounds. *Psychology in the Schools, 42*(8), 837–853.

Handel, R. D. (1999). *Building family literacy in an urban community.* New York: Teachers College Press.

Kuball, Y. E. (1999). A case for developmental continuity in a bilingual K–2 setting. *Young Children, 54*(3), 74–79.

Lake, V. E., & Pappamihiel, N. E. (2003). Effective practices and principles to support English language learners in the early childhood classroom. *Childhood Education, 79*(4), 200–203.

Szecsi, T., & Giambo, D. A. (2004/05). ESOL in every minute of the school day. *Childhood Education, 81*(2), 104–106.

Tabor, P. O. (1998). What early childhood educators need to know: Developing effective programs for linguistically and culturally diverse children and families. *Young Children, 53*(6), 20–26.

Professional Development Resource

NATIONAL CENTER FOR FAMILY LITERACY

325 W. Main Street, Suite 300
Louisville, KY 40202-4237
www.famlit.org

SELF-ASSESSMENT

1. What challenges do English language learners face?

2. What is a dialect?

3. Identify some cultural differences in communication.

4. Name at least five things that you can do as a teacher to create an environment that supports second language acquisition.

5. Describe the five theories of second language acquisition. What type of learning activities are suggested for each theory?

6. Describe the stages of second language acquisition.

Scenario

You are a first-grade teacher who has a native Spanish speaking child in your class. He and his parents are learning English but are not yet fluent. You know a bit of Spanish and you occasionally speak to him in his native language, and he responds in Spanish. In addition, you have sent books to be read at home; most are in Spanish. Through a translator, his mother tells you that she does not want him to speak Spanish at school, nor does she want you to send home books written in Spanish. She feels it will get in the way of his learning English. Defend your practice of speaking and reading in both languages.

REFERENCES

Baca, L. M., & Cervantes, H. (1998). *The bilingual special education interface* (3rd ed.). Upper Saddle River, NJ: Prentice-Hall.

Brown, G., & Yule, G. (1983). *Discourse analysis.* Cambridge: Cambridge University Press.

Cazden, C. (1986). ESL teachers as language advocates for children. In P. Rigg & D. S. Enright (Eds.), *Children and ESL: Integrating perspectives* (pp. 9–21). Washington, DC: Teachers of English to Speakers of Other Languages (TESOL).

Caine, R., & Caine, G. (1994). *Making connections: Teaching and the human brain.* Menlo Park, CA: Addison Wesley.

Canale, M. (1983). From communicative competence to communicative language pedagogy. In J. Richards & R. Schmidt (Eds.), *Language and communication.* New York: Longman.

Chomsky, N. (1959). Review of B. F. Skinner "Verbal Behavior." *Language, 35,* 26–58.

Crawford, J. (Ed.). (1992). *Language loyalties.* Chicago: University of Chicago Press.

Cummins, J. (1984). *Bilingualism and special education: Issues in assessment and pedagogy.* San Diego: College-Hill Press.

Cummins, J. (1994). The acquisition of English as a second language. In K. Spangenburg-Urbschat & R. Pritchard (Eds.), *Kids come in all languages: Reading instruction for ESL students* (pp. 36–64). Newark, DE: International Reading Association.

Cummins, J. (2000). *Language, power, and pedagogy: Bilingual children in the crossfire.* Clevedon, England: Multicultural Matters.

Diaz-Rico, L. T., & Weed, K. Z. *The cross-cultural language and academic development handbook: A complete K–12 reference guide* (2nd ed.). Boston: Allyn and Bacon.

Dicker, S. J. (1996). *Languages in America: A pluralistic view.* Bristol, PA: Multilingual Matters.

Dulay, H., Burt, M., & Krashen, S. (1982). *Language two.* New York: Oxford University Press.

Fox, B. (1987). *Discourse structure and anaphora.* Cambridge: Cambridge University Press.

Gollnick, D. M., & Chinn, P. C. (2006). *Multicultural education in a pluralistic society* (7th ed.). Upper Saddle River, NJ: Merrill Prentice-Hall.

Gopaul-McNichol, S., & Thomas-Presswood, T. (1998). *Working with linguistically and culturally different children: Innovative clinical and educative approaches.* Needham Heights, MA: Allyn and Bacon.

Grant, R., & Wong, S. (1994). Teaching second language learners: Special considerations for content teachers. *Literacy Issues and Practices, 11,* 23–29.

Hart, L. (1983). *Human brain, human learning.* New York: Longman.

Hatch, E. (1992). *Discourse and language education.* Cambridge: Cambridge University Press.

Hollie, S. (2001). Acknowledging the language of African American students: Instructional strategies. *English Journal, 90*(4), 54–59.

Hymes, D. (1962). The ethnography of speaking. In T. Gladwin & W. Sturtevant (Eds.), *Anthropology and human behavior.* Washington, DC: Anthropological Society of Washington.

Krashen, S. (1982). *Principles and practice in second language acquisition.* Oxford: Pergamon.

Krashen, S. (1994). Bilingual education and second language acquisition theory. In D. Durkin (Ed.), *Language issues: Readings for teachers* (pp. 90–115). White Plains, NY: Longman.

Labov, W. (1969). *The study of nonstandard English.* Urbana, IL: National Council of Teachers of English.

Labov, W. (1972). *Sociolinguistic patterns.* Philadelphia: University of Pennsylvania Press.

Lau v. Nichols, 414, U.S., 563–572 (1974, January 21).

Lopez, E., & Gopaul-McNicol, S. (1997). English as a second language. In G. Beor, K. Minke, & A. Thomas (Eds.), *Children's needs II.* Washington, DC: National Association of School Psychologists.

NAEYC. (National Association for the Education of Young Children.) (1995). *Responding to linguistic and cultural diversity: Recommendations for effective early childhood education.* Washington, DC: Author.

Nummela, R., & Rosengren, T. (1986). What's happening in students' brains may redefine teaching. *Educational Leadership, 43* (8), 49–53.

Owens, R. E., Jr. (1992). *Language development.* New York: Macmillan Publishing.

Ovando, C. J., Combs, M. C., & Collier, V. P. (2006). *Bilingual & ESL classrooms: Teaching in multicultural contexts,* fourth edition. New York: McGraw Hill.

Peregoy, S. F., & Boyle, O. F. (2000). *Reading, writing, and learning in ESL: A resource book for K–12 teachers* (3rd ed.). New York: Longman.

Roberts, P. (1985). Speech communities. In V. Clark, P. Eschholz, & A. Rosa (Eds.), *Language, introductory readings* (4th ed.). New York, St. Martin's Press.

Selinker, L. (1991). Along the way: Interlanguage systems in second language acquisition. In L. Malavé & G. Duquette (Eds.), *Language, culture, and cognition.* Clevedon, England: Multilingual Lingual Matters.

Smith, D. D. (2001). *Introduction to special education* (4th ed.). Needham Heights, MA: Allyn and Bacon.

Swank, L. (1997). Speech and language impairment. In P. Wehman (Ed.), *Exceptional individuals in school, community, and work.* Austin, TX: PRO-ED.

Tabors, P. (1997). *One child, two languages: A guide for preschool educators of children learning English as a second language.* Baltimore, MD: Paul H. Brookes.

Thomas, T. N., & Damino, J. (1985). *Specificity of encoding in bilingual memory.* Unpublished manuscript, master's thesis for Hofstra University.

Vygotsky, L. (1978). *Mind in society.* Cambridge, MA: Harvard University Press.

Woffard, J. (1979). Ebonics: A legitimate system of oral communication. *Journal of Black Studies,* 9(4), 367–382.

Wolfram, W., & Christian, D. (1989). *Dialects and education: issues and answers.* Upper Saddle River, NJ: Prentice-Hall.

Wolfram, W., Adger, C., & Christian, D. (1999). *Dialects in schools and communities.* Mahwah, NJ: Lawrence Erlbaum Associates.

Wong-Fillmore, L. (1991). When learning a second language means losing the first. *Early Childhood Research Quarterly, 6*(3), 323–347.

Wong-Fillmore, L. (1999). Reading and academic English learning. Paper presented at the 1999 Regional Conference on Improving America's Schools, Chicago, IL.

Children with Special Needs

11

Typically developing young children benefit from shared experiences in early childhood settings, even though they may be at different stages of development. Other young children develop atypically, however, and need special accommodations in regular early childhood settings or specialized programs for their needs to be met. These children with special needs include those who have intellectual giftedness, superior talents, cognitive disabilities, behavior disorders, sensory impairments, or physical disabilities. Think back on your early years in school or child care. Did you have children with special needs in your classes or care settings? Were they enrolled in any other programs during the day? Did you have opportunities to interact with them? How did you feel about having them in your class? Were any of your friends children with special needs?

We generally refer to any children who are not developing typically in some way (e.g., language or social development) as children with special needs. The term *exceptionalities* is often used to denote those with special needs. The terms *disability* and *impairment* are synonymous and refer to any condition that limits the child's ability to perform certain tasks (e.g., speak, read). It is important to know that the term *handicap* is not used interchangeably with the other two terms. Handicapped refers to problems people with disabilities encounter when they interact within their environments, and individuals can be handicapped in one circumstance but not another. For example, a young child in a wheelchair might be handicapped on the basketball court but not in the classroom. Sometimes the negative attitudes of others limit what a young child with a disability can do, resulting in a handicapping condition.

Gifted young children are those who have exceptional intellectual or creative potential that is more advanced than that of their typically developing peers. A gifted young child might also demonstrate an exceptional talent (e.g., singing, drawing, kicking a football).

Young children can have more than one unusual condition. For example, a deaf child can be gifted. A child can have a physical disability and a learning disability.

After reading this chapter, you will understand:

▶ Causes of exceptionalities.

▶ Types of exceptionalities.

▶ How special needs are diagnosed.

▶ Inclusion.

▶ The role of early childhood educators in regular settings regarding children with special needs.

▶ Instructional strategies for inclusive learning environments.

▶ Antibias environments with regard to children with special needs.

▌} Causes of Exceptionalities

Although scholars argue about the amount of influence nature and environment each have on development, they generally agree that development of individuals is the result of the interaction between nature and the environment. Although many exceptionalities in young children may have a genetic source, it is the interplay between nature and nurture that impedes or advances development.

Gifted children have high IQs, and if their needs are not met, their abilities may diminish (Smutny, 2000). Environmental factors cannot be ignored when identifying the source of giftedness. Environments that include rich, interesting, and diverse experiences are optimal for nurturing giftedness. The development of intellect and talents of young gifted children born into poverty may be at risk if they do not have opportunities for stimulating experiences. On the other hand, young gifted children living in poverty may be faced with daily opportunities to solve problems and to create needed life alternatives (sometimes called streetwiseness or street smarts). If you think about Gardner's theory of multiple intelligences (Chapter 4), young children who are becoming streetwise may have many experiences that support their intellectual development (Gardner, 1991).

Evidence of disabilities can surface at any time during development. Congenital disabilities are present at birth and may or may not be genetic. For example, deafness may be the result of an infection the mother had during pregnancy or it may be genetic. Accidents may also result in a disability.

Causes of disabilities that are not a result of accidents can be classified into three major categories: *genetic, prenatal conditions*, and *birth/postbirth complications*. Following is an overview of causes of disabling conditions.

Genetic

Chromosomes determine individual characteristics including skin color, body size and structure, gender, and facial features. They also determine genetic abnormalities, which account for a small percentage of birth defects. Genetic disorders may be caused by deviations in the chromosomal structure or by abnormal single genes.

▶ Deviations in chromosomal structure are accidents and have no impact on future pregnancies.

▶ Single gene defects are hereditary. They include fragile X syndrome, metabolic disorders, sickle-cell anemia, and cystic fibrosis.

Prenatal Conditions

Disease. The presence of diseases during pregnancy is the cause of about 25% of atypical development in children. Diseases such as rubella, cytomegalovirus, diabetes, and herpes simplex can lead to severe mental and physical disabilities. Modern medical advances have reduced some of these factors. For example, rubella immunizations and careful monitoring of maternal diabetes have significantly reduced these causes of congenital disabilities.

Substance Use and Abuse. There is risk to the fetus if mothers use chemical substances during pregnancy. In fact, expectant mothers should not take any drug, including over-the-counter drugs, unless advised to do so by a physician. Alcohol consumption during pregnancy can result in *fetal alcohol syndrome* (FAS), which has several disabling conditions. Similarly, recreational use of drugs, even occasionally, can result in various disabling conditions for the fetus.

Birth and Postbirth Complications

Complications during birth and infections can lead to disabilities. For example, difficult labor or birth trauma can result in *anoxia*, or lack of oxygen to the brain, which may cause cerebral palsy or other neurological disabilities. Premature infants are at higher risk of breathing problems, heart failure, and infections. Infections such as meningitis and encephalitis attack the brain and lead to disabilities.

Environmental factors may also result in disabilities. For example, lead poisoning and poor nutrition place infants and young children at risk of developing a disability. Young children living in poverty are at greater risk of disabilities than their more affluent peers. The *Advocating for the Child* feature highlights this issue.

❳ Exceptionalities and the Role of Early Childhood Educators

Children with special needs have various exceptionalities that are identified through formal assessment, and assessment may reveal more than one exceptionality. This section provides a brief description of several exceptional conditions, general comments regarding identification of exceptionalities, and the role of early childhood educators who work with exceptional children in regular settings. Following assessment and diagnosis, children are labeled with an exceptionality so that appropriate interventions and services can be provided.

Advocating for the Child

The Health and Well-Being of Children of Poverty

Poverty continues to threaten the health and welfare of millions of young children in the United States. If the pattern continues, one out of three children born in the year 2000 will spend at least a year living in poverty before reaching his/her 18th birthday (Children's Defense Fund, 2001).

Although many children living in poverty develop typically, often atypical development can be related to the impoverished conditions into which infants are born and in which young children live. Poor families experience higher rates of infant death, failure to thrive, cognitive disabilities, learning disabilities, and behavioral disorders. Following are some considerations:

- Children living in poverty are more likely to receive poor nutrition, which impedes healthy development.
- Children living in poverty are more likely to have minimal or no health care.
- Homelessness creates negative life stressors.
- All but the most affluent families face a shortage of high-quality, affordable child care.

Following are some considerations for overcoming the effects of poverty on the healthy development of infants, toddlers, and young children:

- Researchers have found that families who receive nutrition and health services, quality child care, and parent education raise children who score higher on intellectual and developmental assessments than their peers who do not receive the services. Furthermore, the gains hold into later childhood (Campbell & Ramey, 1994).
- The federal WIC program (Chapter 5) provides nutritious food for pregnant and breast-feeding mothers and for their children until the age of 5.
- For infants and toddlers (Campbell & Ramey, 1994) as well as school-age children (Heflin & Rudy, 1991), appropriate care and education where the curriculum is tailored to children's individual needs is the most promising intervention to combat the negative effects of homelessness.

Lawrence Migdale/Photo Researchers.

Assessment of Exceptionalities

Children's exceptionalities are identified via multiple measures including observations and tests. Table 9.1 in Chapter 9 is an overview of several standardized assessments for young children that provide different types of information. Tests and diagnoses are done by qualified professionals (e.g., a psychologist, speech–language pathologist, medical professional, educational diagnostician) who work with a team that includes educators and parents.

IFSPs and IEPs. Outlined in the IDEA legislation, *individualized family service plans* (IFSPs) are required for infants and toddlers and their families, and *individualized education programs* (IEP) are required for preschoolers and school-age children. These plans, based on nondiscriminatory, multifaceted assessment of the child's needs, are designed to increase accountability and parental involvement.

The purpose of the IFSP is to identify and organize resources for children and their families that support the individual child's needs. In the process, the family is contacted and their needs and concerns are assessed. Then, the IFSP document is developed and an ongoing service coordinator is identified. The IFSP outlines the following:

▶ The family's strengths, preferences, and concerns.

▶ The child's levels of development.

▶ Goals and strategies for addressing them.

The purpose of the IEP is to outline learning goals and procedures for individual children. It is developed by a team of appropriate professionals along with the child's parents and teacher. The IEP consists of the following:

▶ The child's present levels of functioning.

▶ Long-term goals.

▶ Short-term objectives that address the long-term goals.

▶ Related services.

▶ Evaluation strategies.

Lauren Shear/Photo Researchers.

Labeling

In order to spend government monies and resources on special education services, children must be diagnosed and labeled with a particular disability (or disabilities). There is great debate in the educational community about the pros and cons of labeling from emotional, political, and ethical perspectives. (See the *Advocating for the Child*.) Whether one supports labeling or not, it is critically important to be certain that the best interests of the child are always the primary consideration. For example, if, on the basis of all accumulated evidence, a child is inappropriately denied full inclusion in a regular early childhood setting, the early childhood educator must advocate for what the evidence suggests is the least restrictive environment.

Attention Deficit Hyperactivity Disorder

Attention-deficit disorder (ADD) or attention-deficit hyperactivity disorder (ADHD) may affect as many as 12% of school-age children (Gordon, 2004). Children with ADD are unable to maintain a normal level of attention and are extremely impulsive. They may be forgetful, easily distracted, disorganized, have difficulty following instructions, and are disinterested in many school tasks (Gordon, 2004). Children with ADHD have high levels of activity and may do things like squirm in their seats, run and climb inappropriately, and avoid quiet activities (Gordon, 2004).

Elizabeth Crews.

Advocating for the Child

Following are some of the arguments for and against labeling children with special needs.

Pros

- Labels assist professionals to communicate with one another as they address an individual's learning needs.

- Many resources are tied to specific categories of exceptionality.

- Labels assist advocates in their efforts to develop programs, promote legislation, and gain support from the public and policy makers.

Cons

- Labels may stigmatize and negatively affect self-esteem.

- Labels may cause educators and parents to focus on what children cannot do rather than on what they can do.

- There is a tendency to stereotype children in a certain category and overlook individuality.

- There may be a tendency to explain inadequate progress as a result of the disability rather than characteristics of the learning environment.

As early childhood educators, we must be cautious not to automatically assume a diagnosis of ADD or ADHD because a child demonstrates difficulty attending or controlling behavior. The diagnosis for ADD and ADHD is a multidisciplinary, team effort. Young children are diagnosed based on criteria found in the *Diagnostic and Statistical Manual of Mental Disorders* (American Psychiatric Association, 1994). The diagnostic team includes a physician who must determine whether the young child consistently demonstrates at least six symptoms based on the criteria for the condition.

The Role of Early Childhood Educators

Children with ADD and ADHD are often off task and disruptive. Their inability to attend can cause them to become frustrated and fall behind in academic progress. This frustration may manifest in aggressive and impulsive behavior.

Communication with parents to achieve consistency between home and the early childhood setting is very important for children with ADD and ADHD. Some additional important considerations are as follows:

- ▶ Allow a somewhat higher level of activity than normally preferred.
- ▶ Immediately and consistently apply consequences for aggressive behavior. Physical proximity and gentle touch often assist a child to maintain control.
- ▶ Provide engaging activities that are interesting to the child.
- ▶ Be clear about expectations.
- ▶ Give clear and concise directions.
- ▶ Be prepared to assist children and head off impulsive behavior during less structured periods of the day (e.g., play, transition times).
- ▶ As discussed in Chapter 8, implement time away rather than time-out.
- ▶ Self-assess frequently to be certain you are meeting the child's needs. Is the curriculum individually appropriate? Is there enough opportunity for movement? Are activities changed frequently enough?

Autism

The rate of autism diagnosed in young children has increased over the past few decades. Although new environmental toxins and other possible causes for the increase cannot be ruled out, it is probably due to improved diagnostic information and methods, and the availability of more programs to meet the needs of autistic children (Sheehan, 2004).

Doctors must rely on behavioral indicators of autism (Sheehan, 2004), which usually appear in young children in the first 2 1/2 years of life. Autistic characteristics include disturbances in (1) rate of development, (2) responses to sensory stimuli, (3) speech/language and cognitive abilities, and (4) the ability to relate to people, events, and objects. Researchers (Mauk, Reber, & Batshaw, 1997) suspect that it has an organic cause.

The primary characteristic of autism is the inability to relate socially and emotionally to others. By age 3 or earlier, autistic children may demonstrate the following characteristics:

- ▶ Lack of interest in affection.
- ▶ Lack of speech except for simple sounds or echolalic speech (repeating what was said rather than responding to what was said).
- ▶ Engagement in self-stimulating behavior (e.g., rocking, flapping hands).
- ▶ Limited self-help skills.

The Role of Early Childhood Educators

Autistic children function best in a predictable environment. Parents are your best resource for understanding their autistic child and how to create a predictable environment for him/her. Frequent and regular communication with the parents will help you understand their child's likes, dislikes, fears, and responses to environmental stimuli. They can help you create a predictable routine, which is very important. With this information, you can structure an optimal environment.

Children with autism will startle easily and may struggle with changes in activity, so it is a good idea to give them warnings about what is about to happen. For example, before touching the child, you might say, "I have your coat here and I'm going to help you put it on now." Before changing the activity say, "We are going to put the toys away and have snack in a few minutes."

It is important to teach young autistic children social and functional communication skills like taking turns, responding to others, and communicating needs. You may find the easiest way to do this is by using gestures and pictures. For example, a touch to your face might be used to communicate that you want the child to look at you and listen. Rubbing your tummy will communicate, "Are you hungry for snack?"

Behavior Disorders

Young children are considered to have behavior disorders if they demonstrate extremely unacceptable behavior on a continuous basis. These children may be a danger to themselves and to other children. It is sometimes challenging for teachers and caregivers to recognize behavior disorders, particularly in toddlers, because of expected behaviors for children of that age. That is, young children in general lack the moral or social development to recognize appropriate behavior and the language development to address their problems in appropriate ways. Thus, they may cry, scream, strike out, and so on. Behavior disordered children are those for whom such behavior is chronic and extreme.

The Role of Early Childhood Educators

Behavior disorders have many and varied causes. As discussed earlier, the younger the child, the more difficult it is to identify behavior disorders. However, extreme and continuous acting out must be addressed. Because behavior disorders are very individual in nature, the approach to addressing the needs of a behavior disordered child is determined on an individual basis. Consultation with the child's parents is critical to fully understand the behavior and to ensure some consistency between home and the early childhood setting.

Regardless of the individual nature of behavior disorders, there are four general guidelines for early childhood educators:

- ▶ Carefully observe and note the antecedent to problematic behavior and then alter the environment to diminish or eliminate the antecedent.
- ▶ Consistently apply consequences to inappropriate behavior.
- ▶ Teach appropriate alternative behaviors (Richey & Wheeler, 2000).
- ▶ Reinforce appropriate behavior.

Developmental Delays

Developmental disabilities are observed when young children perform like a typically developing child of a much younger age. Such disabilities or delays are sometimes characteristic of children born prematurely or to mothers who abused substances during pregnancy. You must be cautious not to confuse developmental disabilities and delays with cultural differences. For example, many children live in families where respect for elders or strangers is shown by remaining silent. It would be easy to quickly label a child from a family that holds this value as language delayed. You will want to get to know the family and their values before assuming that the child has a language delay.

Ellen Senisi/The Image Works.

The Role of Early Childhood Educators

The needs of children with developmental delays can often be met in early childhood settings if educators employ developmentally appropriate practice (DAP) (Chapter 4). In general, DAP for children ages 3–8 calls for practices that include a caring community of learners, active learning experiences, social interaction, rich language experiences, gross and fine motor activities, and experiences with the fine arts. However, DAP alone is not enough; appropriate accommodations for children with special needs must be made.

For example, we know that DAP calls for only a few brief periods of explicit instruction in early childhood classrooms. In the case of children with developmental delays, more frequent, yet still brief, periods of explicit instruction designed to address the goals of an IEP and to accelerate development might be appropriate. These decisions are made based on the needs of individual children.

Upon entrance to an early childhood setting, some children appear to have an undiagnosed developmental delay. In such a case, the responsibility of the early childhood educator who suspects a developmental delay is to first collect observational data and consult with parents. The data will inform subsequent assessment if the child is referred.

Down Syndrome

Down syndrome is a genetic disability most frequently found in babies born to teen mothers or those over 45. Young children with Down syndrome are recognized by their physical appearance, including:

- ▶ Round head.
- ▶ Flattened head in the back and mid-face.
- ▶ Folds at the corner of the eyes.
- ▶ Small ears.
- ▶ Short fingers.
- ▶ Simian crease on the palms of one or both hands.

Down syndrome children typically have cognitive delays to various degrees. They also may have compromised health, including life-threatening congenital heart defects and intestinal abnormalities. They are unusually susceptible to ear infections, which may lead to hearing disabilities.

The Role of Early Childhood Educators

We noted earlier that children with Down syndrome frequently have compromised health issues which must be addressed. It is hoped that general health can be stabilized in the first months or years of life; then, developmental issues can be addressed.

Full inclusion into regular early childhood settings may not be appropriate for all young children with Down syndrome. This is particularly true in kindergarten and the primary grades where more formal instruction takes place. For many, however, motor, communication, and cognitive development is enhanced when they have some learning experiences with typically developing children (Hanson & Lynch, 1995). Many children with Down syndrome will benefit from participating in classroom routines like passing out napkins for snacks, getting in line for a drink of water, or playing outdoors.

Gifted

Young gifted children are precocious and demonstrate a rapid rate of development in one or more realms. Giftedness is more than going through the developmental milestones faster and earlier. Young gifted children think about the world very differently than their peers.

As with any group, there is great diversity among gifted children. Young gifted children are characterized by one or several traits, including: (1) advanced verbal skills, (2) the ability to concentrate and learn rapidly, (3) curiosity, (4) the ability to problem solve, and/or (5) superior artistic, musical, or athletic talents (Smutny, 2000). They often demonstrate intense curiosity and high energy, either of which might also get them into trouble (Smutny, 2000).

Assessment. As with all young children, young gifted children's development is variable. They can often do something today that they could not do yesterday. Thus, testing may be reliable at one time and not another (Smutny, 2000). Furthermore, the cultural bias of tests must be considered. As with other young children, scholars recommend assessment consisting of multiple measures over time to identify young gifted children. Along with appropriate standardized instruments, other assessment measures are listed below. Notice that they are not any different than those used with typically developing children.

▶ *Observation.* Some common characteristics that can be observed in young gifted children ages 4–6 include (1) curiosity and thoughtful questions, (2) advanced vocabulary, (3) use of previously learned things in new context, (4) good memory, (5) unique problem solving ability, and (6) a rapid rate of learning (Smutny, 2000).

▶ *Consult with Parents.* Parents spend far more time with their children than teachers and caregivers and have many insights into their children's strengths and interests. They are often good predictors of their children's abilities and needs (Smutny, 2000).

▶ *Compile a Portfolio.* As discussed in Chapter 9, portfolios document what children can do and their growth over time. With young gifted children, portfolios can document problem solving abilities, linguistic abilities, etc. (Smutny, 2000).

Role of Early Childhood Educators

In child care and preschool settings, young gifted children learn alongside their typically developing peers; public schools often choose this alternative as well. Following are some characteristics of a child-friendly learning environment that will help you meet the needs of gifted young children as well as the needs of their typically developing peers (Smutny, 2000):

▶ Provide an area with hands-on materials, books, etc., to invite inquiry.
▶ Encourage self-initiated projects.
▶ Integrate the curriculum to connect the disciplines.
▶ Provide a wide range of materials and activities.
▶ Have interesting, stimulating lesson-related activities for those who finish an activity or lesson early.

▶ Offer relevant and meaningful learning opportunities that stem from children's interests.

▶ Provide flexible seating. (pp. 3–4)

As part of the assessment team, early childhood educators bring much valuable information to the table as diagnoses are being discussed. Observations of children as they interact with materials and peers in the early childhood setting provide valuable information about children's strengths, challenges, and interests. Information can also be gleaned from observing children during play that includes structured and unstructured components and interaction among children and with parents.

Language and Hearing Disabilities

Language Disabilities. A child with a language disability does not communicate in ways that are easily understandable to others. (Recall from Chapter 5 the discussion of receptive and expressive language.) Some children have receptive language disabilities and are unable to learn some words or follow a sequence of directions. A child with an expressive language disability may have an expressive vocabulary of far fewer words than other same-age children or may have difficulty with the order of sounds in words (e.g., pasghetti for spaghetti). Children speaking in nonmainstream dialects or who are English language learners must not be confused with children who have expressive language delays. The *Focus on Diversity* elaborates on this issue.

Hearing Disabilities. Hearing loss is identified on a continuum from mild to profound and usually interferes with speech and language development. Young children with mild hearing losses need some accommodation to hear and respond to speech, whereas those with profound hearing loss or deafness cannot use hearing to understand speech. Children with profound hearing loss learn to communicate using sign language (Chapter 10).

The Role of Early Childhood Educators

Interactive communication between children and their parents, educators, and other professionals with whom they work is critical to the language development of children with language and hearing disabilities. Adults must engage in interactive

Focus on Diversity

Appropriate Instruction for Children Who Are English Language Learners

Research suggests English language learners (ELL) are overrepresented in special education placements (Artiles, Rueda, Salazar, & Higareda, 2002) and underrepresented in gifted programs (Losen & Orfield, 2002). This phenomenon emerges late in elementary school; however, it may be impacted by poor quality instruction in the early years (and thereafter). Research further suggests that ELL children with strong support in their primary language in school are less likely to receive special education placements (Artiles et al., 2002). It is important for regular educators to understand this issue because they are the ones that make the special education referral.

Multilevel analyses that illuminate cultural, contextual, historical, and political forces (Artiles et al., 2002) are important to inform appropriate instruction for young ELL children. Early childhood educators must be cautious that young children are not misidentified with a learning disability, and thus placed in special education classes where their instructional needs will not be optimally met. Comprehensive assessment is needed to appropriately provide services for ELL children. In the case of ELL, the observation and parent components of assessment are more informative elements than standardized test scores that reflect cultural bias.

Appropriate assessment of young children occurs in natural settings (e.g., home, school setting) and during play. In these contexts, early childhood educators gather information about the child's general development. Observations in the home and interviews with parents provide information about the language and social context in which the child lives. When assessing the child based on norms, comparisons between the child being assessed and others from his/her culture will provide the most accurate assessment.

communication when they are with young children who have language and hearing disabilities. Strategies include these:

▶ Respond immediately to all communication attempts of the young child.

▶ Modify the interaction when the child becomes overstimulated or distracted.

▶ Comment on what the infant or young child is attending to (e.g., "Yes, those are your feet and I'm putting the red socks on them").

▶ Repeat words (e.g., child says, "Doggie," you say, "That's the doggie").

▶ Interpret the child's utterance and verbalize it (e.g., for "da," you respond, "Yes, that's a doll.")

▶ Expand children's words into complete sentences (e.g., for "train," you elaborate, "The toy train runs on the track").

Elizabeth Crews/The Image Works.

Augmentative and Alternative Communication Young children with severe disabilities who are unable to learn to speak intelligibly can learn other forms of communication. Augmentative devices assist children who produce speech to some degree, whereas alternative devices are used to assist children who cannot produce intelligible speech.

Low-tech strategies are nonelectric and include use of sign languages, gestures, picture boards, etc. Examples of high-tech strategies are computerized speech synthesizers and adapted computer boards. Although children may later learn to use highly sophisticated technology, training for very young children should begin with low-tech strategies and devices that meet their communication needs. If you have children in your settings using augmentative or alternative communication, you will want to become as proficient as possible at communicating with those children.

Hearing Aids. Many children wear hearing aids to enhance their hearing. If you have a child with a hearing aid, it is important that you consult with the child's audiologist so that you understand proper care and use of hearing aids. This is particularly important when working with young children who may or may not know whether the hearing aid is working properly.

Lipreading. Many children with hearing disabilities learn to read lips. Following are some tips if you are talking with a young child who is lipreading:

▶ Do not to talk too fast.

▶ Do not move around when you are talking as it makes it more difficult for the child to follow.

▶ Observe children's responses to be certain they understand; repeat if they do not.

▶ Use pictures and gestures to help the child understand.

▶ Nurture language development as you do for all young children in your setting.

Learning Disabilities

The category of learning disabilities encompasses a very wide range of cognitive, social, and emotional disabilities. Because of the number of different learning disabilities, some scholars recommend separating them by definition so that adequate interventions can be identified.

If young children have trouble organizing thoughts and processing information, they may potentially have a learning disability. Another bit of evidence of a learning disability is the inability to think abstractly at the level of their same-age peers. For example, if a child cannot retell an event from the day before or describe something in his home, he may have a learning disability. Given the developmental nature of young children whose thinking processes are still quite immature, young children are often identified as developmentally delayed until further diagnosis at a later time can be conducted.

Dyslexia. The term dyslexia refers to a reading disability that is usually diagnosed in second or third grade. It is easily confused with a language delay in children younger than or 7 or 8. Younger children are often diagnosed with language delays so that intervention can be provided.

The Role of Early Childhood Educators

Learning disabilities are the largest category of disabilities and are usually identified in school-age children. They have many and varied causes and affect growth and development in many different ways. As with behavior disorders, the learning environment and role of the early childhood educator are determined on an individual basis. However, a few guidelines can be considered for working with children with learning disabilities:

- ▶ Use some explicit instruction to help children learn new information.
- ▶ Instruction should be multisensory including visual, auditory, and tactile experiences.
- ▶ Provide adequate opportunities to practice new learning.
- ▶ Provide consistent, specific, and encouraging feedback.
- ▶ Place children's interests at the core of learning experiences.

⟩ Physical Disabilities

Some children have physical disabilities as a result of accidents, whereas others have congenital or genetic physical disabilities. Cerebral palsy is a nonprogressive neuromuscular dysfunction in the central nervous system, and it is the most common physical disability in young children. Another physical disability is hypotonicity, a condition where children lack muscle tone. Infants with this condition have difficulty with head control and, later, with posture. Spina bifida is the result of imperfect development of the spinal cord, and muscular dystrophy is a genetic disability.

Whatever the source of the physical disability, early childhood educators must be cautious about making assumptions about children with physical disabilities. Having a physical disability does not mean a child also has a cognitive disability. For example, a child with severely involved cerebral palsy will have difficulty producing speech, which gives the appearance of a cognitive disability. However, that child probably has an adequate to advanced receptive language vocabulary. The speech production difficulty is the result of the motor impairment.

The Role of Early Childhood Educators

Young children with physical disabilities are often fully included in regular early childhood settings, particularly if they do not have cognitive, sensory, or behavior disabilities. With accommodations for their physical disabilities, they will benefit from many of the same activities as typically functioning children.

The general physical environment must be adapted to accommodate mobility devices. For example, ramps are needed for wheelchair access to learning areas. Adequate space for maneuvering wheelchairs and walkers within the early childhood setting, bathroom, etc., must be available. Railings provide support for children with poor balance. Crutches must have nonskid tips on them.

Creative teachers and caregivers can devise accommodations for children with fine motor disabilities. Simple practices like taping the paper to the table during painting will keep it from slipping around. Gripper devices can be attached to drawing, writing, and eating tools to help children engage in those tasks (e.g., one easy way is to push the marker or utensil through a sponge ball). Velcro closures can replace snaps or buttons. As children mature, there are various types of assistive technologies that enhance mobility and communication and foster independence.

Visual Disabilities

There are both legal and educational definitions of visual disabilities, the only disability addressed by IDEA (Chapter 3) that has two definitions. A young child (or any person) whose visual acuity is 20/200 or less in the best eye with the best possible correction is considered legally blind by the federal government (Social Security Administration, 2000). Also considered legally blind are young children with a severely restricted field of vision, which means they see the world as if they were looking through a tube (Social Security Administration, 2000). The educational definition of blindness extends to any child whose ability to see print or participate in other visual tasks is impaired.

The Role of Early Childhood Educators

As with all disabilities, early childhood educators must communicate regularly with special education professionals who understand how to work with children with visual disabilities. Professionals who are trained to work with children with visual disabilities can help secure available government services and materials, such as books on tape. To optimize the learning experiences of children with visual disabilities, it is important to use other senses to communicate. For example, let the child know you are listening when she speaks by gently touching her arm. Before getting a drink, let her touch her finger to the water stream. Let her feel all parts of an object as well as the whole object.

Early Childhood Environments for Children with Disabilities

Historically, little attention was given to educational needs of children with disabilities. By the late 1960s, however, the federal government was strongly supporting education for children with disabilities, and this included early childhood special education. Recall from Chapter 3 the series of federal legislative actions that addressed the needs of persons with disabilities. Subsequent legislation continued to provide support for children birth to age 8.

Inclusion

Since the PL 94-142 legislation, the federal government has provided funds for states to provide the least restrictive environment for the education of children with disabilities. Determination of the least restrictive environment is made on an individual basis and is designed to provide optimal support for the growth and development of individual children with special needs. For example, the optimal learning environment for a child with a language delay might be full inclusion in a regular early childhood setting where the teacher works in consult with a speech–language pathologist. However, placement in a regular setting may not provide the optimal learning experience for a child with severe or multiple disabilities. That child might optimally benefit from a full-time special placement. Figure 11.1 outlines the continuum from full inclusion to full special placement, and Figure 11.2 is a sample implementation plan for including children with special needs in regular early childhood settings.

The first responsibility for teachers in regular education settings is to learn as much as possible about the particular disabilities of children in their settings.

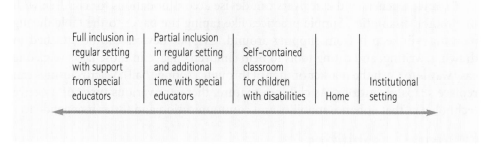

Figure 11.1. **Continuum from full inclusion to full special placement.**

Books, journals, and specialists are good sources of general information. However, because disabilities do not affect all children in exactly the same way, the parents and special educators working with a particular child also provide important information. Regular communication with the child's parents and with educators who specialize in working with particular disabilities (e.g., visual, physical) is critical to working effectively with children with disabilities.

Infants and Toddlers

Infants and toddlers with disabilities are placed in normalized, natural environments, ideally with one primary caregiver. Interacting with their typically developing peers supports the growth and development of infants and toddlers with disabilities. Although accommodations are made to meet their needs, inclusion in an environment with typically developing peers may help educators and parents to establish high, yet reasonable, expectations for them, and to see inclusion as reasonable.

Preschool and Kindergarten

Services for preschoolers and kindergarteners are financially supported with federal funds and fall under the jurisdiction of the state and local school districts. The early years are optimal for inclusion of children with disabilities in regular settings because of the following:

▶ The early years are a time of rapid and varied growth and development, and early childhood educators are accustomed to a wide range of developmental levels among young children in their settings.

▶ Early childhood educators focus more on process than product and offer many opportunities for active engagement and interaction among children with and without disabilities.

▶ Young children have not yet learned to stereotype persons with disabilities.

▶ Early inclusion creates the expectation for parents and educators that inclusion is the norm. It assists children to function positively in typical settings later (Brown, 2001).

It is important to understand that, whether in preschool or formal school settings, merely including children with disabilities is not enough to optimize learning. In addition to continuous consultation with special educators and other professionals, the learning environment for children age 3–5 must include these:

▶ A caring community of learners.

▶ Active learning and developmentally appropriate learning experiences.

▶ Opportunities for interaction among peers and for social development.

▶ Use of functional language to support literacy development.

▶ Ample gross and fine motor activities.

▶ Experiences with art and music.

Child's Name:					
Learning Goal:					
Timeline:					

Learning Activity	Intended Learning Outcome	Regular Educator's Responsibility	Special Educator's Responsibility	Parent's Responsibility	Assessment

Figure 11.2. Inclusion implementation plan.

▶ Collaboration with parents.

▶ Ongoing formative, contextual assessment of progress.

▶ The integrated curriculum.

Primary Grades

Classrooms for primary grade children with disabilities should also have the features mentioned for preschool and kindergarten children. Primary grade children with disabilities also benefit from cooperative learning and peer tutoring experiences.

Cooperative Learning. Recall from Chapters 7 and 8 the discussions on cooperative learning. Although decisions must be made based on needs of individual children, cooperative learning is one successful strategy for including children with disabilities in regular settings. Many of the studies on cooperative learning focus on children with mild disabilities in formal school settings. Research (Fuchs, Fuchs, & Yazdian, 2002; Johnson & Johnson, 1981, 1989; Piercy, Wilton, & Townsend, 2002; Slavin, 1990) suggests that cooperative learning increases academic achievement of children with disabilities (and others) and social acceptance of children with disabilities from their peers without disabilities.

As discussed in Chapter 7, children can contribute to a project or the creation of a product at their individual levels of ability. For example, some children might be researchers and report writers while others are artists or designers.

Peer Tutoring. Children can serve as resources for one another through peer tutoring or peer teaching (Sapon-Shevin, 1996). Peer tutoring can be arranged within or across classrooms. There are benefits for the tutored children, who get one-on-one instruction, and there are benefits for the tutors, who learn as they prepare for instruction. Teachers report that tutors take this work seriously, prepare for it, and demonstrate renewed enthusiasm for the subject (Sapon-Shevin, 1996). Depending on what is being taught and individual strengths, children with and without disabilities can take either role. For example, a child with a hearing disability might be able to teach a math concept she has mastered to another who has not mastered it.

As children work together, they develop understanding and acceptance of differences. Teachers report that teasing almost disappears and that students themselves address problems with teasing when they arise (Sapon-Shevin, 1996).

The importance of teaching social skills to children who are going to work cooperatively or engage in peer tutoring cannot be overemphasized (Sapon-Shevin, 1996). Social skills should be discussed and role played until they become second nature. Children identify appropriate and inappropriate language. For example, asking "How can I help you?" is appropriate, whereas "Oh, just let me do it!!" is inappropriate.

Early Intervention and Early Childhood Special Education

While some use the terms *early intervention* and *early childhood special education* interchangeably, they are different. Early intervention refers to coordinated services for children and their families, birth to age 2, who have developmental delays or are at-risk. Early childhood special education refers to the provision of coordinated services for children ages 3–5.

The purpose of early intervention and early childhood special education is to optimize the learning and daily well-being of infants and young children and to provide opportunities for them to function as part of a community. Effective services are tailored to meet the needs of individuals and their families. An essential component is collaboration with parents where professionals build on what parents already do well and to help them obtain appropriate services.

Activity-Based Intervention. Key to including children with disabilities in natural settings is activity-based intervention, developed from the well-known work of Bricker and Woods-Cripe (1992). Activity-based intervention, like developmentally appropriate practice, is grounded in the theories of Piaget, Vygotsky, and Dewey. In general, the interventions designed to address goals and objectives for individual children are integrated into regular routines.

Head Start. Recall from Chapter 2 that Head Start was the first significant emphasis on education and quality care for young children. Currently, federal regulations require that at least 10% of Head Start enrollment comprise children with disabilities. This inclusion of children with disabilities in early childhood settings with typically developing children has become an integral part of the Head Start program.

Also under the umbrella of Head Start is Early Head Start, which enrolls low-income pregnant women. During pregnancy and the child's infant and toddler years, the mother receives parent and nutrition education and other support services.

Abuse and Neglect

Child abuse affects children across gender, ability, ethnicity, religion, age, and class. In the year 2000, 3 million reports filed on behalf of 5 million children resulted in confirmation of 1 million children as victims of abuse and neglect (National Association for the Education of Young Children, 2003). Some of these children die, most carry emotional scars, and some are physically scarred.

Recall from Chapter 2 our discussion about Maslow's hierarchy of needs. Before children can achieve self-actualization and blossom to their potential, their basic needs must be met. These needs evolve on a continuum beginning with the physical needs of food, water, air to breathe, and the need to feel safe and secure. Children who suffer abuse and neglect have unmet needs at the most basic level.

Treatment is considered abuse or neglect in any of the following conditions (National Association for the Education of Young Children, 2003):

- ▶ Psychological abuse results when children are consistently demeaned, degraded, and devalued. It is perhaps the most difficult to objectively identify.
- ▶ Physical abuse is injury resulting from trauma.
- ▶ Sexual abuse is the result of any sexual contact with a child.
- ▶ Neglect is present when a young child is not appropriately supervised, the child's basic needs for food, clothing, and cleanliness are not adequately met, or health care is not sought when needed.

Associates for Human Services.

{ The Role of Early Childhood Educators

The role of early childhood educators goes far beyond the legal obligation to report abuse or neglect or suspected abuse or neglect. The support and assistance early childhood educators extend to families is vital to preventing child abuse and neglect. Following are guidelines set forth by the National Association for the Education of Young Children (2003) for supporting families and helping to prevent child abuse and neglect.

Provide Quality Care and Education

Teachers and caregivers in high-quality early childhood settings maintain a continuous agenda of professional development so they can understand and implement best practices. They implement practices that value young children as individuals, as developing people, and as members of families. They are family-focused and provide all children with challenging and achievable education. In high-quality early childhood settings, children are physically and psychologically safe at all times.

Develop Reciprocal Relationships with Families

Strong, reciprocal relationships with families are essential to preventing abuse and neglect. Through respectful, cooperative, collaborative, and communicative relationships, you can respond to signs of family stress by providing information or connecting families to school and community services. With a secure reciprocal relationship, difficult issues are more easily discussed. A strong reciprocal relationship develops through the following:

- ▶ Regular, ongoing communication during pick-up and drop-off times.
- ▶ Weekly notes, emails, or phone calls that recognize the contributions and strengths of the child.
- ▶ Invitations to the families to share their cultures and interests.
- ▶ Openness to helping the family.

Recognize When Children Are at Risk

Family stressors place families at risk for child abuse. Early childhood educators must understand and recognize the risk factors for stress, which include these (National Association for the Education of Young Children, 2003):

- ▶ Poverty.
- ▶ Substance abuse and other mental health issues.
- ▶ Inadequate knowledge of good parenting practices.
- ▶ Persistently acting-out children.
- ▶ Challenges of caring for a child with physical, emotional, or cognitive disabilities.

Understand and Assist Families

Early childhood educators are a great resource for families that have a child with challenging behaviors. By learning about the challenges parents face with a child with disabilities, teachers and caregivers can assist families and connect them to school and community resources. Some guidelines for assisting families are as follows:

▶ Model in your setting and talk to parents about the importance of predictable routines.

▶ Share information about what kind of behaviors to expect from their child at his/her developmental stage.

▶ Make suggestions for how to handle difficult and challenging behaviors (e.g., provide examples of language to use, of logical consequences).

▶ Invite parents to observe you as you interact with young children.

Build on Strengths

Recognize and acknowledge the strengths of the child and the family. Provide children with specific and encouraging feedback (see Chapter 8) as they engage in activities. Acknowledge the things parents are doing to support their children and praise them directly. Because you have a reciprocal relationship, parents are likely to be encouraged if you make supportive statements like, "You have been having a rough time lately; I really admire the way you are coping" (National Association for the Education of Young Children, 2003, p. 17).

Be Informed

As an early childhood educator you are obligated to report evidence or suspicion of child abuse or neglect. Reporting puts assistance for children and support for families into motion. Your school counselor or local child protective services can provide you with more detailed information about child abuse and neglect as well as policy and reporting procedures in your state. The *National Child Abuse Hotline* number is 800-422-4453.

Antibias Environments for Children with Special Needs

Very young children have not yet developed negative stereotypes of persons with disabilities. Early interactions with children and adults with disabilities fosters understanding and acceptance (Brown, 2001), and the tendency to create stereotypes of persons with disabilities is lessened.

In antibias early childhood settings, educators use language thoughtfully. For example, a child is not *disabled;* rather, she has a *disability*. When teachers and caregivers comment, "She has autism," rather than saying, "He's autistic," the message is that it is a condition she has, not what she is. Autism does not totally define the child. Similarly, it is appropriate to say, "He has a learning disability," rather than, "He is learning disabled."

Whether young children with disabilities are included in regular early childhood settings or not, the learning environments must be bias free in order to optimally support growth and development. The needs of young children with disabilities in antibias environments are met with the following:

▶ An appropriate fit between the child's needs and educational interventions as determined by multiple assessment data gathered over time.

▶ Practices that are research-based and not driven by personal or social values.

▶ Interventions that are designed collaboratively with families and embrace a multicultural perspective that respects family uniqueness.

▶ Attitudes that children with disabilities are children first and that practices in their learning environments must be developmentally appropriate. Accommodation notwithstanding, materials should be those that typically developing children use.

Teaching about Differences

In environments that are antibias, teachers and caregivers openly address and teach children about differences because not teaching about differences sends children negative messages (Sapon-Shevin, 1996). As an early childhood educator, you become knowledgeable about and accepting of ability differences. Then, you teach the young children about ability differences. An important way to teach understanding and acceptance of ability differences is through interaction among children within the learning environment, discussed earlier (e.g., cooperative learning, peer tutoring).

Community members and high-quality children's books are two resources for teaching about ability differences. Professionals from the community, a speech–language pathologist, for example, can talk about what s/he does to assist those with speech and language difficulties. Furthermore, persons with disabilities can be classroom guests who talk about their work, culture, and interests. Children's books that explain differences and depict persons with disabilities as functional and productive are another resource. Table 11.1 exemplifies some books appropriate for young children that can be used to teach about ability differences. (Recall from Chapter 7, it is critical that books are examined for stereotyping and bias before they are read to children.)

Table 11.1   Books to Engender Understanding and Acceptance of Children with Disabilities

Title	Description	Theme
Talking About Disability by J. Powell	With photographs and simple text, this book explains many different disabilities and depicts persons with disabilities as functional, productive humans.	Various disabilities
We'll Paint the Octopus Red by S. Stuve-Bodeen	Trish looks forward to things she'll do with her new sibling. Her brother is born with Down syndrome and she learns that they can still do things together.	Down syndrome
Thank You Mr. Falker by P. Polacco	Patricia is excited to learn to read but has great difficulty. She has a teacher, Mr. Falker, who understands her challenges and teaches her to read.	Learning disability
A Button in Her Ear by A. B. Litchfield	Angela has difficulty hearing and learns that she needs to wear a hearing aid.	Hearing disability
He's My Brother by J. Lasker	Jamie struggles in school and with making friends. But he loves animals, babies, and beating out rhythms on his drums.	The invisible handicap
Be Good to Eddie Lee by V. Fleming	Eddie Lee is excluded and teased. In the end, he teaches others about acceptance.	Down syndrome

The Early Childhood Environment. The environment should be replete with images of persons with disabilities depicted as contributing, happy members of society. To avoid drawing attention to differences in achievements and skills, star charts and other displays that indicate who has mastered skills, demonstrated the best behavior, etc., should not be used (Sapon-Shevin, 1996). They are demeaning to children who do not function at the same level as others and may engender elitist attitudes for those who do excel.

The Curriculum. Teachers and caregivers must not shy away from differentiating the curriculum or making accommodations for children with disabilities. Being open and honest about the accommodations will assist other children to understand and accept ability differences. For example, "Noah works in a different book because he is learning addition; he's not ready for multiplication yet" is an honest, forthright response to a question (Sapon-Shevin, 1996).

My Developing Professional View

What is your developing view of how to structure an inclusive early childhood learning environment?

SUMMARY

In this chapter, we have examined the types and causes of various exceptionalities. Although there are some commonalities among children with a particular exceptionality, each child has unique needs as well. As with any assessment of young children, multiple assessment measures with data gathered over time is the only way to accurately diagnose an exceptionality. On the basis of the assessment, young children with disabilities are labeled so they can obtain services to support their growth and development.

Gifted children and many children with disabilities are included in regular classrooms on a part- or full-time basis. Young children have not yet formed stereotypes of those who are different. Thus, it is an optimal time for including children with disabilities in classrooms with children who are developing typically. Although many aspects of the learning environment are the same for typically and atypically functioning children, accommodations will need to be made for children with disabilities. Thus, it is vital that early childhood educators understand the nature of various exceptionalities as well as the nature of individual children in order to provide optimal support for growth and development. They must work closely with special educators, parents, and agencies working with the family.

Any early childhood setting must be antibias. Early childhood educators must first check their own biases toward children (or others) with disabilities. Then, it is important to teach young children to understand and accept difference. This happens first through positive interactions with persons with disabilities. Children's books and professionals in the community are also teaching resources.

ENRICHMENT ACTIVITIES

Individual Activities

1. Observe a child with a disability in an early childhood setting. Take field notes during your observation (procedure described in Chapter 9). Following your observation, describe the child, being certain to note the child's strengths and contributions as well as challenges. Also, pay attention to how typically developing children interact with him/her. Think about your role as an early childhood educator working with that child.

2. Interview an early childhood educator who has children with disabilities in his/her setting. Determine his/her perspective on (1) the positive aspects of

inclusion, (2) the challenges, and (3) specific accommodations s/he makes for children with disabilities. Write an overview of your findings.

Cooperative Activities

3. Have each member of your cooperative group select a category of disability (e.g., hearing disabilities, severe cognitive disabilities, physical disabilities). Each group member is to research and identify high-quality children's books that address disabilities in that category, being certain to evaluate the books for accuracy and evidence of acceptance. As a group, build on the books suggested in this chapter to develop an annotated bibliography appropriate for teaching young children about acceptance of persons with disabilities.

4. Have each member of your group select a specific disability to research (e.g., language delays, deafness, cerebral palsy, autism). The websites listed under *Professional Development Resources* are good resources for your research. Focus your research on the causes and characteristics of the disability as well as the uniqueness individuals with the disability might demonstrate. Also examine how early childhood educators in regular settings can support growth and development of a child with that disability. When each of you is an expert on a disability and the role of regular educators, share what you have learned within your group.

Advocacy Activity

5. Select a high-quality children's book that focuses on a disability and a preschool, kindergarten, or primary grade setting. Read the book to the children and facilitate discussion. Older children will be able to write a response to the book. Write a brief overview of the children's response to the book, noting positive and negative attitudes. Consider ways to support positive attitudes about persons with disabilities using children's books as a vehicle.

⟩ FOR FURTHER READING

Curriculum

Sandall, S. R. (2003). Play modifications for children with disabilities. *Young Children, 58*(3), 54–55.

Tournaki, N., & Criscitiello, E. (2003). Using peer tutoring as a successful part of behavior management. *Teaching Exceptional Children, 36*(2), 22–25.

Intervention

Harwood, M., & Kleinfeld, J. S. (2002). Upfront in hope: The value of early intervention for children with fetal alcohol syndrome. *Young Children, 57*(4), 86–90.

Inclusion

Bradley, J., & Kibera, P. (2006). Closing the gap: Culture and the promotion of inclusion in child care. *Young Children, 61*(1), 34–40.

Katz, L., & Schery, T. K. (2006). Including children with hearing loss in early childhood programs. *Young Children, 61*(1), 86–95.

McCormick, L., Wong, M., & Yogi, L. (2003). Individualization in the inclusive preschool: A planning process. *Childhood Education, 79*(4), 212–217.

Olson, J., Murphy, C. L., & Olson, P. D. (1999). Readying parents and teachers for the inclusion of children with disabilities: A step-by-step process. *Young Children, 54*(3), 18–22.

Villa, J., et. al. (2006). A personal story: Making inclusion work. *Young Children, 61*(1), 96–100.

Wolfe, P. S., & Hall, T. E. (2003). Making inclusion a reality for students with severe disabilities. *Teaching Exceptional Children, 35*(4), 56–61.

Professional Development Resources

AMERICAN SPEECH-LANGUAGE-HEARING ASSOCIATION (ASHA)

10801 Rockville Pike
Rockville, MD 20852
http://www.asha.org/

CIRCLE OF INCLUSION

University of Kansas
Department of Special Education
521JR Pearson
Lawrence, KS 66045
http://www.circleofinclusion.org/

FEDERATION FOR CHILDREN WITH SPECIAL NEEDS

1135 Tremont Street, Suite 420
Boston, MA 02120
http://www.fcsn.org/

INCLUSION PRESS

24 Thome Crescent
Toronto, ON M6H 2S5, Canada
http://www.inclusion.com/

NATIONAL INFORMATION CENTER ON DEAFNESS
Gallaudet University
800 Florida Avenue NE
Washington, DC 20002
http://clerccenter.gallaudet.edu/infotogo/

UNITED CEREBRAL PALSY ASSOCIATION OF NASSAU COUNTY
380 Washington Avenue
Roosevelt, NY 11575-1899
http://www.ucpn.org/

SELF-ASSESSMENT

1. Discuss possible causes of different exceptionalities.
2. Choose three exceptionalities discussed in this chapter; describe them and define your role as an early childhood educator as you work with children who have that exceptionality.
3. Explain an IEP and an IFSP.
4. Explain augmentative and alternative communication.
5. What is inclusion? What are some considerations for regular education teachers working in inclusive settings?
6. Discuss the role of early childhood educators regarding issues related to abuse and neglect.

Scenario

You are a kindergarten teacher in an inclusive classroom. David is a child in your classroom who has mild cerebral palsy. He is able to do the things other children do with the exception of fine and gross motor activities. For example, David does not have the coordination needed to be successful at playground games. Over time, you notice that David is not only excluded from playground games but from other activities as well. On one occasion, you even caught some children making fun of him. How can you address this problem?

REFERENCES

American Psychiatric Association. (1994). *Diagnostic and statistical manual of mental disorders* (4th ed.). Washington, DC: Author.

Artiles, A. J., Rueda, R., Salazar, J. J., & Higareda, I. (2002). English-language learner representation in special education in California urban school districts. In D. J. Losen & G. Orfield (Eds.), *Racial inequity in special education* (pp. 117–136). Cambridge, MA: Harvard Educational Press.

Bricker, D., & Woods-Cripe, J. J. (1992). *An activity-based approach to early intervention.* Baltimore: Paul H. Brookes.

Brown, K. (2001). The effectiveness of early childhood inclusion (parents' perspectives). Paper presented at the Special Education Seminar, Loyola College, Baltimore, MD.

Campbell, F. A., & Ramey, C. T. (1994). Effects of early intervention on intellectual and academic achievement: A follow-up study of children from low income families. *Child Development, 65,* 684–698.

Children's Defense Fund. (2001). *Yearbook 2001: The state of America's children.* Washington, DC: Author.

Fuchs, L. S., Fuchs, D., & Yazdian, L. (2002). Enhancing first-grade childrens' mathematical development with peer-assisted learning strategies. *The School Psychology Review, 31*(4), 569–583.

Gordon, D. (2004, September). The latest news on ADHD. *Parents,* 157–158, 160, 258–259.

Hanson, M. J., & Lynch, E. W. (1995). *Early intervention: Implementing child and family services for infants and toddlers who are at-risk and disabled* (2nd ed.). Austin, TX: PRO-ED.

Heflin, L., & Rudy, K. (1991). *Homeless and in need of special education.* Reston, VA: Council for Exceptional Children.

Johnson, D. W., & Johnson, R. T. (1989). *Cooperation and competition: Theory and research.* Edina, MN: Interaction Books.

Johnson, R. T., & Johnson, D. W. (1981). Building friendships between handicapped and non-handicapped students: Effects of cooperative and individualistic instruction. *American Educational Research Journal, 18*(4), 415–423.

Losen, D. J., & Orfield, G. (2002). Introduction: Racial inequity in special education. In D. J. Losen & G. Orfield (Eds.), *Racial inequity in special education* (pp. xv–xxxvii). Cambridge, MA: Harvard Educational Press.

Mauk, J. E., Reber, M., & Batshaw, M. L. (1997). Autism. In M. L. Batshaw (Ed.), *Children with disabilities* (pp. 425–448). Baltimore: Paul H. Brookes.

National Association for the Education of Young Children. (2003). *Building circles, breaking cycles—Preventing child abuse and neglect: The early childhood educator's role.* [Brochure.] Washington, DC: Author.

Piercy, M., Wilton, K., & Townsend, M. (2002). Promoting the social acceptance of young children with moderate-severe intellectual disabilities using cooperative learning techniques. *American Journal on Mental Retardation, 107*(5), 352–360.

Richey, D. D., & Wheeler, J. J. (2000). *Inclusive early childhood education.* Albany, NY: Delmar Thompson Learning.

Sapon-Shevin, M. (1996). Ability differences in the classroom: Teaching and learning in inclusive classrooms. In D. A. Byrnes & G. Kiger (Eds.), *Common bonds: Antibias teaching in a diverse society* (pp. 35–47). Wheaton, MD: Association for Childhood Education International.

Sheehan, J. (2004, July). 6 facts you need to know about autism now! *Parents,* 81–82, 84–85.

Slavin, R. E. (1990). *Cooperative learning: Theory, research and practice.* Englewood Cliffs, NJ: Prentice-Hall.

Smutny, J. F. (2000). *Teaching young gifted children in the regular classroom* (Report No. EDO-EC-00-4). Reston, VA: ERIC Clearinghouse on Disabilities and Gifted Education. (ERIC Document Reproduction Service No. ED445422.)

Social Security Administration. (2000). www.ssa.gov/disability/. Retrieved June 2004.

The Impact of Environments and Technology on Young Children

12

As we go about our daily activities, the environments in which we function influence what we do. For example, think about the environmental characteristics that are unique to a library or a shopping mall. One invites quiet study and reading while the other invites movement, conversation, and eating.

Think back to your experiences in early care and education. What do you remember about the environment? What did it look like? Do you remember small areas to accommodate activities like looking at books, building with blocks, painting, or dramatic play? Were you comfortable with the daily schedule? What was the outdoor environment like? What kind of technology was available? Do you have fond memories of some things and not so fond memories of other things?

The early childhood environment refers to everything that impacts the growth and development of individual children. Environments vary based on program goals; children's family, community, and cultural values; available resources; the sociopolitical climate; and the personal, professional, and cultural values of the early childhood educators.

Previous chapters have integrated some information on environments, particularly in relation to antibias learning environments and political environments at various times. For example, we have discussed characteristics of developmentally appropriate, culturally relevant learning environments and legislation that impacts learning and distribution of resources. Furthermore, in Chapter 8, we discussed characteristics of environments that encourage development of positive self-concept and appropriate behavior.

The focus in this chapter is on indoor and outdoor physical environments and the role of technology in early childhood settings. Teaching for social justice as part of an anti-bias environment is also addressed.

After reading this chapter, you will understand:

▶ Elements of child-centered, indoor early childhood environments for infants and toddlers, preschool and kindergarten, and primary grade children.

▶ Temporal considerations in early childhood environments.

▶ Characteristics of healthy early childhood environments.

▶ Elements of child-centered, outdoor early childhood environments for infants and toddlers, preschool and kindergarten, and primary grade children.

▶ Considerations for teaching social justice in an antibias climate.

▶ The role of technology in early childhood settings for infants and toddlers, preschool and kindergarten, and primary grades.

Indoor Environments

The indoor learning environment includes physical space, materials, procedures, activities, and people. Characteristics of the environment can work to support or impede teaching and learning, so it is critical that teachers recognize the influence the environment has on teaching and learning. High-quality early childhood environments are child-centered.

Child-Centeredness

Child-centered environments for young children are compatible with their developmental stages, cultural identities, and safety needs; they foster growth and development through positive learning experiences. As you create high-quality indoor environments for young children, you will want to consider various aspects related to *safety, health and well-being, compatibility of activities, engaging materials,* and *compatibility for children.*

Safety. Safety must be kept in mind as you organize the early childhood learning environment. In a safe early childhood environment, hazardous materials like cleaning supplies are stored in a secure place out of reach of children. Pathways are kept clear, rugs have no-skid bottoms, and rugs with frayed edges are removed to avoid tripping and falling. Teachers carefully monitor activities that involve scissors, markers, or other objects that children might use carelessly. Materials such as markers, paint, and clay are always nontoxic.

Equipment must be durable, sturdy enough to support the weight of young children, and free of sharp edges. Large equipment must be placed on a forgiving surface such as carpet with rubber padding to minimize the potential for serious injury if children fall.

Health and Well-being. Young children have immature immune systems, which makes them more easily susceptible to illness and infection. As a teacher, you must wash your hands frequently and always after helping children in the bathroom, after diapering, and before preparing food to avoid the spread of germs that can cause illness or infection. Model for and teach children to cough or sneeze into an elbow rather than a hand so they are less likely to pass around germs. Help them develop the habit of washing their hands before eating and after toileting. Sterilize eating areas and manipulative materials regularly.

Young children will also have accidents and sustain cuts and bruises. All teachers must have first aid certification so they can appropriately take care of children after an accident. All adults must understand the procedures for reporting accidents. Emergency numbers should be posted in a prominent spot for easy reference.

Outdoor play is an important part of the day in an early childhood setting. However, children must be protected from harmful exposure to the sun. Consult with parents to learn how they address this issue (e.g., long sleeves and pants, sunblock) and continue it in your setting.

Be prepared if you live in an area where you might experience a natural disaster such as a hurricane, tornado, or earthquake. Establish procedures for responding to such a disaster, and practice them with the children, and encourage parents to do the same in their homes.

Compatibility of Activities. Learning activities in early childhood environments vary. Some are messy while others are neat; some are noisy while others are quiet; some are solitary and others involve groups. It is important to consider the compatibility of activities when you arrange the room, particularly those activities that are in close proximity to each other. For example, exploring books is a quiet, often solitary activity; thus, it should not be placed next to dramatic play, woodworking, or construction where groups of children are actively engaged in noisy activities.

Rugs and furniture arrangements are one way to separate activities and provide boundaries to minimize noise. For example, bookshelves can enclose pillows, beanbag chairs, and tables at a book center to cut off noise from other centers. The block construction area might have a large rug or a few small rugs indicating where construction can take place. Painting easels and other messy activities can be confined to an area that has a washable floor.

Engaging Materials. Children learn best when they have interesting materials and opportunities to investigate, transform, and invent without interruption (Curtis & Carter, 2005). They need a mix of realistic materials and open-ended materials (Chapter 4). For example, a table, chairs, dishes, and menus will encourage restaurant play, while things such as paper towel rolls, blocks, and carpet pieces can be used as play props in a variety of ways. Flexible screens can be added to the play space for children to create small spaces for their play (Curtis & Carter; 2005).

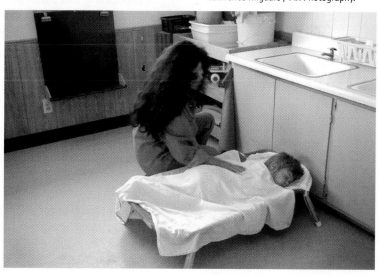

Lawrence Migdale / Pix Photography.

Compatibility for Children. The physical environment encourages all children to feel that they belong there. As discussed in previous chapters, children should be able to see themselves and their families in wall displays and books. All furniture and equipment should be scaled to the size of the children so they can easily sit at tables and get on and off of chairs.

Children need opportunities to function somewhat independently in the environment.

For example, materials are stored so that they can be easily and safely reached. Children will be more able to help with cleanup if storage areas have pictures of items indicating where they belong.

Developmentally Appropriate Activities. In a child-centered environment, the active aspects are consistent with developmentally appropriate practice (Chapter 4). This includes providing for small group activities at learning centers, particularly in pre-kindergarten and kindergarten classrooms. To provide ample choice and minimize conflict, provide one-third more work spaces at centers than there are children (Swim, 2004). That means that if you have 21 children in your class, you need to provide spots for a total of 28 children among the centers. If you have six centers, each would need to accommodate 4–5 children, depending on the activity.

Figure 12.1 is a checklist for child-centered environments for children ages 3–8.

Scheduling Considerations

In previous chapters, we discussed at length the importance of routines in the daily lives of young children. Routines help children know what to expect, and time allotted to each activity communicates its importance. Routines and time allotted to activities vary according to the age and needs of the children.

Child-Centered Early Childhood Environments Checklist

✔ Children can choose many of their activities.

✔ Activities are hands-on and foster higher-order thinking.

✔ Activities are personally relevant to the children's lives.

✔ Diverse interests and needs are accommodated.

✔ Oral and print literacy activities are integrated throughout the day.

✔ Children read and are read to daily.

✔ Activities are purposeful. (e.g., writing/dictating thank-you notes to a class guest, calculating for a purpose).

✔ Appropriate problem-solving is fostered.

✔ Technology is integrated in developmentally appropriate ways. (e.g., word processing calculators).

✔ Drama, movement, music, poetry are integrated throughout the day.

✔ Children frequently work in small groups.

✔ A variety of assessment measures are used (e.g., observation, interviews, artifacts).

✔ Parents are involved in ways that are comfortable for them.

✔ Living things are present in the environment.

Figure 12.1. Checklist for a Child-Centered Environment for Children Ages 3–8
Source: Adapted from: Byrnes, D.A., Dever, M. & Jared, E. (1995). Early childhood practices survey. In: P. Klag (Ed.) *Pioneering innovations in education: Seven strategies for school success.* Logan, UT, Edith Bowen Laboratory School.

Ample blocks of time are needed for children to fully develop, engage in, and learn from their activities. For example, it will likely take children 30 minutes to negotiate a dramatic play theme, identify the characters, and fully engage in the story. They need ample time to explore art materials and express themselves artistically. Through careful and regular observation, teachers learn how much time is ample time.

Focus on Children

Scheduling the Day

Many factors influence class schedules including availability of specialists and classroom aids, scheduling of common areas within the physical facility, and characteristics of the particular teaching context. They also reflect the developmental natures of the children in the setting. Although there are many scheduling variations, following are some possible schedules for young children of different ages.

Toddler Program, 9:00–11:30
- 9:00   Self-selected activities (e.g., large muscle, lap reading, crafts, sensory, blocks)
- 9:45   Whole group story, poems, finger plays
- 10:00 Outdoor play
- 10:30 Self-selected activities
- 10:50 Music and movement
- 11:15 Whole group story
        (Snacks on individual schedules)

Preschool Program, 9:00–11:30
- 9:00   Self-selected activities (e.g., dramatic play, blocks, small group reading, sensory, blocks)
- 9:45   Whole group story, poems, finger plays, class meeting
- 10:00 Outdoor play
- 10:15 Snack
- 10:30 Integrated unit project (includes art, literature, observation, interaction)
- 11:00 Music and movement
- 11:15 Whole group story

Half-Day Kindergarten, 8:30–11:30
- 8:30   Whole group (e.g., calendar, weather, pledge, songs, class meeting)
- 8:45   Language arts, math activities in small groups and includes explicit instruction in phonics, comprehension, vocabulary, number recognition, number sense, problem solving, etc.
- 9:30   Self-selected activities at centers (e.g., blocks, dramatic play, art, listening, discovery, woodworking, books, writing, listening, manipulatives)
- 10:00 Outdoor play
- 10:15 Shared reading
- 10:30 Integrated unit projects (includes observation, interaction, art, literature, writing, math)
- 11:10 Music and movement, whole group story

Full-Day or Extended-Day Kindergarten, 8:30–2:00
- 8:30   Whole group (e.g., calendar, weather, pledge, songs, class meeting)
- 8:45   Language arts in small groups and includes explicit instruction in phonics, comprehension, vocabulary, numerals, number sense, sorting, etc.
- 9:30   Self-selected activities at centers (e.g., blocks, dramatic play, art, listening, discovery, woodworking, books, writing, listening, manipulatives)
- 10:00 Outdoor play
- 10:15 Math activities in small groups and includes explicit instruction in number recognition, number sense, sorting, problem solving, etc.
- 11:00 Music and movement, whole group story
- 11:30 Lunch and outdoor play
- 12:15 Shared reading
- 12:30 Integrated unit projects (includes observation, interaction, art, literature, writing, math)
- 1:30   Music and movement, whole group story
- 2:00   Dismiss

First-Grade Program, 8:30–3:00
- 8:30   Whole group including calendar, songs, poems, and read aloud
- 9:00   Guided reading, includes explicit instruction in comprehension, phonics, fluency, and vocabulary
- 9:30   Independent reading, author studies, book discussions
- 10:15 Outdoor play
- 10:30 Spelling
- 10:45 Writing, fiction/nonfiction; includes explicit instruction in conventions of writing
- 11:45 Lunch and outdoor play
- 12:30 Math, includes explicit instruction in mathematical concepts and problem solving
- 1:15   Specialists (Music, phys ed Art)
- 1:45   Integrated unit projects and discussion (includes observation, interaction, art, literature, writing, math)
- 3:00   Dismiss

James Marshall/The Image Works.

In infant environments, habits vary with individual infants; thus, activities are considered on an individual basis. In toddler environments, most of the time is spent in self-selected, active experiences. Preschoolers are more able to enjoy and benefit from interactive small group activities like co-creating a block structure, dramatic play, and crafts.

A day in kindergarten incorporates both whole group activities and small group experiences. By kindergarten, children are developmentally ready to benefit from brief periods (10–12 minutes) of explicit instruction each day. Primary grade children have fewer self-selected activities, more explicit instruction, and a balance of small group, solitary, and whole group experiences. The *Focus on Children* provides an example of possible time allotments in settings for children of various ages.

ᖗ Room Arrangements

Room arrangements vary based on the needs of the children and available resources. Although there is no one correct room arrangement for any particular age group, following is a discussion of general characteristics of room arrangements in infant, toddler, preschool, kindergarten, and primary grade settings. All settings must be handicap accessible.

Infants and Toddlers

Infants and toddlers have some similar yet some different needs that impact the physical arrangement of their learning environments. Differences pertain to sleeping and eating areas as well as areas designed to accommodate activities.

Infants. If you are an infant caregiver, you will want the environment to be conducive to meeting the infants' individual needs. You will need areas for eating, diapering, sleeping, and playing. Each infant needs a designated crib. Because feeding times may be staggered, a few high chairs in the food preparation area will suffice for several infants. They must, of course, be sterilized after each use.

Infants need space to interact with adults, move around, and explore objects, and that space should be carpeted and clean. Objects can be stored there for easy access. Infants also need a quiet space for lap reading, listening to songs, snuggling, and rocking. Figure 12.2 is a sample environment for infants.

Toddlers. If you are a toddler teacher, you will provide space for children to actively explore, solitarily or in small groups. Figure 12.3 is a sample environment for toddlers.

The large muscle and manipulative areas invite and accommodate movement and noise. They are also the largest areas so the toddlers can move freely and are not crowded during their activities. When the large muscle equipment is moved aside, the area becomes a space for whole group movement and music activities. The manipulatives area will accommodate solitary, parallel, and associative play (cooperative play is uncommon with toddlers, see Chapter 4). It will also accommodate whole group activities such as story time and nap time.

The water and sand tables as well as the art area are for exploring fluid and malleable materials. Materials in the art area can be changed frequently and include clay, play dough, paint, and various materials for projects. Crayons and markers should be available as well.

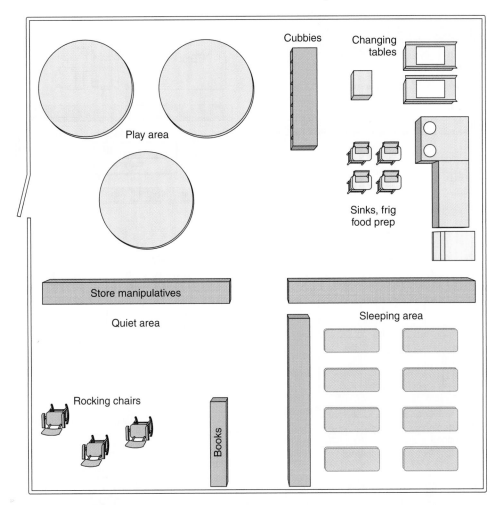

Figure 12.2 Sample physical environment for infants.

The book area is a quiet place where toddlers can go to relax or settle down. The table will have room for several toddlers at once as they explore developmentally appropriate books. A sofa can be used for lap reading, which is a very important toddler activity.

Because toddlers may have very different eating habits, snacks should be provided on individual schedules. A snack table that accommodates five or six toddlers at one time will probably suffice.

Some toddlers will have completed (or be in the process of) toilet learning while others will not. Thus, bathrooms and changing areas with sinks need to be easily accessible. Ideally, toilets and sinks will be child-sized; if not, place stools that will not slide around so children can reach.

Preschool and Kindergarten

Although preschool and kindergarten are often in different contexts (kindergarten is usually part of public school), there are similarities in appropriate learning environments. If you are a preschool or kindergarten teacher, you will arrange your room in learning centers where children can work in small groups for a large part of their day.

Room arrangements may vary but should address the considerations for creating a child-centered environment. Figure 12.4 is a sample environment for preschool or kindergarten. It has two areas where children can

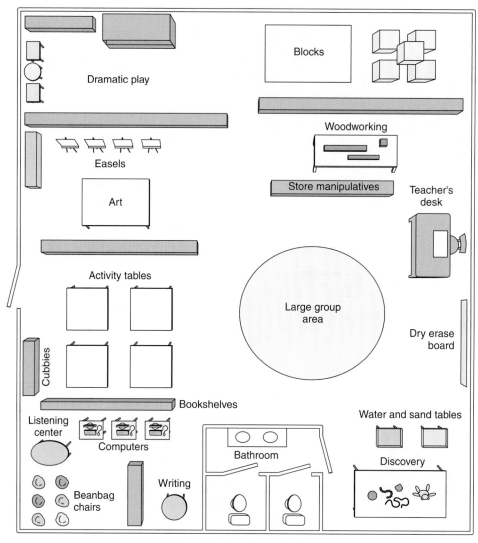

Figure 12.3 Sample physical environment for toddlers.

meet as a large group. The rug area accommodates large group discussions, music and movement activities, and whole group book reading (big books). The table area accommodates large group activities that are relatively quiet. The quiet activity tables are also intended for explicit instruction lessons (kindergarten), individual work, cooperative work, projects, snacks, and for working with small manipulatives.

The other areas accommodate smaller groups of children. The art area is structured so that children can share art materials as they work on art projects, or work individually at easels. Book storage is in close proximity to the reading area. The writing table has writing materials including pencils, papers, rulers, envelopes, etc. The dramatic play, block, woodworking, and art areas are in close proximity, separate from other centers as they tend to be the noisiest centers.

The discovery center houses various materials. It might have incubating eggs, growing plants, or owl pellets to be dissected. Materials at these centers are changed to reflect children's advancing development, changing interests, or content learning themes. The discovery area is a good place to house living things too.

Monika Graff/The Image Works.

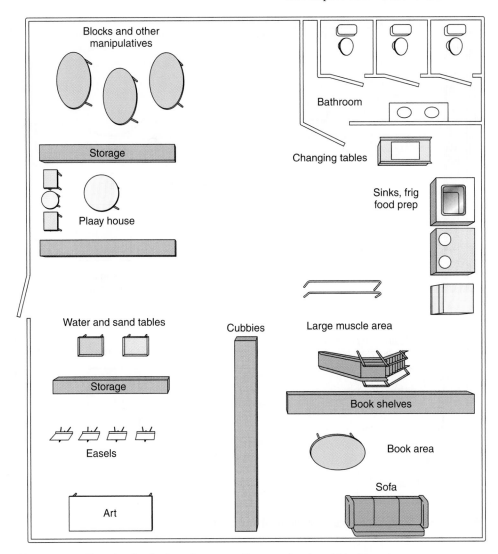

Figure 12.4 Sample physical environment for preschool and kindergarten.

As for toddlers, it is helpful for preschool and kindergarten children to have bathrooms in close proximity. Dividers and storage units create boundaries for each area and help contain the noise. Each child has a cubby space for storing personal items during the day.

Primary Grades

If you are a teacher in the primary grades, you will need spaces for whole group, small group, and solitary work. The individual desks are arranged in groups of four to accommodate both solitary work and cooperative group work. Tables are used for small group instruction, and the large carpet and the desk area can be used for whole group instruction. If you are a primary grade teacher, you will be the only adult in the room during most of the day. That means the room arrangement must be open so that you can easily glance around the room to monitor activities. Figure 12.5 is a sample environment for primary grade classrooms.

A day in a primary grade classroom includes a balance of whole group instruction, small group instruction, skills practice, projects, and self-selected activities. As with preschool and primary age children, noisy and quiet activities are separated so that one activity is not disruptive of another.

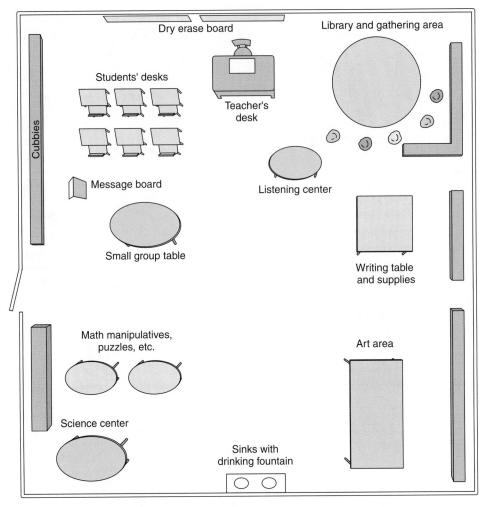

Figure 12.5 **Sample physical environment for primary grades.**

Primary grade classrooms frequently include a message board as a means of communication. The board is used to record lunch count, provide information, share interesting news, etc. Both teachers and students write on it.

The library area serves as a gathering area for discussion and read alouds and as a place for children to read alone. It houses high-interest books that can be used as part of content units, reading instruction, or as a self-selected activity for individual students. Books may belong in the classroom or be checked out from school or community libraries. The library also houses leveled books which are books written for particular reading levels. Thus, children can select books they will be able to read independently. The beanbag chairs accommodate children who wish to visit the class library as a self-selected activity.

The math manipulatives area houses many manipulatives used to teach math concepts. This includes unifix cubes, Cuisenaire rods, counting chips, and collections of items for sorting and classifying. Puzzles, games, and other items used during self-selected activity times can also be stored here.

The writing table houses writing materials including rulers, pencils, paper, scissors, markers, crayons, dictionaries, etc., so children can go there as a self-selected activity. The writing area can also be used for small group instruction. Writing will be both a required and self-selected activity.

Living things and other science artifacts are included in the science area. Children can visit the science area as part of instruction or as a self-selected activity. The art area houses art supplies for children to use as part of project work or a self-selected activity.

Inclusive Environments

Often children with special needs are included in regular early childhood settings. It is vital that accommodations to meet their needs are made. There are many possible accommodations, the nature of which depends entirely on the needs of individual children with disabilities. The *Focus on Diversity* suggests a few examples.

Outdoor Environments

Physically active children have a greater chance of being healthy for a lifetime (Saunders, 2002). In this electronic age, however, outdoor activity often gives way to technology as young children choose to watch movies and play computer games rather than go outside. Furthermore, with the current focus on accountability for achievement and high-stakes testing, teachers may be tempted to replace some outdoor play with more instructional time. Unless the weather is too inclement, young children should go outdoors daily.

High-quality outdoor experiences are not just limited to gross motor activities. The outdoor environment is a great place for creative play. It can become an extension of the classroom to support content learning and help young children gain an

Focus on Diversity

Accommodating Individual Ability Needs

Visual Disabilities

- Use brightly colored containers for storage and pictures to label areas (Wald, Morris, & Abraham, 1996).
- Use tactile and auditory cues (Wald et al., 1996) (e.g., textured surfaces, auditory signals).
- An empty space between containers holding items may assist children with a visual disability to locate materials (Loughlin & Suina, 1982).

Hearing Disabilities

- When you speak, vary your tone (Wald et al., 1996).
- Use visual cues (Wald et al., 1996) (e.g., gestures, pictures).

Motor Disabilities

- Have wide pathways and low sinks and shelves for children in wheelchairs (Bigge, Best, & Heller, 2001).
- Adjust tabletops so wheelchairs can fit under them (Bigge et al., 2001).
- During art, paper mounted on a window or wall might be more accessible for children with motor disabilities (Bigge et al., 2001).
- Provide gripper devices on tools (e.g., push pencil through small Styrofoam ball for gripping).
- Raised edges on work spaces keeps materials from falling to the floor if they are spilled (Loughlin & Suina, 1982).

Learning Disabilities

- Make time accommodations so children have ample time to engage in and complete a particular activity.
- Adjust assignments as needed (e.g., fewer spelling words).
- For children who are easily distracted, provide a work space with reduced sensory stimuli. Clearly display materials with reduced visual stimuli in any one area. Muffle extraneous noise with absorbent material (Loughlin & Suina, 1982).

appreciation of and take responsibility for their natural world. Children who have positive outdoor experiences may be more likely to develop behaviors that are respectful of the natural environment (Arce, 2000).

Gross Motor Activity

The daily time schedules suggested earlier included some time outdoors for all ages of children. Even infants benefit from time outside to crawl and play on blankets or in the grass, swing, and ride in wagons and strollers. Spending time outdoors gives young children the opportunity to learn about and appreciate their natural world. They also need time to engage in gross motor activity to develop basic movement skills like jumping, running, balancing, galloping, skipping, and throwing. These movement activities are easily done outdoors. Any outdoor equipment should be scaled to the size of the children so it can be easily and safely used. For example, children ages 3–8 can use flat seat swings while infants and toddlers need seats that provide support all around.

Outdoor gross motor equipment should include a wide range of activities and apparatus (e.g., climbing, swinging, sliding, riding) as well as balls, Frisbees, etc. As with indoor activities, competition should be avoided.

Creative Play

In addition to manufactured equipment, outdoor play should include materials such as water, sand, pots and pans, shovels and pails, hoes and rakes, and building materials. Such materials invite creative play. Bounded areas for digging, constructing, and even role-play are important elements of the outdoor environment and support creative play (Rivkin, 2002).

Appreciation of Nature

Outdoor play instills an appreciation for the natural environment as children have opportunities to experience it. The outdoor environment can be an extension of the classroom with weather stations, natural animal habitats, gardens, or a collection of native plants. Natural animal habitats can be purposefully created; a bird habitat, for example. Furthermore, as children care for gardens or plots of native plants, they will experience the naturally occurring habitats of insects and worms. Thermometers can be mounted so children can track the temperature daily. The outdoor environment will provide direct experiences that make the integrated curriculum (Chapter 4) meaningful and relevant for young children.

Children of different ages will interact in developmentally expected ways with the natural environment. That is, second graders can more take more responsibility for a garden than preschoolers. Toddlers will give less care to the outdoor environment, but they can watch and talk about changes they observe.

There are many appropriate ways to structure an outdoor environment. Figure 12.6 is one example that is appropriate for kindergarten and primary grade children.

⧙ The Social Environment

Along with the physical arrangement and child-centeredness of the learning environments, the social aspects must also be considered. A healthy social environment is one where everyone is treated with dignity and respect. During the formative early years children are developing social skills and learning how to interact with others in positive ways. It is a time when they are able to learn how to treat others in socially just ways.

Many of you reading this text may recall incidents of name calling and outright bullying from your childhood. Names like "four eyes" or "dummy," racial slurs like

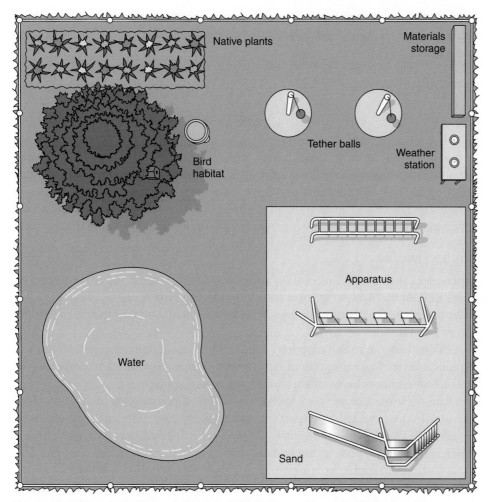

Figure 12.6 Sample outdoor environment for kindergarten and primary grades.

"wetback," and chants like, "fatty, fatty, two by four" are all hurtful comments. They transcend hurtful to demean human beings. A compilation of such experiences has devastating effects for both the name caller and the recipient. While the name caller develops elitist (perhaps even hateful) attitudes, the recipient is developing a negative self-concept. Such behaviors lead to exclusion of others and sometimes even violence.

Teaching for Social Justice

Teaching for social justice begins with an antibias environment, which we have discussed in previous chapters. In Chapter 8, we discussed the merits of teaching conflict resolution strategies, cooperative learning, and prejudice reduction. We also discussed empowering young children by involving them in decision making and providing choices in developmentally appropriate ways. In Chapters 4–7 we discussed the culturally relevant curriculum that is appropriate for children at different developmental levels. Those chapters also identify components of the antibias physical environment (e.g., wall displays). Throughout this text, we discuss communicating with parents to better understand and embrace children's individual family values.

Each of these strategies is designed to teach understanding and foster tolerance and acceptance, and should be the norm in early childhood environments. Using these strategies in infant, toddler, preschool, and primary grade environments will set a trajectory of understanding and tolerance early in the lives of young children.

As young children mature, they are increasingly able to take perspective and think about things not present in their immediate environments. Teachers in kindergarten and the primary grades can teach a critical perspective that helps young children think beyond themselves and learn attitudes of respect and justice.

Teach Questioning

As young children get older, they learn to question their world (Rethinking Schools, 1994). They can grapple with questions like these: Is that fair? Why not? Who is left out or hurt? How can we change the situation? As you pose questions, be certain they stem from the children's personal experience. For example, name-calling incidents or times when someone is left out provide opportunities to talk about difference, who is hurt, and how the situation can be changed. Through guided discussion and adult modeling, young children learn to do this in socially appropriate ways. The *Window into the Classroom* provides an example.

Perspective Taking

Experiences with conflict resolution and cooperative learning support young children's development as perspective takers. In order to resolve conflict or engage in a collaborative project, young children must interact with and take the perspective of other children.

Children's literature also supports young children's development of perspective taking abilities as they take the point of view of characters in stories, both fiction and nonfiction. Some authors have written books from two different perspectives. For example, Tim Paulson wrote *Jack and the Beanstalk/The Beanstalk Incident*, an accounting of the traditional story from Jack's perspective and a retelling from the giant's perspective.

Table 12.1 highlights additional picture books that will not only assist young children to take perspective, but will engender discussion about human rights and social justice. They address issues such as racism and classism in ways that young children can understand. When you use books for this purpose, inform parents of the topics of discussion and content of the books so that they understand the instructional objectives and can reinforce attitudes of respect and justice.

The *Focus on Diversity* describes the response of second graders after hearing the story *Amazing Grace*.

Window into the Classroom

Some of the students in Mr. Ray's first grade class are playing a game of soccer during recess. Marco passes the ball to David who kicks toward the goal and misses. The game ends as recess time is over.

Marco: *[Yelling at David.] You fatty!!!! You made us lose the game!!!!*

Mr. Ray: *Oh Marco, I can see you are quite angry.*

Marco: *Well, David missed the goal and made us lose the game.*

Mr. Ray: *I understand that but do you think calling him a hurtful name is helpful?*

Marco: *Well, if he wasn't so fat he'd kick better!!*

Mr. Ray: *Marco, you don't know that. Now do you think calling him a name is helpful? Does it solve any problem?*

Marco: *No.*

Mr. Ray: *Who was hurt when you called David a name?*

Marco: *David.*

Mr. Ray: *Yes. The soccer game is a team effort. Everyone contributes and you win or lose together. What do you think you will do next time?*

Marco: *I don' know. I guess score more points earlier.*

Mr. Ray: *Well that's one thing you can do. There are lots of things you can do but we've decided name calling isn't helpful, haven't we.*

Marco: *Yeh, I guess so.*

Table 12.1 Books to Engender Discussion about Social Justice

Title	Description	Themes
The Universal Declaration of Human Rights by R. Rocha & O. Roth	This book describes the ideal environment where each person, regardless of differences, enjoys the same human rights.	Human rights
Martin's BIG Words: The Life of Dr. Martin Luther King Jr. by D. Rappaport	This picture book chronicles the life of Dr. Martin Luther King, highlighting his message of *driving out hate with love.*	Civil disobedience, love of humankind
Amazing Grace by M. Hoffman	Grace's classmates tell her that she cannot play Peter Pan in the play because she is a girl and she is black. She does not let them stop her.	Racism, gender bias, determination
The Other Side by J. Woodson	A black girl and a white girl cross the barrier and racial tension created by a fence that separates the black and white sides of town.	Racism
Daddy's Roommate by M. Willhoite	The father of the young boy in this story lives with his gay partner. Their lives are very similar to other families that have experienced an amiable divorce.	Gay Family
The Day Gogo Went to Vote by E. B. Sisulu	Set in postapartheid South Africa, Thembi accompanies her grandmother to vote for the first time.	Oppression
Fly Away Home by E. Bunting	A young boy and his father are homeless, living in the airport.	Economic inequity
The Story of Ruby Bridges by R. Coles	This is the true story of Ruby Bridges, who was the first black child to attend an all white elementary school.	Civil rights

Source: Dever, M. T., Sorenson, B., & Brodrick, J. (2005). Using picture books as a vehicle to teach young children about social justice. *Social Studies and the Young Learner, 18*(1), 19.

Rethinking Curriculum

Curriculum that teaches for social justice may require rethinking what we teach and assume to be true. Recall from Chapter 7 the discussion about integrating issues of diversity into the curriculum, and the importance of transforming it (Banks, 1995) to move beyond superficial study (e.g., holidays, Native American month).

Pause for a minute and think about the holiday *Columbus Day*. What do you know about the meaning and origin of that holiday? Typical curriculum and children's books portray the perspective of Christopher Columbus by chronicling his travels and talking about his feelings and eventual discovery. Most curriculum materials place little emphasis on the perspectives of the Native Americans that Columbus met or the fact that they had been here for centuries. This country was not a *new world* to everyone.

Similarly, the holiday *Thanksgiving* is primarily depicted from the perspective of the European settlers. Often, Native Americans are depicted stereotypically as savages. Little mention is made of the diversity of lifestyles of Native Americans (e.g., they did not all wear feathers in headbands) or the assistance they provided to the first European immigrants. There is seldom discussion of how the arrival of Europeans impacted the lives of Native Americans.

Focus on Diversity

Teaching Young Children about Social Justice

Ms. Baker is a second-grade teacher who embraces the importance of teaching children about social justice. She finds picture books to be an effective medium for raising awareness, engendering empathy, and supporting a developing inclination for advocacy. She regularly reads stories with social justice themes to her students. Following discussion of the stories, the students often write responses. Here are examples of second graders' written responses (original spellings) to the story *Amazing Grace* (see Table 12.1).

Empathy

Most children responded with empathetic support.

> *I would tell her that she could do it and don't listin to them.*
> *You can be Peter Pan.*
> *In fact, you could be eny thin you wanted....*
> *IF I were in Graces class I wanted tell her that she couned be peter and i wanted make fun of her skin.*
> *I would cheer grace on to be peter pan. And I would vot for grace. I would say good job after the play....*
> *I would be nice to Grace and I wood be Grace's bestest friend in the world.*

Advocacy

Several of the second graders demonstrated a basic level of advocacy, showing willingness to advocate on Grace's behalf.

> *I wold have said "let her be peter pan" bcause she has graet imganacon.*
> *If I was in Graces class I would stand up for Grace and say to my class mate that if he was a Girl then what would he feel like and if he would like it if some one said to him you cant be peter pan cause he's black.*
> *I would of said to the prson that told Grace she couldn't do it, that Grace can tryout for wat ever she wated and didn't have to be told wat to try out for.*

Nonempathetic

Only one child of 53 appeared to be non-empathetic.

> *If [I were] where in graces class i whold say your part should be a firiy.*

Source: Dever, M. T., Sorenson, B., & Brodrick, J. (2005). Using picture books as a vehicle to teach young children about social justice. *Social Studies and the Young Learner, 18*(1), 18–21.

Take Action

Recall from Chapter 7, Banks' (2003) highest level of multicultural curriculum development is the *social action* level where children engage in an activity that impacts their social world. At some level, even young children can take action. Calling a peer on a demeaning remark or educating parents about the Native American perspective on Columbus Day and Thanksgiving are forms of social action. Suggesting an action plan to the town council about a problem with littering on the community playground is another example of social action.

Inequity in School Funding

Funding affects the ability of schools to provide optimal learning environments. In 1991, Jonathan Kozol brought national attention to gross inequities in school funding with his landmark work *Savage Inequalities*. Little has changed since that time. Wide gaps in per pupil spending continue, owing in part to unequal property tax bases as one source of school funding (Rethinking Schools, 1997). Districts with the most expensive homes collect the most property tax revenue, whereas districts with less expensive homes have less property tax revenue with which to support schools. This means that children from more educated, affluent families have more adequately funded schools.

Inequitable funding intensifies other issues of inequity. For example, more educated, affluent families typically have more personal time and money to contribute to educating their children. Furthermore, these families tend to represent the cultural mainstream and find school more consistent with their cultural values than children from less educated, less affluent families. Thus, inequities persist.

Inequity in school funding has been debated in legislatures and courts for decades; however, court decisions have failed to bring resolution. Historically, the argument is that reliance on property tax to fund schools supports the idea of local control of schools. However, we are ignoring the notion that the power to eradicate inequities belongs not to the districts themselves, but to the states that oversee the districts and have power over tax allocations (Rethinking Schools, 1997).

Table 12.2 compares the lowest and highest per pupil expenditures in districts by state. Comparisons between states should not be made because we cannot

Table 12.2	Highest and Lowest Funded Districts by State	
State	**School District**	**Spending per Pupil 2000–01**
Alabama	Autauga County Sch. Dist.	5,007
	Homewood City Sch. Dist.	8,191
Alaska	Nenana City Sch. Dist.	3,894
	North Slope Borough Sch. Dist.	22,085
Arizona	Mohave Elementary Sch. Dist.	5,478
	Rainbow Accommodation School	22,600
Arkansas	Emmet Sch. Dist.	4,497
	Lake View Sch. Dist.	7,198
California	Hickman Comm. Charter Sch.	4,664
	San Francisco Co. Off. of Ed.	55,802
Colorado	Lewis-Palmer 38 Sch. Dist.	4,908
	Silverton 1 Sch. Dist.	12,190
Connecticut	Bethany Sch. Dist.	7,586
	Winchester Sch. Dist.	14,788
Delaware	Smyrna Sch. Dist.	7,448
	New Castle Co. Votech Sch. Dist.	12,991
District of Columbia	Dist. of Columbia Public Schls.	12,046
Florida	Nassau County Sch. Dist.	5,391
	Washington County Sch. Dist.	9,990
Georgia	Pike County Sch. Dist.	5,250
	Taliaferro County Sch. Dist.	12,177
Hawaii	Hawaii Dept. of Ed.	6,599
Idaho	Preston Joint Sch. Dist. 201	4,557
	Avery Sch. Dist. 34	34,682
Illinois	Mokena Sch. Dist. 159	4,420
	Township High Sch. Dist. 113	17,004
Indiana	North White Sch. Corp.	6,743
	School City of East Chicago	9,682
Iowa	Treynor Comm. Sch. Dist.	5,286
	Corwith-Wesley Comm. Sch. Dist.	12,932
Kansas	Augusta Sch. Dist.	4,734
	Phillipsburg Sch. Dist.	12,864

Table 12.2   *(continued)*

Kentucky	Anderson Co. Sch. Dist.	4,925
	Anchorage Ind. Sch. Dist.	9,804
Louisiana	Union Parish Sch. Board	5,059
	Saint Charles Union Sch. Board	7,502
Maine	Otis Sch. Dept.	4,404
	Frenchboro Sch. Dept.	13,500
Maryland	Harford Co. Public Schls.	6,958
	Montgomery Co. Public Schls.	9,543
Massachusetts	Southampton Sch. Dist.	6,547
	Gosnold Sch. Dist.	27,333
Michigan	Church Sch. Dist.	4,077
	Benjamin Carson Academy	23,852
Minnesota	Round Lake Sch. Dist.	6,254
	Pine Point Sch. Dist.	15,984
Mississippi	Desoto Co. Sch. Dist.	4,084
	Benoit Sch. Dist.	8,395
Missouri	McDonald Co. R-1 Sch. Dist.	4,571
	Spec. Sch. Dist. St. Louis Co.	28,881
Montana	Avon Elementary Sch. Dist.	3,958
	Trinity Elementary Sch. Dist.	29,200
Nebraska	Garfield Public Sch. Dist.	4,150
	Westside Comm. Sch. Dist.	8,426
Nevada	Clark Co. Sch. Dist.	5,525
	Eureka Co. Sch. Dist.	16,757
New Hampshire	Wentworth Sch. Dist.	5,465
	Waterville Valley Sch. Dist.	19,138
New Jersey	Highland Boro Sch. Dist.	7,220
	South Bergen Jointure Com.	83,454
New Mexico	Rio Rancho Public Schs.	4,783
	Mosquero Municipal Scls.	17,649
New York	Tioga CSD	9,743
	Fire Island UFSD	43,000
North Carolina	Davidson Co. Schls.	5,425
	Hyde Co. Schls.	11,566
North Dakota	Sweet Briar Sch. Dist. 17	4,429
	Twin Buttes Sch. Dist. 37	35,694
Ohio	College Corner Local Sch. Dist.	3,212
	North Bass Local Sch. Dist	51,500
Oklahoma	Bishop Sch. Dist.	4,706
	Albion Sch. Dist.	9,624
Oregon	Echo Sch. Dist. 005	8,186
	Juntura Sch. Dist. 012	33,400
Pennsylvania	Tamaqua Area Sch. Dist.	6,254
	Lower Merion Sch. Dist	13,654

Table 12.2   *(continued)*

Rhode Island	Cumberland Sch. Dist.	7,455
	New Shoreham Sch. Dist.	17,485
South Carolina	Spartanburg Co. Sch. Dist. 04	5,754
	Fairfield Co. Sch. Dist.	8,702
South Dakota	Warner Sch. Dist. 06–5	5,461
	Agar Sch. Dist. 58–1	25,115
Tennessee	Dayton City Elem. Sch. Dist.	3,422
	Franklin City Elem. Sch. Dist.	7,584
Texas	Red Lick ISD	4,798
	Kelton ISD	21,815
Utah	Nebo Sch. Dist.	4,480
	Daggett Sch. Dist.	12,994
Vermont	Richmond Sch. Dist.	5,278
	Dorset Sch. Dist.	16,904
Virginia	Bedford Co. Public Schls.	5,411
	Arlington Co. Public Schls.	11,388
Washington	Kalama Sch. Dist. 402	4,933
	Benge Sch. Dist. 122	22,700
West Virginia	Hardy Co. Sch. Dist.	6,065
	Pleasants Co. Sch. Dist	10,202
Wisconsin	North Cape Sch. Dist.	5,264
	La Du Flambeau Sch. Dist. #1	16,531
Wyoming	Park Co. Sch. Dist. #1	6,683
	Sheridan Co. Sch. Dist #3	13,948

Source: National Center for Educational Statistics. US Department of Education.

account for variance in state economies. We also must be aware that districts' monetary needs within states vary. For example, poverty impacts young children's development; thus, high poverty areas have greater special education needs. However, some large discrepancies can still be noted among districts within states.

Quality Schools for All

All children deserve a high-quality education, and this begs a public school system where districts have equal opportunities to provide for the needs of the children they serve. Funding should be tied to a new vision of schooling where (Rethinking Schools, 1997):

▶ All children's innate curiosities and capacities to learn are respected.

▶ Critical thinking and activism are encouraged.

▶ Social justice is highly valued.

▶ Activities are participatory and experiential.

▶ Children feel valued and cared for.

▶ Environments are culturally sensitive.

▶ The curriculum is academically rigorous.

▶ Parents are important colleagues. (pp. 12–13)

The Role of Technology in Early Childhood Environments

Until the mid-20th century, children needed to develop mathematical and communication literacy to be productive members of society. During the latter part of the 20th century, technology literacy became necessary for one to be a productive member of society. Currently, technology takes many forms including DVDs, audio and video recording devices, digital cameras, computer programs, computer software, CD-ROMs, Internet, electronic toys, and TV. There are also many types of assistive technology to support children with disabilities. Becoming technologically literate involves learning a language, techniques, and skills; this learning begins in early childhood.

©Ellen B. Senisi.

Limited and monitored experiences with computers benefit the growth and development of young children. For example, social and emotional development is enhanced when children interact as they work on computers. Specifically, they talk more and demonstrate positive emotions (Clements & Sarama, 2003). Computers support interactions between children with disabilities and typically developing children (Hutinger & Johanson, 2000). Observed cognitive benefits include higher levels of language and cooperative play when young children use computers (Clements & Sarama, 2003). Computer software supports the development of prereading skills; computerized story books can potentially close the gap between children who are read to often at home and those who are not (Clements & Sarama, 2003).

NAEYC Position on Technology and Young Children

As with anything else, technology must be used in developmentally appropriate ways with young children. Technology experiences for infants and toddlers should be quite limited because they learn through their senses and need primarily active, multisensory experiences. By age 3, children can benefit from limited and monitored experiences with technology.

The NAEYC (1996) set forth the following seven principles regarding computer technology and children ages 3–8. These principles can be applied to other technologies including telecommunications and multimedia, (NAEYC, 1996):

▶ Early childhood educators must use professional judgment to determine whether the use of technology is individually, culturally, and developmentally appropriate. Consider what we know about the nature of young children and how they learn before selecting technology.

▶ Consider how technology supports social and cognitive development. Children are interested in computers when they can make things happen. In addition, when software has increasing complexity, it supports children's cognitive development. Furthermore, studies indicate that children enjoy collaborative computer experiences, seek help from each other, and seem to prefer assistance from peers over adults.

▶ Computers should be integrated into the regular learning environment and used as a tool to support learning. Because computers are another tool for learning, "computer time" separate from classroom activities should be used only for brief periods of skills instruction (keyboarding, for example). Computers should be located in the early childhood setting.

▶ Early childhood educators should promote equitable access to computers. Studies indicate that girls, African-American students, and poor students use computers less and have less access or encouragement to use them.

▶ Technology should affirm children's diverse cultures, languages, and ethnic heritages.

▶ Early childhood educators and parents must advocate for more appropriate technology and applications for all children. Advocacy must focus on easier access to previewing software, easy upgrades, information on benefits of appropriate software, and positive representation of diversity. Software must cater to different abilities, support collaborative experiences, demonstrate nonviolence, and support information sharing. Advocacy must also support national, state, and local policies of equity in access to technology for young children and their families.

▶ Early childhood educators must become active participants in the world of technology and engage in in-depth training in order to make adequate decisions about technology. (pp. 11–15)

Preschool and Kindergarten. Children ages 3–5 years old develop language as they create stories and record them into a tape recorder or dictate them to an adult who types them on the computer. Adults who type the stories should be certain the child is positioned to see the words as they are being created. This supports young children's development of print awareness, letter and word knowledge, and phonics. They should be encouraged to illustrate their stories.

There are software programs appropriate for 3- to 5-year-olds that link words and pictures. Again, emergent literacy is supported as children see the word that names the picture. These stories on computer software are animated and have illustrations that make the characters come alive.

Programs for drawing, creating patterns, and classifying objects are appropriate and support mathematical learning. Early childhood educators should be sure that the programs are open-ended and give some control to the child; programs should not be computerized worksheets.

Primary Grades. Children ages 6–8 will benefit from many of the same types of programs for younger children, particularly if the programs are available in increasing complexity. Furthermore, 6- to 8- year-olds can learn to use word processing and access the Internet. They will learn about the lives of others by becoming *email pals* with children across town, in another state, or in another country. Speech synthesizers are available to provide immediate feedback as children write.

Although primary grade children need to learn mathematical concepts and be able to recite math facts, they also need to learn how to use calculators as a tool. Children in this age group can learn to use digital cameras. They will enjoy taking pictures to illustrate nonfiction books they are writing or to create wall displays.

Media Violence

Whether TV, computers, or another type of technology, some form of technology can be found in most households. There are many advantages to technology, as we have discussed; however, when it portrays violence, it can have a negative effect on young children.

The Facts. In 1984, the Federal Communications Commission deregulated children's television (Levin, 1998). To make matters worse, technology for creating movies and television shows has become more sophisticated, and thus so has the portrayal of violence. Gone are the days of early television when Roy Rogers always conquered the "bad guy" with a couple of good smacks to the jaw. We rarely ever saw blood. Today, media violence is glamorized. Children can view explosions, gun and knife assaults, murder, rape, and so on. Even children's programming is full of violence. For example, children's cartoon and action programs average 20 plus acts of violence per hour (Levin, 1998).

Elizabeth Crews.

Consistent viewing of violence can desensitize young children to violence and its consequences in general. In fact, the consequences of violence are usually not even portrayed in the media as characters walk away from violent encounters.

Children spend an average of 35 hours per week either watching TV or playing video or DVD games (Levin, 1998). As the quantity and quality of violence in the media increases, children will likely have witnessed 8,000 murders and 100,000 additional acts of violence on TV by the time they finish elementary school (Levin, 1998).

Manufacturers contribute to the problem by marketing violent toys, a market that has turned into a billion dollar industry (Levin, 1998). That is, children can watch an action show, purchase replicas of the characters, and enact the violence. Furthermore, many games on video and DVD have violent themes.

The Role of Early Childhood Educators. Early childhood educators can help young children learn to monitor their media viewing. They can also educate parents about the harmful effects of media violence, and help them identify alternative activities. Following are some suggestions for early childhood educators:

▶ Discuss options for TV viewing and other screen activities. Help children make a plan for screen activities—how much and what programs (Levin, 1998).

▶ Educate parents about the dangers to their children of viewing too much media violence. Encourage them to limit viewing violence. Parents should be encouraged to talk with their children when they do view violence and help them to see the consequences of violence.

▶ Discuss activities that are alternatives to movies, TV, and games. Novak's picture book, *Mouse TV*, can be used to start a discussion (Levin, 1998). In the book, the mouse family's TV is broken, much to their distress. After reading the book, brainstorm all the things the mice could do instead of watching TV.

▶ Be an advocate. Write to manufacturers of violent toys and advise them of the harmful effects to children who play out violent media episodes. Suggest more developmentally appropriate toys.

Technology and Parenting

Technology tools exist to enhance parenting. For example, parents can use a filter on their home computers so that their children cannot access certain Internet sites or chat rooms. They can also limit the time children are on the computer.

If the child care or school environment has the appropriate technology, parents can check on their children during the day. With an ID and password, parents can get into the program and actually view their children in the early childhood setting. Most work environments have computers that could be made reasonably available to parents for this purpose.

❭ Antibias Technology Environments

In an antibias learning environment, all children have the opportunity to learn and have their individual needs met. School districts must provide equal access to technology, as well as assistive technology to meet the communication needs for the children who require it.

Equitable Access

Just as with anything, young children have different technology experiences in the early years. Technology is costly, and many families have limited or no technology available to them. Even driving to a library to access technology takes resources. Moreover, parents need an appropriate background of experience to be able to use the technology. In early care and education settings, early childhood educators monitor the use of technology and provide equal opportunity to all children to use it. They integrate it into the curriculum so children see its usefulness (e.g., talking books, research on the Internet).

Elizabeth Crews.

Assistive Technology

Assistive technology is any modification or adaptation used to assist children with disabilities (e.g., Braille printer, communication board, pictures). Assistive technology includes both low-tech (nonelectric) and high-tech (electric) strategies. The appropriate strategy used for a particular child is relative to his/her individual needs and learning goals.

Recommendations for assistive technology and children's training needs are determined by the assessment team and are written into the IEP (Chapter 11). When the use of assistive technology is written into an IEP, the school district is obligated to provide it. School districts, particularly lesser funded districts, often have difficulty finding funds to provide needed assistive technology. Ideally, IDEA funds (Chapter 3) will cover the cost but the federal government usually underfunds the program. Grants, family medical insurance, and Medicare are other possible sources of funding, and educators must diligently pursue needed resources on behalf of children who need them. This stands as another example of how inequities in school funding are costly to the growth and development of young children.

 My Developing Professional View

What are some issues you need to consider as you create an optimal learning environment?

SUMMARY

In this chapter we have examined appropriate learning environments for young children. Appropriate learning environments are consistent with program goals and the developmental and cultural nature of the children in the setting. For example, infants need spaces to carry out their individual schedules for eating, diapering, sleeping, playing, and listening to stories. Toddlers need to be active, whereas preschool and kindergarten children need many small group activities. Primary grade children need spaces for explicit instruction and practice as well as for individual, small, and whole group activities.

Time and activities vary among programs. However, an environment that supports active and quiet activities, including outdoor experiences, is optimal. Early childhood educators must have a plan for addressing health care issues as they arise.

Bias and prejudiced attitudes are learned; similarly, understanding and attitudes of respect and justice are learned. Young children learn about social justice through their daily activities. As their perspective taking abilities mature, conflict resolution, cooperative learning, and prejudice reduction activities are beneficial. Stories that exemplify social justice issues are beneficial as well. Furthermore, early childhood educators plan curriculum that teaches social justice.

Technology is a tool and human beings must become technologically literate if they are to function productively in society. Learning about technology and its uses begins in early childhood. However, early childhood educators must carefully balance technology activities with other developmentally appropriate learning experiences. Furthermore, technology experiences must be carefully evaluated for developmental appropriateness.

ENRICHMENT ACTIVITIES

Individual Activities

1. Observe children in at least two early childhood settings and notice the elements of child-centeredness. Use the checklist provided on page 252 to assist you.

2. Access the website for your state's curriculum guidelines for kindergarten and the primary grades. Select one grade level and assess the following: How is the issue of social justice addressed? Do they have guidelines for character education?

3. Access Early Connections: Technology in Early Childhood Education listed under *Professional Development Resources* in this chapter. Examine some activities for children ages 3–8. In what ways are they developmentally appropriate? Use the Shade (1996) and Clements and Sarama (2003) articles listed in the For *Further Reading* section of this chapter to assist you with your evaluation.

4. Using information in this chapter as a guide, draw a developmentally appropriate learning environment. Be sure you specify the age of children for which your environment is appropriate.

Cooperative Activity

5. Have each group member select a resource to learn more about the story of Columbus, particularly as it relates to the Native American perspective. (Some resources are listed in the *For Further Reading* section.) When each group member has examined a resource, come together to write a children's story about Columbus Day from the Native American perspective.

Advocacy Activities

6. Use the listed resources to learn more about violence in the media. Then go to a local department or discount store and examine children's toys. What types of violent toys are on the market? Identify the manufacturer and write a letter taking a position against media violence; support your position. Suggest some alternatives to violent toys.

7. Illustrate your group's story about Columbus Day from the Native American perspective and read it to a group of young children.

} FOR FURTHER READING

Healthy Environments

Curtis, D., & Carter, M. (2005). Rethinking early childhood environments to enhance learning. *Young Children, 60*(3), 34–38.

Friedman, S. (2005). Environments that inspire. *Young Children, 60*(3), 48–52, 54–56.

National Association for the Education of Young Children. (2004). *Young Children, 59*(2).

Sutterby, J. A., & Thornton, C. D. (2005). It doesn't just happen! Essential contributions from playgrounds. *Young Children, 60*(3), 26–30, 32–33.

Wien, C. A., Coates, A., Keating, B., & Bigelow, B. C. (2005). Designing the environment to build connection to place. *Young Children, 60*(3), 16–22, 24.

Media Violence

Levin, D. (1998). *Remote control childhood? Combating the hazards of media culture.* Washington, DC: National Association for the Education of Young Children.

Physical Environments

Rivkin, M. (2002). Outdoor settings for play and learning. *Young Children, 57*(3), 8–9.

Jensen, B. J., & Bullard, J. A. (2002). The mud center: Recapturing childhood. *Young Children, 57*(3), 16–19.

Sutterby, J. A., & Frost, J. L. (2002). Making playgrounds fit for children and children fit on playgrounds. *Young Children, 57*(3), 36–41.

Social Justice

Dever, M. T., Sorenson, B., & Brodrick, J. (2005). Using picture books as a vehicle to teach young children about social justice. *Social Studies and the Young Learner 18*(1), 18–21.

Flynn, L. L., & Kieff, J. (2002). Including everyone in outdoor play. *Young Children, 57*(3), 20–26.

Gann, C. (2001). A spot of our own: The cultural relevance, anti-bias resource room. *Young Children, 56*(6), 34–36.

Rethinking Schools, Ltd. (1997). *Funding for justice: Money, equity, and the future of public education.* Milwaukee: Author.

Stewart, L. M. (2004). The ABCs of Brown v. Board of Education: A primer of the 50th anniversary. *Social Studies and the Young Learner, 16*(3), 10–13.

Williams, K. C., & Cooney, M. H. (2006). Young children and social justice. *Young Children, 61*(2), 75–82.

Technology

Clements, D. H., & Sarama, J. (2003). Young children and technology: What does research say? *Young Children, 58*(6), 34–40.

Fischer, M. A., & Gillespie, C. W. (2003). Computers and young children's development. *Young Children, 58*(4), 85–91.

Mulligan, S. A. (2003). Assistive technology: Supporting the participation of children with disabilities. *Young Children, 58*(6), 50–53.

Murphy, K. L., DePasquale, R., & McNamara, E. (2003). Meaningful connections: Using technology in primary classrooms. *Young Children, 58*(6), 12–18.

National Association for the Education of Young Children. (1996). NAEYC position statement: Technology and young children—ages three through eight. *Young Children, 51*(6), 11–16.

Robinson, L. (2003). Technology as a scaffold for emergent literacy: Interactive storybooks for toddlers. *Young Children, 58*(6), 42–48.

Shade, D. (1996). Software evaluation. *Young Children, 51*(6), 17–21.

Professional Development Resources

NATIONAL ASSOCIATION FOR MULTICULTURAL EDUCATION

5272 River Road, Suite 430
Bethesda, MD 20816
http://www.nameorg.org/

RETHINKING SCHOOLS

1001 E. Keefe Avenue
Milwaukee, WI 53212
http://www.rethinkingschools.org/

EARLY CONNECTIONS: TECHNOLOGY IN EARLY CHILDHOOD EDUCATION

http://www.netc.org/earlyconnections/

} SELF-ASSESSMENT

1. Discuss the five general considerations for structuring indoor learning environments. How might they differ for different ages of children?

2. Select an age group of children (e.g., toddler, primary grades) and discuss the elements of an appropriate room arrangement for that age group.

3. Discuss some accommodations in your room arrangement you might make for children with motor disabilities.

4. What are some ways you can integrate learning experiences into your outdoor environment?

5. Discuss strategies for teaching young children about social justice. How might appropriate strategies differ for different ages of children?

Scenarios

1. You are a teacher in a pre-K center. During much of your day, children choose activities from the centers in your classroom, including blocks and manipulatives,

books and listening, writing, sensory table, and dramatic play. Over a period of days, you notice that the children at the blocks and manipulatives center seem to get into conflict with the children at the books and listening center which is right next to it. Considering what you know about room arrangements, how might you address this problem?

2. You are a second-grade teacher. You overhear your students talking about stealing cars and other types of robbery. When you query them, you learn that they are playing violent video games at home. How might you respond to this situation?

REFERENCES

Arce, E. M. (2000). *Curriculum for young children: An introduction.* Albany, NY: Delmar Thomson Learning.

Banks, J. A. (1995). Multicultural education: Historical development, dimensions and practice. In J. A. Banks & C. A. McGee Banks (Eds.), *Handbook of research on multicultural education* (pp. 3–24). New York: Macmillan.

Banks, J. A. (2003). *Teaching strategies for ethnic studies* (7th ed.). New York: Allyn and Bacon.

Bigge, J., Best, S., & Heller, K. (2001). *Teaching individuals with physical, health, or multiple disabilities* (4th ed.). Albany, NY: Delmar Thomson Learning.

Byrnes, D. A., Dever, M., & Jared, E. (1995). Early childhood practices survey. In P. Klag (Ed.), *Pioneering innovations in education: Seven strategies for school success.* Logan, UT: Edith Bowen Laboratory School.

Clements, D. H., & Sarama, J. (2003). Young children and technology: What does research say? *Young Children, 58*(6), 34–40.

Curtis, D., & Carter, M. (2005). Rethinking early childhood environments to enhance learning. *Young Children, 60*(3), 34–38.

Dever, M. T., Brodrick, J. and Christensen, B. (2005). Picture books and social justice. *Social Studies and the Young Learner(18)*, 1, 18–21.

Dever, M. T., Sorenson, B., & Brodrick, J. (2005). Using picture books as a vehicle to teach young children about social justice. *Social Studies and the Young Learner, 18*(1), 18–21.

Hutinger, P. L., & Johanson, J. (2000). Implementing and maintaining an effective early childhood comprehensive technology system. *Topics in Early Childhood Special Education, 20*(3), 159–173.

Kozol, J. (1991). *Savage inequalities: Children in America's schools.* New York: Crown Publishers.

Levin, D. (1998). Remote control childhood? Combating the hazards of media culture. Washington, DC: National Association for the Education of Young Children.

Loughlin, C. E., & Suina, J. H. (1982). *The learning environment: An instructional strategy.* New York: Teachers College Press.

NAEYC (National Association for the Education of Young Children) (1996). NAEYC position statement: Technology and young children—ages three through eight. *Young Children, 51*(6), 11–16.

National Council for the Social Studies. (1994). *Expectations of excellence: Curriculum standards for social studies.* Silver Spring, MD: Author.

Rethinking Schools. (1994). *Rethinking our classrooms: Teaching for equity and justice.* Milwaukee: Author.

Rethinking Schools. (1997). *Funding for justice: Money, equity, and the future of public education.* Milwaukee: Author.

Rivkin, M. (2002). Outdoor settings for play and learning. *Young Children, 57*(3), 8–9.

Saunders, S. W. (2002). *Active for life: Developmentally appropriate movement programs for young children.* Washington, DC: National Association for the Education of Young Children.

Swim, T. J. (2004). Basic premises of classroom design: The teacher's perspective. *Early Childhood News,* 34–42.

Wald, P., Morris, L., & Abraham, M. (1996). Three keys for successful circle time: Responding to children with diverse abilities. *Dimensions in Early Childhood, 24*(4), 26–29.

Children and Their Families

13

Culture is a group's way of living and includes shared knowledge, skills, values, expressive forms, social institutions, and ways of surviving. *Cultural knowledge* refers to learned behaviors, beliefs, and ways of relating to people and the environment (King, 2001) and is passed down through generations. What is your family's culture? Do you have family traditions or keepsakes that reflect your culture? Do you have favorite dishes or stories that have been passed down for generations? Did you go to school or play in your neighborhood with children from other cultures?

Families in the United States are increasingly culturally diverse. In 1900, one in eight Americans was from a population other than white, whereas in the year 2000, that statistic was one in four (U.S. Census Bureau, 2002).

Our nation has rich cultural diversity with regard to ethnicity, religion, gender, social class, age, ability, and sexual orientation. It is perhaps this rich cultural diversity that created and sustains the freedoms we enjoy in the United States. In other words, whenever we consider laws or policies, there are so many perspectives to be heard that no one perspective can dominate. Child care and public schools serve culturally diverse populations of young children and their families. Understanding and accepting diverse ways of living is critical if early childhood educators are to provide optimal education and care for young children.

After reading this chapter, you will understand:

▶ Stages of cultural identity.

▶ The progression of several cultures in the United States.

▶ Diverse family values.

▶ The impact of poverty on families in the United States.

▶ Issues related to parental involvement with diverse populations.

▶ The role of early childhood educators working with diverse families.

▶ Strategies for using community resources.

Diverse Family Beliefs, Attitudes, and Practices

Whereas the student population in our nation's public schools is increasingly diverse, the teaching force remains 88% white American (Marshall, 2002). With this disparity, many educators are unfamiliar with the beliefs, attitudes, and practices of many of their students. Because most educators will work with children with a cultural background different from their own, early childhood educators must become familiar with diverse family backgrounds as well as the individual families in their settings. This involves getting to know parents and understanding their cultural backgrounds and identities.

As an early childhood educator, you will be very powerful in your setting. Your expectations and everything you say and do will send a message to children about their self-worth. Often we fear what we do not understand; thus, understanding differences is critical to accepting and valuing young children and their families.

Stages of Cultural Identity

Banks (2003) suggests stages of cultural identity that explain, in part, differences among members of the same ethnic culture. His typology is dynamic rather than static, multidimensional rather than unilinear, and reflects a continuum of human identity. Although the typology is tentative, examining it will help early childhood educators fully embrace diversity (Banks, 2003):

Stage 1: Cultural Psychological Captivity. The individual holds the negative beliefs about his or her cultural group that society has institutionalized. This person is ashamed of his or her cultural group and exemplifies cultural self-rejection.

Stage 2: Cultural Encapsulation. Individuals engage in voluntary separatism by interacting only in their own cultural communities. Many believe their cultural group is superior to other cultural groups. This may describe many members of the dominant culture who are positioned as society's power brokers.

Stage 3: Cultural Identity Clarification. Positive attitudes toward the individual's cultural group characterizes this stage. Also characterized by self-acceptance, individuals are able to respond more positively to other cultural groups.

Stage 4: Biculturalism. Individuals have a healthy sense of cultural identity within their own cultural group. They also have the skills to function positively in other cultural groups.

Stage 5: Multiculturalism and Reflective Nationalism: At this stage, individuals are able to understand and appreciate several cultural groups and to function within them.

Stage 6: Globalism and Global Competency. These individuals have achieved a balance of cultural, national, and global identifications, commitment, literacy, and behaviors. They have internalized the values and rights of humankind and have the commitment and skills to act on those values. (pp. 63–64)

Individuals may experience these stages in a recursive fashion, may skip some stages, and may never reach other stages. An individual's cultural identity may be at one stage in one set of circumstances and another stage in another set of circumstances. For example, members of white groups who may have been at stage 3 or stage 4 became increasingly culturally encapsulated (stage 2) when school desegregation gained momentum (Banks, 2003) in the 1950s.

The Role of Early Childhood Educators. Your task as an early childhood educator is to understand cultural identity and the variance within and across cultural groups. As individuals, teachers must strive for the upper stages of cultural identity themselves and support young children's development toward the upper stages. This process begins with an understanding of self. You will also need to understand various cultures, their progression in our diverse nation, and the oppression many groups have experienced.

Some Cautionary Thoughts. Learning to embrace diversity is not intended to threaten anyone's way of living and being; nor is it about cultures being right or wrong. It is about understanding and accepting *difference* and extending equal *human rights* to all. Each of us is entitled to the way of living and being that is best for us. However, as early childhood educators, when we enter the workplace, we are in a public arena, one that must be accepting of all children and their families. If we are not, we devalue children and families in our care.

Second, it may be difficult for members of the cultural mainstream to read about the historical progression of nonmainstream cultures in our country. However, it is important not to take issues personally; rather, we must strengthen our resolve to become advocates for all children and their families. As early childhood educators, we have the privilege and responsibility to right the wrongs and create a better story about cultural difference.

Finally, it is tempting to lump all members of a culture together as we learn about the historical backgrounds and cultural norms of groups. As we discuss cultural norms, we must consider the great diversity within cultures and avoid stereotyping because it ignores the great individuality of group members. Before reading on, think about a culture of which you are a member (e.g., women, Catholics, gays). Now, make a list of 8–10 stereotypical traits that are used to characterize that group. How many describe you? How many do not describe you? It is unlikely that all of the traits fit you. It is helpful to use the terms *many* or *generally* when talking about group members to note that not *all* members of a group behave in a single way.

Cultural Progression in Our Diverse Nation

To understand cultural diversity among families today, it is important to understand families from an historical perspective. Following is a brief overview of the progression of some cultures in our United States. We have not begun to represent all cultures but have selected some that represent religious, sexual orientation, ability, and ethnic diversity.

European American Families

We begin with a discussion of European families because this group makes up the cultural mainstream and it is the European values against which other groups are typically judged. From the 1600s on, Europeans came to the United States in significant numbers to escape poor economic, social, religious, and political conditions. Although there were many reasons for their continued immigration to the United States, economic opportunity was the most predominant (Banks, 2003).

European immigrants were from mixed backgrounds; however, they were predominantly Anglo-Saxon-Protestant. Thus, English ways shaped the social–political

Nancy Sheehan/PhotoEdit.

institutions and became the dominant culture. It was often necessary for non-Anglo-Saxon-Protestants to deny their ethnic heritage and even Americanize their surnames in order to realize the American dream of prosperity.

Textbooks often romanticize the early European settlers and founders of the United States of America. Books recount the Puritans' quest for freedom to practice their religion and tell the story of the *Mayflower*, hardships, and survival. However, although the Puritans sought their own freedom, they were not open to others' ways of being. They believed their religion was the only right one and were intolerant of other religions.

Our European ancestors founded the United States on the ideal of *rugged individualism* and the concept of responsibility for self (McDermott, 2001). Independence and autonomy were highly valued and instilled in young children. Also embedded in the concept of rugged individualism was the importance of competition, hard work, and punctuality.

By the 1950s, the *melting pot* theory dominated. That is, ethnicity was ostensibly not important or noticed; everyone melted into the mainstream. The *white ethnic movement* changed that attitude. Led by Italians, Jews, Poles, and Greeks, the white ethnic movement highlighted and legitimized ethnic differences. Now, people no longer had to change their names to assimilate and enjoy economic prosperity (Banks, 2003).

European Americans have been the most successful cultural group with regard to gender equality. Today, gender equality has not been fully realized in either overt (e.g., salaries, promotions to top positions) or subtle ways (e.g., gender socialization of young children, equal voice in the workplace), but for decades the American cultural mainstream has been addressing this issue. For example, affirmative action protects against gender discrimination. In the American mainstream, it has become socially acceptable for married couples to share equally in parenting and home-making roles.

African-American Families

How many of you think the arrival of African-Americans in the United States coincided with the rise of slavery? That is often what we think. However, there was a settlement of African-Americans in Florida in the 16th century. More came to the United States with the first Europeans as indentured servants, free at the end of the agreed upon time. The practice of slavery came along later when it became economically desirable to have slaves rather than indentured servants (Banks, 2003).

Dominated by the English, the slave trade was lucrative in Europe, but the practice of slavery did not flourish until European settlements in the colonies were widespread. Abolitionist movements to abolish slavery date back as far as 1775 and continued into the 19th century. The Civil War ended in April, 1865; on December 6, 1865, the thirteenth amendment which abolished slavery in the United States was ratified. All African-Americans were free.

However, African-Americans continued to face challenges as southern whites still wanted them as property. This led to many discriminatory practices. For example, literacy tests and poll taxes were used to keep African-Americans from voting. By the turn of the 20th century, segregation and violence against African-Americans was rampant. To escape discrimination, many African-Americans segregated themselves by building their own towns.

Inequities including segregated schools, denial of housing and employment, and preference given to whites continued for over half of the 20th century. The tide began to turn when the Supreme Court ruled, in the landmark case of *Brown v. Board of Education*, 1954, that segregated schools were *separate and unequal*. By the 1960s, the civil rights movement was in full swing.

Today, African-Americans have made many gains in the areas of education and social–economic status. However, as a result of years of oppression, they are overrepresented in prisons and in poverty living conditions. The cultural values of many African-American families today include high-achievement orientation, strong work orientation, strong kinship bonds, adaptability of family roles, and a religious orientation (Murphy, 2003).

Jim Cummins/Taxi/Getty Images.

Asian-American Families

Asian-Americans, as a group, are very diverse because Asians have immigrated from many different countries, including China, Japan, Vietnam, Korea, and India. Thus, as a group they have great diversity in their ways of living. However, Asians have had some common experiences. First, they left their homes primarily for economic reasons and, second, they encountered racism when they arrived in the United States.

The first Chinese immigrants were men who came to the United States in the 1850s with the promise of gold. It was difficult for many of them to leave their homes because their traditional Confucian teachings taught that young men must value their families over all else and never leave them. However, economic hardships and the prospect of gold drew many young men to the United States (Banks, 2003). Because their dress, skin color, facial features, hair styles, and religious practices were so different from those of Americans, Chinese immigrants encountered hostility and racial prejudice. Many Asians responded to racism by creating their own communities, hence giving rise to Chinatowns and Little Tokyos. Today, many Asian-Americans still live in those settlements.

Japanese immigrants came to United States in the late 1800s to escape overpopulation, depressed farming conditions, and political turmoil (Banks, 2003). Most were men who hoped to earn money and return to Japan. However, most ended up staying in the United States. Some married Japanese *picture brides* who joined them in the United States (Banks 2003). This practice was an arranged marriage where the man saw only a picture of his bride before she joined him in the United States.

When the Japanese bombed Pearl Harbor in December 1941, many Americans feared that Japanese-Americans would be loyal to their mother country. President F. D. Roosevelt authorized the secretary of war to create internment camps where Japanese-Americans were taken to live. Conditions there were abysmal.

Asian-Americans have often been referred to as the *model minority*, a term that is problematic in a couple of ways. First, the term refers to the economic, occupational, and educational success of many Asians today. However, many Asians have historically worked and continue to work long hours for low wages. Second, dubbing them the model minority marginalizes the accomplishments of other ethnic groups (Banks, 2003).

Although it is important to be cautious about making generalizations given the great diversity among Asian-Americans, some common elements can be noted.

In general, many Asian-American families are collectivist (Chapter 8) and place the importance of family above all else. This includes extended family as well. They have a strong work ethic, and *face* (dignity) is very important (McDermott, 2001).

Biracial Multiethnic Families

A family is considered biracial or multiethnic if the parents have different racial or ethnic backgrounds or are themselves biracial or multiethnic. Owing to historically strict social norms regarding marrying outside of one's race or ethnicity, biracial and multiethnic families are a relatively new phenomenon. Historically, when biracial, multiethnic babies were born in the United States, they were considered members of the less dominant race or group. For example, a child born to a black parent and a white parent was considered black. Many biracial and multiethnic children have found it difficult to identify with either cultural group.

As a result of broader social acceptance of marriage among members of different races and ethnicities, the number of biracial, multiethnic babies born since the 1970s has increased 260% compared to a 15% increase in single-race babies (Wardle, 2001). Yet, they still cannot be placed within a traditional racial or ethnic category.

Many psychologists believe that helping young biracial and multiethnic children to identify with both parents at an early age will diminish identity problems for children as they grow older. Early childhood educators must be sure that these children are represented in books and materials in their settings and that they too have an identity label, biracial or multiethnic.

Jeff Greenberg/The Image Works.

Gay and Lesbian Families

Scientists believe that homosexuality is a trait, a characteristic that cannot be changed. Studies estimate that 10% of men and 8% of women are exclusively homosexual (Swall & Swall, 2001). Historically, homosexuals kept their identity quiet for fear of discrimination and violence; this is often referred to as *being in the closet*. With the impact of the civil rights movement, however, gays and lesbians are becoming increasingly visible, *coming out* of the closet.

As parents have children, they expect them to grow up to be heterosexual. Some go as far as to talk about "when you get married" or their future "grandchildren." It is these expectations that shape, in part, the experiences of young children growing up.

Gay and lesbian children may be realizing their difference at a young age and these expectations can be very confusing (Swall & Swall, 2001). As an educator or caregiver, it is important that you do not make assumptions about what children will aspire to do.

Many gays and lesbians choose to have children and live as a family. It is important to understand that in most ways, gay and lesbian families are no different than other families. They encounter the same child raising issues as heterosexual families and have many of the same needs for support and encouragement. They have additional challenges because of a general social prejudice against them. Early childhood educators are in a good position to support and encourage all families, including those that are gay or lesbian.

Tomas Van Houtryve/Corbis Images.

Hispanic American Families

Hispanic Americans immigrated to the United States from many countries, including Mexico, Puerto Rico, and Cuba. Although all Hispanic Americans have Spanish influence in their history, they are a diverse group with different historical, racial, and cultural backgrounds. Mexican Americans comprise the largest group of Hispanic Americans (Banks, 2003).

In the early 19th century, Mexico owned what is now the state of Texas. Concerned over the declining population in Texas, the Mexican government offered land grants to encourage Anglos to settle and take advantage of the rich resources in Texas. This set the stage for the Mexican–American War and the United States taking possession of the Texas territory.

Because so many Americans moved to California during the gold rush in the 1850s, Mexicans were soon outnumbered in the Southwest. They found themselves under Anglo domination. Historically, Mexicans have provided inexpensive labor on the railroads, in the fields, and in the mines.

Myrleen Ferguson Cate/PhotoEdit.

During the civil rights movement of the 1960s, Mexican Americans made many educational and economic gains. A middle-class group of Hispanic Americans emerged, working in the professions and business. The 1980s became known as the *decade of the Hispanic* with a national emphasis on educational and economic development of Hispanic communities. Mexican Americans were given political appointments. At the same time, undocumented immigrants continued to flow into the United States, primarily from Mexico. This triggered nativism (denying immigration so immigrants do not outnumber native born citizens) and racism over an increasing influx of immigrants, many of whom were undocumented Mexican immigrants. The passage of the Immigration Reform and Control Act of 1986, designed to control the flow of undocumented immigrants, prompted some anti-Hispanic sentiment and English-only movements (Banks, 2003). The English-only movement continues today in many states.

Today, a rapidly growing Mexican American population is concentrated in the West and Southwest. The rapid growth is due to a greater birth rate among Mexican Americans and continued immigration from Mexico (Banks, 2003). Many Hispanic American families are collectivist in orientation, placing the good of the group over the good of the individual. Many place high value on family, including extended family. Many families are patriarchal; women raise children and men earn a living. Male elders are highly respected and younger family members defer to them. The primary religion is Catholic, which encourages male dominance and large families (McDermott, 2001).

Jewish American Families

Historically, Jews have made great contributions to our American culture in the areas of education, law, science, medicine, etc. However, they have a history of overcoming great persecution. Driven from Palestine by the ancient Romans, Jews settled in Spain and lived happily until the 13th century when Catholics began brutally forcing them into Catholicism. Many complied but secretly held on to their Jewish beliefs.

When the monarchy expelled Jews from Spain, many came with Columbus to America. Ironically, Jews participated in the American Revolution yet were not given complete religious freedom. For example, as states formed, some states limited candidacy for office to Christians or even just Protestants. It was not until the passing of the 14th amendment in 1868 that religious equality was guaranteed in the states.

Although government policies mandated equality, anti-Semitism flourished during the late 19th and early 20th century. Jews were denied access to social clubs or residential areas and at times denied the opportunity to purchase insurance. Concurrently, many Jews were rising out of the working class to become more affluent. Many were moving into the suburbs and forming Jewish congregations to preserve their Jewish heritage.

Also during the late 19th and early 20th centuries, there was increased anti-Jewish legislation in Europe, which prompted more Jewish immigration to the United States (Banks, 2003). In the early 20th century, the U.S. government placed restrictions on immigration that prevented many Jews from entering our country. As World War II broke out in Europe, anti-Semitism flourished under the German Nazi rule. Because immigration remained restricted in the United States, some ships carrying Jews from Germany were denied entrance to the United States. Six million Jews were killed under Nazi rule (Banks, 2003).

Today, American Jews constitute the largest Jewish community in the world (Banks, 2003). Recently, many Jews have been very active in the civil rights movement, perhaps a proactive reaction to anti-Semitism. Although anti-Semitism has not been completely obliterated, many Jews hold esteemed social and political positions. Although there is great diversity among Jews, as a group they tend to be ideologically liberal.

Native American Families

We often refer to Columbus' discovery of America, yet America has been inhabited by indigenous people for about 40,000 years. Native Americans lived in established communities and civilizations. Although we often depict them in the stereotypical feathered headdress, living in tepees, Native Americans of long ago had very diverse ways of living. Some were farmers, others hunted buffalo for food and clothing, while still others fished for a living.

Lawrence Migdale/Pix Photography.

Although there is great diversity among Native Americans, there are some common values. For example, historically, positions of leadership were earned when talented warriors, medicine men, and spiritual leaders were recognized and respected. Most Native Americans believed in a spiritual world that includes all living things. Through their culture, they learned respect for the earth and living things. Many Native Americans hold these values today.

The Native Americans' respect for the earth was inconsistent with the values of the Europeans who settled in America 400 years ago. Native Americans saw the land as something for everyone to enjoy, respect, and live on, whereas the Europeans wanted to divide it, each owning his own portion (Banks, 2003). Policy makers imposed the European lifestyle by breaking up tribal lands and giving families individual plots, another violation of their tradition. Inconsistencies and intolerance were apparent when Europeans sent Native American youth to boarding schools as a means of assimilating them into the cultural mainstream (Chapter 2). The ramifications of this marginalization are still felt today by many Native Americans.

Today, Native American families are generally collectivist. Many families emphasize interdependent relations and the well-being of the group (Trumbull, Rothstein-Fisch, Greenfield, & Quiroz, 2001). Extended family is very important; in fact, at some level, the entire tribe is considered to be family. All members of a Native American community look out for children (McDermott, 2001). Great respect is shown to elders, and it is common for young children and youth to defer to them. Respect is shown by looking downward, not making eye contact with the elder.

Many Native Americans are noncompetitive and nonmaterialistic, a value that is often interpreted as laziness (McDermott, 2001). Sharing rather than coveting is the norm for Native Americans. Other traditional values still held by many Native Americans today are cooperation, harmony with nature, noninterference, loyalty, and a present rather than future time orientation (McDermott, 2001).

Parents with Disabilities

Historically, parents with disabilities faced barriers as participants in the care and education for their young children. Barriers were both physical and attitudinal (Strong, 1999). Since the civil rights movement and, more recently, the Americans with Disabilities Act (ADA) in 1992 (Chapter 2), many of the physical barriers have come down. The ADA provided protection for persons with disabilities in both private and public settings. Because people may be uncomfortable with those who are different, many attitudinal barriers remain.

Sometimes persons with disabilities are viewed as inferior and are stereotyped as less abled rather than differently abled. On the contrary, parents with disabilities usually lead independent, productive lives. They do not dwell on their disability; it is just one aspect of who they are. With adaptive equipment and other accommodations, parents with disabilities can care for their children just as parents without disabilities do (Strong, 1999). There is little difference between parents with disabilities and parents without disabilities with regard to what they want for their children.

Citizens in the United States enjoy many freedoms; we have many choices. The diverse nature of U.S. society has nurtured freedom and choice. Over the past centuries, many groups have come forward seeking the same opportunities, rights, and freedoms that the cultural mainstream enjoys. Their persistence has in turn led to policy and law mandating equal rights and opportunity. It is, in part, because of diversity in the United States that we are free.

Children of Divorce and Blended Families

In 2002, 38% per year, per capita marriages ended in divorce (http://www.divorcereform.org/rates.html); many of those divorcing families have young children. Although this percentage is on a slight decline, many children are, nonetheless, experiencing divorce; they often become members of new blended families. As parents divorce and families reconfigure, young children will undoubtedly experience some stress as they adjust, even in the best of situations.

As a teacher or caregiver, you can play a very helpful role in situations of divorce and blended families. First and foremost, the child must be helped to feel safe in the school or center setting. Acknowledge and address the child's needs, provide predictable routines, and provide engaging, meaningful activities. Furthermore, you can connect the families to mental health resources if necessary, whether it is school counselors or community agencies. Be sure you involve custodial, noncustodial, and stepparents in conferences and keep them all informed of the child's progress and forthcoming events at the center or school.

Role of Early Childhood Educators. As a future early childhood educator, it is your responsibility to understand and embrace difference and to value the human rights of all children equally. This historical overview was intended to help you understand the history of groups living in our nation today whose children are in early care and education. Where did people live before they came to the United States? Why did they come to this country? What happened when they got here?

It is equally important to understand and accept the individuals in your early childhood setting as they are today. This is best done through careful observation of young children and regular and frequent communication with their parents. For example, some children will prefer using communal materials. Others will seldom look you in the eye. It is vital that we look beyond our own cultural heritage to understand others.

⟩ Families Living in Poverty

Many families in the United States live in the culture of poverty, defined in 2001 as a family of four living on an annual income of $18,104 or less (Payne, 2003). Poverty is sometimes situational, caused by circumstances such as illness or divorce; in other cases, it is generational, a family pattern perpetuated from generation to generation. The *Focus on Diversity* provides some important information about families with young children living in poverty.

This section addresses some of the challenges facing families living in poverty. Also examined is the role of early childhood educators who work with families living in poverty.

©AP/Wide World Photos.

Poverty and Resources

Payne (2003) suggests a working definition of poverty as *the extent to which an individual does without resources.* Although the need for financial resources cannot be minimized, resources needed to live happily, productively, and to secure psychological and physical safety go far beyond financial resources. Many families lack some of the following resources (Payne, 2003):

▶ *Financial.* Having the money to purchase goods and services.

▶ *Emotional.* Having stamina, perseverance, and the ability to make good choices that are not self-destructive.

▶ *Mental.* Having the mental skills to get a job and to deal with daily living.

▶ *Support Systems.* Having family and friends who can assist in the time of need, whether it is providing child care, a temporary home, advice, solace, or financial resources.

▶ *Spiritual.* Those who adhere to belief in a higher power find support through their belief in divine purpose and guidance.

▶ *Physical.* Having a body that enables one to be productive. Most persons with disabilities are productive.

Focus on Diversity

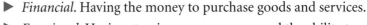

Children in Poverty

Poverty is a serious problem in the United States, particularly for young children who are in their formative years. Did you know:

- In 2001, the poverty rate for the entire U.S. population was 11.7%, while 18.2% of children under 6 lived in poverty.
- The percentage of families living in poverty is increasing.
- Immigrant children are twice as likely to be poor as are native born children.
- Poor children are much more likely than their more affluent counterparts to suffer developmental delays, eventually drop out of school, or give birth during the teen years.
- Children under 6 are particularly vulnerable to poverty.
- Children living with a single mother are five times more likely to live in poverty than children living with married-couple parents.
- The child poverty rate in the United States is substantially higher than in most other Western industrialized nations.

Source: Adapted from Payne, R. K. (2003). *A framework for understanding poverty* (3rd revised ed.). Highlands, TX.

▶ *Role Models.* Having positive role models so the behaviors of productivity can be learned.

▶ *Knowledge of Hidden Rules.* All groups have hidden rules, and when one is unaware of them, they cue others that they do not fit. These rules relate to dress, verbal and nonverbal communication, decorum, etc. (pp. 16–18)

Poverty and Language

All languages have various registers. For example, the *intimate register* occurs between lovers or twins, while the *casual register* occurs among friends (Payne, 2003). The *formal register* is that language needed to secure a well-paying job. It is, in fact, the particular vocabulary, grammar, and syntax of the middle class. Knowledge and use of the formal register allows one to score well on tests, particularly those that lead to entrance into college (Payne, 2003). Most well-paying jobs require the use of the formal register; yet if parents do not have opportunities to interact with someone who uses that register, they are disadvantaged on the job market.

The Role of Early Childhood Educators

Early childhood educators are in a prime position to support and assist families living in poverty. Following are some considerations for you if you are working with children in families living in poverty.

Appropriate Curriculum. Young children living in poverty have not had the same experiences in the early years as those from more affluent families. When they come to school, their language and other skills may be immature. Thus, there is a tendency to overuse explicit instruction in an attempt to catch them up. However, young children, whether poor or affluent, generally learn in the same way. Multisensory, concrete, culturally relevant, interesting, language-rich activities are needed to support growth and development.

Technology. Some children living in poverty do not have access to technology. Even if it is available in libraries, their parents may not have the resources to get them there or know themselves how to use it if they did. Young children living in poverty need access to and support for using technology in developmentally appropriate ways. For example, recall from Chapter 11 that using talking books has the potential to lessen the gap in literacy development between poor children and their more affluent counterparts.

Advocating for the Child

In May 2003, President G. W. Bush signed a Child Tax Credit bill that raised the per-child tax credit from $600 to $1000. The ceiling for eligible families was raised from a family income of $110,000 to include those whose annual income is $200,000. This credit extends no assistance to families whose incomes are low enough that they do not have income tax liability but pay payroll and other taxes.

A $1.6 trillion tax cut over 10 years affects families in the following ways:

• Families with annual incomes over $373,000 (top 1%) receive 45% of the benefits.

• Families with annual incomes over $147,000 (top 5%) receive 52% of the benefits.

• Families with annual incomes below $44,000 (bottom 60%) receive 28.4% of the benefits.

• Families with annual incomes below $15,000 (bottom 20%) receive 0.8% of the benefits.

The Children's Defense Fund (2001) proposed that with the same $1.6 trillion tax cut, we could close the poverty gap by investing in goods and services children need to be happy and healthy, and have billions of dollars left over.

Health Care. Alert parents to health needs of their children and assist them if necessary to obtain health care. Secure the resources to provide nutritional snacks and meals. For example, nutrition programs are available if you work in a Head Start or Title I school (a school with a large number of children living in poverty).

Do Not Be Judgmental. There may be a tendency to label parents living in poverty as noncaring parents. However, it is a rare parent who does not care about his/her children. Rather, they may be consumed with the stress of poverty or single parenthood, or be working extra hours to meet the family's financial needs. If English is not the first language of the family, they may be missing information about their children's needs or be unable to help with homework assignments.

Be an Advocate. Be a social and political advocate for families living in poverty. This might take the form of giving time to a homeless shelter or educating policy makers. For example, the federal government proposed and implemented tax cuts in the interest of boosting the sagging economy of the early 21st century. The *Advocating for the Child* highlights the problems of this action relative to families living in poverty.

Involving Parents from Diverse Populations

Involving parents in their children's care and education has a positive impact on achievement (Eldridge, 2001; Henderson & Berla, 1994; Marcon, 1993). Yet, issues such as poverty, ethnicity, family structure, family stressors, parenting styles, family language, and parental education influence parents' abilities to be involved in their children's education.

How involved in your school experiences were your parents? Do you think their involvement or lack of involvement related to their level of comfort in being at school, helping with homework, and so on? Recall from Chapter 8 some of the general differences in family styles and parental expectations. For example, some parents place higher value on independence and personal achievement whereas others highly value an individual's contributions to the group. Some parents feel they are out of bounds in their role as a parent if they teach their children at home. Others feel they lack the education to teach their children properly. Some parents feel praise singles a child out and prefer the normative effect of focusing on areas in which the child can improve. Yet, other parents are eager to hear about their child's accomplishments.

Involving parents productively in their children's care and education requires early childhood educators to maintain meaningful connections with families. Research suggests the following guidelines:

> *Serve Families, Not Just Children.* The impact on families as well as information from or involvement of family members must be considered when policies and practices are implemented (Powell, 1998).

> *Align Practices with Families.* Methods of working with families must be shaped by their needs (Powell, 1998).

> *Parent and Teacher Confidence.* Many opportunities must exist for parents and educators to get to know each other. Parents must feel confident that teachers and caregivers are skilled, knowledgeable, and caring. Educator training should focus on taking perspectives of all families in the setting (Powell, 1998).

> *Communication.* Early childhood educators must continually refine their communication skills (Swick, 2003). Communication must be frequent, personal, and consistent. If the educator and parents do not speak the same language, interpreters must be utilized (Powell, 1998).

Parents Are People. Programs must find ways to address a range of parental interests (Powell, 1998). A positive attitude about the needs and strengths of all families must be maintained (Swick, 2003).

Parental Roles. Parents need a clear understanding of the role they play in their children's education. Cultural values must be embraced as parents have beliefs about the appropriateness of parental involvement in their children's education (Powell, 1998).

Parents as Partners. Engage parents as partners with a variety of family-friendly strategies that encourage active and meaningful partnerships (Swick, 2003).

Parent Perspectives in Program Quality Assessments. When programs are assessed for quality, parent perspectives and parent–staff relations must be considered (Powell, 1998).

Places for Parents. Maintain places in the setting that are especially designed to meet the needs of parents and families and encourage their participation (Swick, 2003). This might include a library of parenting books (in needed languages if possible), a library of children's books (in needed languages if possible), bus schedules, and community events for young children.

Multicultural Learning. Engage families and staff in multicultural learning (Swick, 2003). For example, invite parents to talk about a cultural practice or artifact. Read about the histories of cultures.

Professional Development. Early childhood educators need special training in working with parents in a diverse society. State licensure and certification must emphasize working with parents (Powell, 1998; Swick, 2003).

Types of Parental Involvement

When early childhood educators involve parents in their children's care and education, they must consider the influence of parents' cultures, time, skills, and dispositions. Epstein (1995) identified six types of parental involvement—*parenting, communicating, volunteering, learning at home, decision making, collaborating with community*—and redefined each to embrace multiple parent perspectives.

Parenting. Parenting refers to helping families establish home environments to support their children's learning. To do this *all* parents must be able to receive information, not just those who can attend a meeting or event. Redefined, *parenting* means that information is available in a variety of forms (e.g., read, viewed) and can be accessed at anytime and in anyplace (Epstein, 1995).

Communicating. Communication serves the purpose of learning about the home culture, sharing information about the early childhood program and policies, understanding the parents' perspectives, and discussing how the child is growing and developing. Communication takes many forms including notes, phone calls, meetings, sharing of artifacts and cultural experiences, and so on.

Communication is redefined as recursive. That is, communication is two-, three-, and four-way among parents, educators, children, and the community. Interpreters are used if needed (Selden, 1991). Home visits are implemented so early childhood educators can become better acquainted with families and visit them in their familiar environment. If parents seem uncomfortable with home visits or with coming to the early childhood setting, a neutral place should be identified (Epstein, 1995).

Don Smetzer/PhotoEdit.

©Ellen B. Senisi.

Richard Hutchings/PhotoEdit.

Volunteering. Historically, parents have volunteered to help with activities in the early childhood setting. This was particularly prominent when fewer mothers were working outside of the home. Volunteering has been redefined to include anyone who does anything to support the activities in the school or center. The new definition also values the diversity of knowledge, skills, and talents parents have and provides ways for them to share what they have to offer (Epstein, 1995).

Learning at Home. Learning at home historically encompasses involving families in supervising homework, even with young children (primary grades). This has been redefined to include interactive activities within the home or community. It may include parents encouraging, listening, or discussing, not just teaching at home (Epstein, 1995). Learning at home activities acknowledge parents' skills and comfort levels with learning activities.

Decision Making. Involving parents in decision making at the school, district, and state levels has been redefined to mean a partnership aimed at shared goals, not merely arguing opposing ideas (Epstein, 1995). It should include parents from diverse backgrounds. All parents should have a way to provide input and receive information.

Collaborating with the Community. Incorporation of community resources strengthens programs and family practices. Information on community health, cultural, recreational, and social resources should be available. Community is redefined to mean all who are affected by the quality of education. All neighborhoods that influence the quality of learning and support the education and care of young children are included (Epstein, 1995).

Barriers to Parent Involvement

High-quality early childhood educators are careful not to assume all parents have the same interests, abilities, and resources for becoming involved in their children's care and education; this assumption creates barriers to parent involvement. There is no *one size fits all* strategy for involving parents. Rather, there are many ways parents can become involved. Considerations related to parent involvement must address parents' concerns and resources related to time, money, and parents' literacy, home language, and lifestyles.

Consider, for example, a mothers' luncheon hosted by the center or school. (You have decided to hold a different event for fathers.) Mothers will pay a small fee to come to the luncheon and a brief program. On the surface, this sounds like a great way to get parents and others involved in school. However, it is critical to consider the following barriers: (Kieff & Wellhousen, 2000)

▶ There is no mother in the home.

▶ The mother does not speak English.

▶ The mother does not eat the type of food being served.

▶ The family has recently immigrated and the mother is uncomfortable in the school culture.

▶ The mother cannot read the invitation that the child brought home.

- ▶ The family cannot afford the small fee to attend the luncheon.
- ▶ The mother has no transportation.
- ▶ There is no one to care for younger siblings in the mother's absence.
- ▶ The mother has disabilities that make it difficult for her to go out.
- ▶ The mother cannot leave work at the scheduled time.

It is likely that the list could go on, but it highlights some of the many barriers to parent involvement at school. Thus, it is critical that early childhood educators consider other ways to involve parents. Furthermore, by carefully analyzing the concerns and resources of parents in the particular early childhood setting, educators can address barriers. Returning to our example, following are some modifications to the event that would support parent attendance.

- ▶ Specify *guest* rather than *mother*.
- ▶ Use interpreters as needed.
- ▶ Provide telecommunication devices, Braille, etc., as needed (Strong, 1999).
- ▶ Extend the invitation via the phone rather than in printed material.
- ▶ Have a potluck or serve a buffet with various dishes.
- ▶ Get a business partner to financially sponsor the event.
- ▶ Provide child care and transportation.
- ▶ Hold events at various times to accommodate various schedules (Kieff & Wellhousen, 2000).

Communicating with Difficult Parents.   Anytime you communicate with parents, it is critical that you do as much listening as talking. Parents have valuable information about their children's strengths, talents, interests, and challenges. This is information that will assist you in working effectively with young children. Sometimes, however, communication becomes difficult when parents are confrontational or argumentative. Following are some guidelines for communicating with a parent in a difficult situation. They should be implemented in the order listed:

Bob Daemmrich/The Image Works.

1. Remain calm and professional.
2. Do not become defensive or engage in a heated argument.
3. Use active listening (Chapter 8) so the parent feels his/her concerns have been heard.
4. Offer to reschedule the conference at a better time.
5. Enlist the assistance of a mediator if necessary.

The *Window into the Classroom* feature on p. 291 highlights a case study of a kindergarten classroom that is inclusive of many family lifestyles.

Antibias Environment

Many children's books are available that depict and describe the lives of various types of families. Including these books in your early childhood setting will teach young children about families' different ways of living and being. It will also help young children see themselves as a valued member of the group. Table 13.1 lists a few children's books that depict diversity among families. These books can be added to the other aspects of the antibias learning environment discussed in previous chapters.

Table 13.1   Books about Different Kinds of Families

Title	Description	Theme
Fly Away Home by E. Bunting	This homeless father and his son live in the airport.	Single father, poverty
Families Are Different by Nina Pellegrini	Two Korean girls are adopted by parents of European descent in the United States.	Adoption
Adoption Day by J. McCutcheon	These happy parents fly to another country to adopt their children.	Adoption
Daddy Makes the Best Spaghetti by A. Grossnickle	Daddy and Cory enjoy making dinner together.	Nontraditional family roles
Just Plain Fancy by Patricia Polacco	Naomi worries that her peacock is too fancy to be Amish.	Amish values and traditions
Dim Sum for Everyone by Grace Lin	Jie-Jie and Mei-Mei go with their family to a dim sum restaurant.	Chinese culture
Families by Ann Morris	This book depicts all kinds of families.	Many cultures
The Trees of the Dancing Goats by Patricia Polacco	This is a warm story of kindness shared between a Jewish family and a Christian family.	Religious difference
Dinosaurs Divorce: A Guide for Changing Families by Krasny Brown and Marc Brown	This book invites young children to express their feelings about and reactions to divorce.	Divorce
Heather Has Two Mommies By L. Newman	Heather lives with her two mommies in a house with a big apple tree in the yard.	Gay families

Family Literacy

Literacy learning is the cornerstone of early childhood education, and we know that parent involvement is critical to children's literacy learning. As early childhood professionals, it is important that we incorporate the many literacy skills of parents in our classrooms. It is unfortunate, however, that nonmainstream parents are sometimes viewed as unable or unwilling to support their children's literacy learning. On the contrary, many culturally and linguistically diverse parents see literacy acquisition as their children's hope for growing into productive citizens (Nieto, 2002), and they want to support their children's literacy development.

The *Theory into Practice* feature suggests some guidelines for family literacy initiatives.

Using Community Resources

Captured in the proverb, *It takes a village to raise a child*, communities have some responsibility for the care and education of the children within it. Moreover, communities are a rich resource for early childhood centers and schools. In fact, the

Window into the Classroom

When Alice took a position as a kindergarten teacher in an urban school with a culturally diverse student population, she vowed to make *meeting the needs of all children and families in her classroom* a priority. In conversations with teachers experienced with culturally diverse populations, she was dismayed to see many negative attitudes. Alice knew that if she were to be successful, she would have to learn a lot about individual families. Alice did just that.

In her fourth year, Alice's full-day kindergarten program had 18 young children including 9 European Americans, 1 Asian-American, 3 Mexican Americans, 4 African-Americans, and 1 mixed race child. Four of the children were living in single or stepparent families and one had a mother who was deaf. Two families were native Spanish speakers; one was bilingual. One family was Jewish, one was Buddhist, one was atheist, and the others were Christian. Most families were low- or low-middle socioeconomic status.

Alice began her year by making home visits to get acquainted with the families and the children in her class. During home visits, Alice interacted with each child and learned a lot about their interests, temperaments, and developing skills. Parents were also a focus of the home visit. By talking with them, she gained insights about what they wanted for their children and their expectations for her as a teacher. She also asked the parents about their preferred means of communication with her (e.g., email, phone).

Alice decided to have both public and private communication with parents. Because all but two families had access to a computer, at home, the library, or at work, she developed a website to communicate information about what the children were doing in class, upcoming events, and school and community resources for parents. The site included a discussion board where parents posed questions and comments and others responded. For private communication, Alice used email or the phone, depending on parental preference. For example, email was the best way to communicate with the deaf mother, and phone, with the assistance of a translator worked to communicate with a Spanish-speaking family.

Alice strived to acknowledge different family values in her classroom. For example, when children were working on individual projects (e.g., writing a story, completing an art project), they could choose to sit at a table with others and share materials, or work more independently at their individual desks. There were other times during the day, cleanup for example, that she permitted children to work together or independently.

Alice was very flexible when she gave the children activities to do at home. She knew that some parents did the activities with their children whereas others, for one reason or another, did not. Alice encouraged parents who did not do homework with their child to listen to their child tell about the day's events at school and the homework activity.

Alice created a warm and welcoming atmosphere in her program. Her walls and bulletin boards reflected the cultural diversity of the classroom, community, and nation. Children learned about a variety of religions along with other social studies content. She made parents feel comfortable talking with her and welcomed divorced parents to participate equally in school events and activities.

---

community should become an extension of the early childhood program. Young children benefit when the community becomes involved. Following are some ways that a community can support the care and education of its young children.

Family Friendliness

Employers' rules, regulations, and policies affect the lives of families they employ. Employers must acknowledge the importance of parental involvement in young children's care and education and establish a family-friendly atmosphere. That is, needs of the workplace must balance with the needs of employees and their families. Needs might include maternity and paternity leave, time during the day to visit the center or school, starting and ending the work day to fit with family schedules, job sharing, sick leave to care for ill children, and so on. Employers consider the needs of both men and women in their employ and look for ways to provide these benefits.

Picture Partners/Alamy Images.

Theory into Practice

Family Literacy Initiatives

- Do not take the deficit perspective; recognize the rich language skills of parents who may not be native English speakers.
- Reflect on your expectations for the involvement of all parents in your early childhood setting in ways that are comfortable for them. Recognize that not all parents are able to come to school events or feel comfortable at school.
- Through interviews, conversations, and home visits, learn about the literacy backgrounds of the families in your setting.
- To help young children identify with the story, provide culturally and linguistically relevant reading material and language activities in your classroom and for use at home. For example, some books are made available in other languages, yet reflect the values and lifestyles of the mainstream.
- Value the family's home language by sending home books and notes in that language.
- Value and encourage storytelling, dialogue, and language play, particularly for parents who are not proficient readers and writers.
- Provide ways for parents to help their children with special needs develop literacy.
- Envision literacy as a means of empowering families; build a community of learners through parent events.
- Help parents see the value of the many literacy activities in which they engage daily.

Source: Ordonez-Jasis, R., & Ortiz, R. W. (2006). Reading their words; Working with diverse families to enhance children's early literacy development. *Young Children, 61*(1), 42–47.

Resources

Community businesses and service organizations are great resources for early childhood educators and worthy partners in the care and education of young children. They can provide materials and financial support for projects. The benefit is reciprocal when the business receives advertising because their involvement is reported in the newspaper or appears on a program or brochure. Furthermore, most communities have organizations that engage in various philanthropic projects. Your local chamber of commerce or information center can provide a list of potential partners.

Michael Newman/PhotoEdit.

Invited Guests

Tapping into cultural resources begins with the parents and family members of young children in your setting. Many family members are willing and able to share something from their culture with young children (e.g., a favorite story, recipe, tradition). Furthermore, communities are culture-rich; even in the most homogeneous communities, diversity exists. Many groups are willing to provide a knowledgeable person to talk with young children about their culture. This might include various churches, cultural centers, historical centers, nature centers, zoos, an aquarium, dance studio, etc. Immigrants or descendants of immigrants can share their home culture.

 My Developing Professional View

> What are some key issues you will consider when you involve families in their children's education?

SUMMARY

Culture is knowledge, skills, values, expressive forms, social institutions, and ways of surviving that are shared among members of a group; the United States is made up of many different cultures. Native Americans and some African-Americans preceded the settlement of Europeans in the United States. Immigration from all continents as well as differences in ability, religion, and sexual orientation have created a rich and diverse society in the United States.

Although some came for religious freedom, most immigrants, including the early settlers, came to the United States for economic opportunity. Anglo-Saxon-Protestant is the largest group of immigrants and, thus, the group whose values have shaped the cultural mainstream of the United States. It is the group against which all others are measured. Cultures that are different than the mainstream have historically been victims of racism and discrimination.

Poverty is a culture that continues to threaten the healthy growth and development of approximately 18% of children under the age of 6. Early childhood educators must be cautious that they do not stereotype children of poverty and assume their parents do not care about them. Furthermore, early childhood educators must understand the lived experiences of children of poverty, provide needed support and resources to their families, and advocate on their behalf. Children of poverty need developmentally appropriate care and education and rich learning experiences.

Parental involvement in the care and education of their children supports achievement and healthy growth and development. Early childhood educators must find ways to involve parents that are appropriate for individual families. Furthermore, businesses and other agencies within the community are a rich resource for early childhood educators. Their potential as partners should be explored.

ENRICHMENT ACTIVITIES

Individual Activities

1. Reflect on your own culture. Identify a book, tradition, practice, or belief that is very important to you. Write a reflective paper about how you would feel if: (1) your book, tradition, practice, or belief was in the minority; (2) you were

asked to give up the book, tradition, practice, or belief; (3) you were told you can retain the book, tradition, practice, or belief as long as you don't tell anyone about it or share it with anyone.

2. Interview a parent from a culture other than your own whose young child is attending an early childhood program. Identify the parent's expectation for his/her child's teacher or caregiver. Identify the perception of the teacher or caregiver of the parents' role in their children's education. Write a brief overview of your findings.

3. Access the online professional development resources listed on the next page. Pay particular attention to resources and advice for teachers and parents in a diverse society. Write a brief overview of your findings.

4. Access a database of children's books. Identify books about families to add to the brief list found on Table 13.1. Be certain to evaluate them for antibias characteristics using the guidelines on page 290.

Cooperative Activity

5. It is important to understand the cultural knowledge of families with whom you will work in early childhood settings. This chapter has provided you with a brief overview of some cultures. To enrich your understanding, each member of your cooperative group will select a culture to learn more about and share the findings with the group. You may choose cultures discussed in this chapter or another culture. You may focus on ethnicity, religion, ability, class, age, gender, or sexual orientation. Remember to be cautious about stereotyping a culture; use the terms *generally* or *many* to avoid implying that all members of the culture have identical values, attitudes, and beliefs.

Advocacy Activity

6. Volunteer to read stories to young children at a homeless shelter. Pay particular attention to the types of stories that engage their attention so you can select interesting, culturally relevant books. You can also assist those homeless children who are in school with their homework.

⟨ FOR FURTHER READING

Understanding Families

Brickmayer, J., Cohen, J., Jensen, I. D., & Variano, D. A. (2005). Kyle lives with his granny—Where are his mommy and daddy?: Supporting grandparents who raise grandchildren. *Young Children, 60*(3), 100–104.

Joshi, A. (2005). Understanding Asian Indian families: Facilitating meaningful home–school relations. *Young Children, 60*(3), 75–79.

Murphy, J. C. (2003). Case studies in African American school success and parenting behaviors. *Young Children, 58*(6), 85–89.

Ordonez-Jasis, R., & Ortiz, R. W. (2006). Reading their words; working with diverse families to enhance children's early literacy development. *Young Children, 61*(1), 42–47.

Regan, R. (2005). *Non-Western educational traditions: Indigenous approaches to educational thought and practice (3rd ed.).* Mahwah, NJ: Lawrence Erlbaum Associates.

Strong, M. F. (1999). Serving mothers with disabilities in early childhood programs. *Young Children, 54*(3), 10–17.

Wardle, F. (2001). Viewpoint: Supporting multiracial and multiethnic children and their families. *Young Children, 56*(6), 38–39.

Parent Involvement

Eldridge, D. (2001). Parent involvement: It's worth the effort. *Young Children, 56*(4), 65–69.

Epstein, J. (1995). Schools, family, community partnerships: Caring for the children we share. *Phi Delta Kappan, 77*(9), 701–712.

Kieff, J., & Wellhousen K. (2000). Planning family involvement in early childhood programs. *Young Children, 55*(3), 18–25.

Trumbull, E., Rothstein-Fisch, C., Greenfield, P. M., & Quiroz, B. (2001). *Bridging cultures between home and school: A guide for teachers.* Mahwah, NJ: Lawrence Erlbaum Associates.

Professional Development Resources

PROJECT HOPE: VIRGINIA EDUCATION FOR HOMELESS CHILDREN AND YOUTH PROGRAM

College of William and Mary
School of Education
PO Box 8795
Williamsburg, VA 23187-8795
http://www.wm.edu/hope/homeless.php

MEGA SKILLS ONLINE EDUCATION CENTER

1500 Massachusetts Avenue NW
Washington, DC 20005
http://www.megaskillshsi.org/

FAMILY EDUCATION

20 Park Plaza, 12th Floor
Boston, MA 02116
http://www.familyeducation.com/home

{ SELF-ASSESSMENT

1. Learning about the history of a cultural group helps us understand the general social and political norms of that group today. Select a group discussed in this chapter and briefly describe their history and how that might influence their lives today.

2. Discuss some things to consider as an early childhood educator if you were working in a setting that serves children living in poverty.

3. Identify some barriers to parent involvement. Discuss ways to break down the barriers.

4. Discuss some ways to involve the community in early care and education.

Scenarios

1. You are a pre-K teacher in an urban community, and the children in your setting come from very diverse ethnic backgrounds. You are having a difficult time engaging the children's interest in story time even though you have selected high-quality children's books to read. For example, you read stories about the major holidays at the appropriate time (e.g., Halloween, Easter) and stories about families doing things together. What might you consider as you make accommodations to better engage the children in story time?

2. You are a first-grade teacher in a school that serves a diverse population. Aware of the importance of parent involvement, you have sent a note home inviting parents to help in your classroom and to visit the classroom. However, parental response to your invitation is minimal; only one parent volunteered to help in your classroom. How might you involve other parents in their children's education?

REFERENCES

Banks, J. A. (2003). *Teaching strategies for ethnic studies.* New York: Allyn and Bacon.

Children's Defense Fund. (2001). *The state of America's children yearbook 2001.* Washington, DC: Author.

Eldridge, D. (2001). Parent involvement: It's worth the effort. *Young Children, 56*(4), 65–69.

Epstein, J. (1995). Schools, family, community partnerships: Caring for the children we share. *Phi Delta Kappan, 77*(9), 701–712.

Henderson, A., & Berla, N. (Eds.). (1994). *A new generation of evidence: The family is critical to student achievement.* Washington, DC: National Committee for Citizens in Education, Center for Law and Education.

Kieff, J. & Wellhousen K. (2000). Planning family involvement in early childhood programs. *Young Children, 55*(3), 18–25.

King, J. E. (2001). Culture-centered knowledge: Black studies, curriculum transformation, and social action. In J. A. Banks & C. A. M. Banks (Eds.), *Handbook of research on multicultural education* (pp. 265–290). San Francisco: Jossey-Bass.

Marcon, R. A. (1993). Parental involvement and early school success: Following the "class of 2000" at year five. Paper presented at the Biennial Meeting of the Society for Research in Child Development, New Orleans, March 1993. ERIC, ED 357881.

Marshall, P. L. (2002). *Cultural diversity in our schools.* Belmont, CA: Wadsworth/Thomson Learning.

McDermott, D. (2001). Parenting and ethnicity. In M. J. Fine & S. W. Lee (Eds.), *Handbook of diversity in parent education: The changing faces of parenting and parent education* (pp. 73–96). New York: Academic Press.

Murphy, J. C. (2003). Case studies in African American school success and parenting behaviors. *Young Children, 58*(6), 85–89.

Nieto, S. (2002). *Language, culture, and teaching: Critical perspectives for a new century.* Mahwah, NJ: Lawrence Erlbaum Associates.

Ordonez-Jasis, R., & Ortiz, R. W. (2006). Reading their words; Working with diverse families to enhance children's early literacy development. *Young Children, 61*(1), 42–47.

Payne, R. K. (2003). *A framework for understanding poverty* (3rd revised ed.). Highlands, TX: aha! Process.

Powell, D. R. (1998). Reweaving parents into the fabric of early childhood programs. *Young Children, 53*(5), 60–67.

Seldin, C. A. (1991). Parent/teacher conferencing: A three-year study to enrich communication. Report no. 140. ERIC, ED 338597.

Strong, M. F. (1999). Serving mothers with disabilities in early childhood programs. *Young Children, 54*(3), 10–17.

Swall, D., & Swall, F. (2001). Teaching about sexual diversity: A new frontier for parenthood educators. In M. J. Fine & S. W. Lee (Eds.), *Handbook of diversity in parent education: The changing faces of parenting and parent education* (pp. 37–71). New York: Academic Press.

Swick, K. J. (2003). Working with families of young children. In J. P. Isenberg & J. R. Jalongo (Eds.), *Major trends and issues in early childhood education: Challenges, controversies and insights.* New York: Teachers College Press.

Trumbull, E., Rothstein-Fisch, C., Greenfield, P. M., & Quiroz, B. (2001). *Bridging cultures between home and school: A guide for teachers.* Mahwah, NJ: Lawrence Erlbaum Associates.

U.S. Census Bureau. http://www.census.gov/prod/2002pubs/censr-4.pdf, retrieved Jan. 18, 2005.

Wardle, F. (2001). Viewpoint: Supporting multiracial and multiethnic children and their families. *Young Children, 56*(6), 38–39.

Issues and Advocacy in Early Childhood in the Twenty-first Century

14

Have you ever thought about what society might be like 35 years from now? As older persons who qualified as teachers well over 35 years ago, we have often reflected on the world and society in which the children we taught now live as adults. The children in the first classes we taught will now be in their late forties. Did the education they experienced then prepare them for life today in the 21st century? Cell phones, ATMs, photos of Mars and the rings of Saturn are just a few aspects of life that were the stuff of science fiction in those days. It is not only the technology and material goods that are different, the fabric of the family, people's expectations, relationships, and opportunities that are part of contemporary society have changed as well.

When asked to brainstorm and list what they thought society would be like 35 years in the future, some teacher education students came up with the following list: increased violence and crime, drug problems, racial unrest, terrorism, increased reliance on technology, more families living in poverty, more homelessness, higher divorce rates, schools where students take classes programmed by computers and taught over the Internet, increased isolation of the individual, more mental illness, and so it went on. They were then asked the obvious next question, "What do you want society to be like in 35 years?" Here the story was quite different: a greater focus on the needs of the individual; a stronger sense of community; schools and teachers that foster creativity and academic progress for all; teachers that truly care about the children; happy families; social justice; less crime, poverty, and drug abuse; and so it went on. A follow-up discussion on this issue elicited the realization that the education system is the major influence and catalyst in shaping the kind of society in which we live. If we want to change the vision of the future, we must influence the children of today through our schools. This is especially true in the case of the young children, from birth to age 8. Four hundred years ago, the Jesuits had a mantra, "Give me a child until the age of seven, and I will show you the adult." The influence of the early years on a person's development has always been acknowledged.

As early childhood educators, what issues must we be prepared to address, and which negative influences must we attempt to counteract so that we can realize our hope for a better world and society? The issues evident in the neonatal years of the 21st century can be framed by the five themes that have been woven through the pages of this text. In this chapter we begin with the most central theme of *children*, and then look at how *sociopolitical influences, diversity, advocacy*, and our *professional development* impacts their lives.

After reading this chapter, you will understand:

▶ The contemporary view of childhood.

▶ The sociopolitical influences such as poverty, the market model for schooling, and on-going concerns of high-stakes testing and others that impact families, early care, and education.

▶ The impact of increasing cultural and linguistic diversity on early care and education.

▶ Strategies for advocating for young children.

▶ Considerations related to professional development for early childhood educators in the 21st century.

View of the Child

The contemporary view of the child has echoes of the child as a miniature adult (Chapter 1). Take a walk through the children's clothes section of any department store and look closely at the outfits designed for children, particularly for young girls. The clothes emulate those worn by Britney Spears, the Olsen twins, and other pop culture icons. The styles are overtly "sexy" for girls and "macho" for boys. Children are being hurried into mimicking adult behavior.

As mentioned in Chapter 1, David Elkind wrote extensively on the late 20th century view of childhood that continues today into the 21st century. He claimed that modern images of childhood lead to the miseducation of young children (Elkind, 1993) and included the *sensual child*, the *malleable child* (Elkind, 1993), and the *hurried child* (Elkind, 1981). His theory is still relevant today. Children are "hurried" into growing up in many ways. They have computers, cell phones, iPods, TVs in their bedrooms, and more disposable money than previous generations; however, the responsibilities that should accompany adult behavior are missing. Watch many of the pop-psychology TV programs and talk shows, such as *Dr. Phil, Honey We're Killing the Kids*, or *Supernanny*, and you will notice how many address the issue of parents who are unable to control their children's behavior and who are at their children's beck and call.

Conversely, changes in families often present challenges; for example, some one-parent families are challenged to meet the demands of daily life. Some blended families face challenges as they integrate each family member into the unit. The number of children living in poverty and without adequate medical care is rising. Also increasing are the number of abused children. At a recent gathering to remember those killed by childhood abuse, four candles were lit to represent the number of children who die each day in the United States from abuse. At a similar event the previous year, only three candles were used. The tragic numbers are increasing.

Elizabeth Crews.

The tendency to ignore the affective side of education in favor of stressing the mastery of basic skills to the exclusion of aesthetics or critical thinking is indicative of the view of children as miniature adults. As in the early years of civilized society, the focus is on preparing children for the workplace. If we wish to raise children who will make a positive contribution toward creating a better society 35 years hence, we must advocate for a return to educating the whole child. To do this we have to keep in mind what is developmentally and culturally appropriate, cognitively, socially, and emotionally. This must be done regardless of the social, political, and economic forces that influence our view of childhood today.

Grace/zefa/Corbis Images.

⸨ Sociopolitical Influences

As we have read in previous chapters, those dedicated to the welfare of young children have historically promoted early care and education as a means of counteracting the effects of poverty, family disintegration, and disease in the cities of the recently industrialized world. For example, in the United Kingdom, the living conditions during the early 20th century were appalling for the poor in the larger cities. Many children were abandoned, lived on the streets, and/or went hungry and neglected. Margaret McMillan (1860–1931) opened her nursery school in London, in 1914, with the express aim of improving the health and the cognitive and emotional development of the children.

SUPERSTOCK.

This was also a time when scientific knowledge about psychology, brain development, and mental wellness was burgeoning. In the book *The Nursery School* (E. P. Dutton, 1919), McMillan tells how the early childhood educators under her training are expected to "nurture" the children, keeping them clean, well-fed, rested, and safe. In addition, it is interesting to note that she says the nursery school (preschool) teacher is going "to modify or determine the structure of the brain." Does this sound familiar even today? One hundred years later, in the wealthiest nation on earth, we are still facing the specters of poverty, child abuse, family disintegration, homelessness, lack of health care, and drug addiction among our youngest citizens.

⸨ Poverty

Thirteen million children in the United States live in poverty and 3 out of 5 of those children live in extreme poverty (Children's Defense Fund, 2005a). The projected outcomes for these children are not optimistic; poverty will affect not only the quality of their lives but also their educational attainment. Table 14.1 illustrates the problem clearly. The prognosis for children of poverty to become productive and effective contributors to the nation or their communities is poor. Early childhood educators are in a key position to support children and families living in poverty.

Early childhood professionals must adjust the learning environment and activities to meet the needs of children of poverty. Recall that Maslow's hierarchy

Table 14.1	The Effects of Childhood Poverty

Health Outcomes for Children Living in Poverty

Children living in poverty are:

Five times more likely to have fair to poor health,

Three times more likely to have unmet health needs,

Three times more likely to be uninsured,

Two times more likely not to have seen a doctor in two years,

One and one half times more likely to miss ten days of school for illness or injury.

Source: Children's Defense Fund, 2005b

Educational Outcomes for Children Living in Poverty

Children living in poverty consistently achieve at lower levels than their more affluent peers. By the time they reach grade four:

Children Eligible for Free/Reduced Lunch	Peers Ineligible for Free/Reduced Lunch
15% write at grade level	42% write at grade level
46% are on grade level in math	79% are on grade level in math

Source: Children's Defense Fund, 2005c

Tony Freeman/PhotoEdit.

of needs suggests that food, shelter, and feelings of security and safety are basic needs that children have (Chapter 2). As early childhood professionals, we must advocate for programs (e.g., nutrition programs) and policy (e.g., subsidized high-quality child care) that support families living in poverty. Furthermore, we must understand the background of experiences that individual children bring to their learning and build on those experiences to support their success (Chapters 4–7). Early childhood professionals must communicate effectively with parents (Chapter 10) and assist them to receive available services (Chapter 13).

Health and Well-being

As we enter the 21st century, the health and well-being of young children is increasingly becoming a concern. Children in our nation are at risk as victims of violence and unhealthy lifestyles.

Obesity. No one who reads a newspaper or magazine or watches news shows on television could fail to be aware of the obesity issues now prevalent in our society. That these issues also include alarming statistics on childhood obesity should make all early childhood educators sit up and take notice. A 2002 report from the Pediatric Nutritional Surveillance System (U.S. Department of Health and Human Services, 2004) states that childhood obesity has reached epidemic proportions. The percentage of children who have a body mass index (BMI) above or at the 95th percentile on growth charts (Centers for Disease Control 2006) continues to increase. Almost 3 million (15%) of our nation's children between the ages of 6 and 19 are overweight according to 1999–2000 data. This number is three times higher than in 1980. The same data show that the percentage of overweight children in the 2- to 5-year-old age group is over 10%, an increase of 7% since 1994

(National Center for Health Statistics 2002, http://www.cdc.gov/nchs/press-room/02news/obesityonrise.htm). Table 14.2 shows the rates of overweight children broken down by ethnic group.

The risks of obesity in children are a high incidence of the following:

▶ Type 2 diabetes, originally an adult onset disease.

▶ Sleep apnea, which leads to learning and memory problems.

▶ High cholesterol and blood pressure levels, which are factors for heart disease.

▶ Orthopedic problems, liver disease, and asthma.

Research done by the National Institutes of Health indicates that although genetics do have a role in childhood obesity, the rapid and large increases over the last few decades can be traced to poor diet, overeating, and lack of exercise. Recommendations to reverse the trend are as follows:

▶ Encourage more breast-feeding.

▶ Increase physical activity.

▶ Promote consumption of fruits and vegetables.

▶ Decrease television viewing.

▶ Routinely screen children for weight problems.

Najlah Feanny/Corbis Images.

Educators of young children have a great responsibility in modeling and establishing healthy habits in young children, particularly in the areas of nutrition and physical activity. Early childhood educators should not only provide healthy food, but teach children the connection between nutrition and physical health. In addition they must provide young children frequent opportunities for running, jumping, climbing, kicking, throwing, and dancing. These activities are often excluded from daily life in this age of technology and electronic entertainment. Regular and ample outdoor play is a must. Such activities will not only help offset weight gain, but they also have the added benefits of improving eye–hand coordination and small and large muscle control.

Safety. Although the United States leads industrialized nations in many ways (gross domestic product, for example), the picture for its children remains grim with regard to their safety. In the United States each day (Children's Defense Fund, 2006):

4 children are killed by abuse or neglect,

35 children or teens die from auto accidents,

77 babies die before their first birthdays,

1,900 public school students are corporally punished,[*]

2,482 children are confirmed as abused or neglected.

[*] *Based on per school day (180 seven-hour days) calculations*

Table 14.2	Percentage of Children Who Are Overweight	
Ethnicity	Preschool age	Age 6–11
African-American	8%	20%
Latino-American	11%	24%
Euro-American	10%	12%

Source: National Center for Health Statistics: October 8, 2002 (http://www.cdc.gov/nchs/pressroom/02news/obesityonrise.htm).

In their position statement on violence in the lives of children, the National Association for the Education of Young Children notes that the causes and effects of violence in our society are complex (NAEYC, 1993). Much violence results from issues discussed throughout this text—poverty, prejudice, abuse, and social injustice. Strategies for addressing those inequities have also been addressed in this text. For example, we have discussed the critical importance of creating antibias environments, teaching for social justice, and engaging children in cooperative activities while limiting competitive activities, to name a few. In addition, early childhood educators must

- Support families by advocating for job training, health care, early childhood education, and parent education programs.
- Advocate against corporal punishment and other behaviors that model violence (NAEYC, 1993).
- Advocate for resources for the prevention of violence (NAEYC, 1993).
- Support family-friendly policies in the workplace.

Media. Violence in young children is also the result of frequent exposure to violence on TV and in other forms of media. Violent programming contributes significantly to children's violent behavior. When children view violent programming regularly and excessively, they

- Are more likely to behave in aggressive ways to others because they learn that violence is an acceptable way of solving problems (Horton & Zimmer, 1994).
- Are less likely to show remorse for aggressive and violent behavior (Horton & Zimmer, 1994).
- May become desensitized to the harmful effects of violence, which are often not shown on TV.
- Do not always differentiate between fantasy and reality, which affects their interpretation of violent programming.

As advocates for the well-being of young children, a great responsibility falls to early childhood educators to combat the effects of violence in the lives of young children. As knowledgeable and resourceful people in the lives of young children, early childhood educators must

- Educate parents about the harmful effects of too much TV viewing, particularly regular programming and cable channels. Encourage parents to support play and other creative activities at home and to limit TV viewing primarily to PBS programs.
- Advocate for policies that regulate TV programming, marketing of violent toys, and availability of firearms and weapons (NAEYC, 1993).

Disaster. Throughout history, disaster has struck communities in the United States and around the world; some communities have experienced more than others. Conflicts (e.g., civil war, terrorist attacks) and natural disasters (e.g., earthquakes, hurricanes) have profound effects on young children and their families. When disaster strikes, children need support as they try to make sense of what has happened and to recover from fear and terror. Early childhood educators need to not only create a supportive environment in the early childhood setting, they need to assist parents as they interact with their young children in the face of disaster. Some general guidelines include the following:

- Maintain a normal routine as much as possible.
- Acknowledge children's fears while reassuring them that you will keep them safe; avoid telling them they are not fearful (e.g., "I know that preparing for the hurricane is a little scary, but I will keep you safe").

▶ Respond to children's questions and concerns in clear and concrete ways (e.g., "Preparing for the hurricane is how we keep ourselves safe," or, "Yes, there are people who do bad things but I won't let anything happen to you").

▶ Encourage children to talk openly about their concerns.

Commerce, Industry, and Business

The dawn of the 21st century saw increased numbers of families with young children living in poverty. Child care is a critical need for low-income working families as well as those leaving welfare for work. Without access to child care, many parents simply cannot work. Some parents with jobs are forced to take time off or to quit because they cannot find reliable and safe care for their children. In 1995–96 private industry extended child care benefits to only 1 in 25 employees, and the majority of these were professional and technical workers, not blue-collar workers (Issues in Labor Statistics, August 1998, http://www.bls.gov/opub/ils/pdf/opbils24.pdf).

Recall from Chapter 3 that employer subsidized child care like the Kaiser Shipbuilding Nursery emerged when approximately one-third of U.S. women went to work on behalf of the war effort in the 1940s. Today there are companies that offer on-site child care through employer sponsored programs. In fact, businesses have emerged that assist companies to do this. One of these is the Children's Creative Learning Centers (CCLC). This nationwide group offers comprehensive services to employers, which include (a) on-site and near-site child care programs, (b) resource and referral, (c) backup child care, and (d) family child care networks. Among their clients are several Fortune 500 companies that have created innovative programs for their employees in partnership with CCLC. More information can be found on the Internet at http://www.cclc.com/corp_fam/index.html.

There are usually three types of child care benefits:

▶ Employer funds child care, regardless of location.

▶ Employer manages child care center on the work site.

▶ Employers, or group of employers, manage a child care center away from the work site.

Many of the on-site centers allow parents to visit the children during the day and also may have video access for parents to monitor the child's well-being.

One criticism that has surfaced regarding on-site, employer sponsored child care is quality. Because high-quality child care is expensive, some businesses try to circumvent state rules and regulations, arguing that parents are on site and thus are technically not away from their children. In such situations, employers may argue that rules and regulations can be reasonably relaxed. Early childhood educators must remain diligent overseers of high standards for early care and education.

Metaphor of the Market for Schooling

Peter Crookson, (1994) suggests two competing metaphors for schooling; one is democracy and the other is the market. In the democratic relationship, human interactions are communal, whereas in the market relationship, human interactions are exchanges. The former values the primacy and efficacy of citizenship; the latter values the primacy and efficacy of consumership (Crookson, 1994).

Because we are a capitalist, democratic society that values free enterprise, many Americans are easily drawn to the market model for schools. After all, it reflects the rest of our society. The notion of school choice for families is embedded in the market model and continues to garner support in the 21st century.

Vouchers. Under a school voucher system, parents can choose the school they want their children to attend and submit their vouchers to that school. Schools then submit the vouchers to the government which pays a predetermined amount to the school for each voucher. Many view this strategy as a means of holding schools accountable for providing a quality education for all children because schools will be forced to compete for tax monies.

The concept of school vouchers is not new; this market model practice dates back to the 1950s when, following the *Brown vs. Board* decision, many families in the South sought a way to take their children out of integrated schools. Concurrently, economist Milton Friedman was advocating that schools would be better in a free-market system. That is, competition would force them to improve.

Historically, wealthy parents could select elite private schools over public education for their children; vouchers have emerged as a means of providing the opportunity to all parents to place their children in the best schools. Proponents of the voucher system claim that the market model is sufficient to establish the effectiveness of schools. That is, schools of highest quality will naturally be desirable to families and all families will have the opportunity to choose the best school.

In reality, school choice is not egalitarian. Moreover, the practice fails to consider the broader educational context as it gives way to the wishes of individual families. First, higher quality schools cannot accommodate all who wish to attend; thus, admission can become subjectively selective. In other words, schools can select only the least challenging students.

Another consideration is that the market model assumes there is profit for which all schools compete; however, our schools are supported by a finite number of tax dollars, and there is no profit to share. Furthermore, marketing and price cutting, key to being competitive, do not constitute a good model for schools. Our finite number of tax dollars must be used to create good schools for all children. The *Advocating for the Child* exemplifies this frightening thought about the market model for schools.

In reality, children from low-income families are less likely than their middle- and upper-class counterparts to attend schools deemed *the best*. First, parents have differing abilities to discern which school will best meet their children's particular learning needs. Furthermore, it is difficult for parents whose own school experiences were unsatisfactory to identify the school most likely to meet the needs of their children. In fact, they may have little confidence that any school will meet their children's needs. Finally, many parents do not have the resources (time off of work, money) to transport their children to a school out of their attendance area.

Perhaps the greatest concern related to vouchers is that they take money from less successful schools and divert it to more successful schools. (Success is usually determined by standardized test scores.) This takes attention away from the real problems that schools are facing. That is, teachers need education and resources to provide the best education for all children. This includes teacher education programs and professional development opportunities where early childhood educators learn how to identify and address the needs of all children, and where they learn to develop an engaging and innovative curriculum. It also includes appropriate support services (e.g., mental health professionals, translators).

Magnet Schools. Magnet schools are public schools that offer unique educational emphases. The emphasis might be in the area of fine arts, science, and so on. Magnet

Billy E. Barnes/PhotoEdit.

Advocating for the Child

The Market Model of Schooling
In the true spirit of the market model, ads like this are a possibility.

schools are open to all children in the district, usually on a lottery basis. Magnet schools exemplify the primacy of consumership because, even though students living outside of the magnet school's attendance area have increased choice, many living within the attendance area must be denied to accommodate the transfers.

Charter Schools. Another response to inadequate schools takes the form of charter schools. Initiated by businesses, parents, or teachers, and in agreement with the local and state school board, a charter school is technically a public school that is exempt from certain rules and regulations. In agreement with the local and state governments, charter schools provide agreed-upon new, creative, or unusual approaches to education. Charter schools cannot possibly meet the needs of all children because they are not available to all children.

High-Stakes Testing

Recall from Chapter 2 that standardized testing emerged during the progressive era as a relatively inexpensive and easily understandable means of documenting intelligence. The tangibility of numbers and ease of scoring bubble sheets has fostered continued use of standardized measures, most recently into the prekindergarten, kindergarten, and primary grades. Policies such as the No Child Left Behind (NCLB) legislation elevate standardized testing to high-stakes because the tests are used to determine adequate yearly progress (Chapter 2).

In Chapter 9, we discussed several considerations related to standardized testing with young children. First, valid, reliable results are difficult to achieve with young children. Perhaps of greater concern are the narrowing of the curriculum as teachers teach to the test and the failure of standardized scores to illuminate the specific needs of individual children. Early childhood educators in the 21st century must remain diligent advocates for the value of other forms of assessment that are grounded in the daily activities of young children (e.g., portfolios, observation). With the prominence of digital technology, this is an achievable goal.

Diversity

This nation is becoming increasingly diverse. Early in the 21st century, more than 50% of children in school will be non-white, non-middle-class, and non-native English speakers. In contrast, the child care workers and teachers are becoming less diverse as fewer minority group members join the teaching and child care professions. It is therefore of paramount importance that early childhood educators see the richness of diversity and become cross-culturally aware and understand how to teach inclusively.

Culture influences how both early childhood educators and children behave, learn, and think. It affects values and interactions, both essential components of a learning environment. Many who are part of the mainstream Euro-American

Michael Newman/PhotoEdit.

group find it difficult to understand the perspectives of those whose lives have been marginalized by society. Many early childhood educators have never lived in or experienced the communities in which their students live. In such situations the challenge of learning about the cultures that have formed the experiences of their students is challenging, but not impossible. It is important for early childhood educators to be curious, to read articles and books, to observe groups and individuals, to become acquainted with families of children in their settings, and to participate in community activities (Gollnick & Chinn, 2002; Banks, 2001). This is how you will build an understanding and acceptance of other perspectives.

Teaching in a Diverse Society

The issue of diversity encompasses class, ethnicity, language, religion, ability, and gender/sexuality. As our society becomes more diverse, so do the children in our classrooms. An education that is multicultural has long been the ideal of many educators, and the 21st century is the time to fulfill this ideal.

Multicultural education is not a curriculum; rather, it is a philosophy. There are three commonly accepted goals for a multicultural education (Gollnick & Chinn, 2002; Banks, 2001):

▶ To ensure that students from diverse backgrounds have the opportunity to experience success in education: educational equity.

▶ To promote intercultural and intracultural understanding among all groups.

▶ To prepare students to participate in a fully democratic society.

The idea of *educational equity* is that all students should be taught in a way that supports their potential for academic success. The curriculum should be inclusive, examining issues, information, and knowledge from the perspectives of all cultural groups. In addition, the instructional strategies used should meet the needs of all learners' learning styles, learning approaches, and intelligences.

Cultural understanding does not refer to merely learning about ethnic groups; it encompasses the need to understand one's own culture (intracultural) as well the culture of others (intercultural). When people can participate in a variety of cultural groups they benefit from the richness of this nation's heritage and develop a broad human perspective, which includes the ability to see their own culture from other points of view (Banks, 2001).

Living in a democracy entails great responsibility for one's decisions. In order to truly vote with confidence, each person has to critically analyze the statements and claims of the politicians running for election. The history of the world is littered with the debris of evil leaders, often voted in by a democratic voting system. Hitler and Mussolini are two examples. People are not born with the ability to discern truth and critically analyze; they learn those skills through education. In doing so, they also learn to empathize with those who have been victimized and oppressed, both in other countries and in the United States. The ability to evaluate the actions of one's own people from the perspective of others calls for a high level of reasoning and ethics that can be fostered in the early years if democratic principles are present in care and education settings.

Linguistic Diversity. Addressing the varied linguistic needs of young children is another issue that has already had an impact on education, and will continue to do so through the 21st century (see Chapter 10). The number of English language learners will increase, which will pose a challenge to early childhood educators who are not equipped to work effectively with young children who do not speak Standard English. Early childhood educators must work to educate legislators and other policy makers about the importance of providing resources for teacher education and public schools to supply appropriate education and materials for working with non-speakers of Standard English.

Families. Family values and lifestyles continue to vary from traditional two-parent, two-gender, same race parents (Chapter 13). Mixed race families and those headed by same gender parents are increasingly present in our society. Furthermore, owing to loss of a spouse, divorce, adoption, and other decisions to embark on single parenthood, families are increasingly headed by a single parent, father or mother. Although many single fathers are heads of household, more households are headed by a single female. The *Focus on Diversity* illuminates the educational implications and the need for men in early childhood education.

As early childhood educators, we must accept and extend human rights to all children, regardless of our personal values. All children, and their families, must be welcomed and nurtured in our early childhood settings.

Religious Diversity. Many in the United States have suggested that putting religion back in public education settings is a way to improve the moral character of children and combat society's negative influences. Some argue that it will help us diminish violence and hate in our society; however, the United States is very diverse with regard to family beliefs and practices, including families that do not embrace religious beliefs and practices. Integrating religion into the public establishments of a diverse society serves only to acknowledge particular beliefs and practices while ignoring others. The *Focus on Diversity* feature on p. 309 exemplifies the problem.

Rather than promoting a particular religion, early childhood educators must teach the principles of human rights (values espoused by most religions). All humans have the right to be physically and psychologically safe. Early childhood educators must create environments that honor each child's right to feel safe, secure, and valued.

©Ellen B. Senisi.

Advocacy

One theme that permeates this text is the influence of the social and political environment on care and education of young children. After examining history, we can probably safely assume that things in the 21st century will be no different. That is, as society in the United States continues to transform, so does early education and care. As advocates for the rights and well-being of young children and their families, we must view inequities in schooling,

Focus on Diversity

Men Wanted for Teaching Young Children

Jeanette Riley
Assistant Professor of Early Childhood and Elementary Education at Murray State University - Kentucky

The U.S. Census Bureau figures (Fields, 2003) show that 14.7 million children live in households with no father figure. Having a man teacher offers children a chance to experience a positive male role model. A male teacher may be the only man many young children see reading, writing, playing, and modeling positive behaviors for them. He also may be the only model of a male caregiver some children have in their lives. Nevertheless, according to Milloy, (2003), over 90% of elementary school teachers are women and the percentage is even higher at the preschool level. Traditionally, the teaching of young children has been considered a job for women. The teachers of these children are expected to show motherly love and nurturing qualities; therefore, it has always been believed that women were best suited to the task (Beatty, 1995). Our society expects women to naturally want to take care of and teach young children (King, 1998), whereas men entering the field have to overcome society's beliefs. Teaching young children has been considered a woman's job for so long that society often finds it difficult to accept that men would want to work with younger children. This stereotypical thinking contributes to the lack of male teachers in the classrooms of younger children (Thornton, 1999).

Men who wish to teach young children may have their motives questioned. All teachers have become more aware of how actions such as giving a hug to a child might be perceived. The behaviors of men teachers are examined more closely than are the behaviors of women, and some schools have differing policies for men and women about touching children (Sargent, 2001). Consequently, men who teach young children must negotiate living under constant suspicion while finding ways to give children the emotional closeness they need (Sargent, 2001).

The low status and low salary typical of jobs considered women's work discourages men from teaching young children (Thornton & Bricheno, 2000). Often, when men enter the teaching profession, it is with the intention of eventually moving into the more lucrative, more male-oriented world of administration (Montecinos & Nielson, 1997; Thornton & Bricheno, 2000). Unlike the expectations for women teachers, men are expected to want to move up the career ladder.

Although women often choose to teach prior to graduating from high school, men tend to make the decision after entering college (Montecinos & Nielsen, 1997) or later. This may be partially due to the problems men assume they will encounter but also because of the lack of opportunities men have early in life to care for children. Men who want to teach young children often worry that they do not have adequate background experiences to work with young children. Girls usually have more opportunities at a young age to take care of younger siblings or do babysitting jobs. Boys are less frequently given these opportunities. Once men decide to pursue a career in teaching, they often find jobs working in summer camps, with sports teams, or for after school programs to gain experience working with children (Sargent, 2001).

Educators are becoming more aware of the benefits children receive from both women and men taking part in their lives (Gadsden & Ray, 2002; Sanders, 2002). With encouragement, more men may begin to choose teaching young children as a career option, providing young children with more diversity in their learning environments.

access to high-quality care, and support for working families as central concerns as we strive to make the world safe and nurturing for all children.

Consider these demographics from the Children's Defense Fund (2006). To which nation do you think they refer?

Each day:

▶ 1 mother dies in childbirth,

▶ 367 babies are born to mothers who received late or no prenatal care,

▶ 888 babies are born at low birth weight,

▶ 1,154 babies are born to teen mothers,

▶ 1,701 babies are born without health insurance,

▶ 2,252 babies are born to mothers who are not high school graduates,

▶ 2,337 babies are born into poverty.

If you said a country in Africa or South America, you are incorrect. This happens each day in the United States of America. How can we as teachers of young children stand by without making our voices heard in protest? If we do not advo-

Focus on Diversity

Religion and Public Schools

Following is a conversation between Mary and Rebecca. Mary's young son Jimmy has just started kindergarten.

M:*You know we lobbied the school board to get prayer back into our schools and they've agreed. They decided to do it, and children whose parents don't want them to pray can go sit in the media center until the prayer is over.*

R:*Really! Well, how's it going?*

M:*Well, on the first day of school I asked Jimmy if they had a prayer. He indicated they did and, after the prayer, the teacher said, "There is but one God, Allah; Moses, Jesus, and Mohammed are His prophets."*

R:*Oh dear!! That's not what we believe. What did you do?*

M:*I went to the principal and told him I had no problem with Muslims but I asked to have Jimmy moved to another classroom! I waited for him after school and asked again about the prayer. He said they prayed alright. They all looked up, raised their palms in the air, and hummed!!*

R:*Oh my!!*

M:*Yes, well I went to the principal and asked to have Jimmy put in a class with a Christian teacher.*

R:*So is that where he is now?*

M:*Yes, he's in Ms. Johnson's class.*

R:*You must be so relieved.*

M:*Not exactly; he came home this time and told me that she began the prayer with "Hail Mary, Mother of God!"*

R:*What are you going to do now?*

M:*Well, my Jimmy is going to sit in the media center until we can get prayer out of our public school!!!!!!!!!!!!!!!!!*

---

cate for young children, who will? How will we explain ourselves as professionals to the surviving adults 35 years from now?

We have already discussed the characteristics of personal, public policy, and private sector advocacy. As part of our *personal* advocacy, we must continue to assert our informed voices as we talk with each other and with informal groups in our families, schools, and communities. We must study the issues and cast our vote for policy and laws that keep children and their families central.

Meyer (2005) suggests grabbing people's attention by wearing a message. For example, when he had T-shirts printed with the words "Raise a child, not a test score" on the front and "High-Stakes Testing" written in a red circle with a line through it on the back, people stopped him in stores to inquire about the message. Some even ordered a shirt. It was a small action that gave him the opportunity to educate others.

As a *public policy* advocate, remember that public officials work for you, a taxpayer. You can share your informed insights as easily as writing an email note or sending a formal letter. Contact information for government officials is easily accessible on state and federal government websites.

As part of your *private sector* advocacy, connect to community organizations that may not be fully informed about schools and ways to support the education of all children (Meyer, 2005). Use your knowledge to educate them about high-quality early education and care.

Professional Development

Always be mindful that you will live and teach in an ever changing world. As a high-quality early childhood professional, it is critical that you remain knowledgeable about both your professional and social worlds. Be a wise consumer of international, national, state, and local news to best understand the world in which you are working. Understand the impact of the social world on the lives of children in your early childhood setting.

As an advocate for children and families, you will need to be aware of the latest research, theories, and conventional wisdom of early childhood professionals. Maintain professional memberships and continue to access professional journals. Learn about your local education association and how it can support you as a developing professional.

Curriculum

Simply defined, the curriculum is what is taught to learners. The curriculum is different than *instruction*, which refers to activities that impart knowledge or skill (Merriam-Webster 2006). It is also different than *learning*, which is the cognitive process of acquiring knowledge or skill (Merriam-Webster, 2006). What is taught, or the curriculum content, depends on how the purpose of education is perceived. There are several ideas about the purpose of education that influence early childhood curriculum (Sowell, 2005):

▶ To develop cognitive attainment and understanding.

▶ To increase intellectual and thinking processes.

▶ To reform society.

▶ To prepare children to live in a changing and volatile world.

▶ To help children reach their full potential.

The concept of developmentally appropriate practice (Chapters 4–7) encompasses all five of these purposes, with an emphasis on the latter three. It calls for a curriculum that is both experience based and outcome based; however, the emphasis is on experiential learning. Experience based learning emanates from a curriculum that aims to help children reach their full potential and to prepare them to live in a world of ever changing expectations and realities. It is based on the premise that the cognitive, affective, and psychomotor growth of individuals is important. The curriculum content and instruction are based on individual needs, interests, and past experiences.

Photodisc Green/Getty Images, Inc.

In contrast, the NCLB Act limits its emphasis to an outcomes based approach to learning as reflected only in the first purpose for education that we mention. Emphasizing only the first purpose raises little concern about the context of learning by focusing primarily on content. With this emphasis the learners are assessed on how well they have mastered the intended outcomes, with no attention to the learning process (Sowell, 2005). The curriculum remains fixed regardless of the individuals.

What is not taught in school can be as significant as what is taught. Omitting certain content or disciplines sends a definite message about their relative importance in life. When the fine arts or physical education and activity is not part of a child's day, they learn that they are not essential.

The Null Curriculum. Elliot Eisner (1994) contends that in addition to the explicit (that which is intentionally taught) and implicit curricula (that which is taught unintentionally), there is also a *null curriculum*. Eisner defines this as "the options students are not afforded, the perspectives they may never know about, much less be able to use, the concepts and skills that are not part of their intellectual repertoire . . . their absence will have important consequences on the kind of life that students can choose to lead" (p. 107). Schools serving low-income populations and high-risk students often gear the curriculum to the basic facts and skills. In some cases, the curriculum for students of apparently different ability levels and social backgrounds differ even if they attend the same school.

John Dewey, in his book *The Child and the Curriculum* (1902), reveals that the link between the purpose of education and the curriculum is not a contemporary idea; it was burgeoning in the late 19th century when Dewey began his writing. It continued through the 20th century, and we are still addressing it in the 21st century. Dewey contended that children are motivated by the urge to (a) socialize, (b) investigate, (c) construct, and (d) express themselves artistically. If we, as early childhood educators, have as our purpose the development of the child's total potential and, in addition, aim to prepare each child to cope with a changing world, then we must espouse these as a framework for an appropriate curriculum for young children. The curriculum should place equal emphasis on each of these four functions, using them as a guide to what should be taught.

We return again to the question, "What is the purpose of education?" Surely the answer should be the same for all students, and therefore the available curriculum and services should also be the same. Educational equity must be an important issue for child advocates and all educators.

 ## My Developing Professional View

> Describe your role and responsibilities as an early childhood educator in the 21st century.

SUMMARY

We began this text by noting that it is an exciting time to be an early childhood educator, and it truly is! Throughout this text, we have examined the social, political, historical, and contemporary trends and issues related to early education and care. We have examined the ebb and flow of ideas and practices over time in an increasingly complex society. As we cultivate our greatest natural resource, young children, we get to be the change agents that set the trajectory for a just and caring society in which each individual's human rights are valued. We do not have to do more than early childhood educators have done in the past; we merely have to do it differently as we address the changing needs of children and families. As we go forth and do our work, we have the privilege of leaving our mark on the future. We must ensure that it is for the good of all children.

ENRICHMENT ACTIVITIES

Individual Activity

1. After thinking about the social issues that affect young children, what do you believe is the purpose of early childhood education? Your answer will determine what you believe should be the nature of the curriculum and, accordingly, the instructional approach used with young children. Revisit Chapters 4–7 to review ideas about teaching and then write a 2- to 3-page response to the question.

Cooperative Activities

2. Each member of your group will select an early childhood educator from a care center or public school to interview on an issue discussed in this chapter

(e.g., childhood obesity, high-stakes testing). Seek his/her perspective on the issue, including ideas about what is needed to adequately address the issue in the coming years or decades. Synthesize your findings to identify themes in the teachers' responses.

3. In your groups, address the following questions. (a) What do you think life will be like in 25 years when you are veteran teachers? (b) What would you like for it to be like? (c) What can you do to help set a trajectory for high-quality early care and education for all children in your charge?

Advocacy Activity

4. Write a letter to the president or your state governor taking a position on an issue in early care and education. Discuss considerations for policy makers and changes you wish to see. Provide a clear rationale for your position.

⸔ SELF-ASSESSMENT

1. What are some considerations for early childhood educators who work with children living in poverty? What are some considerations for early childhood educators who work with children who are obese?

2. Compare and contrast the metaphors of democracy and the market for schooling.

3. Identify some educational issues about which you will need to be aware as an early childhood educator in the 21st century. Briefly explain each.

4. Explain the *null curriculum*.

Scenario

You are a second-grade teacher. You and your colleagues are sensitive to religious diversity and, although you teach about religion, you do not celebrate it in any way, even to the extent that there are no holiday parties in your school. You learn that a group of parents is circulating a petition to present to the school board mandating that holiday parties be reinstated in the school. As the most senior faculty member, you have been asked to go before the board to present a reasoned argument against the practice of holding holiday parties. What will the key elements of your argument be?

⸔ FOR FURTHER READING

Glickman, C. (2004). *Letters to the next president: What we can do about the real crisis in public education.* New York: Teachers College Press.

Meyer, R. J. (2005). Viewpoint: Taking a stand: Strategies for activism. *Young Children, 60*(3), 80–85.

Rethinking Schools. (1996). *Selling out our schools: Vouchers, markets, and the future of public education.* Milwaukee, WI: Rethinking Schools.

Washington, V., & Andrews, J. D. (1998). *Children of 2010.* Washington, DC: National Association for the Education of Young Children.

Professional Development Resources

CENTERS FOR DISEASE CONTROL AND PREVENTION

1600 Clifton Road
Atlanta, GA 30333
http://www.cdc.gov/

CHILDREN'S DEFENSE FUND

25 E Street NW
Washington, DC 20001
http://www.childrensdefense.org/

CHILDREN'S CREATIVE LEARNING CENTERS

794 East Duane Avenue
Sunnyvale, CA 94086
http://www.cclc.com/

RETHINKING SCHOOLS

1001 E. Keefe Avenue
Milwaukee, WI 53212
http://www.rethinkingschools.org/

REFERENCES

Banks, J. A. (2001). *Cultural diversity and education* (4th ed.). Needham Heights, MA: Allyn and Bacon.

Beatty, B. (1995). *Preschool education in America: The culture of young children from the colonial era to the present.* New Haven: Yale University Press.

Center for Disease Control. (2006). Prevalence of Overweight Among Children and Adolescents: United States, 2003–2004. http://www.cdc.gov/nchs/products/pubs/pubd/hestats/obese03_04/overwght_child_03.htm

Children's Defense Fund. (2006). Each Day in America. http://www.childrensdefense.org/site/PageServer?pagename=research_national_data_each_day

Children's Defense Fund. (2005a). Family income & jobs: Raising children out of poverty. http://www.childrensdefense.org/site/DocServer/Greenbook_2005.pdf?docID=1741

Children's Defense Fund. (2005b). Children's health: Fighting poverty and poor health. http://www.childrensdefense.org/site/DocServer/Greenbook_2005.pdf?docID=1741

Children's Defense Fund. (2005c). Education: The path out of poverty. http://www.childrensdefense.org/site/DocServer/Greenbook_2005.pdf?docID=1741

Children's Defense Fund. (2006). http://www.PageServer?pagename-research_national_data_each_day???

Crookston, Jr., P. (1994). *School choice.* New Haven: Yale University Press.

Dewey, J. (1902). *The child and the curriculum.* Chicago: University of Chicago Press.

Eisner, E. W. (1994). *The educational imagination: On the design and evaluation of school programs* (3rd ed.). New York: Macmillan.

Elkind, D. (1981). *The hurried child.* New York: Addison-Wesley.

Elkind, D. (1993). *Images of the young child.* Washington, DC: National Association for the Education of Young Children.

Fields, J. (2003). *Children's living arrangements and characteristics: March 2002.* Retrieved July 20, 2004, from U.S. Census Bureau website: http://www.census.gov/prod/2003pubs/p20-547.pdf.

Gadsden, V., & Ray, A. (2002). Engaging fathers: Issues and considerations for early childhood educators. *Young Children, 57*(6), 32–41.

Gollnick, D. M., & Chinn, P. C. (2002). *Multicultural education in a pluralistic society.* Upper Saddle River, NJ: Merrill Prentice-Hall.

Horton, J., & Zimmer, J. (1994). *Media violence and children: A guide for parents.* [Brochure.] Washington, DC: National Association for the Education of Young Children.

Issues in Labor Statistics. (1998) Employer-sponsored childcare benefits. http://www.bls.gov/opub/ils/pdf/opbils24.pdf

King, J. R. (1998). *Uncommon caring: Learning from men who teach young children.* New York: Teachers College Press.

Marriam-Webster. (2006) Webster's Online Dictionary. http://www.mw.com/dictionary/curriculum

McMillan, M. (1999). The nursery school. In K. M. Paciorek & J. H. Munro (Eds.), *Sources: Notable selections in early childhood education* (2nd ed.).

Meyer, R. J. (2005). Viewpoint: Taking a stand: Strategies for activism. *Young Children, 60*(3), 80–85.

Milloy, M. (2003). The guy teacher. *NEA Today, 22*(2), 22–31.

Montecinos, C., & Nielson, L. E. (1997). Gender and cohort differences in university students' decisions to become elementary teacher education majors. *Journal of Teacher Education, 48,* 47–54.

NAEYC. (National Association for the Education of Young Children.) (1993). NAEYC position statement on violence in the lives of children. *Young Children, 48*(6), 80–84.

National Center for Health Statistics. (2002). Obesity still on the rise, new data show. http://www.cdc.gov/nchs//pressroom/02news/obesityonrise.htm

Sanders, K. (2002). Men don't care? *Young Children, 57*(6), 44–48.

Sargent, P. (2001). *Real men or real teachers? Contradictions in the lives of men elementary school teachers.* Harriman, TN: Men's Studies Press.

Sowell, E. J. (2005). *Curriculum: An integrative introduction.* Upper Saddle River, NJ: Merrill Prentice-Hall.

Thornton, M. (1999). Reducing wastage among men student teachers in primary courses: A male club approach. *Journal of Education for Teaching, 25,* 41–53.

Thornton, M., & Bricheno, P. (2000). Primary school teachers' careers in England and Wales: The relationship between gender, role, position and promotion aspirations. *Pedagogy, Culture and Society, 8,* 187–206.

Webster's Online Dictionary: The Rosetta Edition. http://www.websters-online-dictionary.org/.

Index

A

A National at Risk, 59
Abecedarian Early Intervention
    Project, 130
*Abington School District v.
    Schempp* (1963), 65
Abuse, child, 242–243
Academic redshirting, 77,
    132–134
Accents, 212
Accidents, 251
Accountability movement, 45–46
Active listening, 173–174
Activity-based intervention, 242
Adaptation, 36
Additive approach to diversity, 147
Adequate yearly progress (AYP),
    48, 60–61
Administrative reform, 54–55
Adult/child ratios, 104–105
Advocacy, 86–87, 307–309
Affective side of education, 299
African-American children, 6–7,
    11, 26–28, 32–33. *See also*
    Cultural diversity
African-American families,
    278–279
African-American vernacular
    English (AAVE), 211
Age groups. *See* Six- to eight-year
    olds; Three- to five-year
    olds
Alertness to aggression, 182
Alternative communication, 237
American Civil Liberties Union
    (ACLU), 65
American Sign Language (ASL),
    212–213
Americans with Disabilities Act
    (1990), 60
Ancient Greeks view of
    childhood, 4
Ancient Romans view of
    childhood, 4–5
Ancient views of childhood, 2–5
Anecdotal notes, 189
Antibias environments
    assessment and, 202
    celebrations and, 148
    classroom guests and, 150
    communities and, 148–149

conflict resolution and,
    146–147
content integration and,
    147–148
cooperative learning and, 146
educational materials and, 150
exclusion and, 127
family literacy and, 290
friendships and, 149–150
hidden curriculums and, 150
for infants and toddlers,
    107–109
instructional strategies and,
    146–150
literacy and, 144–146
literature and, 128
prejudice reduction activities
    and, 146
for primary grades, 144–150
similarities and differences
    and, 126
special need children and,
    244–246
teaching antibias attitudes,
    126–128
technology and, 271
for three- to five-year olds,
    126–128
Aristotle, 4
Asian-American families,
    279–280. *See also* Cultural
    diversity
Assessment
    anecdotal records, 189
    antibias assessment, 202
    audio recordings, 190
    authentic, 188
    child's nature and, 196–197
    cultural experiences and,
        200–201
    cultural issues in, 199–202
    cultural values and, 201
    event samples, 189–190
    of exceptionalities, 230–231
    field notes, 189
    formative, 188
    home visits, 194
    language barriers and, 201
    linguistically diverse children,
        200

linking with curriculum,
    195–196
observation, 188–191
photographs, 191
portfolios, 191–194
program evaluation, 202–203
standardized tests, 195,
    197–199
time samples, 189
video recordings, 190–191
work sampling system, 194
Assimilation, 79
Assistive technology, 271
Association for Childhood
    Education International
    (ACEI), 71
Associative play, 82
Attachment in infants and
    toddlers, 101–102
Attention-deficit disorder
    (ADD), 231–232
Attention deficit hyperactivity
    disorder (ADHD), 231–232
Audio recordings, 190
Augmentative communication,
    237
Autism, 232–233

B

Babbling, 96
Balanced literacy, 151–153
Bank Street, 33, 123
Basic interpersonal
    communicative skills
    (BICS), 220
Battelle Developmental
    Inventory, 195
Bayley Scales of Infant
    Development, 195
Before and after school
    programs, 154
Behavior disorders, 233
Behavior guidance
    children with special needs,
        177–178
    choices and, 169
    cultural considerations,
        178–181
    for infants, 170–171
    for kindergartners, 173–175

praise and, 169–170
    for preschoolers, 173–175
    for primary grade children,
        175–177
    punishment and, 170
    strategies for, 170–178
    supporting nonviolent
        behavior, 181–183
    for toddlers, 171–173
Behavior modification, 15
Behaviorism, 37–38, 76–77
Behaviorist theory of language
    acquisition, 92
Bell, Alexander Graham, 33
Bell, T.H., 47
Bibliotherapy, 182
Biculturalism, 276
Bilingual education, 213–215
    history of, 61–62
    legislation related to, 63
    student assessment and, 201
Bilingual Education Act
    (1968), 63
Binet, Alfred, 31
Biracial multiethnic families, 280
Birth reflexes, cognitive
    development and, 99
Black English, 211
Blank slates, children as, 8
Blended families, 283
Blindness, 239
Bodily/kinesthetic children,
    74–75
Brain-based development, 73
Brain research theory, 218
BRIGANCE Diagnostic
    Inventory of Basic Skills,
    195
British infant school, 29
Brown v. Board of Education
    (1954), 40, 279
Bullying, 183
Bureau of Indian Affairs
    (BIA), 28
Bush, G.W., 48, 60, 200, 285

C

Callier-Azusa Scale, 195
Calm environments, infants
    and, 162

Capabilities, three-to five-year olds, 117–118

Castaneda v. Pickard (1981), 63

Celebrations, diversity and, 148

Center based child care, 128–129

Centralized governance, 56

Cerebral palsy, 238

Charter schools, 305

Checklists, 191, 194

Child abuse, 242–243

Child Care Development Block Grants (CCDBG), 60, 130

Child care programs. *See also* Three-to-five year olds
center based, 128–129
church or temple centers, 129
employer sponsored, 129, 303
home child care, 129
for infants and toddlers, 104–105
low-income families and, 303
nannies, 129
professional preparation for, 70
quality in, 129–130
types of, 128–129

Child-centered learning environments, 16, 151, 250–259

Child Development Associate (CDA) certificate, 70

Child guidance, past and present, 6–7, 11–14

Child neglect, 242–243

Child study movement, 34–39, 188
behaviorism, 37–38
children with disabilities and, 39
constructivism, 35–36
early childhood programs, 39
early childhood theories, 35–39
maturationism, 38–39
self-actualization theory, 38
social, political environment, 34–35
testing movement, 35
Waldorf schools, 39

Child Tax Credit bill, 285

Childhood, views of
ancient Greek view of, 4
ancient Native American view of, 3–4
ancient Roman view of, 4–5
children as blank slates, 8
children as children, 8–11
children as miniature adults, 5–6
children as our future, 16–17
children as sinful, 6–8
contemporary views, 13–16, 298–299
standardization of childhood, 11–13

Children's Creative Learning

Centers (CCLC), 303

Children's Defense Fund, 71, 154, 285, 308

Choices, giving children, 169

Chomsky, Noam, 216

Church and state relationship, 62–66. *See also* Religious diversity
colonial era, 62–63
history of Roman Catholic schools, 64
industrial era, 63–64
progressive era, 64–65
separation of church and state today, 66
twentieth century, 65–66

Church or temple care centers, 129

Circular reactions, cognitive development and, 99

Civil Rights Act (1964), 40–41, 58

Civil Rights Language Minority Regulations (1980), 63

Civil Rights movement, 40–41

Class meetings, 176–177

Classical conditioning, 37

Classification, children and, 82

Classroom guests, 150

Clinton, Bill, 59

Cognitive academic language proficiency (CALP), 220

Cognitive development
six- to eight-year olds, 140–142
three- to five-year olds, 99–100, 116–117

Cold War, 40

Collectivism, 179–180

Colonial era, 24–25
church and state relationship, 62–63
Dame schools, 25
early childhood education, 25
Latin grammar schools, 25
social-political environment, 24–25

Comenius, John Amos, 23–24

Common schools, 26–27

Communication, with difficult parents, 289

Communicative competence theory, 217

Communities, diversity and, 148–149

Community resources, 288, 290–293

Conceptual understanding, 142–143

Concrete operational stage of development, 37

Conflict resolution, 146–147, 174–175, 181–182

Conservation, 82

Constructivism, 35–36, 76

Contemporary views of childhood, 298–299

Continuity concept, 32

Contributions approach to diversity, 147

Cooperation
versus competition, 165, 167–168
by three-to five-year olds, 117

Cooperative learning
antibias instructional strategies and, 146
elements of, 168
in primary grades, 241
violence and, 182

Cooperative play, 82

Coupling mobility, infants and toddlers, 101

Creationism *vs.* evolution, 64–65

Creative play, 260

Crookson, Peter, 303

Crying, 96, 171

Cultural diversity. *See also* Antibias classrooms; Families; Linguistically diverse children
assessment and, 199–202
behavior guidance and, 178–181
celebrations and, 148
classroom guests and, 150
communities and, 148–149
content integration and, 147–150
contributions approach to, 147
cultural encapsulation and, 276
cultural psychological captivity and, 276
culturally relevant environments, 164
curriculum transformation and, 147
educational materials and, 150, 180
embracing of, 277
friendships and, 149–150
hidden curriculum and, 150
individualism *vs.* collectivism, 179–180
integrating into curriculum, 147–150
multicultural education, 306–307
opinion expression and, 180
parenting advice and, 181
praise and, 181
school work help and, 180–181
social-emotional development and, 102
in the twenty-first century, 306
understanding roles and, 180–181

Cultural identity stages, 276–277

Curiosity, infants and, 171

Curriculum, 83–86
children ages three to eight, 84

children in poverty and, 285
developmentally appropriate practice and, 310
educational purpose and, 310
general guidelines, 83–84
infants and toddles, 84
integrated curriculum, 85–86
integrating diversity into, 147–150
kindergarten, 134–135
linking assessment to, 195–196
null curriculum, 310–311
primary grades, 150–154
social justice and, 263
for special needs children, 246
test driven, 199

D

Dame schools, 25

Darwin, Charles, 64–65

Decision making, parental involvement in, 288

Delayed language development, 98

Democratic environments, 169

Demographics, 308–309

Development
checklists for, 194
developmental disabilities, 233–234
developmental kindergartens, 133
Piaget's stages of, 37
standardized testing and, 197–198

Developmentally appropriate practice (DAP), 78–86
in child-centered environments, 252
children's play and, 82–83
cultural relevance and, 79
curriculum development and, 83–86, 310
development delays and, 234
theories and, 49
value of play and, 79–82

Developmentally inappropriate practice (DIP), 49

Dewey, John, 12, 32, 123, 311

Diagnostic Inventory for Screening Children, 195

Dialects, 210–211
Black English, 211
dialect errors, 210
educator role and, 211

DIBELS test, 195

Dictation, 152

Differences, teaching about, 245

Direct instruction, 151

Disabilities. *See* Special needs children

Disasters, effects on children, 302–303

Discourse theory, 218

Discrimination, poverty and, 145

Disease, atypical development and, 229
DISTAR, 42, 151
Diversity. *See* Antibias classrooms; Cultural diversity; Linguistically diverse children
Divorce, children of, 283
Down syndrome, 98, 234–235
Dreikurs, Rudolf, 15, 172
Dyslexia, 238

E

e-mail, 269
Early childhood theories
    behaviorism, 37–38, 42
    constructivism, 35–36
    in electronic age, 48–49
    maturationism, 38–39
    psychosocial theory, 42
    self-actualization theory, 38
Early Head Start programs, 106, 242. *See also* Head Start programs
Early intervention special education, 242
Ebonics, 211
Economic Opportunity Act (1964), 44, 58
Education for All Handicapped Children Act (1975), 60
Education for Handicapped Children (1966), 58
Educational equity, 306
Educational theories, progressive educators, 31–32
Egocentrism, 100, 116
Eisner, Elliot, 310
Electronic age, 47–49
    early childhood programs, 49
    early childhood theories, 48–49
    immigration and, 47
    social, political environment, 47
    technology and, 47
    terrorism and, 47
    testing movement, 47–48
Elementary and Secondary Education Act (1965), 58, 59
Elkind, David, 13, 41, 298
Employer-sponsored child care, 129, 303
Encouraging environments, 162–168
    for grade children, 166–168
    for infants, 162
    for kindergartners, 163–166
    for preschoolers, 163–166
    for toddlers, 162–163
Engel v. Vitale (1962), 65
Engelmann, Siegfried, 151
English as a second language (ESL), 214–215
English language learners (ELL), 47, 213, 236. *See also* Linguistically diverse children

Entrance age, kindergarten, 133
Environmental issues, poverty and, 145
Environments. *See also* Antibias environments
    child-centerdness and, 250–254
    democratic, 169
    encouraging, 162–168
    inclusive, 259
    indoor, 250–259
    outdoor, 259–260
    play, 83, 260
    room arrangements, 254–259
    scheduling considerations, 252–254
    school funding and, 264–267
    social, 260–264
    technology and, 268–271
Equilibration, 36
Equitable access to technology, 271
Era of accountability, federal policies and, 59
Erikson, Erik, 42
Erikson's stages of psychological development, 43
European American families, 8, 277–278. *See also* Cultural diversity
European influence, in precolonial times, 22–24
Event samples, 189–190
Evolution *vs.* creationism, 64–65
Exceptionalities. *See* Special needs children
Existentialist children, 76
Explicit instruction, 151
Expressive language, 96–97

F

Families. *See also* Cultural diversity; Parental involvement
    African-American families, 278–279
    antibias environments and, 289–290
    Asian-American families, 279–280
    biracial multiethnic families, 280
    blended families, 283
    books about, 290
    children of divorce, 283
    community resources and, 290–293
    cultural identity stages, 276–277
    employers and, 291
    European American families, 277–278
    gay and lesbian families, 280
    Hispanic American families, 280–281
    Jewish American families, 281–282

literacy and, 290, 292
    Native American families, 282
    parent involvement, 286–289
    parents with disabilities, 283
    poverty and, 284–286
    special need children and, 243–244
    values and lifestyles of, 307
Family Support Act (1988), 60
Farrell, Elizabeth, 33
Federal policies, 57–61. *See also* Governance
    children with disabilities, 58
    entering twenty-first century, 59–61
    era of accountability, 59
    Great Society era, 59
    postwar years, 57
Fetal alcohol syndrome (FAS), 229
Field notes, 189
Fine motor development, 100, 118
First Amendment, 66
First intentional behaviors, cognitive development, 99
Formal operational stage of development, 37
Foundling homes, 5
Free School Society, 64
Freedman's Bureau, 28
Freedom with limits, toddlers and, 163
Friendships, 117, 149–150
Froebel, Friedrich, 10, 11, 29–30
Full-day kindergartens, 134
Funding, of quality child care, 130
Future, children as, 16–17

G

Gardner, Howard, 74
Gay families, 280
Genetic abnormalities, 229
Gesell, Arnold, 34, 38–39, 77
Gifted children, 201, 235–236
Glasser, William, 15
Global competency, 276
Globalism, 276
Goals 2000, Educate America Act (1993), 59–60, 61
Goddard, Henry, 31, 39
Governance. *See also* Federal policies
    administrative reform, 54–55
    centralized governance, 56
    governance today, 55–56
    nursery schools, 55
    oversight for early care and education, 54–56
    scientific management, 55
Grade retention, 77
Graduate degrees, 70
Grammar development, 97
Great Depression era, 54

Great Society era, 40–41, 58–59
Gross motor activity, 260
Gross motor development, 118
Guidance. *See* Behavior guidance
Guided reading, 152
Guided writing, 152

H

Hailmann, Eudora, 34
Half-day kindergartens, 134
Hall, Stanley G., 34
Handicapped Children's Early Education Assistance Act (1968), 58
Harris, William, 30
Hayakawa, S.I., 208
Head Start programs, 41, 44, 70, 119–121, 242
Head Start Reauthorization Act (1995), 106
Health and well-being, 251, 300–303
    disasters and, 302–303
    obesity and, 300–301
    poverty and, 145, 286, 300
    safety and, 301–302
    violence in media and, 302
Hearing aids, 237
Hearing disabilities, 98, 236–237, 259
Helpfulness, cultural considerations and, 180
Hidden curriculums, 150
High/Scope approach, 44, 121–123
    child-directed activities and, 122–123
    key experiences and, 122
    teacher-directed activities and, 123
High/Scope Perry Preschool Longitudinal Study, 130
High-stakes testing, 198–199, 305
Hispanic American families, 280–281. *See also* Cultural diversity
History of early childhood programs, 32–34
    Bank Street approach, 33
    for children of color, 32–33
    for children with disabilities, 33, 39
    in colonial times, 25, 28–30
    in electronic age, 49
    High/Scope approach, 44
    kindergarten, 33–34
    Montessori education, 34
    nursery schools, 33
    open education, 46
    Reggio Emilia school, 42–44
    Waldorf schools, 39
Holophrasic speech, 96
Home child care, 129
Home learning, 288
Home visits, 194

Homeless children education, 157
Homeschooling, 155–156
Housing and Urban
    Development Act (1968), 58
Human interactions
    infants and, 162
    toddlers and, 163
Human rights, 307
Hunt, J. McVicker, 12, 41
Hurried child, 13–14

I

I messages, 175
Immigration, 47
Immigration Act (1965), 63
Immigration Restriction League,
    62
Impulse control, in infants and
    toddlers, 101
Inappropriate labels,
    standardized testing and,
    198
Inclusion, special needs children,
    239–242
Independence, cultural
    considerations and, 180
Independent writing, 152
Individualism vs. collectivism,
    179–180
Individualized education
    programs (IEP), 230–231
Individualized family service
    plans (IFSP), 230–231
Individuals with Disabilities Act
    (IDEA) (1990), 60
Indoor environments
    compatibility for children,
        251–252
    developmentally appropriate
        activities and, 252
    engaging materials use, 251
    health and well-being issues,
        251
    room and physical
        arrangements, 254–259
    safety issues and, 250
    scheduling considerations and,
        252–254
Industrial era, 25–28
    African-American education,
        27–28
    church and state relationship,
        63–64
    common schools, 26–27
    early childhood education,
        28–30
    Native-American education, 28
    origins of kindergarten, 28–30
    social, political environment,
        25–28
    testing movement origins, 27
Inequitable funding, 264–267
Infants. See also Toddlers
    antibias environments and,
        107–109

appropriate behavior guidance
    and, 170–171
appropriate toys and, 103
assessment of, 197
calm environments and, 162
caregivers and, 93–94
child care programs and,
    104–105
cognitive development and,
    99–100
curiosity and, 171
curriculum development
    and, 84
with disabilities, 240
human interactions and, 162
language development and,
    92–98
physical development and,
    100–101
play and, 103
response to crying and, 171
routines and, 162
sensory learning and, 162
social-emotional development
    and, 101–102
Information processing
    six- to eight-year olds, 142
    three- to five-year olds,
        116–117
Inherent goodness, 169
Insecure ambivalent infants, 102
Insecure avoidant infants, 102
Integrated curriculum, 85–86
Intelligence quotient (IQ)
    origins, 27
Interactive writing, 152
Interpersonal children, 76
Intrapersonal children, 76
Invented spelling, 142
Invited guests, 293

J

Jewish American families,
    281–282. See also Cultural
    diversity
Johnson, Lyndon, 40
Journaling, 71

K

Kalamazoo case of 1874, 27
Kennedy, Robert, 108
Kindergarten students, 130–135.
    See also Three-to five-year
    olds
    academic readiness and
        redshirting, 132–134
    active listening and, 173–174
    alternatives to kindergarten,
        133–134
    appropriate behavior guidance
        and, 173–175
    assessment in, 197
    at close of 19th century, 33–34
    conflict resolution and,
        174–175

cooperation vs. competition,
    165
culturally relevant
    environments and, 164
curriculum for, 134–135
developmental kindergartens,
    133
with disabilities, 240–241
entrance age, 133
expectations and, 165
half-day/full day kindergarten,
    134
I messages and, 175
origins of, 28–30
play and, 165
readiness for, 131–132
responsibility and, 165
room arrangement and,
    165–166
routines and, 164
self-confidence and, 164
sense of self and, 164
states requiring attendance,
    131
technology and, 269
transitional first grades, 133
transitions and, 164–165
Klu Klux Klan, 65
Kozol, Jonathan, 264

L

Labeling of special needs
    children, 231–232
Language, poverty and, 285
Language acquisition device
    (LAD), 216
Language barriers, 201. See also
    Cultural considerations
Language development, 92–98.
    See also Linguistically
    diverse children
    behaviorist theory of, 92
    cultural aspects of, 98
    delayed development, 98
    Down syndrome and, 98
    expressive language, 96–97
    hearing impairment and, 98
    language delays, 98
    nativist theory of, 92–96
    private speech, 97
    reading to infants and toddlers
        and, 97
    receptive language, 96
    signing, 97
    social interaction and, 114
    stages of, 96–97
    theories of language
        acquisition, 92–96
    three-to five year olds, 114–116
Language disabilities, 236–237
Lanham Act, 57
Latin grammar schools, 25
Lau Remedies (1975), 63
Lau v. Nichols (1974), 63, 209
Learning activities, in early

childhood environments,
    251
Learning by doing, 116
Learning disabilities, 237–238,
    259
Learning theories, 72–78
    behaviorism, 76–77
    brain-based development, 73
    constructivism, 76
    maturation, 77–78
    multiple intelligences, 74–75
Lesbian families, 280
Linguistically diverse children.
    See also Cultural diversity
    accents, 212
    bilingual education, 213–214
    challenges regarding, 208–209
    controversy regarding,
        208–209
    dialects, 210–211
    English as a second language,
        214–215
    nonverbal communication,
        215
    second language acquisition,
        215–223
    sign language, 212–213
    twenty-first century issues, 307
Lipreading, 237
Literacy. See also Reading
    antibias classrooms and,
        144–146
    balanced, 151–153
    initiatives, 290, 292
    six- to eight-year old
        development, 140
    three- to five-year old
        development, 114–116
Locke, John, 8
Logical consequences, 172,
    175–176
Looping, 155
Loss of first language, 222–223
Low scores, standardized tests,
    199
Luther, Martin, 22–23

M

Magnet schools, 304–305
Malaguzzi, Loris, 43–44
Male teachers, 308
Malleable child, 13
Managing behavior. See Behavior
    guidance
Mann, Horace, 64
Market model for schooling,
    303–305
Maslow, Abraham, 38
Maslow's hierarchy of needs, 38
Materials, educational
    cultural considerations and,
        180
    diversity and, 150
    engaging materials, 251
    play, 83

Maternal Child Health and Mental Retardation Act (1964), 45
Mathematical/logical children, 74
Maturation, 77–78
Maturationism, 38–39
Maturationists, 131
McCollum v. Board of Education (1948), 65
McMillan, Margaret, 299
Media, violence in, 183, 269–270, 302
Medicaid, 58
Medicare, 58
Meisels, Samuel, 194
Melting pot theory, 79, 278
Mental age (MA) concept, 27
Metropolitan Achievement Test, 195
Middle ages, 5–6
Miniature adults, children as, 5–6
Mitchell, Lucy Sprague, 34–35, 123
Modern views of childhood, 13–15
Monitor model theory, 217
Montessori, Maria, 12, 34, 106, 125
Montessori schools, 34, 106–107, 125–126
Mothers, participating in workforce, 14
Motor disabilities, 259
Multiage grouping, 154–155
Multicultural education, 120, 276, 306–307. *See also* Cultural diversity
Multiple intelligences, 74–75
Musical/rhythmic children, 74

N
Nannies, 129
Nation at Risk, 48
National Association for the Education of Young Children (NAEYC), 48–49, 71, 83–86, 196
National Association of Early Childhood Specialists in State Departments of Education (NAECS/SDE), 196
National Board certification, 70
National Commission on Excellence in Education, 47–48
National Council for Exceptional Children, 33
National Reading Panel Report, 153
Native-American children, 3–4, 6–7, 11, 12, 26, 28, 32–33
Native-American families, 282. *See also* Cultural diversity
Nativist theory of language acquisition, 92–96
Natural consequences, application of, 172, 175–176
Natural disasters, 251
Naturalist children, 76
Naturalization Act, 62
Nature appreciation, 260
Neglect, child, 242–243
No Child Left Behind Act (2001), 48, 59, 60–61, 70, 154, 200
Nonverbal communication, 215
Nonviolent behavior, supporting, 181–183
    alertness to aggression, 182
    bullying, 183
    conflict resolution and, 181–182
    cooperative learning and, 182
    encouraging discussion and, 182
    redirecting violent play, 182–183
    role models and, 181
Norm-referenced tests, 199
Northwest Ordinance (1787), 63
Null curriculum, 310–311
Nursery schools, federal involvement in, 55

O
Obesity, 300–301
Object permanence, 99
Observation, 188–191
    anecdotal notes, 189
    audio recordings, 190
    checklists, 191
    event samples, 189–190
    field notes, 189
    photographs, 191
    time samples, 189
    video recordings, 190–191
Open education, 46
Operant conditioning, 42
Opinion expression, cultural considerations and, 180
Outdoor environments, 259–260
Owen, Robert, 10

P
Parallel play, 82
Parental involvement, 286–289. *See also* Families
    barriers to, 288–289
    communication and, 287
    community collaboration and, 288
    conferences, 193
    decision making and, 288
    difficult parents, 289
    guidelines for, 286–287
    learning at home and, 288
    parenting, 287
    types of, 287–288
    volunteering and, 288
Parenting advice, cultural considerations and, 181
Parents with disabilities, 283
Parker, Francis A., 31
Paulson, Tim, 262
Pavlov, Ivan, 37
Peabody, Elizabeth, 30
Peer tutoring, 241–242
Perry Preschool Project, 44
Personal advocacy, 87
Perspective taking, 262
Pestalozzi, Johann Heinrich, 9–10
Philosophies of learning
    behaviorism, 76–77
    brain-based development, 73
    constructivism, 76
    maturation, 77–78
    multiple intelligences, 74–75
Photographic assessment, 191
Physical abuse, 243
Physical development
    fine motor development, 100
    six- to eight-year olds, 143
    three- to five-year olds, 100–101, 118
    toileting and, 101
Physical disabilities, 238–239
Physical environment. *See* Room arrangements
Piaget, Jean, 35–36, 37, 41
Piaget's theory, 76
Plan-do-review, 122
Plato, 4
Play
    cognitive development and, 82
    constructivism and, 36
    creative, 260
    infants and toddlers and, 103
    inside environments and, 83
    materials for, 83
    outside environments and, 82–83
    preschoolers and kindergartners and, 165
    primary grades and, 153–154
    social-emotional development and, 81–82
    suggestions and, 83
    value of, 79–82
Plessy v. Ferguson, 33
Portfolios, 191–194
    age appropriate, 193–194
    assessment of, 201
    parent conferences and, 193
    purposes of, 193
    reflection and, 192–193
    show portfolios, 193
    work sampling system and, 194
    working portfolios, 193
Post World War II education, 39–44
    behaviorism, 42
    children with disabilities and, 41, 44
    civil rights movement and, 40–41
    early childhood programs, 42–44
    early childhood theories, 41–44
    federal policies and, 57
    Great Society and, 40–41
    Head Start, 44
    High/Scope Educational Research Foundation, 44
    psychosocial theory, 42
    Reggio Emilia early childhood program, 42–44
    social, political environment, 39–41
    testing movement and, 41
    War on Poverty and, 40
    women's role and, 41
Postbirth complications, dysfunctions and, 229
Poverty
    adjustments and, 299–300
    advocating for, 286
    appropriate curriculum and, 285
    assessment materials and, 201
    biological issues and, 145
    childhood needs and, 108
    discrimination and, 145
    educational outcomes and, 300
    effects of, 300
    environmental issues, 145
    family issues and, 284–286
    health and well-being and, 230, 286, 300
    language issues and, 285
    lasting effects and, 107
    resources and, 284–285
    substandard child care and, 59
    technology and, 285
Praise, 169–170, 181
Precolonial times, 22–24
Prejudice reduction activities, 146, 177–178
Preoperational stage of development, 37
Preparation. *See* Professional preparation
Preschool and Kindergarten Behavior Scales, 195
Preschool children. *See also* Three-to-five year olds
    active listening and, 173–174
    appropriate behavior guidance and, 173–175
    assessment of, 197
    conflict resolution and, 174–175
    cooperation *vs.* competition, 165
    culturally relevant environments and, 164
    with disabilities, 240–241
    expectations and, 165
    I messages and, 175
    natural and logical consequences and, 175
    play and, 165